1434

ALSO BY GAVIN MENZIES

1421: The Year China Discovered America

THE YEAR
A MAGNIFICENT CHINESE FLEET
SAILED TO ITALY
AND IGNITED THE RENAISSANCE

GAVIN MENZIES

HarperCollins*Publishers*

HarperCollins*Publishers*
77–85 Fulham Palace Road,
Hammersmith, London W6 8JB

HarperCollins' website address is:
www.harpercollins.co.uk

First published in 2008 by William Morrow,
an imprint of HarperCollins*Publishers*
This edition 2008

3

A catalogue record of this book is
available from the British Library

ISBN-13 978-0-00-726937-2 (hardback)
ISBN-10 0-00-726937-4 (hardback)
ISBN-13 978-0-00-727586-1 (paperback)
ISBN-10 0-00-727586-2 (paperback)

Printed and bound in Great Britain by
Clays Ltd, St Ives plc

This book is dedicated to my beloved wife, Marcella,
who has traveled with me on the journeys related in this book
and through life

CHINESE NOMENCLATURE

Most names are rendered in Pinyin, which is now standard in China—for example, the modern spelling Mao Zedong, not Mao Tse-tung. For simplicity, however, I have retained the older form of Romanization known as Wade-Giles, for names that have long been familiar to Western readers. The *Wu Pei Chi,* for instance, is more readily recognized than the *Wu Bei Zhi.* I have also kept the more established spellings of Cantonese place-names, writing of Hong Kong and Canton, rather than Xianggang and Guangzhou. Inscriptions on navigational charts have been left in the older form, as have academic texts in the bibliography.

CONTENTS

CONTENTS

III China's Legacy

INTRODUCTION

One thing that greatly puzzled me when writing *1421* was the lack of curiosity among many professional historians.

After all, Christopher Columbus supposedly discovered America in 1492. Yet eighteen years before he set sail, Columbus had a map of the Americas, which he later acknowledged in his logs. Indeed, even before his first voyage, Columbus signed a contract with the king and queen of Spain that appointed him viceroy of the Americas. His fellow ship's captain Martín Alonso Pinzón, who sailed with him in 1492, had too seen a map of the Americas—in the pope's library.

How do you *discover* a place for which you already have a map?

The same question could be asked of Magellan. The strait that connects the Atlantic to the Pacific bears the great Portuguese explorer's name. When Magellan reached that strait in 1520, he had run out of food and his sailors were reduced to eating rats. Worse, they were convinced they were lost. Esteban Gómez led a mutiny, seizing the *San Antonio* with the intent to lead part of the expedition back to Spain. Magellan quashed the mutiny by claiming he was not at all lost. A member of the crew wrote, "We all believed that [the Strait] was a cul-de-sac; but the captain knew that he had to navigate through a very well-concealed strait, having seen it in a chart preserved in the treasury of the king of Portugal, and made by Martin of Bohemia, a man of great parts."[1]

Why was the strait named after Magellan when Magellan had seen it on a chart before he set sail? It doesn't make sense.

The paradox might be explained had there been no maps of the strait or of the Pacific—if, as some believe, Magellan was bluffing about having seen a chart. But there *were* maps. Martin Waldseemüller published his map of the Americas and the Pacific in 1507, twelve years before Magellan set sail. In 1515, four years before Magellan sailed,

Johannes Schöner published a map showing the strait Magellan is said to have "discovered."

The mystery only deepens when we consider the two cartographers, Waldseemüller and Schöner. Were these two hoary old sea captains who had made heroic voyages across the Pacific before Magellan? Should we rename the strait after Schöner? Hardly.

Schöner never went to sea. He flunked his exams at the University of Erfurt, leaving without a degree. He became an apprentice priest in 1515 but for failing to celebrate mass, was relegated to a small village, where his punishment was officiating at early-morning mass. So how did a young man from rural Germany with no maritime tradition produce a map of the Pacific well before Magellan discovered that ocean?

Like Schöner, Waldseemüller had never seen the sea. Born in Wolfenweiler near Freiberg in 1475, he spent his working life as a cannon at Saint-Dié in eastern France—a region famed for its plums but completely devoid of maritime tradition. Waldseemüller, too, left university without a degree. Yet his map of the Americas showed the Sierra Madre of Mexico and the Sierra Nevada of North America before Magellan reached the Pacific or Balboa reached its coast.

These two rustic mapmakers were not the only Europeans with an uncanny prescience about unseen lands. In 1419, before European voyages of exploration even began, Albertin di Virga published a map of the Eastern Hemisphere that shows northern Australia. It was another 350 years before Captain Cook "discovered" that continent. Similarly, Brazil appeared on Portuguese maps before the first Portuguese, Cabral and Dias, set sail for Brazil. The South Shetland Islands were shown on the Piri Reis map four hundred years before Europeans reached the Antarctic.

The great European explorers were brave and determined men. But they discovered nothing. Magellan was not the first to circumnavigate the globe, nor was Columbus the first to discover the Americas. So why, we may ask, do historians persist in propagating this fantasy? Why is *The Times Atlas of World Exploration,* which details the discoveries of European explorers, still taught in schools? Why are the young so insistently misled?

After *1421* was published, we set up our website, www.1421.tv, which has since received millions of visitors. Additionally we have received hundreds of thousands of e-mails from readers of *1421,* many bringing new evidence to our attention. Of the criticism we've received, the most frequent complaint has concerned my failure to describe the Chinese fleets' visits to Europe when the Renaissance was just getting under way.

Two years ago, a Chinese Canadian scholar, Tai Peng Wang, discovered Chinese and Italian records showing beyond a doubt that Chinese delegations had reached Italy during the reigns of Zhu Di (1403–1424) and the Xuan De emperor (1426–1435). Naturally, this was of the greatest interest to me and the research team.

Shortly after Tai Peng Wang's 2005 discovery, my wife, Marcella, and I set off with friends for Spain. For a decade, we've enjoyed holidays with this same group of friends, traveling to seemingly inaccessible places—crossing the Andes, Himalayas, Karakorams, and Hindu Kush, voyaging down the Amazon, journeying to the glaciers of Patagonia and the high Altiplano of Bolivia. In 2005 we walked the Via de la Plata from Seville, from where the conquistadores sailed to the New World, north to their homeland of Extremadura. Along the way, we visited the towns in which the conquistadores were born and raised. One of these was Toledo, painted with such bravura by El Greco. Of particular interest to me were the medieval pumps by which this fortified mountain town drew its water from the river far below.

On a lovely autumn day, we walked uphill to the great cathedral that dominates Toledo and the surrounding countryside. We dumped our bags in a small hotel built into the cathedral walls and set off to explore. In a neighboring Moorish palace there was an exhibition dedicated to Leonardo da Vinci and his Madrid codices, focusing on his pumps, aqueducts, locks, and canals—all highly relevant to Toledo.

The exhibit contained this note: "Leonardo embarked upon a thorough analysis of waterways. The encounter with Francesco di Giorgio in Pavia in 1490 was a decisive moment in Leonardo's training, a turning point. Leonardo planned to write a treatise on water." This puzzled me. I had been taught that Leonardo had designed the first European canals and locks, that he was the first to illustrate pumps and fountains. So what relevant training had he received from Francesco di Giorgio, a name completely unknown to me?

My research revealed that Leonardo had owned a copy of di Giorgio's treatise on civil and military machines. In the treatise, di Giorgio had illustrated and described a range of astonishing machines, many of which Leonardo subsequently reproduced in three-dimensional drawings. The illustrations were not limited to canals, locks, and pumps; they included parachutes, submersible tanks, and machine guns as well as hundreds of other machines with civil and military applications.

This was quite a shock. It seemed Leonardo was more illustrator than inventor and that the greater genius may have resided in di Giorgio. Was di Giorgio the original inventor of these fantastic machines? Or did he, in turn, copy them from another?

I learned that di Giorgio had inherited notebooks and treatises from another Italian, Mariano di Jacopo ditto Taccola (called Taccola: "the Crow"). Taccola was a clerk of public works living in Siena. Having never seen the sea or fought a battle, he nevertheless managed to draw a wide variety of nautical machines—paddle-wheeled boats, frogmen, and machines for lifting wrecks, together with a range of gunpowder weapons, even an advanced method of making gunpowder and designing a helicopter. It seems Taccola was responsible for nearly every technical illustration that di Giorgio and Leonardo had later improved upon.

So, once again, we confront our familiar puzzle: How did a clerk in a remote Italian hill town, a man who had never traveled abroad or obtained a university education, come to produce technical illustrations of such amazing machines?

This book attempts to answer that and a few related riddles. In doing so, we stumble upon the map of the Americas that Taccola's contemporary Paolo Toscanelli sent to both Christopher Columbus and the king of Portugal, in whose library Magellan encountered it.

Like *1421,* this book is a collective endeavor that never would have been written without the help of thousands of people across the world. I do not claim definitive answers to every riddle. This is a work in progress. Indeed, I hope readers will join us in the search for answers and share them with us—as so many did in response to *1421*.

However, before we meet the Chinese squadron upon its arrival in Venice and then Florence, a bit of background is necessary on the aims of the Xuan De emperor for whom Grand Eunuch Zheng He served as ambassador to Europe. A Xuan De imperial order dated June 29, 1430, stated:

> . . . Everything is prosperous and renewed but the Foreign Countries distantly located beyond the sea, still had not heard and did not know. For this reason Grand Directors Zheng He, Wang Jinghong and others were specially sent, bearing the word, to go and instruct them into deference and submission . . .

The first three chapters of this book describe the two years of preparations in China and Indonesia to fulfill that order, which required launching and provisioning the greatest fleet the world had ever seen for a voyage across the world. Chapter 4 explains how the Chinese calculated longitude without clocks and latitude without sextants—prerequisites for drawing accurate maps of new lands. Chapters 5 and 6 describe how the fleet left the Malabar Coast of India, sailed to the canal linking the Nile to the Red Sea, then down the Nile into the Mediterranean. Some have argued that no Chinese records exist to suggest that Zheng He's fleets ever left the Indian Ocean. Chapters 5 and 6 document the many records in China, Egypt, Dalmatia, Venice, Florence, and the Papal States describing the fleets' voyage.

In chapter 21 I discuss the immense transfer of knowledge that took place in 1434 between China and Europe. This knowledge originated with a people who, over a thousand years, had created an advanced civilization in Asia; it was given to Europe just as she was emerging from a millennium of stagnation following the fall of the Roman Empire.

The Renaissance has traditionally been portrayed as a rebirth of the classical civilizations of Greece and Rome. It seems to me the time has come to reappraise this Eurocentric view of history. While the ideals of Greece and Rome played an important role in the Renaissance, I submit that the transfer of Chinese intellectual capital to Europe was the spark that set the Renaissance ablaze.

The internet has revolutionized the historian's profession, and though it is not necessary for readers to visit the *1434* website, it does contain a great deal of additional information about China's role in the Renaissance. On occasion in the text, I make reference to specific subjects that are discussed in greater detail on the website. I believe that many will find this interesting. The *1421* website has also become a forum for discussion, and I hope the same will be true for *1434*. When you have read the book, please tell us whether you agree with its conclusions.

Gavin Menzies
New York
July 17, 2007

I

Setting the Scene

1

A
LAST VOYAGE

In the summer of 1421 the emperor Zhu Di lost a stupendous gamble. In doing so, he lost control of China and, eventually, his life.

Zhu Di's dreams were so outsized that, though China in the early fifteenth century was the greatest power on earth, it still could not summon the means to realize the emperor's monumental ambitions. Having embarked on the simultaneous construction of the Forbidden City, the Ming tombs, and the Temple of Heaven, China was also building two thousand ships for Zheng He's fleets. These vast projects had denuded the land of timber. As a consequence, eunuchs were sent to pillage Vietnam. But the Vietnamese leader Le Loi fought the Chinese with great skill and courage, tying down the Chinese army at huge financial and psychological cost. China had her Vietnam six hundred years before France and America had theirs.[1]

China's debacle in Vietnam grew out of the costs of building and maintaining her treasure fleets, through which the emperor sought to bring the entire world into Confucian harmony within the Chinese tribute system. The fleets were led by eunuchs—brave sailors who were intensely loyal to the emperor, permanently insecure, and ready to sacrifice all. However, the eunuchs were also uneducated and frequently corrupt. And they were loathed by the mandarins, the educated administrative class that buttressed a Confucian system in which every citizen was assigned a clearly defined place.

Superb administrators, the mandarins recoiled from risk. They disapproved of the extravagant adventures of the treasure fleets, whose far-flung exploits had the added disadvantage of bringing them into contact with "long nosed barbarians." In the Yuan dynasty (1279–1368), mandarins were the lowest class.[2] However, in the Ming dynasty, Emperor Hong Wu, Zhu Di's father, reversed the class system to favor mandarins.

The mandarins planned Hong Wu's attack on his son Zhu Di, the Prince of Yen, whom Hong had banished to Beijing (Nanjing then being the capital of China). The eunuchs sided with Zhu Di, joining his drive south into Nanjing. After his victory in 1402, Zhu Di expressed his gratitude by appointing eunuchs to command the treasure fleets.

Henry Tsai paints a vivid portrait of Zhu Di, also known as the Yongle emperor:

> He was an overachiever. He should be credited for the construction of the imposing Forbidden City of Beijing, which still stands today to amaze countless visitors from lands afar. He should be applauded for sponsoring the legendary maritime expeditions of the Muslim eunuch Admiral Zheng He, the legacy of which still lives vividly in the historical consciousness of many Southeast Asians and East Africans. He reinforced the power structure of the absolutist empire his father the Hongwu emperor founded, and extended the tentacles of Chinese civilisation to Vietnam, Korea, Japan, among other tributary states of Ming China. He smoothed out China's relations with the Mongols from whom Emperor Hongwu had recovered the Chinese empire. He made possible the compilation of various important Chinese texts, including the monumental encyclopaedia *Yongle dadian*. . . .
>
> Yongle [the alternative name for Zhu Di] was also a usurper, a man who bathed his hands in the blood of numerous political victims. And the bloodshed did not stop there. After ascending the throne, he built a well-knit information network staffed by eunuchs whom his father had specifically blocked from the core of politics, to spy on scholar officials [mandarins] who might challenge his legitimacy and his absolutism.[3]

Under Zhu Di, the mandarins were relegated to organizing the finances necessary to build the fleet. But for generations of mandarins who governed the Ming dynasty and compiled almost all Chinese historical sources, the voyages led by Zheng He were a deviation from the proper path. The mandarins did all they could to belittle Zheng He's achievements. As Edward L. Dreyer points out, Zheng He's biography in the *Ming-Shi-lu* was deliberately placed before a series of chapters on eunuchs "who are grouped with 'flatterers and deceivers,' 'treacherous ministers,' 'roving bandits' and 'all intrinsically evil categories of people.'"[4]

As long as the voyages prospered, and tribute flowed back to the Middle Kingdom to finance the fleet's adventures, the simmering rivalry between mandarins and eunuchs could be contained. However, in the summer of 1421, Zhu Di's reign went horribly wrong. First, the Forbidden City, which had cost vast sums to build, was burned to ashes by a thunderbolt. Next, the emperor became impotent and was taunted by his concubines. In a final indignity, he was thrown from his horse, a present from Tamburlaine's son Shah Rokh.[5] It appeared that Zhu Di had lost heaven's favor.

In December 1421, at a time when Chinese farmers were reduced to eating grass, Zhu Di embarked on another extravaganza. He led an enormous army into the northern steppe to fight the Mongol armies of Aruqtai, who had refused to pay tribute.[6]

This was too much for Xia Yuanji, the minister of finance; he refused to fund the expedition. Zhu Di had his minister arrested along with the minister of justice, who had also objected to the adventure. Fang Bin, the minister of war, committed suicide. With his finances in ruins and his cabinet in revolt, the emperor rode off to the steppe, where he was outwitted and outmaneuvered by Aruqtai. On August 12, 1424, Zhu Di died.[7]

Zhu Gaozhi, Zhu Di's son, took over as emperor and promptly reversed his father's policies. Xia Yuanji was restored as minister of finance, and drastic fiscal measures were adopted to rein in inflation. Zhu Gaozhi's first edict on ascending the throne on September 7, 1424, laid the treasure fleet low: he ordered all voyages of the treasure ships to be stopped. All ships moored at Taicang were ordered back to Nanjing.[8]

The mandarins were back in control. The great Zheng He was pensioned off along with his admirals and captains. Treasure ships were left to rot at their moorings. Nanjing's dry docks were flooded and plans for additional treasure ships were burned.

Then suddenly, unexpectedly, on May 29, 1425, Zhu Gaozhi died. He was succeeded by his son Zhu Zhanji, Zhu Di's grandson.

Zhu Zhanji seemed destined to be one of China's greatest emperors. Far more cautious than Zhu Di, he was nonetheless extremely clever. He quickly realized that China's abdication as Queen of the Seas would have disastrous consequences—not least that the barbarians would cease paying tribute. What's more, the dream of a world united in Confucian harmony would be dashed and the colossal expenditure that had enabled China to acquire allies and settlements throughout the world would be wasted.

Zhu Zhanji also realized that the eunuchs disfavored by his father had their virtues. He set up a palace school to instruct them[9] and appointed eunuchs to important military commands. He reversed his father's plan to move the capital south to Nanjing, restoring it to Beijing, once again facing the Mongols. Yet he also believed in the Confucian virtues espoused by the mandarins and cultivated their friendship over bottles of wine. In many ways Zhu Zhanji combined the best of his father, including his concern for farmers, with that of his grandfather, whose boldness he emulated in approaching the barbarians.

The new reign would be known as Xuan De, "propagating virtue." For Zheng He and the eunuchs, it marked a return to center stage. Soon another great sailing expedition would be launched, to bear the word to the barbarians to instruct them into deference and submission.

2

THE EMPEROR'S
AMBASSADOR

In 1430 the young emperor empowered Admirals Zheng He and
Wang Jinghong to act on his behalf, issuing them a specially
minted brass medallion, in a mix of zhuanshu[1] and kaishu[2] scripts,
inscribed AUTHORISED AND AWARDED BY XUAN DE OF THE GREAT MING.

The emperor appointed Zheng He as his ambassador. Here is the
edict from the *Xuanzong Shi-lu,* dated June 29, 1430: "Everything was
prosperous and renewed but the Foreign countries, distantly located
beyond the sea, still had not heard and did not know. For this reason
Grand Directors Zheng He, Wang Jinghong and others were specially
sent, bearing the word, to go and instruct them into deference and
submission."[3]

This voyage to "instruct" the foreigners was the zenith of Admiral
Zheng He's great career. Before departing, he had two inscriptions
carved in stone to document his achievements. The first inscription,
dated March 14, 1431, was placed near the temple of the sea goddess at
Taicang, downriver from Nanjing near the estuary of the Yangtze.

From the time when we, Cheng Ho [Zheng He] and his companions at the
beginning of the Yung Lo period [1403] received the Imperial commission as
envoy to the barbarians, up until now, seven voyages have taken place and
each time we have commanded several tens of thousands of government soldiers and more than a hundred oceangoing vessels. Starting from Tai Ts'ang

and taking the sea, we have by way of the countries of Chan-Ch'eng, Hsienlo, Quawa, K'ochih, and Kuli [Calicut] reached Hulu mossu [Cairo] and other countries of the western regions, more than 3,000 countries in all.[4]

The other inscribed stone was placed farther down the Chinese coast at the mouth of the Min River in Fujian. It is dated the second winter month of the sixth year of Xuan De, which makes it between December 5, 1431, and January 7, 1432. It is called the Chang Le epigraphy.

> The Imperial Ming dynasty in unifying seas and continents surpassing the three dynasties even goes beyond the Han and Tang dynasties. The countries beyond the horizon and from the ends of the earth have all become subjects and the most western of the western or the most northern of the northern countries however far they may be, the distance and the routes may be calculated.[5]

Liu Gang, who owns a Chinese map of the world from 1418, a critical document that we will revisit later, has translated the Chang Le epigraphy as it would have been understood in the early Ming dynasty. His translation differs in some key respects from the modern translation produced above.

> The Imperial Ming dynasty has unified seas and the universe, surpassing the first three generations [of Ming emperors] as well as of the Han and Tang dynasties. None of these countries had not become subjects, even those at the remotest corners in the west of the western region of the Imperial Ming and the north of the northward extension from the Imperial Ming are so far away, however, that the distance to them can be calculated by mileage.[6]

The full import of the distinctions become apparent once we understand what the terms "western region of the Imperial Ming" and "northward extension from the Imperial Ming" meant at the time the stones were carved. "The term 'western region' originated during the Han dynasty and at that time referred to the region between Zhong

Ling (now in the northern Xian Jiang autonomous region) and Dun Huang (at the edge of the Takla Makan Desert)," Liu Gang explains.

> By the Tang dynasty, the extent of the "western region" had been extended to North Africa. The books written in the Ming dynasty describing travel to the western region adopt an even broader definition: *Records of Journeys to the Western Region* and *Notes on the Barbarians,* both books published during Zheng He's era, extended the western region much further westwards. This is reflected in the Taicang stele, which refers to reaching "Hu lu mo Ssu (Cairo) and other countries of the western regions." The second stele in Fujian mentions reaching "the remotest corners in the west of the western region," i.e., far west of Cairo."[7]

The phrase "the north of the northward extension from the Imperial Ming" is even more pregnant with meaning. As Liu Gang has explained, in Zheng He's era the Chinese had no concept of the North Pole as the highest point of the earthly sphere. Accordingly, when they traveled north from China to the North American continent, traversing the North Pole (great circle route), they believed the journey was always northward. The modern geographic understanding is that the great circle route from China to North America runs north to the North Pole, then south to North America. This concept was unknown to the Chinese.

To the Ming Chinese, "in the north of the northward extension from the Imperial Ming" means a place beyond the North Pole. This understanding is reflected in the 1418 world map, which shows a passage through the polar ice across the North Pole leading to America. (According to the Dutch meteorological office, there were three exceptionally warm winters in the 1420s, which could have melted the Arctic sea ice.)[8]

Thus, if we take the two steles at their word, it appears that Zheng He's fleets had already reached three thousand countries as well as the North Pole and North America beyond the Pole.

The emperor's order to Zheng He to instruct distant lands beyond the seas to follow the way of heaven now seems awesome. Zheng He is being ordered to return to all three thousand countries he had visited in his life at sea. The task would require a huge number of ships—several great fleets readied for voyages across the world. This explains the lengthy delay between the imperial edict and the fleets' actual departure from Chinese waters some two years later.

Each month, a wealth of evidence comes to our website from sources in about 120 different countries. Taken together, the evidence, which includes the wrecks of Chinese junks in distant waters, has convinced me that my original estimate of the size of Zheng He's fleet—some one hundred ships—was far too low.

Over the past three years, two researchers, Professor Xi Longfei and Dr. Sally Church, have found references in the *Ming Shi-lu* to the number of junks built in the years 1403 to 1419. The figures are subject to interpretation, particularly with regard to the number that can be assigned specifically to Zheng He's fleets. But it seems the low estimate of the size of Zheng He's fleets is as follows: 249 ships completed in 1407 "in preparation for sending embassies to the Western Oceans"; plus five oceangoing ships built in 1404, which the *Ming Shi-lu* explicitly states were ordered because envoys would soon be sent abroad; plus 48 "Treasure ships" built in 1408 and another 41 built in 1419. That makes a total of 343 ships constructed for Zheng He's voyages.[9]

A middle estimate would include "converted" ships, the purpose of which is unspecified in the *Ming Shi-lu*. Of these, there were 188 in 1403; 80 in early November 1405; 13 in late November 1407; 33 in 1408; and 61 in 1413. Adding these converted ships to the 343 ships described above would give Zheng He a total of 718 ships.

The high estimate includes 1,180 *haizhou*, ordered in 1405, whose purpose is unspecified, and two orders of *haifeng chuan* (ocean wind ships)—61 in 1412 and the same number again in 1413. All together, that would mean a fleet of 2,020 ships out of a total construction program of 2,726. Even at this high estimate, Zheng He's fleet would still have been smaller than Kublai Khan's, though of better quality.

Based on Camões's account of the Chinese fleet that reached Calicut eighty years before Vasco da Gama, my guess is that Zheng He had at his disposal more than 1,000 ships. "More than eight hundred sail of large and small ships came to India from the ports of Malacca and China and the Lequeos (Ryuku) Islands with people of many nations and all laden with merchandise of great value which they brought for sale . . . they were so numerous that they filled the country and settled as dwellers in all of the towns of the sea coast."[10]

The emperor's massive ship-building program was accompanied by major improvements in the junks' construction. Professor Pan Biao of the College of Wood Science and Technology of Nanjing Forestry University has carried out groundbreaking work into the types of tim-ber found in the Nanjing shipyards where the treasure ships were built. About 80 percent of the material was pine, 11 percent hardwoods other than teak, and 5.5 percent teak.

The pine—soft, humidity- and decay-resistant, and long used for building both houses and ships—was largely from south China. Teak, which is hard, heavy, and resistant to insect attack, is ideal for main frames. However, it was foreign to China and a new material for Chi-nese shipbuilders.

What astonished Professor Pan Biao was the volume of hardwood and teak that was imported. "Before Zheng He, hardwood had never left its countries of origin in a single step," he said. "But during Zheng He's voyages, and in the one or two hundred years following his voy-ages, hardwood was not only massively used in shipbuilding but was also brought into Southeast Asia and transplanted there for the first time." Professor Pan Biao argues that Zheng He's voyages contributed greatly to large-scale international trade in hardwood and to the re-markable progress in Southeast Asia's shipbuilding industry.[11]

In each of the years 1406, 1408, 1418, and 1432, fleets of a hundred or more Chinese vessels spent lengthy periods refitting in the ports of East Java. The Chinese who settled in Java played a major part in the development of Javanese shipbuilding. Professor Anthony Reid sug-gests that the flowering of Javanese shipbuilding in the fifteenth cen-tury was due to "creative melding of Chinese and Javanese marine technology in the wake of Zheng He's expeditions."[12]

The new building program in China, aided by better timber and the huge refitting endeavor in Java, would gradually have improved the quality of Zheng He's fleets. We know from detailed research initiated by Kenzo Hayashida that Kublai Khan's fleets, wrecked in Tokushima Bay in Japan in 1281, were doomed as much by the poor quality of their construction as by the fury of the *kamikaze* winds.

With their superior wood and construction, Zheng He's ships would be capable of crossing the stormiest oceans. However, the scale of these vast fleets would have created enormous command and control problems, as I can attest from personal experience.

In late 1968, before taking command of HMS *Rorqual,* I was appointed operations officer to the staff of Admiral Griffin, who then commanded the Royal Navy's Far East Fleet. My duties were the day-to-day operation of the fleet—an aircraft carrier, fuel tanker, supply ships, destroyers, frigates, and submarines.[13] I quickly learned just how difficult it is to control a fleet of twenty ships, not least in the sudden squalls of the South China Sea, which can reduce visibility to a few yards. Changes in visibility constitute a threat, which requires that the fleet be continuously repositioned.

This experience was repeated when I was in command of HMS *Rorqual.* By tradition, the first Royal Navy vessel on the scene of a sunken submarine takes charge of the recovery operation, irrespective of the seniority of her captain. When HMS *Onslaught* was simulating a sunken submarine on the seabed, the *Rorqual* was the first ship there.[14] So, for a brief period, I exercised operational control of the British Far East Fleet, a task that led me to greatly appreciate the value of wireless and satellite communications.

Zheng He's admirals had no such technology. Instead, they would have relied on bells, gongs, drums, carrier pigeons, and fireworks to coordinate their movements. Consequently, they would have been unable effectively to control more than perhaps twenty junks of various types and capabilities, such as treasure ships supplied by water carriers and grain ships protected by fighting ships. For a short period, in calm seas with unchanging good visibility, they might have been able to control as many as fifty ships. But these conditions do not last long at sea. As the weather changes, so does the threat. Capital ships, such as Zheng He's treasure ships, are protected more closely inshore than in the open ocean. Likewise, the threat of pirates requires a different disposition than that required for landing troops on an exposed beach.

With approximately one thousand ships under his overall command, Zheng He probably would have appointed at least twenty, and quite possibly fifty, rear admirals. On his final voyage, I believe there were four full admirals (Zheng He, Wang Jinghong, Hong Bao, and Zhou Man), eight vice admirals (Wang Heng, Hou Xian, Li Xing, Wu Zhong, Yang Zhen, Zhang Da, Zhu Liang, Zhu Zhen), and another twelve rear admirals[15] in command of a total of twenty-four fleets, which is the minimum number of fleets I would expect given the number of ships.

In my opinion, the case for broad-based leadership of the fleets is reflected in the Taicang stele, which uses the first-person plural to describe the command of men and ships. ("Each time we have commanded several tens of thousands of government soldiers and more than a hundred oceangoing vessels.") The implication is that Zheng He is acting in concert with his team of admirals.

The scope of the shipbuilding program—more than 2,700 ships—undermines the notion that Zheng He commanded just one fleet of a hundred oceangoing vessels. However, a single fleet of a thousand junks would have been impossible to control. Chinese records listing dates for outbound and returning voyages make it clear that different fleets departed and returned under different commanders often years apart.

In sum, the scale of Zheng He's voyages would have required many independent fleets to be simultaneously at sea. Some fleets were no doubt carried off by storms to unexpected destinations. Others, as evidence I'll present in chapter 22 suggests, were surely wrecked, sometimes in the most spectacular fashion. In any case, it should come as no surprise that many, perhaps even a majority, of destinations reached by the fleets were never recorded in official Chinese records. Seafaring in the fifteenth century was an even more hazardous profession than it is today. Many ships never returned home to tell their tales. The loss of life was terrible, as was the economic and intellectual devastation of the wreckage around the world.

This voyage, from which few junks returned, was the most ambitious of them all. Zheng He's fleets were sent to every country in the known world. Consequently the preparations would have been awesome, as I can vouch from my experience in 1969 on the staff of Admiral Griffin's Far East Fleet.

Zheng He's fleet was multinational and multifaith, as was the British fleet in 1969. Our ships had Ethiopian, Iranian, Indian and Pakistani officers, Maltese stewards, Goanese engine-room stokers, Chinese laundrymen, Tamil engineers, Christians, Muslims, Taoists, Hindus, Confucians, Zoroastrians, Buddhists, and Jews. The British Admiralty took great pains to ensure that captains would know of the religion, history, culture, background, and customs of all the crew as well as of the countries the fleet would visit. In the same way the Xuan De emperor and his predecessor, Zhu Di, would also have briefed Zheng He in great detail. They had the ideal tool with which to do so—the *Yongle Dadian*.[16] This massive encyclopedia was completed in 1421 and housed in the newly built Forbidden City. Three thousand scholars had worked for years compiling all Chinese knowledge from the previous two thousand years, in 22,937 passages extracted from more than 7,000 titles, a work of 50 million characters. The encyclopedia was of a scale and scope unparalleled in history and to my mind Zhu Di's monumental legacy to humankind. It was contained in 11,095 books, each 16 inches high and 10 inches wide, requiring 600 yards of shelf space, 5 rows high or one third of one deck of his flagship. The encyclopedia covered every subject on the planet: geography and cartography, agriculture, civil and military engineering, warfare, health and medical care, building and town planning, steel and steel production, ceramics firing and painting, biochemistry including cross-fertilization, alcohol production, silk making and weaving, gunpowder making, ship construction, even codes, cyphers, and cryptography. We know this from the contents pages, of which there are copies in the National Libraries in Beijing and Taipei, the British Library in London, the Bibliothèque Nationale in Paris, and the Asian Libraries of Oxford and Cambridge Universities.

Fortunately, one part of the *Yongle Dadian* remains more or less whole at Cambridge University, where it has escaped the ravages of the Boxer uprising and more recently the lunacy of Mao's Red Guards, who burned any intellectual book they could lay their hands on. The Cambridge book is about mathematics. Joseph Needham describes the truly amazing depth of Chinese mathematical knowledge shown in this book, which contains knowledge from the year A.D. 263 onward.[17]

There are chapters giving practical advice on using trigonometry to determine heights of buildings, hills, trees, and towns on cliffs, and the circumference of walled cities, the depth of ravines, and the breadth of river estuaries.

No fewer than ninety-five mathematical treatises of the Song dynasty are mentioned, some on such specialized subjects as the Chinese remainder theorum and cryptoanalysis—the use of mathematics to break codes. There are mathematical methods for calculating the area and volume of circles, spheres, cones, pyramids, cubes, and cylinders and for determining magic numbers and constructing magic squares, and the principles of square-root extraction and negative numbers. It was lucky Zheng He had a prodigious memory—he could recite the entire Koran by heart in Arabic at the age of eleven.

As Needham points out, the discoveries made on the voyages of Zheng He's fleet were incorporated into the *Yongle Dadian*. One can go further and say that one of Zhu Di's leading objectives was to acquire knowledge gained from the barbarians. This is epitomized in the instructions given to the three previous eunuchs, Zheng He, Jang Min, and Li Qi in 1403—to be described in the next chapter.[18]

The best way to acquire knowledge, Zhu Di knew, would be to share it—to show the barbarians how immensely deep, wide, and old was Chinese knowledge and Chinese civilization. Zheng He and his captains were thus key players in compiling the knowledge contained in the *Yongle Dadian*. For this of course they needed to have copies of the encyclopedia aboard their junks, and they needed also to brief interpreters about the contents so the message could be propagated. Zhu Di made enormous strides in improving Chinese printing methods, which enabled parts of the *Yongle Dadian* to be reproduced.[19]

Even "Pascal's" triangle was included in the *Yongle Dadian*—centuries before Pascal. The Chinese have always been practical. Mathematics was applied to surveying and cartography. By the Eastern Han dynasty (A.D. 25–A.D. 220), Chinese surveyors were using compass and squares, plumb lines and water levels. By the third century they were using the trigonometry of right-angle triangles, by the fourteenth century the Jacob's staff to measure heights and distances.

Ch'in Chiu-shao in his book *Shu-Shu Chiu-Chang* of 1247[20] (included in the *Yongle Dadian*) used knowledge of Chinese mathematics and Chinese surveying instruments to calculate the areas of rice fields, the volume of water required to flood those fields, and hence the size and flow rate of dykes that would be required. He gave different methods of building canals and the strength of lock gates that would be needed.

One could carry out a similar exercise for military machines available to Zheng He and how these had been developed over the centuries. The *Yongle Dadian* included details on how to build mortars, bazookas, cannons, rocket-propelled missiles, flamethrowers, and all manner of gunpowder bombs. This vast encyclopedia was a massive collective endeavor to bring together in one place Chinese knowledge gained in every field over thousands of years. Zheng He had the immense good fortune to set sail with priceless intellectual knowledge in every sphere of human activity. He commanded a magnificent fleet—magnificent not only in military and naval capabilities but in its cargo—intellectual goods of great value and sophistication. The fleet was the repository of half the world's knowledge.

He also had well-educated officers who through interpreters could speak to the leaders of foreign countries in seventeen different languages including Arabic, Persian, Hindi, Tamil, Swahili, and Latin.[21] Zheng He's fleet resembled a floating university and probably had more intellectual knowledge in its library than any university in the world at that time.

THE FLEETS ARE PREPARED
FOR THE VOYAGE TO
THE BARBARIANS

I n order for the barbarians to follow the way of heaven, they would first need to find their way to the wellspring of Confucian virtue, the Middle Kingdom. Such a journey would require both maps and the ability to establish position at sea. Thus the provision of accurate charts and a viable system of navigation was of paramount importance— not only to facilitate the safe passage of Zheng He and his fleets but also to encourage the barbarians to return tribute to the new emperor.

Zhu Di and his father, Hong Wu, had encouraged the development of every aspect of navigation. A handbook titled *Notebook on Sea Bottom Currents,* found in Quanzhou, states that, after announcing the ascension of the Yongle emperor (Zhu Di) to the throne, Zheng He and his admirals were instructed to search for navigation charts, collecting all the information about currents, islands, mountains, straits, and the positions of stars. They used this data to revise their navigation charts, including compass points and the cross-references of stars.

The Chinese cultivated Arab navigators and astronomers, especially during the Yuan dynasty (1279–1368). According to Gong Zhen, in 1403, two years before the first formal expedition, Zheng He, Jang Min, and Li Qi were sent by Zhu Di to visit countries of the western oceans. Their mission included recruiting foreign navigators capable of deep-sea navigation. For this and much other information in chapters 3 5, and 6, I am indebted to Tai Peng Wang's research.[1]

The writer Yan Congjian stated in *Shuyu Zhouzi Lu* (Compiled information about the remotest foreign countries):

In the first year of the reign of the Emperor Hong Wu of the Ming dynasty (1368) the Emperor converted the Bureau of History into the Bureau of Astronomy. He also established the Bureau of the Chinese Islamic Astronomy. In the second year (1369) the Hong Wu Emperor summoned eleven Chinese Muslims including Zheng Ah Li, the Chinese Muslim Astronomical Officer, to the capital, Nanjing, "on a mission to improve on the Islamic calendars and to observe the astronomical-phenomena. They were each conferred upon with gifts and official titles accordingly.

In 1382 the emperor summoned a group of scholars, including the Islamic observatory official Hai Da Er and a master of Islam named Ma Sa Yi Hei, to choose the best astronomy books among several hundred volumes of *Xiyu Shu* (Books from the western regions) at the Yuan court in Beijing. The next year, a Chinese translation of the selected books, *Tian Wen Shu* (Works of astronomy), was published.

According to the Ming translator Ma Ha, the *Tian Wen Shu* was originally written by Abu Hassan Koshiya (A.D. 971–1029), a Yuan mathematician who played a dominant role in the development of spherical trigonometry. Ma Ha praises Koshiya as "one of the greatest scholars of all times who explained the ultimate theories of astronomy in all its great profundity and simplicity."

The *Tian Wen Shu* explained the Islamic concepts of longitude and latitude. So it is clear that early Chinese concepts of latitude, longitude, and a round earth go back at least to this Ming translation of Islamic geography books. In about 1270 the Arab astrologer Jamal ad-Din had made a terrestrial globe of the earth that correctly depicted the proportions of land (30 percent) and sea (70 percent). He gave the globe to Guo Shoujing, as will be described in later chapters.

A reliance on Islamic navigators continued in Zheng He's era. Zheng He himself was a Muslim, and given the advanced state of navigation and astronomy in the Islamic world, it's no wonder he recruited other Muslims to his fleets. According to Chen Shuiyuan, a Taiwanese historian, many were located in Quanzhou, one of the most cosmopolitan cities in the world and home to special graveyards reserved for Muslim sailors. Zheng He and his team also searched the provinces of Fujian, Guangdong, and Zhejiang for superior navigators.

Foreign navigators and astronomers who voyaged on Chinese ships were given Chinese names, such as Wang Gui, Wu Zheng, and Ma Zheng. When they returned after a successful mission, they were rewarded. In 1407, for example, foreigners returning to Quanzhou received notes equivalent to fifty taeles of silver as well as rolls of embroidered silk. In 1430, when a foreign Muslim named Sheban returned from the final expedition, the Xuan De Emperor promoted him to deputy battalion commander.

In a paper titled "Instruments and Observation at the Imperial Astronomical Bureau During the Ming Dynasty," Professor Thatcher E. Deane states:

> As with the development of the calendric systems . . . were most evident at the beginning of a dynasty, less so at the beginning of an individual emperor's reign, and almost never at any other time when such expenditures were not direct investments in legitimising state and ruler. Hong Wu had an urgent need to improve the calendrical system because he was the first of the dynasty; Zhu Di was accused of usurping the throne so he also had a very strong need.

Gifts for Foreign Rulers

This obsessive focus on improving navigational techniques enabled Zheng He's fleets to reach foreign countries, where, after presenting their credentials, the Chinese ambassadors would supply maps and astronomical tables to the rulers. The gift of knowledge was intended to make it possible for them to return tribute to the Middle Kingdom.

We know from recent excavations at the Jingdezhen kilns (where the bulk of the ceramics carried in Zheng He's fleets were fired) and from excavations in Cairo beside the Red Sea Canal, as well as from collections in Europe, that Chinese delegations offered personal gifts to foreign leaders. Ceramic copies of Mamluk candlesticks were given to the Mamluk sultans, along with blue and white flasks, ewers, porcelain cups, and pen boxes. A ewer cover decorated with an armillary sphere in cobalt was fired for the king of Portugal, as were ceramic tiles for Ottoman sultans.

Gifts for more ordinary folk made the journey as well. Playing cards, chess, and mah-jongg sets were given to merchants. Children's whirligig toys, kites, and hot-air balloons were dispensed.

The saddest cargo of the great fleets were women. Traditionally, foreign rulers were each presented with one hundred slave girls. When the fleets returned, the Xuan De emperor observed: "Ten thousand countries are our guests." The number of concubines and slave girls embarked must have been staggering. In a subsequent chapter, we'll show how, after the Chinese squadron reached Venice, female slaves and their offspring made a significant impact on the domestic life and population of Venice, Florence, and Tuscany.

Finally, a word about the most valuable part of the fleet—the sailors.

Like their modern counterparts, their most prized possessions were mementoes of their loved ones at home—drawings, locks of a wife's or children's hair, little presents, perhaps a pet dog, a tub of roses, or a tame, flightless bird or pet duck. Chinese sailors were avid gamblers; playing cards and dice were part of everyday life, as was mah-jongg.

Like today's sailors, they would have been keen to better themselves. As the voyage progressed and boredom set in, they would have put aside novels for progressively more serious reading. By Zheng He's era, printed popular books were widely available and all kinds of pocket encyclopedias were sold. Reference books (*jih yung lei shu*) with illustrations and descriptions covered all manner of practical subjects: agriculture; salt and sugar manufacture; collecting ceramics and bronzes; ship and cart making; coal and fuel use; paper making and printing; welding technology; alcohol fermentation; pearl and jade collecting.

The *Nung Shu,* a popular encyclopedia first published in 1313, provided descriptions and illustrations of agricultural machinery, including tilt and trip hammers; rotary grinding mills; winnowing fans; bellows powered by piston rods, connecting rods, and horizontal water wheels; flour-sifting machinery drawn by a water wheel; vertical water wheels for driving textile machinery; winders or windlasses with cranks for cranes, wells, and mine shafts; salt mills; pearl-diving apparatus; scoop wheels; pallet chain pumps driven by animals; chain pumps powered by horizontal water wheels; chain pumps operated solely by the current; rotary grinding mills operated by horizontal windmills; double-edged runner mills operated by horizontal water wheels; roller mills; cotton gins; and mills for grinding rice or corn. (See examples on pages in later chapters.)

Doubtless these descriptions of how to make a wide variety of useful farm machinery would have had value to farmers in other countries. Once the Chinese sailors were ashore, they could have supplemented their wages by selling these books, just as sailors in my time would sell cigarette rations to the locals or give their rum tots to pretty girls.

Another pocket encyclopedia, the *Wu-ching Tsung-yao,* a collection of the most important military techniques, gave detailed accounts of the construction and functions of a vast array of military machines. Here is Professor Joseph Needham's translation of the text next to an eleventh-century description of how to make a flamethrower:

> On the right is the naphtha flame thrower (*fang meng huo yu*). The tank is made of brass and supported on four legs. From its upper surface arise four vertical tubes attached to a horizontal cylinder above. They are all connected with the tank. The head and tail of the cylinder are large, (the middle) of narrow diameter. In the tail is a small opening the size of a millet grain. The head end has two round openings.

The description continues for another six lines before instructions are given for loading the machine:

> Before use the tank is filled with rather more than three catties of the oil with a spoon through a filter (*sha lo*). At the same time gunpowder (*huo yao*) is placed in the ignition chamber at the head. When the fire is to be started one applies a heated branding-iron (to the ignition chamber) and the piston rod is forced fully into the cylinder.[2]

Subsequent instructions describe how to cope with misfiring or break-down.

There are equally detailed descriptions of other military hardware in this remarkable book. The most formidable weapon described is a water-wheeled battleship dating from the Song dynasty (A.D. 960–1279). It details a twenty-two-wheeled ship commanded by rebels and an even bigger one owned by the government. "Against the paddle wheel fighting ship of Yang Yao, the government force used live bombs thrown from trebuchet catapults. For these they used pottery containers with very thin walls, within which were placed poisonous drugs, lime and fragments of scrap iron. When these were hurled onto the rebel ships during engagements, the lime filled the air like smoke or fog so that sailors could not open their eyes."[3]

What is extraordinary is that this military information seems to have been unclassified—it could have been acquired by anyone. It must have been of considerable value to realms that lacked sophisticated gunpowder weapons in the 1430s, including Venice and Florence. Perhaps Chinese officers supplemented their incomes by selling these military pocket encyclopedias.

We can be confident that Zheng He's fleets had every weapon then known to the Chinese: sea-skimming rockets, machine guns, mines, mortars, bombards for use against shore batteries, cannons, flame-throwers, grenades, and much more. His fleets were powerfully armed and well supplied by water tankers and grain and horse ships, which enabled them to stay at sea for months on end. In addition, the ships were repositories of great wealth—both material and intellectual.

Of equal importance were the calendars carried by the fleets. Given the order to inform distant lands of the commencement of the new reign of Xuan De, an era when "everything should begin anew," a calendar was essential to Zheng He's mission.

Today, calendars are little more than holiday presents—Pirelli Tire calendars, featuring beautiful women, gardening calendars awash with color, others that remind us of bank holidays, when to celebrate Easter and file our tax returns. In the 1430s, Europeans had no unified calendar, for they had not yet agreed how to measure time. The Gregorian calendar did not come into use until a century later. To Islamic people, however, a unified calendar was essential. The Muslim calendar was based on lunar months rather than the solar year. Each month had a different purpose, such as the month to make the hajj, the pilgrimage to Mecca, which began on the first day of the new moon. The Muslim calendar also provided the times of the five daily prayers.

The calendar was likewise of great political and economic importance to the Chinese, who for thousands of years had led the world in calendar making. In *Ancient Chinese Inventions* (page 67), Deng Yinke describes their meticulous approach.

In 1276 Kublai Khan, the first emperor of the Yuan dynasty, assigned the task of compiling a new calendar to astronomer Guo Shou Jing so that his new empire would have a unified calendar from north to south and the errors in previous calendars could be corrected. Guo was a scientist with an exceptional talent and dedication. On taking over the task, Guo said "a good calendar must be based on observations and observations depend upon good devices." He went on to examine the Hun Yi (armillary sphere), the only instrument in the observatory of the capital Dadu (Beijing), and found that the North Star of it was set at 35° which was at the latitude of Kaifeng where the Hun Yi was made. This meant that the instrument had not been adjusted when it was transported to Dadu from Kaifeng. . . . Guo thus made it a priority to develop new devices. Within three years of strenuous efforts he worked out twelve astronomical devices which were far better in function and accuracy than previous ones. He also made a number of portable instruments for use in field studies outside Dadu.

As part of the calendar project, Guo presided over a nationwide programme of astronomical observations. He selected twenty-seven sites for astronomical observation throughout the country, which covered a wide area from latitude 15° N to 65° N and longitude 128° E to longitude 102° E. The items of observation included the length of the shadow of the gnomon, the angle of the North Star from the ground surface, and the beginning times of day and night on the vernal equinox and the autumnal equinox. . . . Guo also examined nearly nine hundred years of astronomical records from 462 to 1278 and selected six figures from the records for calculating the duration of the tropical year. Guo's result was 365.2425 days, which was the same as that of the Gregorian calendar, the calendar now widely used across the world. . . .

Guo Shou Jing and the other astronomers worked for four years and completed the calendar in 1280. They made numerous calculations converting the data of the ecliptic coordinate and the equatorial coordinate systems, and used twice interpolations to solve the variations in the speed of the sun's movement, which affected the accuracy of the calendar. The calendar was unprecedented in accuracy. It adopted the winter solstice of the year 1280, the ninth year of the Yuan dynasty, as the epoch, the point of reference for the calendar, and established the duration of a tropical year of 365.2425 days and that of a lunar month 29.530593 days. The error between the duration of its tropical year and that of the revolution of the earth around the sun was only 26 seconds. The calendar was named the *Shoushi,* meaning "measuring time for the public."

Issuing calendars was the prerogative of the emperor alone. Accuracy was necessary to enable astronomers to predict eclipses and comets—a sign that the emperor enjoyed heaven's mandate. If predictions proved incorrect, the astronomer responsible was severely punished, often with death.

The *Shoushi* calendar produced by Guo Shoujing was officially adopted by the Ming Bureau of Astronomy in 1384. This is the calendar that Zhu Di and the Xuan De emperor would have ordered Zheng He to present to foreign heads of state (discussed in detail in later chapters).

The Shoushi calendar can be viewed in the *Yuan shi-lu,* the official history of the Yuan dynasty. However, copies also came into the possession of Europeans, notably the diarist Samuel Pepys and the famous scientists Robert Boyle and Robert Hooke. The Japanese and Koreans also copied the calendar, and translations from those languages can be viewed on our website.

The calendar contained the length of a solar day at the latitude of Beijing. This is the duration from the time when the sun is at its maximum height (altitude) in the sky from one day to the next. We tend to think of this as twenty-four hours. It is not. The earth rotates around its own axis every twenty-three hours and fifty-six minutes while also traveling round the sun. The combination of the two movements means that the earth's position relative to the sun, compared with its position relative to the stars, varies by about four minutes each day. Moreover, the earth's trajectory around the sun is not a circle but an ellipse. The sun is not at the center of this ellipse, so that as the earth nears the sun it accelerates. As the earth recedes from the sun, on the longer leg of the ellipse, it decelerates. Its rotation also speeds up approaching the sun and slows down receding from the sun.

Thus, the length of the solar day varies throughout the year. The difference of this length is called the equation of time of the sun. To predict the length of the year at 365.2425 days, which is accurate to within ten seconds a year, Guo Shoujing had to take into account four of these movements. In order to accomplish that, he must have known how the solar system worked, including the facts that the earth travels around the sun in an ellipse and is not at the center of the universe and that the earth is attracted to the sun's much bigger mass.

Guo Shoujing's calculations for the lunar month of 29.530593 days

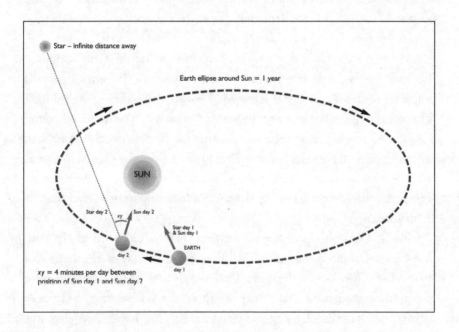

A diagram showing how the earth travels in an ellipse around the sun.

were even more impressive, requiring a more complex trigonometry. The moon travels around the earth as the earth is moving in an ellipse around the sun. This means that as the earth approaches the sun, the moon's attraction to the sun's mass increases, so the speed at which the moon travels around the earth accelerates. Then, as the earth recedes from the sun on its elliptical path, the moon decelerates. Hence, to make his extraordinarily accurate calculations, Guo had to be aware not only that the earth travels around the sun in an ellipse but also that the moon circles the earth. He had to have understood spherical trigonometry and to have employed calculus and have had an accurate idea of the respective masses of earth, sun, and moon.

However, there are further ramifications to Guo Shoujing's achievements. The earth's trajectory around the sun is not constant: it changes over the years. Guo knew of these changes, which he had gathered from Chinese observations stretching back eight hundred years. The great French astronomer Pierre-Simon Laplace credited Guo Shoujing with knowledge of what Laplace called the "diminution of the ecliptic"—essentially, the fact that the earth's ecliptic path around the sun had grown flatter over the centuries.

Even further refinements were taken into account by Guo Shoujing. The earth is not a perfect sphere but an oblate spheroid with flattened poles. Its center of gravity is somewhat below the center of its volume. This means the earth has a slight wobble, which can be deduced by the apparent position of the stars—in particular by Polaris, the Pole Star, which apparently moves over a 26,000-year period. This movement had been compensated for by the Chinese before Guo Shoujing's era. Templates had been made to adjust for the apparent movement of Polaris.

Finally, Guo Shoujing knew of the planets' orbits around the sun, and even of Jupiter's rotation and its circling moons. The American writer Rosa Mui and colleagues Paul Dong and Zhou Xin Yan have kindly informed me of the work of Professor Xi Zezong, a Chinese astronomer based in Beijing, who has found that Jupiter's satellites or moons were first discovered two thousand years before Galileo by the Chinese astronomer Gan De.

Since A.D. 85, Chinese astronomers have made accurate observations of the period of planetary revolutions around the sun (synodic intervals). They are correct to within a few hours—Mercury 115 days, Venus 584 days, Mars 779 days, Jupiter 398 days, Saturn 378 days. (In later chapters, we provide evidence that Copernicus, Galileo, Kepler, Hooke, and Newton were aware of the Chinese astronomers' work.)

In their published paper entitled "Calendars, Interpolation, Gnomons and Armillary Spheres in the Works of Guo Shoujing (1231–1314)," Ng Say Tiong and Professor Helmer Aslaksen of the Department of Mathematics, National University of Singapore, note that the inconsistent motions of the moon and sun were discovered in the Eastern Han period (A.D. 25–200), and during the North and South dynasty (A.D. 386–589), respectively. The method of interpolation employed by A.D. 554–610 was the equal interval second difference method. (Please refer to our *1434* website for further explanation.) Guo Shoujing improved on this by using a third difference method of interpolation, which enabled him to determine the equation of time of the sun and moon and hence to predict their positions. Guo Shoujing had developed the forward distance method of interpolation subsequently further developed by Newton into calculus.

The *Shoushi* calendar, which Zheng He's fleets presented to heads of state, based upon Guo Shoujing's pioneering work, contained a mass of astronomical data running to thousands of observations. It enabled comets and eclipses to be predicted for years ahead, as well as times of sunrise and sunset, moonrise and moonset. The positions of the sun and moon relative to the stars and to each other were included, as were the positions of the planets relative to the stars, sun, and moon. Adjustments enabled sunrise and sunset, and moonrise and moonset, to be calculated for different places on earth for every day of the year. As described in detail in chapter 4, the calendar enabled longitude to be calculated by using the slip between solar and sidereal time, by eclipses of the moon, or by the angular distance between the moon and selected stars or planets. Please refer to the *1434* website and to the endnotes for further explanation.

Tai Peng Wang has found the specific stars by which Zheng He's fleet navigated. We can set these up on the "Starry Night" computer program for the dates when Zheng He's fleet was transiting the Indian Ocean en route for the Malabar Coast of India and Cairo. We can also compare these stars with those included in Zheng He's navigational tables and the almanac for the year 1408, now in the Pepys Library at Cambridge. (The 1408 tables contain similar astronomical information as that contained in the *Shoushi* calendar.)

Thus Zheng He was able to provide Europeans with maps, navigational tools, and an astronomical calendar beyond anything they had yet been able to produce on their own. Supplied with this revolutionary knowledge, the barbarians would be able to make their way to the Middle Kingdom, appropriately "with deference."

ZHENG HE'S NAVIGATORS'
CALCULATION
OF LATITUDE
AND LONGITUDE

There are no signposts in the open ocean. The only way a navigator can determine his position is by using the stars, planets, sun,
and moon.

As a first step, a navigator must have a system of providing markers
across the oceans. This system of markers, adopted by all seafaring
civilizations for millennia, is latitude and longitude. It involves drawing
imaginary horizontal and vertical lines over the globe. Horizontal lines
are called latitude lines, and the vertical are longitude lines.

Latitude lines are parallel with the equator; each longitude line
passes through both the North and South Poles. So a navigator's precise position can be fixed on the globe using a common system.

In order to have produced an accurate map of the world by 1418,
the Chinese fleets must have had such a system to determine their positions at sea. Without an accurate system, captains could not have
known the true locations of newly discovered lands, and any map derived from their disparate calculations would have been an incoherent
mess.

Unlike the Europeans, who followed Babylonian astronomers with
360 degrees of longitude, the Chinese employed 365¼ degrees. The
Chinese used latitude degrees below Polaris (at 90° elevation). The

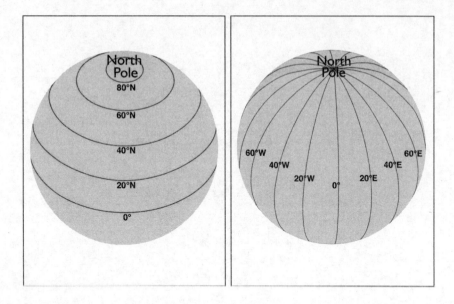

Diagrams showing the lines of latitude and longitude around a globe.

Europeans used latitude above the equator (Polaris 0° elevation). The results are the same for both systems.

After establishing a common system for the earth, the Chinese next had to establish a common map of the heavens. Each navigator would have had to use the same name for the same star as well as the same star map from which longitude would have been determined.

How the Chinese Fixed the Stars' Positions in the Sky

In the thirteenth century, the astronomer Guo Shoujing fixed the positions of key stars relative to Polaris (the Pole Star). Polaris appears on an extension of the earth's axis, billions of miles away above the North Pole. Because of the earth's rotation, the heavens appear to rotate around Polaris. The farther north one goes, the more of the heavens one can see.

In 1964 I was navigator of HMS *Narwhal,* a submarine operating

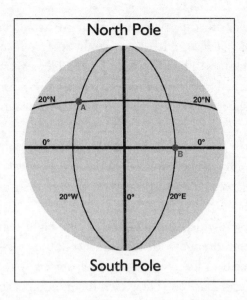

Diagram showing the positions of ships A and B on a globe.
Ship A is at 20° N 20° W, Ship B is at 0° N 20° E.

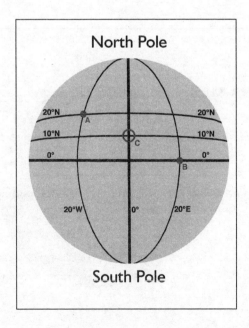

Ships A and B discovering new lands at point C will have the same
position for the new land: 10° N 0° E.

under the polar ice cap. Now and then we would find clear-water "lakes," called *polynyas,* where we would surface in order to fix our position by the stars. The heavens appeared like a vast globe above us. As we approached the North Pole, we seemed to be inside a bowl looking at a hemisphere of stars spreading in an arc down to the horizon all around us.

At the North Pole, the Chinese could fix the position of every star in the Northern Hemisphere relative to Polaris. The stars are so far away that to an observer on earth they never change their positions relative to one another.

The Chinese divided the sky into twenty-eight segments or mansions. Picture an orange with its skin sliced; the cuts start where the orange was fixed to its tree and continue vertically downward. They called each mansion a *hsiu.* They fixed the position of stars at the top of each of the twenty-eight mansions relative to the Pole Star (*ABC*).

Then they fixed stars in the lower part (DEF) of each segment rela-

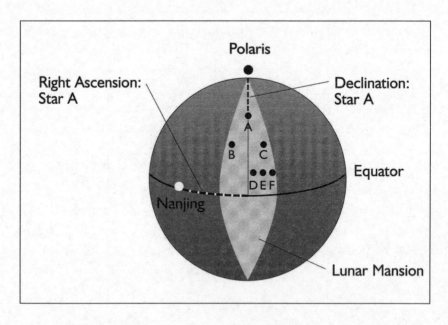

The Chinese fixed the position of stars at the top of each
of the 28 lunar mansions relative to the Pole Star.

tive to those in the upper part (ABC). Because stars never change their position relative to one another, even if the Chinese were not near the North Pole and hence could not see the stars in the lower part of each segment (because these stars were below the horizon), they always knew the stars' positions. So they could produce star maps.

They noted the vertical positions of each star below Polaris (none can be above Polaris) and the horizontal position of each *hsiu* relative to Nanjing (longitude). The Chinese called the vertical height of each star below Polaris "declination" and its position around the equator from Nanjing "right ascension." So for the stars in the sky, the Chinese had the same system of measurement they used to determine latitude and longitude. This system was called the equatorial system—vastly simpler than the equinoctial system, used in medieval times before Guo Shoujing, which relied on the ecliptic or the horizon. After 1434, Europeans adopted the Chinese system, which remains in use today.

Next, the Chinese needed precise instruments to measure each star's position. Guo Shoujing provided the tools. A sighting tube was first positioned by pointing it at Polaris at precisely the angle of the observer's latitude—that is, if the observer was at the North Pole, the sighting tube would be at 90° elevation (see page 34). On this diagram, the instrument is aligned to Polaris at 39°49 N, the latitude of Beijing. Once positioned, the instrument was bolted down—because if the angle changed from the latitude of the observer, it became useless.

The observer then selected a star, looking at it through another tube attached to a circle marked in degrees. The movement of the tube along the circle gave the number of degrees below Polaris of the selected star (the arc y-z), which is the star's declination.

The horizontal angle, the angle from Nanjing, was found by rotating the ring around the equatorial circle, which gave the horizontal angle of the star from Nanjing (its right ascension). The position of the star then was entered in the star tables. The Chinese entered 1,461 stars in their tables, a process that required many astronomers and hundreds of years.

Tables were printed and, along with a star map, given to each navigator. Thus all navigators possessed a common system of latitude and

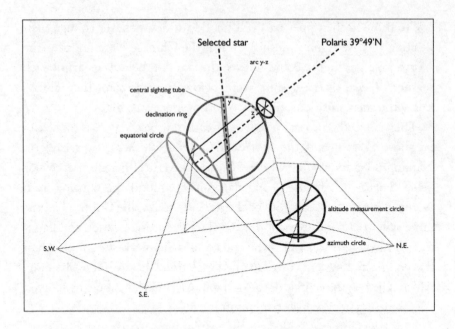

Selected star

arc y-z

Polaris 39°49'N

central sighting tube

declination ring

equatorial circle

altitude measurement circle

azimuth circle

S.W.

N.E.

S.E.

A torquetum based on the equatorial system, as used by Zheng He's
navigators and pioneered by Guo Shoujing.

longitude to fix their positions on the globe, and an identical map of
the heavens, which enabled them to recognize each star.

How the Star Tables Allowed Longitude to Be Calculated

For the following description, I am indebted to Professor Robert Cribbs,
who has tested the method described to prove its efficacy. This method
allows longitude to be determined on any clear day without waiting for
a lunar eclipse and without sending messages back to the observer in
Beijing. It is a much more advanced method than that described in my
book *1421* (that method, kindly explained to me by Professor John Oliver and Marshall Payn, is dependent on eclipses of the moon, which do
not happen all that frequently).

Professor Cribbs's method is based on the fact that the earth not only
rotates on its own axis every twenty-three hours and fifty-six minutes

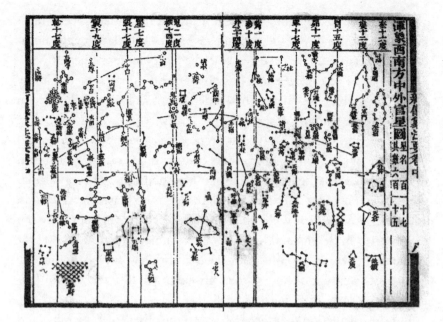

This is a typical star map as used by Zheng He and his navigators.

but also travels in an ellipse around the sun—something Guo Shoujing had worked out back in 1280. The combination of these two movements means there is a slip of four minutes each day between the time when the earth is in the same position relative to the sun (solar time, twenty-four hours) and the time when the earth is in the same position relative to the stars (sidereal time, twenty-three hours and fifty-six minutes). This slip between sidereal time and solar time amounts to one day every 1,461 days, or four years. The effect is that every midnight, twelve hours after the sun has hit its highest point in the sky, a different star will be in line with Polaris than the day before.

Astronomers in Nanjing observed the night sky for every day of the 1,461-day cycle and noted the star in line with Polaris at precisely midnight. They produced a table of 1,461 days, which was dispensed to navigators. The 1408 astronomical calendar covers 366 days of that cycle. A copy of a page of the 1408 astronomical tables is reproduced later in the color insert of this book.

With the tables in hand, a navigator in, say, the Indian Ocean must know only which day of the cycle it is, which he calculates by the number of sunsets that have occurred since he left Nanjing. If he left Nanjing on day 61 of the cycle and has noted eighty sunsets, then it is day 141. On the tables, he can see that Aldebaran is in line with Polaris on day 141 (to the Nanjing observer).

However, in the Indian Ocean he observes another, unrecognized star in line with Polaris. He consults his star map and confirms from the tables that it is Betelgeuse. He can now make one of two calculations: he can note the difference in right ascension between Aldebaran and Betelgeuse, which will equal the difference in longitude between the observer in Beijing and himself; or he can note the time it takes for Aldebaran to come into line with Polaris. If this is, say, six hours (one quarter of twenty-four hours), then his longitude difference from Beijing is 90 degrees (one quarter of 360°).

For the calculation to be accurate, both the observer in Nanjing and the navigator in the Indian Ocean must be looking due north at Polaris. If they wish to use the second method to calculate longitude, both must have precisely the same midnight. They do this as follows: First they use a vertical stick to measure the sun's shadow. When the shadow is shortest, the sun is at its maximum height at midday and is due south. Both observers build a trench running due north-south, a trench that can be flooded to see the reflection of Polaris at night and emptied of water to measure the sun's shadow at midday.

The sun's shadow when at its shortest can be measured on the trench. To get the precise second, the shadow is sharpened by employing a pinhole camera atop a pole called a gnomon (described on the website). By using identical gnomons and a standardized pinhole camera, the observers in Nanjing and the Indian Ocean can each determine the same due south/north and the same instant when the sun is at its highest—that is, midday. Our experiments described on the *1434* website have shown that they can calculate this to within two seconds. They can now use a standardized clock to calculate midnight, twelve hours after midday. The *1434* website explains how this Chinese clock worked and how, in Zheng's era, refinements were built to compensate for different temperatures and air pressures, which would otherwise have affected the number of drips coming out of the clock. Thus time was accurate to within two seconds.

Using the water clock, the observer in Nanjing and the observer in the Indian Ocean establish the same midnight. After sunset the trench is flooded and two poles are placed on either side of the trench; a line is suspended horizontally between the poles. Another line is hung vertically so the observer can see the reflection of the vertical string in the water of the trench in line with Polaris. At the instant of midnight, the navigator in the Indian Ocean looks at the star in line with Polaris reflected in the water, which is in line with the string. (In our example, on day 141 this star is Betelgeuse.) His tables for day 141 say that in Nanjing the star is Aldebaran. From that, he can determine his longitude. According to Robert Cribbs, the method is accurate to within two seconds, which amounts to a maximum error of three degrees in longitude, negligible for mapping the world.

This method requires the navigator to be on land. However, Professor Cribbs has also developed a method of determining longitude at sea by using the equation of time of the moon and the angular distance between the moon and a selected star. To deploy this method (see *1434* website) some calculus is required to establish the future position of the moon for the 1,461-day cycle. By 1280, Guo Shoujing had established a system very similar to calculus. The results appeared in his tables and calendar, which were adopted by the Ming in 1384. Consequently, they were available to Zheng He's fleets, as were tables of declination of the sun.

Thanks to Tai Peng Wang, who brought the matter to my attention, and to the work of Xi Feilong, Yang Xi, and Tang Xiren, who have recently discovered the star maps of Zheng He's voyages, we know which stars Zheng He's fleet actually used to determine latitude and longitude on their passage to India. They sailed with the monsoon winds, starting across the Indian Ocean from the northwest tip of Sumatra at Pulau Rondo, now called Banda Atjeh, on October 10, 1432, determining latitude and longitude as follows: "Gauging the vertical positions of the given stars above the horizon in the east, west, north and south, they reached Sri Lanka." Using Vega, Sagittarius, Gemini, and Poseidon, they arrived at Calicut (11° N, 76° E) on December 10. See the TPW paper "Zheng He's delegation to the Papal Court at Florence" on the *1434* website.

Finally, how accurate were Zheng He's navigators? Two answers produce the same result: their measurement of declination at 22°2330" (correct to within two miles) and the accuracy of the eye, which can be judged to within a quarter of a degree—the full moon appears large but its diameter is under half a degree (thirty miles).

It is my submission that Zheng He's navigators were able to calculate latitude to within half a degree, or thirty miles, and longitude to within two seconds, or three degrees. When the fleets arrived in Venice and Florence, their methods of calculating latitude and longitude were transferred to Europeans. In due course, Columbus and Vespucci used them to reach the New World.

5

VOYAGE TO THE RED SEA

On January 19, 1431, the fleets left Nanjing, China. They invariably sailed in January because of the free power provided by the monsoons, which to this day determine sailing patterns from China across the Indian Ocean to India and Africa.[1]

Monsoons are caused by the difference in temperature between the massive Himalayan plateau and the sea. In summer the Asian landmass becomes hotter than the ocean, sucking winds and water vapor off the sea. In April the southwest monsoon is heralded by westerly winds in the Indian Ocean. By May the southwest monsoon hits Indochina to reach its peak and constancy in July, by which time winds reach thirty knots in the South China Sea. By now India is flooded with monsoon rain. During September the temperature drops, and by November, when the Himalayas have become bitterly cold, air is drawn off the mountains by the warmer seas.

The northeast monsoon starts in late December, after which the wind gradually abates until April, when the cycle begins again. Ships sailing between China, India, and Africa took advantage of these monsoons to sail before the wind, returning on the next monsoon to their respective countries. They awaited the change of monsoon in some sheltered harbor. For example, in Southeast Asia, by the time Indian ships had arrived in the Malacca Strait with the southwest monsoon winds, Chinese junks had not yet departed their home ports. By the time the Chinese arrived, the Indian ships were gone. Hence the need for harbors around the Indian Ocean where goods could be stored from one monsoon season to the next. The Chinese and Arabs built entrepôt ports in Southeast Asia and around the Indian Ocean where goods were warehoused en route to their final destinations.

Monsoons were so predictable—and important—that they were incorporated into Arab calendars, which illustrated the highly synchronized system of regular shipping between Egypt, East Africa, India, and the Gulf. For example, one such calendar describes day 68 (March 16): "End of sailing of Indian ships from India to Aden: no-one ventures after this day." (See research of Tai Peng Wang in notes).

Zheng He's fleets took advantage of this Islamic navigational calendar, joining the regular schedule of shipping. As the historian Paul Lunde points out in "The Navigator Ahmad Ibn Majid," on day 100 (April 15) the last fleet from India was scheduled to arrive in Aden. The departure from Egypt of the first ships of the convoy, owned by the Karimi merchants, was timed so the convoy's arrival coincided with the Indians'. Four months later, on August 14 (day 220), the last ships from Egypt arrived in Aden. Six days later, ships from Sri Lanka and Coramandel set out on their voyage home. The last departure from Aden, powered by the monsoon, was on day 250 (September 13).

In Zheng He's era, ocean trade was dominated by the Arabs and Chinese. The Chinese made goods that the rest of the world craved—principally, porcelain and silk. Chinese junks carried these valuable cargoes to Malacca, India, and Cairo. Malacca was virtually a Chinese colony. In Calicut, on the Malabar Coast of India, Chinese and Arab traders met in equal numbers.

Relations between the Chinese and Arabs had been friendly for centuries. In Cairo the Chinese were an established minority. Likewise, there was a substantial Arab quarter in the Chinese port of Quanzhou. Many Arab navigators and interpreters joined Zheng He's fleets.

In every respect—numbers, ship construction, cargo capacity, range, defense, communications, supplies, the ability to navigate in the trackless oceans, and the repair and maintenance of ships at sea for months on end—the Chinese were centuries ahead of Europe. The most powerful fleet after China's belonged to Venice, which possessed around three hundred galleys—fast, light, shallow ships rowed by oarsmen. Venetian galleys, the largest of which carried around fifty tons of cargo, were suitable for calm summer days in the Mediterranean—but not for anything like the travails of the Chinese fleets.

Zheng He's treasure ships were oceangoing monsters, capable of sailing through storms across the oceans of the world for weeks at a time. Carrying more than a thousand tons of cargo, they could reach Malacca in five weeks, the Strait of Hormuz in twelve. Staterooms were provided for ambassadors and their staffs returning to India, the Persian Gulf, and Africa. More than 180 medical officers were on the admiral's staff; each ship had a medical officer for every 150 men, and they took on sufficient citrus and coconuts to protect them from scurvy for two months. Caulkers, sailmakers, anchor repairers, scaffolders, carpenters, and specialists in tung oil application maintained the ships during the voyage. In addition, the ships carried interpreters who could communicate with rulers in India, Africa, and Europe—in Hindi, Swahili, Arabic, and Romance languages. As with all Chinese expeditions, astrologists and geomancers accompanied the fleets.

While Venetian galleys were primarily protected by archers, Chinese ships were armed with gunpowder weapons—bombards, fragmentation mortars, cannons, flaming arrows, even shells that sprayed excrement over their targets. With these awesome weapons, Admiral Zheng He would have no difficulty destroying pirate fleets. A contest between a Chinese fleet and a rival navy would resemble that between a shark and a minnow. In his final voyage, Zheng He commanded fleets more than ten times the size of Nelson's at Trafalgar.[2]

However, there were two major distinctions between this final voyage and previous trips. First, huge improvements in cartography, navigation techniques, and ship construction made the voyages safer and their destinations more likely to be reached. Second, the principal purpose of this voyage was to present foreign rulers with the Xuan De calendar and with charts and navigational aids to enable foreign rulers to return tribute to China. When Zheng He's junks returned in 1434, the Xuan De emperor, Zhu Zhanji, was able to claim that "ten thousand countries [are] our guests."[3] In the years immediately thereafter, a dozen countries paid tribute to the emperor, including an enormous delegation from Egypt.

Thanks to the research of Tai Peng Wang, we are able to follow the precise route of Zheng He's and Hong Bao's fleets to Calicut. Xi Feilong, Yang Xi, and Tang Xiren, in their recent discovery and analysis of *The Charts of Zheng He's Voyages,* have reproduced Zheng He's route and identified the specific stars his navigators used to determine latitude and longitude on the way to India.

Sailing with the monsoons across the Indian Ocean, their point of departure on October 10, 1432, was Pulau Rondo (Banda Atjeh) on the northwest tip of Sumatra (6°04′ N, 95°07′ E). Zheng He's book of charts describes how by "gauging the vertical positions of the given stars above the horizon in the east, west, north, and south (they) reached Sri Lanka."

The choice of stars (more accurately star groups—some contain multiple and binary stars) used by Zheng He's navigators for their Indian Ocean crossing at first appears baffling. The right ascensions ("longitude in the heavens") are Poseidon, twenty hours, Vega, eighteen hours, Sagittarius, nineteen hours, and Gemini, seven hours. So the positions obtained from their measurements would correspond to their right ascension and the distances from the stars illustrated by the lines CD, EF, GH, and IJ on Fig 6 on our website. That is, an approximate line of 015/195 (seven hours/nineteen hours). Why do all the chosen stars have approximately the same right ascensions? Why not select different stars from different parts of the heavens?

The answer becomes clear when Polaris is considered. Polaris is at 90° elevation at the North Pole and 0° at the equator. Thus the height of Polaris in the sky (altitude) equals latitude—the line AB, Fig 6 on our website. By measuring Polaris's height, a navigator could ascertain his latitude. The best stars to determine longitude would be at right angles to Polaris, that is, stars with right ascensions of 90 and 270 degrees (six and eighteen hours).

This discovery of Tai Peng Wang and his colleagues enables us to refine how Zheng He's sailors determined latitude and longitude. For

latitude, they used the sun at midday (meridian passage) and Polaris by
night in the north. For longitude, they used those stars in the ephemeris tables that had right ascensions nearest six or eighteen hours or,
alternatively, the moon. (I was a submarine navigator for four years and
never thought of such an ingenious solution. One would have needed
only two looks through the periscope—when one was at most risk—
one at Polaris another at Pollux.)

Wang Jinghong, another admiral, would lead his fleet to the Persian
Gulf.

In this chapter, we describe the passage of Zheng He and Hong
Bao, then follow the voyage of a much smaller detachment from
Hong Bao's fleet, which sailed up the Red Sea to Cairo and the
Mediterranean—following in the wake of Zheng He's 1408 voyage to
the Mediterranean.

On November 18, 1432, when the fleets were south of Sri Lanka,
Zheng He ordered Hong Bao to lead the fleet to Calicut, their next
port of call. A commander-in-chief does not order one of his flag officers to lead the fleet into harbor if he himself intends to be present.
This means that Zheng He was detaching part of his fleet under the
command of Hong Bao.[4]

We know from the charts of Zheng He's voyages that Hong Bao
left Calicut for Dandi Bandar farther up the coast (16° N, 73° E),
crossing the Arabian Sea on a course of approximately 330 to make
landfall at Jebel Khamish (22°25′ N, 59°27′ E). After a few days he
pushed on to Bandar 'Abbas, arriving on January 16, 1433. Hong
Bao's fleets returned to Calicut on March 25 and sailed for China on
April 9, reporting there the sad news that Zheng He had "passed
away."

How did Hong Bao know that Zheng He had passed away? After
his order to Hong Bao, Zheng He seems to have vanished. In my view,
for reasons to be described in a later book, after detaching Hong Bao,
Zheng He sailed for Africa and North America, settling near what is
now Asheville, North Carolina, where he died.

Ma Huan, the historian aboard Zheng He's fleet,[5] describes Calicut
in detail. Almost a tenth of Ma Huan's book is devoted to this city-

state, which had become a very important forward base for Zheng He's fleets. Ma Huan, a Muslim, was delighted to find there were more than twenty mosques for a Muslim population of thirty thousand. He gives a detailed account of how trade was conducted between representatives of the treasure fleet and local merchants and brokers. After negotiations, all parties would clasp hands and swear that the agreed prices would never be repudiated.

These fascinating accounts are mirrored in those of Niccolò da Conti, who had reached Calicut in 1419. As Richard Hall points out in *Empires of the Monsoon,* Ma Huan and Niccolò da Conti's descriptions are almost the same word for word,[6] not least in the descriptions of the Indian test for guilt (the accused's finger was dipped in boiling oil; if the finger was burned, it signified guilt).

Niccolò accurately describes construction of the Chinese junks, so I am confident that he boarded one of Zheng He's junks in 1421, which would have given him the ideal opportunity to acquire a map. Just such a map, as I will describe later, turned up in Venice before 1428, and a copy can be seen today in the Doges' Palace. (Although Niccolò da Conti may not have returned to Venice until 1434, in the 1420s he had entrusted his mail to a friend, Piero Tafur, who took it to Venice on his behalf.)

On his 1432 voyage, Hong Bao did not stay long in Calicut. When he arrived, Calicut merchants were about to leave for Tianfang (Egypt) in their own fleet. Hong Bao seized the opportunity, detaching two junks and seven senior officers for a trade delegation laden with silks and porcelains, which joined the Calicut fleet.[7]

The story is taken up by Ibn Tagri Birdi, the celebrated Egyptian historian, in his history of Egypt, *Al Nujun AzZahira Fi Mulek Misr Wal Kahira,* who writes in 1432:

A report came from Mecca, the honoured, that a number of junks had come from China to the seaports of India and that two of them had anchored in the port of Aden, that their goods, chinaware, silks, musk and the like were not disposed of there because of the disorders of the State of Yemen. . . . The Sultan wrote to them to let them come to Jedda and to show them honour.[8]

As Tai Peng Wang points out, there were very good reasons why the Chinese envoys should rush to Mecca—Zheng He and many of his eunuch captains were Muslims. The Ming envoys had been ordered by the emperor to announce the imperial edict of the Xuan De emperor to the kingdoms of Maijia (Mecca), Qian Lida (Baghdad), Wusili (Cairo), Mulanpi Kingdom (Morocco), and Lumi (the Papal States), to inform them that they were all his subjects.

According to the *Ming Shi-lu* (the official Ming history), Egypt and Morocco were among those foreign countries that in Zhu Di's reign (1403–1424) had already received the Chinese imperial edict and gifts (the 1408 visit—*Ming Shi-lu*) but had failed by 1430 to return tribute to China. However, the *Ming Shi-lu* noted that the Papal States and Baghdad were among the foreign countries that had already sent tribute to Ming China during the reign of the emperor Zhu Di.

In 1432, Mecca was part of the Mamluk kingdom of Egypt. The Mamluks ruled by far the richest country in the Western world at that time; Cairo was the world's largest port outside China. The ships that Hong Bao had dispatched to Mecca had also been ordered to Cairo,[9] which lay farther up the Red Sea through the Red Sea–Nile canal. Evidence of the Chinese visit to Cairo comes from the description of the Pyramids on the 1418 Chinese map and in other contemporary Chinese records.

We get a vivid description of earlier Chinese junks from Ibn Battutah who wrote of the immense size of the ships, their petroleum weapons, the luxurious quarters for merchants, and the poor slave girls.

Descriptions of the Chinese Vessels

The Chinese vessels are of three kinds: large ships called junks, middle-sized ones called zaws, and smaller ones called kakams. The large ships have anything from twelve down to three sails which are made of bamboo rods plaited like mats. They are never lowered, but they turn them according to the direction of the wind; at anchor they are left floating in the wind. A ship carries a complement of a thousand men, six hundred of whom are sailors and four hundred men-at-arms, including archers, men with shields and arbalists, that is, men who throw naphtha. Each large vessel is accompanied by three smaller ones, the half, the third, and the quarter. These vessels are built only in the town of Zaitun in China or in Sin Kalan which is Sin al Sin [Canton]. . . . At the side of these baulks are their oars, which are as large as masts, ten or fifteen men joining together to work each of them, and they row standing on their feet. In the vessel they build four decks, [with] cabins, suites and salons for merchants. A set of rooms has several rooms and a latrine: it can be locked by its occupant, and he can take along with him slave girls and wives. . . . Some of the Chinese own large numbers of ships on which their factors are sent to foreign countries. There are no people in the world wealthier than the Chinese.[10]

Ibn Battutah also described the exchange of slaves among the potentates: "The King of China has sent to the Sultan [of India] a hundred Mamluks and slave girls, five hundred pieces of velvet cloth. . . . [The sultan] requited the present with an even richer one . . . a hundred male slaves, a hundred Hindu singing and dancing girls."[11]

Trade delegations between Egypt and China had been commonplace not only centuries before Zheng He's voyages but also centuries before Ibn Battutah's. They were led by the Karim, a formation of Egyptian Jewish merchants who specialized in trade between Cairo, India, and China.[12] A certain Bazaldeen Kulami Karimi,[13] born in 1149, went to China five times, amassing a great fortune from the Chinese ceramic and silk trade. Thirteenth-century chronicler Zhao Ruqua mentions a wealthy Tazi merchant sojourner who financed an Arab cemetery in the southeast quarter of the Chinese port of Quanzhou, so that Arab merchants could be buried facing Mecca.[14]

Chinese merchants imported huge quantities of Arabic frankincense. Song records indicate that Chen Xin Lang, a merchant, imported frankincense valued at 300,000 guan. Karimi merchants in China lived in luxurious houses and were big spenders, the envy of all in the trading port. In consequence, the emperor instructed local officials to watch for "untoward unruly behaviour."

Trade between Calicut and the Egyptian Mamluks flourished in the 1420s. Historian Stanley Lane Poole tells us that in 1425, a captain convoyed fourteen vessels with rich cargoes to Jeddah. The following year, no fewer than forty ships sailed from India to Cairo and Persia, paying duties to the value of seventy thousand dinars.[15]

Reciprocal visits were not restricted to merchants. The kingdom of Mecca sent a delegation to pay tribute to China after Zheng He's visit in 1414; the sultan himself appeared in person with tributes of a lion and a *quilin* (giraffe) to be presented to Zhu Di. In 1433 the sultan sent a delegation led by Shu Xian to accompany the Chinese delegates returning to China.[16]

Liu Gang, owner of the 1418 map, points out a very interesting pattern in several Chinese records, including the *Captivating Views of the Ocean's Shores*; *Notes on the Barbarians in the Western Oceans*; *Records on Tributes from Western Oceans*; and the *Ming Shi-lu* itself.[17] Each of the four books provides a description of Hormuz that cannot possibly correspond to the Hormuz we know today. They describe vegetation that blossoms in spring, leaves that fall in autumn, and winter with frost, little rain, and much dew. The books also state that Hormuz is one of the biggest kingdoms in the western oceans, and that businessmen from barbarian countries arrive by sea or road. Hormuz, they add, is close to the seashore at the end of the Western Sea. People are white-skinned and tall. Society is highly developed in literature, medical knowledge, astronomy, art, and technique—far superior to other barbarians. Indeed, they compare the level of civilization there to that of Zonghua (China).

None of this is applicable to Hormuz, which we know from many fifteenth-century merchants' accounts as a small island in the Strait of Hormuz, between the Persian Gulf and the Gulf of Oman, with little vegetation and no frost, a tiny, inaccessible place so intolerably hot it was inhabited only three months a year. Civilization, including astronomy and medical techniques, was hardly developed at all.

In my view, the "Hormuz" described by the Chinese books of the fifteenth century can only mean Cairo. This is substantiated by the *Ming Shi Waigua Zhuan* (Profiles of foreign countries in Ming history) compiled by You Ton of the Qing dynasty.[18] It states that Mosili (Cairo) was called upon by Chinese envoys, including Zheng He, but that it failed to reciprocate. Descriptions of Chinese trade with Cairo proliferate. The Chinese scholar Li Anshan, in *Feiizhou Hualiko Huarem* (A history of Chinese overseas in Africa) identifies the Mosili kingdom as Egypt and the Jiegantou Kingdom as the port of Alexandria. Mosili was again denoted as Egypt in the pioneering research of Zhang Xing Gang and Han Zhenghua. They also identified Jiegentou as Alexandria, a Chinese transliteration of the Arabic name Zuilkarnain, which was used by the Arabs to refer to Alexander the Great. In *Chinese Religions and National Minorities,* the Chinese historian Bai Shouyi writes, "Mi Xi en [contemporary Egypt] had all regularly sent their merchants and envoys to China and China sometimes would send its envoys or merchants to these countries."

The *Ming Shi-lu* says, "Year 6 [1408] Zheng He went to Hormuz and other countries returning home in Year 8 [1410]." Further corroboration that Zheng He's fleets visited Cairo is found in maps. The 1418 map has this description: "There is a huge city here built with stone, the dimensions of stones can be compared to those used in tombs of the Qin dynasty Emperor." The volume of Emperor Qin's pyramid tomb and the volume of the Pharaoh Khufu's pyramid at Giza are about the same—Qin's has a larger base area, while Khufu's is higher. The Map of Southwest Maritime Countries, from Zheng He's era, also describes the Egyptian Pyramids.

So Egypt was not a new frontier to Zheng He: his forebears had been traveling there for centuries. They had reached Cairo through the shallow Red Sea–Nile canal, which Zheng He's smaller junks would have used as well. From Cairo, the Mediterranean—and southern Europe—were well within reach.

6

CAIRO AND THE
RED SEA-NILE CANAL

The best place to understand the importance of the River Nile to Cairo and Egypt is from the Windows on the World on the 36th floor of the Ramses Hilton. Every time I visit Cairo, I make a point of quaffing lager there surrounded by swifts and swallows twittering at sunset. To the west, highlighted by the setting sun, are the plateau and the Pyramids. The Moqattam Hills are to the east. North and south, the great river storms out of Africa, traveling in a great curve past the Hilton to the green smudge of the delta up north.

Between the Pyramids and the Moqattam Hills rests the large, wide valley over which modern Cairo sprawls. This valley was once more than eight hundred feet below the sea and some thirty to forty miles across. The enormous river gradually dried up thousands of years ago and became heavily forested and rich in game—elephants, hippopotamus, antelope, and all manner of deer and birds. The river, then as now, teemed with fish. Beautiful sunshine for most of the year coupled with the endless flow of water made life easy for hunters.[1] This is why Egypt has one of the oldest civilizations in the world, comparable to that of China along the Yangtze and Yellow Rivers or Mesopotamia between the Tigris and Euphrates.

Over the centuries the silt brought down through Africa by the mighty river has gradually been deposited on the eastern and western banks of what is now modern Cairo. As the river narrowed, the ports have moved steadily north.

The first Europeans here were Greeks, who built a city at Heliopolis, about four miles south of the Ramses Hilton on the east bank of the Nile. The Romans built Babylon, north of Heliopolis; the Arabs built Al-Fustat/Misr (Cairo) still farther north, and in the late Middle Ages the port moved north of where the Hilton stands now—first to Maks and then to Bulaq, which is now opposite Cairo's main railway station. As the ports migrated, so did the entrance to the Red Sea–Nile canal from the river. By the 1420s, the entrance was below what is now the Hilton. Looking to the northeast from the Windows on the World, one can still see its outline. When it was filled in 1899, the walls on either side were left, allowing it to retain water. Today the tramway passes right over this forgotten canal—a green pencil line stretching from the Hilton to the railway station.[2] One can travel beside the canal today from Cairo to Zagazig, as Marcella and I did in 2006; it remains about one hundred feet wide the entire way.

To see how the river has gradually narrowed, you can take a felucca up the Nile, sailing with a gentle breeze against the current, which in autumn is about half a knot. The old Roman fortress of Babylon is still visible, with a very old Coptic church on top of it. A little group of Coptic churches and a synagogue surround the remains of the Roman city. Here the Egyptian authorities, have erected a sign stating: THIS WAS THE ENTRANCE TO THE RED SEA NILE CANAL.

A mass of information exists about the evolution of the canal from the time of the Pharaoh Necho II (610–595 B.C.). Herodotus tells us (*Histories*) that four steles were erected by Darius (522–486 B.C.) to commemorate the canal's construction. Berkeley professor Carol A. Redmount in "The Wadi Tumilat and the Canal of the Pharaohs" writes that the steles were placed on elevations so they could be seen by boats on the canal. The westernmost stele was discovered at Tell el-Maskhuta; the others were found along the canal, ending about six kilometers north of Suez. One face of each stele features hieroglyphs, the other cuneiform (in Persian, Elemite, and Babylonian characters).[3]

Professor Redmount tells us that Herodotus, who visited Egypt in the mid-fifth century B.C., was the first classical author to mention explicitly the canal connecting the Nile to the Red Sea. He said the canal was started by Necho II and completed by Darius. Aristotle, writing in the fourth century B.C., cites Sesostris as the canal's creator. Ptolomy II, Philadelphus (reigned 285–246 B.C.), records the cutting of the canal through the Wadi Tumilat. He is followed by Diodorus Siculus, who, on a visit to Egypt in 59 B.C., confirmed that the waterway was begun by Necho, continued by Darius, and finally completed by Ptolemy II, who provided a lock to compensate for the rise and fall of the Nile. According to Strabo (64 B.C.–A.D. 24), the canal was 46 meters wide and of sufficient depth to accommodate large ships. In his *Natural History,* Pliny states that the canal was 100 feet wide and 40 feet deep for a distance of 37½ Roman miles up to the Bitter Springs. The Alexandrian astronomer Claudius Ptolemaeus, or Ptolemy, called the canal "the River of Trajan" and indicated that it started from the main Nile stream upriver from Babylon—that is, from Heliopolis. Lucien, an Egyptian official under the Antonine emperors, in about A.D. 170 described a traveler who sailed the canal from Alexandria to Clysma on the Gulf of Suez:

Then came the Arabs.

[The] Caliph Muiz had invested a fortune of his own to conquer Egypt, so he obviously wanted to get back his investment as quickly as possible, and as always the Red Sea Canal was to be implement of his wealth. The customs port of Al Maks, which means "customs tax," lay in the bend of the river which came almost up to the walls of Kahira on the west side near the canal, and this Mu'iz immediately took over and expanded into a proper dockyard, keeping its tax collecting character but also laying the foundations there for a new port of his own, which immediately took away much of the business that usually went to Fustat-Misr.

Here Mu'iz built six hundred ships and about 77 years later, when Nasir Ibn Khusrau came to Cairo [in the 11th century], seven of his ships were still lying on the river bank. "I, the author of this narrative, Ibn Khusrau says: 'I have seen them'". They measured thirty erich by sixty arech (275 feet long by 110 feet abeam). These ships were no doubt a brilliant investment because they could move large quantities of cargo at one time, rather like the modern monstrous oil tankers. Nothing that could make money escaped Mu'iz, and he reorganised the whole tax system into a central collecting body which did away with the local collectors, who used to take a considerable rake-off of their own. In one day he collected over 475,000 US dollars (modern equivalent) in taxes from Fustat-Misr alone.[4]

In *A History of Egypt in the Middle Ages,* Stanley Lane Poole tells us, One hundred and twenty thousand labourers were kept at work winter and summer in maintaining and improving dams and canals. The old canal traditionally called the Amnis Trajanus connecting Babylon (Cairo) with the Red Sea was cleaned and reopened in less than a year and corn was sent to Medina by ship instead of by caravan as in the previous year.[5]

In short, a wealth of evidence from Greek, Roman, and Arab writers states that the canal enabled ships to carry goods from the Nile to the Red Sea and vice versa. Grain was transported from the wheat fields of the Sudan to Rome, Mecca, Arabia, and India. Chinese porcelain and silk could be brought to Rome, Venetian glass to India.

In 642, Amir ibn Al-As dredged out the old canal, which was filling with silt brought down by the Nile. A century later there was a rebellion in Mecca and Medina, and in 767 the Abbasid Abu Ja'far al-Mansur blocked the canal to stop corn supplies from reaching Mecca. Shortly afterward, in 780, during the caliphate of Al Mahdi the canal was reopened. Then in 870 Ahmad ibn Tulun dredged the canal once again, and a further expansion took place in 955.

The next huge improvement to the canal was caxrried out by Sultan al-Malik an-Nasir in 1337, who assigned no fewer than 100,000 men to the job. He also built the Nilometer on the south of Roda island, which can be seen to this day. It measured the height of the river and thus served as a flood warning.

This final canal widening and dredging is summarized by historian James Aldridge in *Cairo: Biography of a City,* based on descriptions by the fifteenth-century Egyptian historian al-Madkrizi:

The land which emerged round Elephant Island was marshy and soft and Makrizi, who tells us all this, says the Mamluks used to practise archery there. But in the middle of the fourteenth century Al Nazir joined the Red Sea canal to the new bank of the river through this new swampy land, thus draining it. This new exit for the old canal was called Khalig Al Nasir, and it remained the exit of the Red Sea canal until this century, although it was later diverted again and called the Ismailiya Canal. It met the river where the Egyptian Pharaonic Museum is now, near the Nile Hilton. This final version of Nazir's canal was only filled in at the end of the nineteenth century to make what is now Rameses II Street, and anyone with a moment to spare on top of the Nile Hilton can look down on this street and trace the line of the old canal right up to the station square which was once the port of Al Maks.[6]

As we have noted, one of the Chinese names for Cairo was Misr, a name derived from the pharaonic name for the river port in Babylon. As time passed, Al-Fustat and Misr became interchangeable names for the port and the city of Cairo, "no doubt because all trade with Egypt was directed eventually to the river port of Misr or it came from Misr," Aldrich explains. "So it seems logical that sooner or later it was all known as Fustat-Misr (which is what al-Makrizi often calls it) and then simply as Misr. Today, Egyptians still call both their country and Cairo simply Misr."

On November 26, 2004, the Oriental Ceramic Society of France held a conference in Paris on trade between China and the Mediterranean prior to the sixteenth century. The conference produced a wealth of fascinating detail about the export of Chinese ceramics to Egypt, the Middle East, and the Mediterranean.[7]

Excavation sites in the southern suburbs of Cairo have produced Chinese ceramics dating from the tenth to the fourteenth centuries. In "Chinese Porcelain from Fustat," archaeologist R. L. Hobson describes the significance of the porcelain and ceramics finds:

> . . . Turning over the piles of fragments stored at Fustat and in the Arab Museum in Cairo . . . we realise most clearly the extent and antiquity of the trade

between Egypt and the Far East. There are, for instance, pieces of buff stone-
ware with cream glaze mottled with green and brownish yellow, which came
from China in the Tang dynasty; there are several varieties of celadon porcelain which tell of Sung traders. And there are blue and white porcelains ranging from the Yuan to the end of the Ming period. . . .

The typical Lung ch'uan and ch'u-chou celadons of the Sung, Yuan and
Ming periods abound, bowls and dishes with carved designs or with reliefs of
fishes or rosettes, things too well known to call for detailed notice. . . .

It was only natural that the volume of trade with China should increase in
the Ming dynasty. . . . This is evidenced in Egypt by the large quantity of blue
and white porcelain, of which fragments abound not only at Fustat, but all
around Cairo.

. . . Among the earliest specimens is the bottom of a bowl with the reign-
mark of Yung Lo (1403–1424)"—viz Zhu Di.[8]

This extraordinary trade in porcelain and ceramics was lubricated
by the Karim. The Karim had their own warehouses (*fonduqs*) stretching from Cairo to India and beyond. They built their own ships and
sometimes leased them to others. They also operated as bankers, which
proved to be their undoing.

In 1398 the Karim made a massive loan to the Mamluk sultan, to
finance an army to halt Tamburlaine's march toward Cairo. When the
loans were called, the sultan came up short. Al-Ashraf Barsbay nation-
alized the Nile–Red Sea canal to replenish his coffers, setting the prices
at which goods brought through Egypt could be bought and sold.
With a single stroke, the security for the Karim's loans—trade through
the canal—unraveled. The Karim were ruined within decades. When
China withdrew from the world stage in the 1430s, after Zheng He's
final voyage, Chinese goods came no more.

Cairo: The Quintessential Timeless Islamic City

Cairo stands today just as it did in 1433. The fortified city has withstood invaders for five centuries. During the Mongol wars, Saladin's

fortifications provided a refuge for all of Islam, making Cairo a haven not only for the caliph but for philosophers, artists, craftsmen, and teachers as well as hundreds of thousands of ordinary people fleeing Genghis Khan and his successors. Enormous wealth flowed into the city and was deployed on a sumptuous array of mosques, madrassahs, mausoleums, and hospitals. This is the domed medieval Cairo that Zheng He would have found.[9]

At first sight, Islamic towns and cities appear chaotic to Western eyes, with their elaborate, twisting streets leading higgledy-piggledy in all directions. They had, however, a master plan. At "the centre of the Islamic city stands the Friday Mosque; to it and from it everything flows as if it were a heart."[10] Next to the mosque stands the madrassah, where Islamic law and theology are taught, the forerunner of the Western university. Around mosque and madrassah sprawls the bazaar with its khans and caravanserais where merchants rest, feed their camels, and store their goods in safety.

Trade and religion go hand in hand under Islam, which affords merchants great prestige (Muhammad was one). The status of the merchant was evidenced by the distance of his shop from the Friday mosque: perfume, spice, and incense shops were nearest, followed by gold merchants and silversmiths. Cobblers were farthest away. Mosque and market were both within easy reach of the caravanserais.

The central square played host to all manner of entertainment, resounding with the cries of snake charmers, bears, dancers, and storytellers. Radiating outward beyond the bazaar was a jumbled assortment of residential districts divided by race and religion. Surrounding them was a defensive wall (in Cairo it was Saladin's) to keep out Mongols and robbers.

At the center of medieval Cairo was the city's Friday mosque, Al-Azhar, founded in 970, as soon as the enclosure walls of Al-Qahira were completed. It is perhaps the most prestigious mosque in the world and is connected to the world's oldest university. For more than a thousand years Al-Azhar University has provided Muslim students from around the world with free board and a theological education focused on the Koran and Islamic law, logic, grammar, rhetoric, astronomy, and science.

For centuries, the mosque on Fridays has been packed. As it overflows, men lay their mats outside on the pavement. They pray in uniform lines, rich and poor side by side, old men and young, golden cloaks next to dirty kashmaks. All men are equal in Islam; no boxes are reserved for the gentry. Inside, Al-Azhar resembles London's Southwark Cathedral, though it is not quite as tall and rather more austere. Gowned students, seated between gray marble columns, are taught by a wizened imam perched in a high chair. (The gowns of Oxford and Cambridge were copied from those worn by Islamic students, just as our university "chair" is derived from the imam's perch.)

The Al-Azhar competes with the mosques of Sayyid Hasan, al-Ghoury, and Sultan al-Ashraf Barsbay—all within a stone's throw. The Egyptian president worships at the Mosque of Al-Azhar. Their muezzins call the faithful to prayer five times a day. Traditionally, muezzins are chosen from the blind, who cannot see down into the houses where unveiled women are dressing.

In the square, Cairo's festivals, the *moulids,* are held and the Sufi brotherhood prays with banners and drums; music blasts all night long. Vast crowds come up from the delta for the holiday of Eid, congregating at the cafés around the square, each one favored by a particular delta village.

One can readily understand why Cairo would have been a magnet for all peoples of Islam, including Zheng He and his fellow Muslims returning from Mecca. In broad terms, foreigners lived in Cairo, white native Egyptians, the *fellahin,* lived on the delta and in the Nile Valley. With the holiest mosque in the world situated next to the largest market in the world, the city had everything. Here they could study the Koran, sell their goods, and enjoy the city's storied evening delights.

Today, as in the Middle Ages, Cairo is a city of good-natured people living in close quarters, bustling and jostling from one corner to the next. To motorists and pedestrians making headway through the crowds, a few hundred yards can seem like a mile. Cairo's population is polyglot, full of the offspring of Sudanese, Armenian, Jewish, Georgian, Persian, North African, and Indian merchants. Indeed, Egyptians intermarried with the descendants of conquerors and merchants to such an extent that today it is difficult to find a "pure" Egyptian.

Zheng He's sailors would have seen, alongside Al-Azhar Mosque, two imposing complexes: the madrassah and the Wikala of al-Ghouri, named after one of the later Mamluk sultans. *Wikala* is the Egyptian name for a caravanserai. Both caravanserai and madrassah complemented the mosque and were frequently funded by a charity, or *wakf*, set up by the sultan or a wealthy merchant.

Cairo's madrassah, typical of an early Islamic university, is a large, rectangular building with an open courtyard at its center, surrounded by broad cloisters. In the cloisters, small groups of students debate with teachers; great importance is placed on mental agility. While Europe stumbled through the Dark Ages, Cairo safeguarded the world's largest library. Here, the great books of the ancients, including Aristotle and Plato, were stored before at last being summoned to aid the Enlightenment.

In the caravanserai of al-Ghoury, merchants from China laden with gold, silk, and ceramics could rest in simple, clean surroundings, a stone's throw from the cool mosque. In Zheng He's time, there were eleven caravanserais in Cairo, twenty-three markets for international trade, fifty smaller markets (souks) for local trade, and eleven race courses.

Al-Madkrizi gave a vivid account of life in the caravanserais in the 1420s. Every sort of spice was for sale, along with all manner of silks and more mundane goods—fruits, nuts, and jams galore. Merchants carried with them their chests of gold and silver, all their worldly wealth. Theft was common. The punishment (still enforced in Saudi Arabia) was severing of the right hand.

In the late Middle Ages, Cairo was the world's leading emporium for three of the most important commodities of international trade—gold, spice, and perfume. Cairo had become bullion capital of the world as a result of Islam's expansion. Arab caliphs, needing ever more gold to lubricate trade, initially adopted Byzantine coins, overstamping them with the caliph's head. After Arab armies overran North Africa, they captured the gold trade from Mali and Guinea, which had by far the largest gold seams.

Arabs' domination of the gold trade led to the gold dinar becoming the currency of Mediterranean trade. The rulers of Castile, Aragon, and León copied Almoravid dinars, which they called *morbetinos*.

Cairo's spice bazaar, the Khan el-Khalili, faces the Al-Azhar Mosque. It was built by a wealthy Mamluk of that name in 1382 and still teems with business six hundred years later. The most prestigious part of the bazaar, nearest the mosque, is where the fabled incense is found. Brought from the wadis of southern Arabia, these concentrated essences are sold by the ounce, diluted with alcohol one part to nine for perfume, one to twenty for eau de toilette, one to thirty for eau de cologne. Cairo's shops still maintain the medieval tradition of selling perfumes in large bottles alongside herbs and spices, and Egypt remains a source for many of the essences used by French couture houses.

In the Middle Ages perfume and spice were equally valuable. The spice trade with the East, transacted through Cairo, was the cornerstone of Venetian wealth.

Europeans devoured spices, the better to make palatable their salted meat and dried fish. In addition to enlivening food, spices were extensively used by apothecaries. Purges were accomplished by cassia or rhubarb; theriac, made of an assortment of herbs and spices, was a panacea for ills ranging from constipation to fever and even the plague. Ginger jams were said to encourage the flow of urine. Cinnamon assisted menstruation and was valuable for windy colic; nutmeg relieved coughs and asthma. As Iris Origo points out in *The Merchant of Predo,* there was hardly an Eastern spice, however rare or expensive, that did not reach the cooking pots or medicine chests of Italian bankers and merchants.

Walking outward from the spice market today, one encounters the brass and copperware shops, stacked with Arab coffeepots, water jugs, tabletops, coal scuttles, and trays. Tiny pieces of mother-of-pearl, bone, and ebony are inlaid in intricate mosaic patterns on wooden boxes.

Although amber prayer beads are used to count the mercies of Allah, much as Catholics use rosaries, amber appears less valuable in the marketplace than copper.

Farther out, there are leather and clothing stalls. Egyptian men, like their medieval predecessors, wear *galabayas,* collarless tunics resembling large, floppy nightshirts. (Caftans are the more colorful version, embroidered at the front and on the hems.) Women seek dowry dresses made by desert Bedouin. The market encompasses a world. Remarkably, almost everything sold here today was available to Zheng He's sailors and Chinese merchants as they passed through Cairo in 1433. It is an easy passage downstream from Cairo with the current. Just north of Cairo the Nile divides, the Western Rosetta Channel leading to Alexandria, linked to the Nile by a canal. In Alexandria the Mamluk authorities insisted all passing ships deposited maps they had used for their journey. These were copied and the originals returned. That done, the Chinese drifted into the Mediterranean.

II

China Ignites

the Renaissance

TO THE VENICE OF NICCOLÒ DA CONTI

I n the Middle Ages, sea traffic between Egypt and Europe was determined by the geography of the Mediterranean.[1] Surrounding the Mediterranean are mountain ranges—in the southwest the Atlas Mountains of Morocco, then moving clockwise, the Sierra Nevada in southern Spain; the Pyrenees; the French, Italian, and Yugoslav Alps; the mountains of Greece, Bulgaria, and Turkey; and finally the Anti-Lebanon Range between Lebanon and Syria.

These mountains dictate the Mediterranean climate. Between the September and March equinoxes, a high anticyclone builds over the Azores, allowing Atlantic depressions to rush through the Strait of Gibraltar and then scurry west to east, the length of the Mediterranean. As these warm, wet winds reach the cold mountains on the coast, they create blustery winds and rain. The mistral in France is perhaps the best-known, but every Mediterranean region has gusty wet squalls in winter that make sea voyages hazardous.

The whole Mediterranean shares a common climate; wet winter is followed by calm, hot summer. As regular as clockwork, the sun moves north each year, carrying with it the anticyclone over the Azores until it stops opposite the Strait of Gibraltar. The wet Atlantic winds are now shut out of the Mediterranean, and the air is still. By July, the whole sea is flat as glass, without a breath of wind. Dry Saharan air marches north, the skies clear to infinity, and searing hot summer winds—typically the terral in southern Spain—blow across the coast. The three major seafaring powers of Europe—Aragon, Genoa, and Venice, exploited this geography to conduct trade with the east through Alexandria and Cairo. Venice and Genoa were entirely dependent on trade for their huge wealth. The Venetian ceremony of La Sensa, which takes place on Ascension Day, suggests just how passionately Venice embraced the sea.[2]

The doge embarks at Saint Mark's in his great gilded ship, the Bucintoro. Perched on a golden throne, he sits high above a crew of 150 oarsmen, who row across the lagoon to the Lido. The doge's golden robes are embroidered with the Lion of Saint Mark's and he wears a diamond-studded cap, *la renza*—the same hat worn by Chinese admirals in the early Ming. Silk standards flutter above his head. After a short service, the doge casts a golden ring into the lagoon. As it sinks through the azure sea he proclaims: *"Mare, noi ti sposiano in segne del nostro vero perpetua dominio"* (O Sea, we wed thee in sign of our true and everlasting dominion).

By 1434, the marriage ritual was already more than four hundred years old. It originated when Pope Alexander III gave the doge a ring and told him: "Receive this ring as the symbol of your empire over the sea. . . . You and your successors be married to her each year, so that succeeding generations may know that the sea is yours, and belongeth to you as a spouse to a husband."[3]

Venice's wealth was rooted in her capture of Byzantium. In 1204 a Crusade had been launched to take Jerusalem. Financing for the Crusade was hard to come by until the Doge Dandolo offered support—provided the Crusaders would capture Zara (contemporary Zadar in Croatia) on their way south. The Crusaders agreed, becoming mercenaries in the process.

The temptation to capture Byzantium for Venice, as well, proved irresistible to the Crusaders, who initiated the sack of the Orthodox Christian capital by another Christian state.[4] When Byzantium fell, her empire was divided amongst the victors. Venetian spoils, exemplified by the four bronze horses and marble on the façade of Saint Mark's Basilica, included Byzantine islands and ports from the Black Sea through the Aegean to the Ionian Sea. Venetian galleys thus had friendly harbors all the way to Byzantium and Alexandria.

Venice now controlled the Adriatic. In 1396, six years after she had defeated Genoa and fourteen years after the Cretan revolt, she acquired Corfu. To Venetians, Corfu was of vital importance due to its strategic location. Corfu became the fortified base from which Venetian galleys policed the strait leading to the Adriatic.

Venice built lovely colonial towns on these Adriatic islands. Her ports, modeled in her own image, each with its campanile, cathedral, piazza, and evening promenade, line the Dalmatian coast. From Ulcinj in the south to Piran in the north, the ports of Bar, Dubrovnik, Korcula, Hvar, Split, Zadar, Rab, Krk, Pula, and Porec are sublime legacies of Venetian architecture. By 1433 they were havens for the armadas carrying ceramics, silk, and spices from Alexandria and Cairo to the warehouses of Venice. While the Slavic chants of Orthodox churches resound in the mountains, on the coast Sundays are punctuated by bells summoning Catholics to mass.[5] Saint Jacob's in Sibenik, Saint Mark's in Piran, Saint Laurence's in Trogir, and Our Lady's in Rijeca are superb by any standard. They are among the sights that greeted Zheng He's ships on their passage from Alexandria to Venice. Even with fifteen men to each oar it would have been a ten-day slog from Alexandria to Crete across an airless sea. Once in the Adriatic they would have picked up a light evening breeze blowing on shore. What a relief that would have been!

I know those islands well following a visit in 1966. In December 1965 I had met Marcella; we became engaged in June and decided to take a holiday traveling through the Dalmatian islands to Montenegro and Serbia. In the four years before meeting Marcella I had been navigating officer of HMS *Narwhal,* a submarine. It was the eve of the cold war and our patrols were spent in the North. Winters were drab and cold; the sun shone for an only hour or so, at midday; most of the time one looked at ice, sea, and sky in everlasting shades of gray.

In August 1966, Marcella, my uncle Edward, and I boarded a ferry in Venice bound for Dubrovnik, en route wending through the Dalmatian archipelago. We passed Marco Polo's home on Korcula, Diocletian's vast palace at Split, and honey-colored Hvar. The searing colors of azure sea and sky emphasized by the brilliant white Karst of the coastline, the red campanile towers, and the russet and gold of drying tobacco are etched on my brain and will remain with me all my life.

We slept on the upper deck under the stars, swam off remote beaches watched only by seagulls, and feasted on local seafish washed down by Dingaz, a rough, full-bodied, almost black wine.

The same idyllic scene would have greeted Zheng He's sailors and female slaves as his junks rowed slowly up the coast. They would have seen the outlines of these mini "Venices" from miles out to sea, dotted along the coast all the way from Dubrovnik to Trieste to Venice itself. They would have noticed Diocletian's enormous palace, Hvar's spectacular harbor, and the glistening white fortress walls of Dubrovnik, and would have surely called at some of those ports.

So in my view we should find evidence of Zheng He's fleets' visits in museums along the Dalmatian coast. Over the years, Marcella and I have visited the most likely museums—the old maritime school at Perast, the Matko family museum at Orebic, the Seamans' Guild (Museum) in the Gulf of Kotor, Ivo Vizin's Museum at Prcanj, and the Maritime Museum in Kotor itself. We found nothing.

However, my interest was renewed and sharpened in 2004 after meeting Dr. Gunnar Thompson in Seattle. He had brought Albertin di Virga's world map to my attention. This map had been found in a secondhand bookshop at Srebrenica near the Dalmatian coast. It was dated to between 1410 and 1419 and showed the world from Greenland to Australia, including Africa, accurately drawn decades before Europeans knew Africa's shape and centuries before they knew the shape and relative positions of China, Japan, and Australia. The map had been authenticated by Professor Franz Von Wieser, the leading cartographer of his day. It must have been copied from a non-European map, and in the opinion of Dr. Thompson and me, it could only be a copy of a Chinese map that had been published before 1419. Moreover, Dr. Thompson had found evidence that ships from the Dalmatian coast had sailed to North America in the 1440s and settled near the Roanoke River in Virginia—the famous "Croatans."[6] In my view, Dalmatian ships would not have visited America fifty years before Columbus unless they had maps showing the way—once again pointing to Zheng He's fleets having visited Dalmatia and leaving maps. By 2005 we had sold Serbo-Croat literary rights to *1421,* which I hoped would lead to new evidence of Chinese visits along the coast, but alas, none emerged.

Then out of the blue on October 21, 2007, I received two e-mails from Dr. A. Z. Lovric, a geneticist whose old family name was Yoshamya (names were forcibly changed after the Ottoman invasions in the sixteenth century). Dr. Lovric told me that his distinguished predecessor Professor Mitjel Yoshamya had published a lengthy paper (of nearly twelve hundred pages) claiming that a Dalmatian admiral, Harvatye Mariakyr, had sailed the world before Ottoman invasions. He had done so having received world maps from a Chinese admiral who had visited the Dalmatian coast. Copies of the e-mails are included on the *1434* website.

Here is a summary of the points made in Dr. Lovric's e-mails:

1. A legend persists among island people off the Adriatic that prior to the Ottoman invasions (prior to 1522) foreign sailing ships manned by "Oblique-eyed yellow Easterners" (in old Dalmatic: *pashoglavi zihodane*) visited the Adriatic.
2. After the oriental naval visits the medieval Dalmatian admiral Harvatye Mariakyr with seven Adriatic ships reciprocated the visit by sailing through the Indian Ocean (Khulap-Yndran) to the Far East to Zihodane in Khitay (Cathay).
3. On his return from the Far East, Admiral Mariakyr, having learned of a new land in the West, decided to sail there with his fleet to Semeraye (South America); he lost his life in medieval Parané (Patagonia). This voyage was recorded in medieval Glagolitic script.
4. Recent DNA studies have confirmed that in some Adriatic islands (Hvar, Korcula) and on the adjacent coasts (Makarska) certain families have East Asian genotype.
5. Up until the twentieth century some of these Adriatic

islanders had surnames of non-Slavic and non-European origin, for example, Yoshamya, Yenda, Uresha, Shamana, Sayana, Sarana, and Hayana. In 1918 when the Austro-Hungarians were defeated, the islanders were obliged to Slavicize such foreign surnames, but they persist to this day in nicknames and aliases.

6. Medieval Dalmatian-colored symbols for maps were the same as those used by the Chinese: black = north, white = west, red = south, blue and green = east.

7. Adriatic islanders have until recently used a non-European nomenclature for America and the Far East based on translations of Chinese nomenclature.

8. American cactuses (chiefly *Opuntia*) in medieval Dalmatia, at Dubrovnik and elsewhere, were said to have been brought by early ships from the Far East.

Dr. Lovric's e-mails referred to Professor Mitjel Yoshamya's research in Croatian, published in Zagreb in 2004. The lengthy paper covers the spread of old Dalmatian names across the Pacific before the Spanish explorers; Sion-Kulap (Pacific): Skopye-Kulapne (Philippines), Sadritye-Polnebne (Melanesia), Sadritye-Zihodne (Micronesia), Skopye-Zihodne (Japan), Artazihod (Korea), and Velapolneb (New Zealand). Goa was the main Dalmatian base for Far East trade. (These old Dalmatian names were used on German maps of the Pacific until Germany was defeated in World War II, after which they were expunged and replaced by Spanish, French, and Portuguese names.) I hope that young scholars will translate the whole of Professor Yoshamya's manuscript into English, since only excerpts have yet been translated.

As will be seen when we reach Venice, tens of thousands of Asian slave girls and women were brought to Venice. Doubtless many of these would have escaped as the fleets berthed at the islands en route to Venice, and this will be shown up in the mitochondrial DNA.

The first step in setting up a DNA research program for Venetian and Dalmatian people was to see what existing DNA research had already been carried out. Dr. Lovric, who works in the Department of Molecular Genetics, kindly provided me with the information. There were a dozen local DNA reports of people on Adriatic islands, which were all summarized in Lovorka Bara, Marijana Perii et al., "Y Chromosomal Heritage of Croatian Population and its Island Isolates."[7] As may be seen in the abstract, Professor Bara et al. state: "In one of the Southern Island (Hvar) populations, we found a relatively high frequency (14%) of lineages belonging to P* (xM 173) cluster, which is unusual for European populations. Interestingly, the same population also harboured mitochondrial haplogroup F that is virtually absent in European populations—indicating a connection with central Asian populations, possibly the Avars."

Then at paragraph 3 on page 6 of their report:

Worthy of note is the finding of considerable frequency haplogroup P* (xM 173) in the population of the island of Hvar. According to Wells et al (44—see footnotes) this lineage displays a maximum in central Asia while being rare in Europe, Middle East and East Asia. Its presence in Hvar recapitulates our finding of MtDNA haplogroup F on the island of Hvar and in mainland Croatian population that is virtually absent in Europe but, again, common in populations from central and Eastern Asia (51—see footnotes). There are several possibilities for the occurrence of the ancestral lineage of M 173. One is the well documented alliance of Avars (a Mongol people) and Slavs (Croatians) that followed Avar arrival to the Eastern Adriatic in 6th Century AD. The other is the expansion of the Ottoman Empire from the 16th to 18th Century AD when refugees from the Western Balkans frequently immigrated to the islands. Lastly, the ancient Silk Road linking China with Western Asia and Europe could be a possible path of P(xM 173) lineage too. Any of these migratory patterns could have introduced the mutation to the investigated population.

As may be seen, the distinguished professors do not include a fourth possibility: that the inheritance of Chinese and Asian (Mongol) genes came by sea from sailors on ships sailing from Alexandria to Venice. Looking at a map reveals this is by far the most likely method. The

Avars settled near the Drava River on the Hungarian border—why should they then decide to migrate westward across some of the most rugged mountains on the planet to reach Hvar? Why choose the most extreme island, the farthest out in the ocean, on which to settle?

Second, if they had followed this bizarre route, their genes would be seen in the populations between where they settled on the Drava and Hvar; they are not. The same could be said for the Ottoman invasions down the Danube. Why should they choose a remote place out at sea to settle when they had the fertile Danube plain? The amount of Asian DNA, 14 percent, is remarkable; well-documented Danish invasions of Britain reveal a comparable 7 percent. Also, in my view, the fact that both Asian men (Y chromosome) and women (mitochondrial) settled on Hvar means men and women from Asia arrived together. Mongol armies invading from the East would have taken women where they found them. They would not have brought their wives and concubines along. Quite the opposite prevailed on Chinese junks, where female slaves and sailors lived side by side.

There are no Dalmatian accounts of Asian people trekking overland across the Dinaric Alps to Hvar, but there are local accounts (collated by Professor Lovric) that prior to the sixteenth century Ottoman invasions, foreign sailing ships manned by "Oblique-eyed yellow Easterners" visited the coast. Hvar, as may be seen from the map, is smack on the direct route from Alexandria (via Corfu) to Venice. In my submission, the DNA results are part of a logical sequence of events. Zheng He's squadron arrives in the Mediterranean in late 1433 or early 1434. One or more of his ships berths at Hvar when sailors and slave girls jump ship. The other ships proceed to Venice, where they unload the slaves. Officers then travel on to Florence, where they meet the pope in 1434. The squadron returns via Dalmatia in late 1434, when a Dalmatian fleet joins them for passage back through the Red Sea–Nile canal to China. On arrival in China the Chinese fleet is impounded: Admiral Harvatye Mariakyr takes his seven ships into the Pacific and "discovers" thirty Pacific islands, to which he gives Dalmatian names. He brings his fleet back home in the late 1430s/early 1440s with a Chinese map of the Americas and sails for America in the early 1440s. If this scenario is correct, the DNA of Venetians should reflect that of the people of Hvar, as should the DNA of indigenous Native Americans where Admiral Mariakyr's fleet visited (and left Glagolitic inscriptions recording their voyages around New England and Nova Scotia).

This DNA research will be pursued, and results will be posted on our website. We hope the Glagolitic manuscripts will also be translated.

Now to return to Zheng He's squadron leaving Hvar for Venice, a few days voyage to the north. Here the Chinese would have found excellent repair yards, which would have been of the greatest importance to them, for their ships had by now been away from their home bases for nearly three years. The Chinese were lucky—Venice had been building and repairing galleys for hundreds of years.

To develop trade between Alexandria, Cairo, and Venice, Venice built galleys and manned them with skilled seamen. The Arsenal, the greatest medieval dockyard of Europe, was the key to Venetian maritime supremacy. By 1434, Venice could put thirty-five large galleys to sea along with three thousand smaller craft manned by 25,000 sailors. At the beginning of the fifteenth century, the ship workers' guild had more than 6,000 members out of a total Venetian population of 170,000. The Senate passed stringent laws to control shipbuilding. The number of galleys built for export was restricted. Any foreigner wishing to place an order first had to obtain authorization from the Great Council.

Galleys were built on a "conveyor belt" on which ships were towed past a succession of stations, where they acquired ropes and sails, armaments and dry provisions.[8] When Henry III of France visited Venice, the Arsenal's shipwrights assembled a galley weighing six thousand pounds in the time it took the doge and his royal visitor to eat their way through a state banquet. Galleys were built to standard specifications so that replacement parts could be stored in Venetian yards down the Adriatic and across the Mediterranean.

Financial incentives were given to shipbuilders and owners to keep the Arsenal productive with experienced shipwrights on the job. Bankers were discouraged from charging exorbitant interest. The public bank had authority to grant soft loans: in the event that it was necessary to accelerate construction, costs could be subsidized. Almost every citizen had a stake in maritime commerce with the East—even the galley oarsmen had the right to trade on their personal accounts. A single voyage to Alexandria or Cairo could enrich a vessel's entire company.

Venice was equally committed to training her naval officers, pilots, and ratings. The admiral and fleet navigator of Venetian armadas were usually graduates of the Venetian naval college at Perast, a port in the Gulf of Kotor in southern Dalmatia near Hvar. The port had an international reputation[9]: Czar Peter the Great of Russia sent his first officer cadets there. The armadas' in-shore navigation was handled by professional pilots, trained at Porec on the north Dalmatia coast. The cream of these mariners, the *pedotti grandi,* would steer an armada into the lagoon at the end of its journey from Alexandria.

For centuries Dalmatia has been renowned for her seafarers. The names of her illustrious officers crop up time and again in tales of epic battles—from Coromandel to the Spanish Main. Venetian galleys were built almost entirely from Dalmatian wood—pine for planks, resin for caulking, oak for rudders, keels, and straits. Roughly half the crew of each galley would be Dalmatian.

Venice brilliantly exploited her maritime assets. With the acquisition of ports on the Dalmatian coast, she gained abundant timber. Centuries of history and tradition had bred skillful and hardy seamen. Journeying north from Alexandria, Zheng He's fleets would have found numerous ports, first in Crete, then across the Ionian Sea to the Adriatic. It was an easy journey, even in the calms of summer when the Chinese oarsmen—fifteen to an oar—would eat up the miles. The Chinese could have expected to be guided by experienced local pilots.

Cairo's contact with Europe was through Venice, which had entered a commercial treaty with the Mamluks giving them exclusive trading rights. The two cities were joined by their pursuit of a monopoly on east-west trade.

The link with Cairo opened up additional possibilities of trade with China and new ways of reaching that distant land. A stream of merchants and Franciscan missionaries left Venice for China. Oriental adventures were relayed via chroniclers including the Polos; Giovanni da Pian del Carpine in his *Historia Mongalorum* (1247); William of Rubruck who wrote *Itinerarium* (1255); *Raban Sauma* (1287) and Odoric of Pordenone (1330); and Jordan de Sévérac's *Mirabilia* (c. 1329). The Jews had their own traveling merchants, notably Jacob of Ancona prior to Marco Polo. Venice was intimately acquainted with China. Her merchants, the Polos in particular, made fortunes trading exotic Chinese silks and drappi tartareschi. Popes and emperors were buried wrapped in Chinese silk.

Small wonder, given their centuries of trade with China, that Venetians were the first Europeans to obtain world maps from their trading partner. Di Virga's map of the Eastern Hemisphere was published in 1419, and Pizzigano's map of the Caribbean appeared in 1424. Today, you can see on the wall of the Doges' Palace a world map published prior to 1428 that includes North America. As the roundels on the walls testify, this map was created from evidence brought back from China by Marco Polo and Niccolò da Conti. The inscription relating to da Conti says: "ORIENTALIS INDIAS HAC TABULA EXPRESSUS PEREGRATIONIBUS ET SCRIPTIS ILLUSTRAUNT EN NARATIS MERCANTORIAM AD JIUVIERE SAECOLO XV NICOLAUS DE COMITIBUS. EDITO ITENERARIO LUSITANE POST MODUM VERSO NOVAM LUCEM NAUTIS ALLATURO." My translation: "Oriental India [viz China and the Indies in fifteenth-century terminology] as drawn in this way is clearly a result of the foreign travels and illustrated writings not least the narratives of the merchant of the fifteenth century, Niccolò da Conti. Publication of this itinerary sheds new light on the [travels of] mariners."

This map was probably completed before 1428 (inauguration of Doges' Palace) but destroyed by fire in 1486; the original maps (of which a copy was given to Dom Pedro) were hung on the walls. According to Lorenzetti, the map was repainted by Ramusio in 1540 after the fire—the same Ramusio who had said that Fra Mauro's world map was copied from one in the Camolodensian Monastery on the (current) Island of the Dead in the lagoon. Giovanni Forlani's map shows Oregon and the Bering Straits before Bering or Vancouver. Zatta's map shows Vancouver Island also before Cook or Vancouver and places on it "Colonia dei Chinesi" (Chinese Colony).

By 1418 Venice had become the richest state in Europe. The city's mule caravans could tramp unmolested through Venetian territory to the Brenner Pass.[10] As the seaport nearest the heart of Europe, Venice exploited her access to Lake Constance, which was the principal trading center for merchants from France, Germany, Austria, Poland, and Russia.

For more than 150 years before Zheng He appeared, Venetian bankers had been using a cashless giro system, crediting one merchant and debiting another.[11] Italian bankers led by the Bardis and Peruzzis pioneered international banking the length and breadth of Europe. Almost every citizen of the Venetian Republic was involved in some aspect of trade[12]—shopkeepers in retail markets, porters and fish traders in wholesale markets, dockers to load and unload, shipwrights in the Arsenal, oarsmen in the galleys. There were few beggars and hardly any unemployment.

Essential to the Contis, the di Virgas, the Corrers (the family of Pope Eugenius IV's mother), and the Contarinis were the great oared galleys that left the Rialto for Alexandria, Beirut, Cairo, Flanders, and London. The galley routes to Alexandria and the East resemble the spokes of a vast spider's web.[13] The Magistrates of the Waters issued detailed sailing orders with which merchants were required to comply. The following order, issued to a galley departing for Aigues-Mortes in Provence, underscores the importance of the silk trade.

> The galley will load cloths and spices of Venice up to the 13th of January next; she is to leave Venice on the 15th of the same month. These terms may not be extended, suspended or broken under penalty of a fine of 500 ducats. No silken goods may be loaded or shipped on this galley, anywhere in the Gulf of Venice or outside it, apart from veils, taffetas and Saracen cloth. If the master of the galley loads or permits the loading of any silken goods, he will be suspended for a period of five years during which time he may not command any of the galleys of the state or private persons.[14]

The Magistrate of the Waters tightly controlled the movement of ships and where they were permitted to load and unload. Each type of good had its designated loading wharf—stone barges at the Incurabile, timber ships at the Misericordia and the Fondamente Nuove. Zheng He's junks from Alexandria would have tied up at the Riva degli Schiavoni. Venetian merchants submitted to this discipline knowing that it benefited all. The dominant families appointed agents in Crete, Alexandria, Cairo, and every important harbor to facilitate their international trade.

Today, the area around Saint Mark's Basilica still swarms with boats unloading passengers, vegetables, fruit, and wine. I have been to Venice innumerable times since first visiting as a young officer on the HMS *Diamond* fifty years ago. My most vivid memory was a sultry August evening twenty years ago, after Marcella and I had attended vespers at Saint Mark's, the finest Byzantine building in the world, the epitome of medieval Christian art, and the symbol of Venice's trade with Alexandria and the East.

For more than one thousand years this glorious cathedral has been the most important building in Venice. Here Crusades were blessed, including the one financed by the blind old doge Dandolo, who implored Saint Mark to deliver Byzantium to Venice. Here Venetians met to pray for deliverance in times of danger or to thank God in victory. Generation after generation of Venetian merchants have poured their wealth into the city's fabulous cathedral.[15]

Built in the shape of a Greek cross, the cathedral overlooks the lagoon, allowing one to enjoy the view from either land or sea, in changing light as the day progresses. The finest artists have endowed the exterior and interior with masterpieces of marble and mosaics. The west façade is a blaze of green, purple, gold, and blue marble collected from across the Venetian empire.

Within, worshippers see the residue of wealth in the gold ceilings. The basilica is at its best by candlelight at vespers, from a pew beneath the central dome. From here Jesus appears to ascend to heaven, carried by four angels surrounded by the apostles and the Virgin. Every inch of the vast ceiling, walls, and floors is encased in mosaics. Treasures lie sprawled before one. An altar of solid gold is studded with rubies and emeralds. Panels depict scenes from the lives of Christ and Saint Mark. Chinese silk and ceramics, Byzantine reliquaries, cut Persian glass, crystal goblets, and silver swords from Tartary fill the museum. All of this resulted from centuries of seaborne trade.

The wealth of fifteenth-century Venice is captured in the speech delivered by the dying doge Tommaso Mocenigo:

> This city now stands out in the way of business to different parts of the world. Ten millions of ducats were earned yearly by ships and galleys and the profit is not less than two million ducats a year. In this city there are three thousand vessels of one, two hundred amafore with seventeen thousand seamen. There are three hundred large ships with eight thousand sailors. Every year there go to sea forty-five galleys with eleven thousand sailors and there are three thousand ship carpenters and three thousand caulkers. There are three thousand weavers of silk and sixteen thousand weavers of common cloth. Houses are estimated to be worth seven million five hundred thousand ducats. The rents are five hundred thousand ducats. There are one thousand noblemen whose income is from seven hundred to four thousand ducats.[16]

Venice prided herself on wealth but also on a republican government enshrined in a written constitution replete with complex checks and balances. Although the doge was head of state, he was constrained by various committees and councils. When Genoa was defeated in 1380, the Italian city-states of Verona, Vicenza, and Mantua willingly accepted the Pax Venetica. Their governing bodies were added to the Great Council. By 1418, Venice had outmaneuvered the Holy Roman Emperor and expanded her territories southward. Representatives of Istria, Friuli, and Dalmatia further swelled the Great Council. Gentile da Fabriano, Antonio Veneziano, and Jacobeló del Fiore were retained by the procurators of Saint Mark to adorn the walls of the Great Council Chamber with paintings of the glorious history of the Serenissima. Roberti carved his wonderful marble capitals, which adorn the façade. In 1419, Pisanello's frescoes were unveiled.

The Doges' Palace was designed for different functions. At the front, overlooking the lagoon, is the Great Council Chamber. At the far end, next to Saint Mark's, the doge's quarters are linked to the legislative areas by golden staircases. At the heart of the Doges' Palace is the map room—the biggest in his quarters.

The map room might well be described as the heart of the Venetian Empire. Here the doge would receive visiting heads of state, including Chinese delegations. The two long walls of the room are covered with eleven painted maps of the world. Facing the visitor is a map of the Venetian Empire in the eastern Mediterranean showing the route to China and the East. To the left is the Venetian Empire in the western Mediterranean. Neither of these maps shows latitude or longitude. They cover the same area as maps on the opposite wall showing the rest of the world. The Venetian Empire is thus shown far larger than it was.

The opposite wall is divided by the door into the Sala del Filosofi. To the left of the door is a map of central Asia from Crete to Tibet—the former trading empire of Byzantium. To the right is a map of the world from Arabia across the Pacific to California. India and the Indies, China, Japan, the Pacific, and North America from Alaska to California are depicted with general accuracy. Other maps show the Northeast Passage from the Faeroes to the rivers of Siberia; North and South America; the Red Sea and Arabia; the Atlantic coast of North America to 55° N, and central Asia. The whole world is there save for southern Australia.

Of greatest interest is the world map showing the Pacific and North America. There are two roundels on this map: one describes the part that Marco Polo played in gathering the information; the other recounts the role played by Niccolò da Conti. These are the world maps that Dom Pedro was given during his state visit to Venice between the fifth and twenty-second of April 1428. A host of Venetian records describes that visit: *Les Chronique Venetienne: The Diaries of Antonio Morosone from 1416–1433; the manuscript Zorsi delfine.* An extensive bibliography exists in F. M. Rogers's marvelous book *The Travels of the Infante, Dom Pedro of Portugal.*

There are no material differences among the various accounts, which Professor Rogers summarizes: "In March of 1428, Mario Dandolo, the Venetian Ambassador to the King of Hungary, reported that the Infante Don Pedro had left for Venice. The Doge (Francesco Foscari) and the Council decided to receive the Portuguese prince and his companions in regal fashion as their guests and at their expense.... the Doge received Dom Pedro on board the *Bucintoro* (royal barge)."

Of the gifts bestowed upon Dom Pedro during his visit to Venice, Professor Rogers cites several accounts,[17] the first by the celebrated historian Antonio Galvão:

In the year 1428 it is written that Dom Peter [Pedro], the King of Portugal's eldest son, was a great traveller. He went into England, France, Alamaine, from thence into the Holy Land and to other places; and came home by Italy, taking Rome and Venice in his way; from whence he brought a map of the world which had all the parts of the world and earth described. The streight [*sic*] of Magellan was called in it the Dragon's Tail; the Cape of Bona Sperança [Good Hope], the forefront of Afrike and so forth of other places; by which map, Dom Henry, the King's third sonne was much helped and furthered into his discoveries. ...

It was told me by Francis de Souza Tavares that in the year 1528 Dom Fernando, the King's son and heir, did show him a map which was found in the study of the Alcobaza which had been made one hundred and twenty years before [1408] which map did set forth all the navigation of the East Indies with the Cape of Boa Esperanza as our later maps have described it; whereby it appeareth that in ancient times there was as much or more discovered than now there is. (*Tratado Dos Diversos e Desayados Caminhos*, Lisbon, 1563).

Further corroboration is provided by Professor Rogers: "In early 1502 in Lisbon the famous German printer Valentin Fernandes published a beautiful volume of the Indies of the East [China]. ... He included Portuguese translations of the Indies based on information gathered in Florence from Nicolo da Conti and delegates to the Council [presided over by Eugenius IV] and included in Book IV of his treatise *De Variaetate Fortunae*." Later Professor Rogers writes:

In the second part of his lengthy introduction to Marco Polo, Valentin Fernandes makes the following statement pregnant with meaning from several points of view: "Concerning this matter I heard . . . that the Venetians had hidden the present book for many years in their Treasure House. And at the time that the Infante Don Pedro of glorious memory, your uncle, arrived in Venice [1428] . . . offered him as a worthy gift the said book about Marco Polo that he might be guided by it since he was desirous of seeing and travelling through the world. They say this book is in the Torre de Tombo." (p. 47)

Professor Rogers also summarized Marco Polo's and da Conti's contributions to world maps:

With the Cape [Good Hope] rounded, the all-water route to India lay revealed. Valentin Fernandes could think of no greater service to his monarch than the publication in Portuguese translation the three best available descriptions of the world over which King Manuel now assumed dominion. One was that of Marco Polo; another was the description of the Indies (viz China) written by Pogio the Florentine, based on the information supplied to him by the delegates to the Council of Florence and by Nicolo da Conti." (p. 266)

It seems to me beyond argument that the world map on display today in the Doges' Palace is, as the Venetians claim, based on information that reached Venice from Marco Polo and Niccolò da Conti and that this was the same world map taken to Portugal by Dom Pedro in 1428. Consequently, both the Venetians and the Portuguese knew the contours of the whole world before the Portuguese voyages of exploration even started. We know that da Conti was in Calicut the same time as Zheng He's fleets, for he describes the junks and his description tallies with those of Ma Huan, Zheng He's historian, who was in Calicut in 1419.[18]

As noted, in 1419, Pisanello (1395–1455) had painted murals in the Doges' Palace. Pisanello came from Verona, which by then had joined the Pax Venetica—her grandees were elected to the Great Council of Venice. In about 1436 Pisanello painted another fresco in the church of Saint Anastasia at Verona entitled *Saint George and the Princess of Trebizond*. In the left-hand section is a group of horsemen. Seated on a

A sketch of Mongol faces by the Veronese artist Pisanello, 1430s.

richly caparisoned horse is a Mongol general with facial features, clothes, and hat very similar to the carvings of Zhu Di's generals that line the road that leads to Zheng He's tomb north of Beijing. The Mongol dignitary wears rich silk clothes. Pisanello's sketches of the hard, powerful Mongol face can be seen separately in the Louvre in Paris. The sketch and painting are so vivid that its seems to me inescapable that Pisanello painted what he saw in the late 1430s—a Mongolian general in Venice or Verona, a captain or admiral of one of the Chinese junks.[19] (See note 20 for Pisanello's other sketches of Chinese visitors to Venice in the 1430s). In my view Pisanello's sketches depict

Admiral Zheng He, a pioneer of global exploration, who was in great part responsible for this remarkable adventure.

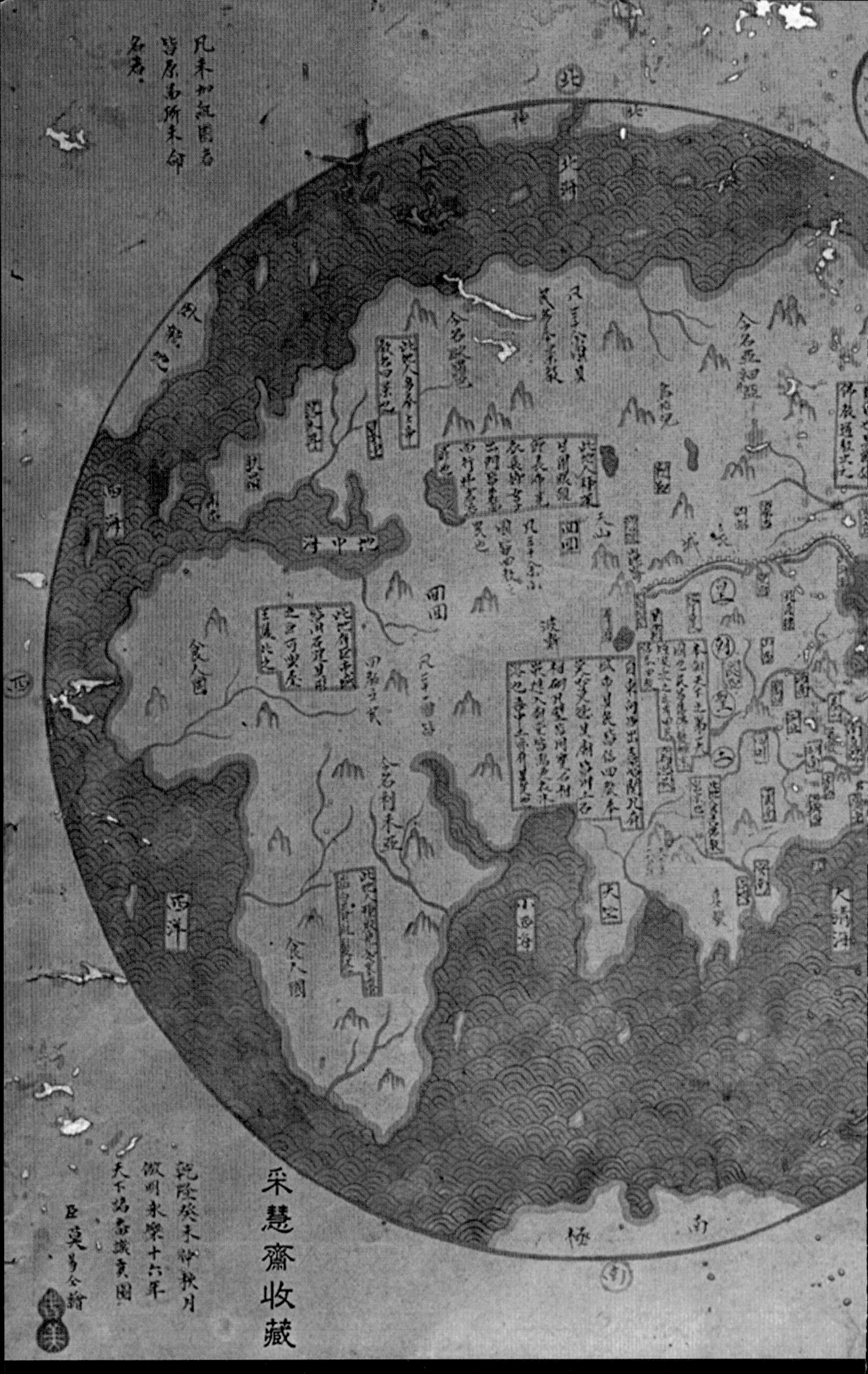
凡未加紙圖者
皆原畫所未命
名者。
乾隆癸未仲秋月
倣明永樂十六年
天下諸番識貢圖
莫易仝摹
采慧齋收藏

The Liu Gang 1418 /1763 map—a tribute to Zheng He's courageous voyages of discovery.

Bronze Chinese lion figure at the entrance to the Emperor's Summer Palace, Beijing.

Visitors at the Summer Palace, Beijing, c. 1902.

A delicate piece of
beautiful Ming porcelain,
as traded around the world
by the Treasure fleet.

A view of the magnificent Forbidden City,
Beijing, whose construction flourished under
the great emperors of the Ming dynasty.

A view of the Great Wall of China snaking along the rugged mountain ridge at Simatai.

A vast fleet of Chinese junks could carry a considerable amount more than a caravan of camels!

The fleet journeyed northward up the
crystalline Red Sea waters, through to the
bustling souks of Cairo, and beyond.

the Chinese Admiral and his senior Mandarin advisor in their formal dress when they met the Doge. As captain of HMS *Rorqual* I would wear my ceremonial sword when calling on local dignitaries at the start of an official visit. The Chinese admiral would have carried his ceremonial bow.

The Chinese junks berthed at the Riva degli Schiavoni, or Quay of Slaves, would have created little fuss—Chinese and Arab ships were there as a matter of course. The ambassador and the captains would have presented their credentials to the doge in his palace a few hundred yards away, together with the *Shoushi* astronomical calendar giving details of the Xuan De emperor's conception and birth. Ceremonial gifts of silk and blue-and-white imperial porcelain would have followed, and finally maps of the voyage from China. The barbarians would now be able to return tribute.

Fresh meat, fruit, fish, vegetables, and water would be embarked, paid for partly in Venetian ducats (which the Chinese would have acquired in Cairo) and partly in rice. Zheng He's fleets would have disposed of the poor concubines and slaves who had not died in transit or been given away at a previous port, dispatching them to the slave market or shipping them on to Florence.

A date would have been set for a regulation to fix the price for the sale of the ceramics that crammed the holds. Tampions would have been placed on the guns; then the sailors could begin their shore leave. We can imagine Chinese sailors preparing to go ashore in a manner very similar to that of my fellow sailors fifty years ago when the HMS *Diamond* berthed opposite the Riva degli Schiavoni: we trimmed our beards, cut our long hair, gave ourselves a good wash. For the Chinese, perhaps first a swim in the Lido before donning their best clothes, having a drink, and collecting presents to give out to the girls. In 1434 these were likely to have been children's toys or miniature carts, junks or whirligigs, or perhaps one of the pocket encyclopedias such as the *Nung Shu*, showing how to design farm machinery.

Once ashore, the Chinese sailors could have been excused if they thought they were back in Quanzhou—their Mongolian counterparts were everywhere. Venice was the gateway to Tuscany and the funnel through which slaves reached Europe. Lazari writes: "Many of the slave girls described in the *Registro degli Schiavi,* mostly in their teens were sold in a state of pregnancy and later used as nurses. . . . In this way a large influx of Asiatic blood penetrated into the Tuscan population."

Lynn White quotes Lazari: "Lazari, who has studied most carefully the records of these unfortunates in Venice, assures us that the largest number came from the regions bordering Tibet and China in the north. 'As they came in their thousands and were rapidly absorbed by the indigenous population, a certain Mongolian strain could not have been rare in Tuscan homes and streets.' "[20]

Iris Origo paints a vivid picture of the slaves who reached Florence from Venice:

A traveller arriving in Tuscany at this time might well have been startled by the appearance of the serving-maids and grooms of the Florentine ladies. Mostly small and squat, with yellow skins, black hair, high cheek-bones and dark slanting eyes . . . they certainly seemed to belong to a different race from the Florentine . . . and if the traveller had friends in one of the Florentine *palazzi* and went to call, he found several other exotic figures there too: swarthy or yellow little girls of eleven or twelve . . . acting as nursemaids or play-mates for the little Florentine merchant-princes.

All these were slaves: most of them Tartars. . . .

Even a notary's wife, or a small shopkeeper's, would have at least one, and it was far from uncommon to find one among the possessions of a priest or nun. And a glimpse of them—perhaps slightly romanticised—even appears in a popular song describing little slaves shaking the carpets out of the windows on the Lungarno:

"La schiavette amorose Scotendo le robe la mattina Fresche e giorose come fior di spina"*

[*"The charming little slave-girls—shaking out the clothes in the morning—as fresh and joyful as hawthorn buds."][21]

Now let us follow the rich Chinese ambassador and the poor slave girls across the wooded plains of Tuscany to Florence.

PAOLO TOSCANELLI'S

FLORENCE

Arriving in Florence, the Chinese delegations would have seen towering above them the massive dome of the Cathedral of Santa Maria del Fiore, a symbol of religious faith and a tribute to Florence's brilliant architects and engineers.

An argumentative, opinionated genius, Filippo Brunelleschi, was the cathedral's architect. To build his creation, he had designed a lift to hoist up the four million bricks the job required. A novel invention, the lift could operate at two speeds, depending on the load, and was capable of reversing direction without stopping the bullocks that supplied its power. Once the bricks arrived at the base of the cupola, giant cranes, another ingenious design, shifted them into place.

The dome was unique, resembling a lemon with the bottom sliced off. Standing a sliced lemon upright, with the severed section as the base, one sees the curve increase as the dome rises. Initially, the cathedral bricks rise vertically, then they curve more and more as the tiers get higher, until, at the top, they are almost horizontal. Without internal supports to secure them, one would have expected the bricks to fall inward. But Brunelleschi solved this problem by deploying complex, three-dimensional mathematics applicable to the volume of inverted cones—an extraordinary solution he reached with the assistance of Paolo Toscanelli.[1]

Brunelleschi designed and organized everything concerned with this huge structure, at the time the largest in the world after Santa Sofia in Byzantium. He supervised the kilns where the bricks were made; he specified the proportions of lime and sodium bicarbonate for the mortar; he designed new forms for molding the bricks. He even built his own ships—articulated to facilitate sailing along the shallow, twisting Arno loaded with marble from Carrara quarries. He was granted a patent for this invention, accompanied by the right to burn rival boats! For three years, all marble was carried in Signor Brunelleschi's barges. It appeared that Brunelleschi, like Leonardo da Vinci, never went to university yet he became a genius who could turn his hand to anything.

The city that sprawled around the cathedral in the 1430s was one vast building site, a frenzy of civic works.[2] The dome alone created thousands of jobs; bricklayers, masons, carpenters, blacksmiths, winchers, plasterers, and tool sharpeners toiled like worker bees. Contractors quarried stone from the surrounding hills, providing marble from Carrara, Siena, Monsummano, and Campiglia. Florence's lead furnaces fired full blast; tile and brick factories in Castinno, Lastra, Campi, and Impruneta worked in shifts at full capacity. Farmers planted new vines, sank new wells, and raised more barns.

Between the acquisition of the port of Pisa in 1406 and that of Livorno in 1421, Florence had enjoyed a continuous economic boom. Merchants made fortunes and patronized a stream of architects, sculptors, painters, and engineers. In this extraordinary era, Florence reached her apogee, "throwing up geniuses with the ease of a juggler."[3] Or so it seems.

Italy in the fourteenth century was a patchwork of small, independent states of negligible political and military weight. Dialect, money, even weights and measures varied from state to state. Florence itself was a backwater. Yet from 1413 to 1470, Florence produced a series of works so majestic that nearly six centuries later they can still take your breath away. Why did the Renaissance suddenly explode in this small Italian town? What caused Gothic architects, sculptors, and painters to adopt the radical style we call Renaissance? How did such a bounty of genius emerge from obscurity in the space of a few years? Why there? Why then?

One explanation begins with the fact that Nature was very kind to northern Italy. The Alps sweep in a defensive semicircle around her northern frontiers; in spring, their melting snows feed the Po and its tributaries, which meander across the plain of Lombardy to the Adriatic. Rain falls throughout the year; even in high summer the hay fields are lush and green, the sweet corn nine feet high. Three or four crops provide winter fodder for animals. Brilliant sunshine, abundant water, and rich alluvial soil produce crops of every description: walnuts and chestnuts in the mountains; apples, pears, grapes, and peaches in the foothills; on the Riviera, oranges, lemons, and persimmons. From Alexandria to Mantua stretch mile upon golden mile of rice fields. Four thousand square miles of intensively cultivated land in the Po Valley provide plentiful food for everyone.

Italy enjoyed other blessings, as well. Throughout the Middle Ages, life there differed from life in the barbarian north.[4] The urban life created by the Romans survived the Ostrogoth and Hun invasions. After the fall of the Roman Empire, Italians (unlike the brutish English) were not driven back into forests. Feudalism did not take root (Italy provided few warriors for the Crusades).

Northern Italy had a far more dense population than elsewhere in Europe. Urban wealth and commerce had encouraged an inflow of labor from the countryside, stimulating further economic growth. Old Roman walled cities afforded protection. Cities, rather than states or kings, dominated northern Italy's life. People were born, lived, fought, and died as individuals.

For millennia, Venice had been the hub of European trade, exchanging the riches of the East for raw materials from the north. Venice's wealth spilled over into the Veneto and along the valley of the Po. Genoese, Florentine, and Venetian merchants set up business in Alexandria, Byzantium, and Trebizond. In northern Europe, by contrast, generations struggled to eke out a living in the cold forests and marshes surrounding them. There was little surplus labor for commerce.

Florence, nestled in the lee of the Apennines, enjoys a host of natural advantages. An easy journey from Venice, she is approached through lush, green valleys, their gentle, undulating slopes covered with oaks, sweet chestnuts, mountain ash, and acacia. Despite calamitous floods, on balance the River Arno has profited the city, providing an abundance of fish while transporting sewage and building materials downstream. Florence has never been much troubled by the water shortages that limited growth in the hill towns. Almost every aspect of the wool trade—separating fleeces, tanning hides, washing, spinning, and fulling—required copious amounts of water.

By the fourteenth century an all-weather road had been built beside the Arno. Traffic from Venice and the Lombard plain converged at Bologna, from which the shortest route to Rome lay across the Apennines. Florence occupied both trade routes—from the Adriatic to the Mediterranean and from Venice to Rome.

Florence's access to Venice enabled her to reap some of the benefits of Venice's trade with the East. It also exposed the city to an influx of Chinese and other Asians, as we can see from period paintings and sculpture. "About this time," explained art historian Bernard Berenson in *Essays in the Study of Sienese Painting,* "the arts and crafts of the contemporary orient were beginning to invade Italy."[5]

Ambrogio Lorenzetti, who never left Tuscany, painted *The Martyrdom of the Franciscan Friars* in the church of San Francesco Siena, depicting Chinese merchants with conical hats. Previously, oriental eyes had appeared in faces painted by Giotto and Duccio. As Leonardo Olschki wrote in "Asiatic Exoticism in Italian Art of the Early Renaissance," "the impression has been given that Tuscany was almost a neighbouring country of the great Mongolian Empire and that Mandarins, Khans and Oriental dignitaries were almost as much at home in Florence and Siena as in Peking, Tabriz and Calicut."[6]

There was a very substantial Chinese and Mongolian population in Florence in the decades after 1434, which Olschki describes here:

By this [slave] trade the Mongolian type became very familiar in Northern Italy and especially in Florence where the most conspicuous families such as the Adimari, Alberti, Cavalcanti, Medici, Strozzi, Vespucci and many others had their servants "*de genere Tartarorum*" and were emulated by notaries, priests, physicians, merchants and finally craftsmen and artists. . . . An ancestor of Alesso Baldovinetti bought three of those exotic girls whose portraits he drew on the margin of his still unpublished Journal. . . . The Mongolian slave girls seem to have been attractive enough to the Florentine male folk to become a disruptive element in the family life and general morality of the town. It is symptomatic that a lady of the rank of Alessandra Macinghi Strozzi wrote jocosely, in 1464, about a girl slave flirting with her son and behaving like a lady of his household. There is evidence enough for the important part played by these women in the amorous life of the town. Figures speak an impressive language. Among the 7534 infants delivered between 1394 and 1485 in the Florentine foundling hospital up to 32 percent were illegitimate children of those oriental slaves.

In this way a large influx of Asiatic blood penetrated into the Tuscan population during the most brilliant epoch of its cultural and economic evolution.[7]

Florentine families were able to keep Asian slave girls due to the wealth generated by the wool and silk trade. But that trade would never have flourished without the innovations of Italian banking.

Florence produced two bankers of genius: Giovanni de' Medici and Francesco di Marco Datini.[8] From 1398 until his death in 1410, Datini devised a range of new financial instruments that revolutionized European banking. Giovanni de' Medici took over where Datini left off,[9] leading his family to become the wealthiest in Florence and far and away the most important patrons of Renaissance learning and art. The Medicis funded artists, astronomers, engineers, architects, and cartographers on a grand scale.

In addition to art, the family purchased power, assiduously courting the papacy. During the schism that resulted in two competing popes, one in Avignon and the other in Rome, a pirate rejoicing in the name of Baldassare Cossa was elected Pope John XXIII. The Medicis had bought Baldassare his cardinal's hat with a loan of ten thousand ducats. When Baldassari became pope, the Medicis promptly became principal bankers to the papacy. (For a short period the Spinis replaced them, but at the end of 1420, the Spini bank became insolvent and the Medicis acquired their business.)

In 1421, for the statutory two-month period, Giovanni de' Medici occupied the office of *gonfalonieri,* the head of Florence. Within a few years not only did the Medici bank became the most successful commercial enterprise in Italy but the family became the most profitable in the whole of Europe. For the next 150 years, Medici power and money fired the Renaissance.

The Renaissance produced an enormous appetite for talent— engineers, astronomers, mathematicians, and artists whose individual works were so widely acclaimed that others were inspired to follow with confidence. In this, Florence once again had an ideal climate.

While the Medicis and other wealthy patrons provided the funds, substantial projects were overseen by the *operas,*[10] committees comprising of a cross section of society. Artists, engineers, and bankers sat alongside lawyers, astronomers, and aristocrats, just as they did in the city's governing body, the Signoria. This relaxed communication among different social classes took place in a society that valued diversity. The Medicis counted the pope, the chancellor of Florence (Leonardo Bruni), Toscanelli, Brunelleschi, Leon Battista Alberti, and Nicholas of Cusa among their friends. They ate, drank, and prayed together, frequently meeting every day. They examined almost every aspect of human endeavor with a cold, inquisitive eye. If man could explain the fundamental workings of the heavens, he could expound with equal comfort on sculpture, painting, drama, poetry, music, medicine, civil engineering, and warfare.

A very important tradition, which bound the Florentine hierarchy together, was their private group meal, the *mensa,* held twice a day at the headquarters of the Signoria in the Palazzo Vecchio. As Timothy J. McGee wrote in "Dinner Music for the Florentine Signoria, 1350– 1450":[11] "The Mensa took place in the civic office building now known as the Palazzo Vecchio which has served as the seat of Florentine government since its construction in 1300. . . . The Signoria was the executive branch of the city government. . . . Present at the mensa itself were a few senior members of the signoria staff (the famiglia), occasional distinguished visitors and guests of the city. . . ."

The Chinese delegation, with their new ideas, fabulous inventions, and depth of culture, would have made a very forceful impression on Florentine intellectuals meeting for the *mensa,* including Paolo Toscanelli. Florence was the ideal loam for Chinese intellectual seeds.

By pure chance, the Chinese arrived in Florence just as the Medicis returned from exile. In September 1433 the Signoria had exiled Cosimo de' Medici along with most of his family. However, in the elections of September 1434, the conservative faction in the Signoria was routed. The Strozzis, opponents of the Medicis, were exiled or barred from office.

Finance for the winning side had been provided by Cosimo, who had become chief executive of the family bank in 1420. He proved to be a brilliant banker. Profits for the years 1420–1435 totaled 186,382 florins and rose to 290,791 florins between 1435 and 1450. It was a huge sum, more than the income of some European states. Cosimo opened branches in Ancona, Pisa, Genoa, Lyons, Basel, Antwerp, Bruges, and London, becoming the first European international bank. He financed the Council of Florence (1438–1439) and provided the funds to topple the Viscontis in Milan, Florence's old rival.

As Mary Hollingsworth has shown, Cosimo took a dramatic turn after 1434, embarking on an orgy of patronage. He financed exotic palaces and chapels—San Lorenzo, San Marco, and the Medici Palace—fitting them with magnificent libraries. He financed the production of new books, maps, and scientific instruments to fill them. Vespasiano da Bisticci, a leading Florentine bookseller, described Cosimo employing fifty-five scribes to copy two hundred texts—a small undertaking by the standards of Zhu Di's encyclopedia but vast by European standards. (Henry V of England owned twenty books when he died in 1422.)

The Medici family spent 663,755 florins on patronage between 1434 and 1471. Recipients included Pope Eugenius IV, Toscanelli, Alberti, Poggio Bracciolini, Friar Mauro (for the world map of 1459), Christopher Columbus (described in chapter 10), and the young Amerigo Vespucci.[12]

The family supported Florentine humanists such as Toscanelli and Alberti, who showed a new approach to the world, explaining it through reason rather than mysticism. Cosimo financed artists who used perspective and proportion and scientists who argued that the earth was a globe, who could envision new lands full of riches that could be reached by sailing across the seas and never falling off the edge. He supported and financed scientists who could explain man's place in the universe.

Mary Hollingsworth cites Cosimo and his brother Lorenzo's embellishment of the sacristy at San Lorenzo as a notable insertion of science into the very heart of the church:

> In the little dome above the altar, an astronomical fresco depicted the position of the sun, moon and stars for 6 July 1439, the official day of Union between the Eastern and Western Churches signed at the Council of Florence. . . . His choice of such an explicitly modern theme to commemorate this event was significant. Ceilings painted blue and studded with gold stars to represent Heaven were common in medieval churches. But this scientifically accurate depiction of a particular day's sky was unfamiliar. . . . [13]

The position of the sun, moon, and stars for July 6, 1439, as seen in Florence may be checked by setting up the software package "Starry Night" for that day at latitude 43°48′ N. The puzzling question is, how did Cosimo's artist—without the benefit of computer-based astronomical tables—know the position of the sun, moon, and stars for that day?

My first thought on seeing the painted heavens on the blue dome above the altar was that the artist must have had some sort of camera to photograph the sky so accurately. The mystery deepened after I studied color photographs of the dome, which displayed detailed celestial information.

Someone knew the precise positions of the stars relative to one another, as well as the positions of the sun and moon relative to each other and to the stars. Whoever painted that fresco understood the solar system. Author Patricia Fortini Brown, in *"Laetentur Caeli: The*

Canis Major as depicted in Alberti's night sky in the Sacristy
of San Lorenzo.

Council of Florence and the Astronomical Fresco in the Old Sacristy,"
states: "This is not just another star-patterned vault: with its carefully
defined celestial meridians and graduated band of the ecliptic, dis-
tinctly marked off in measured degrees, it represents a dated and located sky with apparent 'scientific' exactitude."

As described in chapter 4, the apparent position of the stars relative
to sun and earth changes daily over a 1,461-day cycle. Because of the
astonishing accuracy of the fresco, it is possible to date the day in this
cycle that the fresco represents. Brown explains:

> The recent development of computer based astronomical tables which accord
> a degree of accuracy unavailable to Warburg's astronomer [a previous attempt
> at dating] now makes it possible to ascertain with certainty the date indicated
> by lunar and solar positions in the old Sacristy fresco. . . . Professor John Hei-
> lbron has been able to verify independently the 6 July 1439 dating first men-
> tioned by Bing and to fix the time of day at approximately 12 noon.[14]

At noon on July 6, 1439, a mass celebrated the triumph of Pope Eugenius IV, who, at the Council of Florence the day before, had sealed the union of the western and eastern Christian churches. (With the union achieved, Venice's navy subsequently defeated the Ottoman navy and lifted the blockade of Byzantium.) July 6 was named a public holiday, and the Cathedral of Santa Maria del Fiore was prepared with thrones for the Catholic and Orthodox bishops. Pope Eugenius IV celebrated a pontifical mass at noon with the epistle and gospel read in both Latin and Greek. The Decree of Union was then proclaimed in a papal bull, which began, *"Laetentur caeli,"* Let the heavens rejoice.

The dome was later painted to depict the moment of heavenly rejoicing. But how was it painted with such accuracy, and by whom?

My first thought was that the painting was done by observation of the sky. On examination, I realized this was impossible. It was broad daylight; although the stars were indeed in the positions revealed by the dome, they could not have been seen at noon.

What if the sky had been observed on the night of July 6, and the star positions extrapolated backward? This suggestion fails for two reasons. First, the fresco shows sun, moon, and stars, but the sun, of course, is not visible at night. Second, an army of observers would have been necessary to measure precisely the angles between stars and between the stars, sun, and moon—all at a time when the sun was not visible. Florence in 1439 had neither an army of qualified observers nor sufficient measuring instruments.

This complex painting required years to execute, during which the position of the stars relative to the earth would have changed according to the 1,461-day cycle. Thus it could not have resulted from piecemeal observations over the course of the job. Instead, the inescapable conclusion is that the artist had access to accurate astronomical tables.

From the financial accounts (quoted by James Beck, listing payments to the artists in *Leon Battista Alberti and the Night Sky at San Lorenzo*),[15] it appears that the painting was started after the death of Giovanni and his wife, Piccarda Bueri, in April 1433, possibly halted during the Medicis' exile (October 1433–October 1434) and started again in 1435, later payments being made in May 1439 and January and

September 1440. The painting thus took at least six years. The explanation for the astonishingly accurate dating seems to me that the constellations with their figures (the major part of the work) were painted over six years up until the Union of the Churches, after which specific stars were painted in positions they would have occupied at noon on July 6, 1439—a relatively minor and easy piece of work if the declination and right ascensions of the stars were known.

Beck, has shown that the painter was Leon Battista Alberti, perhaps assisted by his friend Paolo Toscanelli. These two were Florence's leading astronomers and mathematicians in 1439. Alberti in 1434 had accompanied Eugenius IV to Florence, where he met Toscanelli.

As we shall shortly discover, the most likely explanation of the fresco mystery is that Alberti, who served as the pope's notary, met the Chinese delegates and obtained a copy of the astronomical calendar presented by the Chinese to Eugenius IV. The calendar provided the necessary information of right ascensions and declinations of stars to draw the night sky for a particular day and hour.

TOSCANELLI MEETS THE CHINESE AMBASSADOR

Here is a translation of Paolo Toscanelli's letter, written in Florence on June 25, 1474, to Canon Fernan Martins (Martinez de Roriz), King Alfonso of Portugal's confessor at the court in Lisbon.

Canon of Lisbon, Paulus the physician [i.e. Toscanelli] It pleased me to hear of your intimacy and friendship with your great and powerful King. Often before I have spoken of the sea route from here to India, the land of spices: a route which is shorter than that via Guinea. You tell me that His Highness wishes me to explain this in greater detail so that it will be easier to understand and take this route. Although I could show this on a globe representing the earth, I have decided to do it more simply and clearly by demonstrating the way on a nautical chart. I therefore send His Majesty a chart drawn by my own hand, on which I have indicated the western coast line from Ireland in the north to the end of Guinea, and the islands which lie upon this path. Opposite them, directly to the west, I have indicated the beginning of India [i.e., China, using the nomenclature of the 15th century], together with the islands and places you will come to: how far you should keep from the Arctic pole and the equator; and how many leagues you must cover before you come to these places, which are most rich in all kinds of spices, gems and precious stones. And be not amazed when I say that spices grow in lands to the West, even though we usually say to the East: for he who sails west will always find these lands, in the west and he who travels east by land will always find the same lands in the east.

The upright lines on this chart show the distance from east to west, whereas the cross lines show the distance from north to south. The chart also indicates various places in India which may be reached if one meets with a storm or head wind or any other misfortune.

That you may know as much about these places as possible, you should know that the only people living on any of these islands are merchants who trade there.

There are said to be as many ships, mariners and goods there as in the rest of the world put together especially in the principal port called Zaiton where they load and unload one hundred great ships of pepper every year, not to mention many other ships with other spices. That country has many inhabitants, provinces, kingdoms and innumerable cities all of which are ruled by a prince known as the Grand Khan, which in our language means "The King of Kings," who mainly resides in the Province of Cathay. His forefathers greatly desired to make contact with the Christian world, and some two hundred years ago they sent ambassadors to the Pope, asking him to send them many learned men who could instruct them in our faith; but these ambassadors [the Polos] met with difficulties on the way, and had to turn back without reaching Rome. In the days of Pope Eugenius [1431–1447], there came an ambassador to him, who told him of their great feelings of friendship to all the Christians, and I had a long conversation with the ambassador about many things: about the vast size of the royal buildings, about the amazing length and breadth of their rivers, and about the great number of cities on their banks—so great a number that along one river there were two hundred cities with very long, wide bridges of marble that were adorned with many pillars. This country is richer than any other yet discovered, not only could it provide great profit and many valuable things, but also possesses gold and silver and precious stones and all kinds of spice in large quantities—things which do not reach our countries at present. And there are also many scholars, philosophers, astronomers, and other men skilled in the natural sciences who govern that great kingdom and conduct its wars.

From the city of Lisbon to the west, the chart shows twenty-six sections, of two hundred and fifty miles each—altogether nearly one-third of the earth's circumference before reaching the very large and magnificent city of Kinsai. This city is approximately one hundred miles in circumference and possesses ten marble bridges and its name means "the Heavenly City" in our language. Amazing things have been related about its vast buildings, its artistic treasures, and its revenues. It lies in the Province of Manji, near the Province of Cathay, where the King chiefly resides. And from the island of Antillia which you call "the Island of the Seven Cities," to the very famous island Cipangu are ten sections, that is, two thousand five hundred miles. That island [Cipangu] is very rich in gold, pearls and precious stones and its temples and palaces are covered in gold. But since the route to this place is not yet known, all these things remain hidden and secret; and yet one may go there in great safety.

I could still tell of many other things, but as I have already told you of them in person, and as you are a man of good judgement I will dilate no further on this subject. I try to answer your questions as well as the lack of time and my work [would] have permitted me, but I am always prepared to serve His Highness and answer his questions at greater length should he so wish.

Written in Florence on the twenty-fifth of June 1474.[1]

Pope Eugenius IV was born Gabriele Condulmer in 1383 in Venice.[2] He was pope from March 3, 1431, until his death on February 23, 1447. His mother's side was a rich merchant family, the Corrers, whose magnificent palaces can be seen alongside the Grand Canal in Venice to this day.[3] He was crowned pope at Saint Peter's in Rome on March 11, 1431. After June 1434, he spent his pontificate in Florence until he moved to Ferrara in 1438.

A short while after his letter to Canon Martins, Toscanelli wrote to Christopher Columbus:

Paul, the Physician to Christopher Columbus, greeting. I received your letters with the things you sent me, and with them received great satisfaction. I perceive your magnificent and grand desire to navigate from parts of the East to the West [i.e., to sail westward to China] in the way that was set forth in the letter that I sent you [a copy of the letter to Canon Martinez] and which will be demonstrated better on a round sphere. It pleases me much that I should be well understood: for the voyage is not only possible it is true, and certain to be honourable and to yield incalculable profit, and a very great fame among all Christians. But you cannot know this perfectly save through experience and practice as I have had in the form of the most copious and good and true information from distinguished men of great learning who have come here in the Court of Rome [i.e., Florence at that time] from the said parts [China] and from others being merchants, who have had business for a long time in those parts, men of high authority. Thus when that voyage shall be made it will be to powerful kingdoms and cities and most noble provinces, very rich in all manner of things in great abundance and very necessary to us, such as all sorts of spices in great quantity and jewels in greatest abundance.[4]

In these two letters Toscanelli tells Canon Martins and Christopher Columbus that the earth is a sphere and that China can be reached by sailing west from Spain. Toscanelli writes that Eugenius IV received an ambassador from China and that he, Toscanelli, obtained this information from him and from men of great learning who came to Florence in the time of Eugenius IV (1434 or later).

Yet in 1474, when Toscanelli wrote these letters, Europeans had not reached southern Africa, and it was another eighteen years before Columbus set sail for the Americas. So how did Toscanelli know China could be reached, not only via the east around Africa, but via the west?

Toscanelli's claims to Columbus about the map or globe seem extraordinary.[5] He asserts that the chart shows that the distance, sailing westward, from Lisbon to Kinsai in China is only one-third of the earth's circumference and that from Antilia (Island of the Seven Cities) to the "very famous island Cipangu" is a distance of 2,500 miles. He implies in his letter to Columbus that the information is on a round sphere and that the lands of spices can be reached by sailing westward.

The famous island Cipangu is Japan. So Toscanelli's claim that it is only 2,500 miles from Japan to Antilia, in the Caribbean, seems absurd. So does his claim that the map shows the distance from Lisbon westward to China is one-third of the earth's circumference; in fact, it is nearer two-thirds. If Toscanelli's account is true, it must have been a very distinctive map.

I have searched for this map for twelve years, starting with an investigation into the maps of Toscanelli's friend Regiomontanus. As described in later chapters, Regiomontanus worked closely with Toscanelli. Some historians, notably Ernst Zinner, the leading authority on Regiomontanus, and Gustavo Uzielli, believe the map Toscanelli sent to Columbus was drawn up with help from Regiomontanus.[6] Here is Zinner:

> Toscanelli was famous for his 1474 letters to Columbus and Canon Martins in which he advised them about reaching the Indies by crossing the world ocean and suggested a map for the journey. It is possible that there was a prototype of this map in one of Bessarions's nautical charts which contained islands similar to those found by Columbus; this was reported by Marco Parenti in March 1493. Now Bessarion [backer of Regiomontanus and friend of the pope] died in 1472, so Uzielli who described Toscanelli's work took the position that the map had been designed by Regiomontanus with Toscanelli's assistance. Such a collaborative work is not impossible for . . . the two men were in correspondence.[7]

At first this seemed a fruitful line of enquiry. In 1471, Regiomontanus received permission to make Nuremberg his home, and the next year he set up a printing press to print documents. In 1472 he stated his intention to publish maps: *"et fiet descriptio totius habilitatis note quam vulgo appellant Mappam Mund Ceteru germanie particularis tabula; ite Itali; Hispanie: gallie universe; Greciq."* (My translation: "to make a description of the entire habitable world commonly called a mappa mundi. Germany is described in detail, likewise Italy, Spain, Gaul, and Greece.")

For the next three years Regiomontanus was preoccupied with ephemeris tables and calendars. In 1475 the pope summoned him to Rome, where Regiomontanus died, probably of the plague. He never got around to publishing his world map. Zinner, in his lengthy book on Regiomontanus, does not mention publication of a world map. So that line of enquiry ended in a cul-de-sac.

Then, out of the blue, in April 2007 I received an e-mail from Mr. A. G. Self, a friend of our website, who attached ten pages from a book on Magellan by F. H. H. Guillemard.[8]

In the book, Guillemard exhibited globes that Johannes Schöner published in 1515 and 1520.[9] The author wished to demonstrate that before Magellan set sail, European globes had been published showing the strait leading from the Atlantic to the Pacific, which we now call the Strait of Magellan. The globes also showed the Pacific and China. The authenticity of Schöner's globes of 1515, 1520, and 1523 has never been challenged.

I studied Schöner's 1515 globe with the greatest interest. It was virtually identical to the copy of a globe shown on Waldseemüller's 1507 world map. Both are shown in the second color insert of this book.

Then the lightning bolt struck. Schöner's 1515 globe corresponded exactly with the description of the globe in the letters Toscanelli sent to the king of Portugal and Columbus. It is as if Toscanelli had Schöner's globe in front of him when writing the letters. Below I have quoted Toscanelli (Q) and followed with my remarks (R). Please have Schöner's globes to hand.

1. Q: "Often before I have spoken of the sea route from here to India, the land of spices, a route which is shorter than that of Guinea." R: This is what Schöner's 1515 and 1520 globes show.

2. Q: "Although I could show this on a globe representing the earth, I have decided to do it more simply and clearly by demonstrating the map on a nautical chart [i.e., Toscanelli, like Schöner, is copying from a globe, putting the copy on a chart]."

3. Q: "I therefore send His Majesty a chart drawn by my own hand."
R: Schöner's 1515 and 1520 maps (or charts) are copies of a globe.

4. Q: "on which I have included the western coast line from Ireland in the north to the end of Guinea, and the islands which lie upon this path."
R: This part is shown on the 1515 globe's eastern hemisphere.

5. Q: "Opposite them, directed to the west, I have included the beginning of India."
R: China is shown as "India," "India Superior," and "India Meridconalis" by Schöner.

6. Q: "The upright lines on this chart show the distance from east

to west, whereas the cross lines show the distance from north to south."

R: There are more upright and cross lines on Schöner's 1520 globe, but both of Schöner's have these.

7. Q: "From the City of Lisbon to the west, the chart shows 26 sections of 250 miles [6,500 miles] each—altogether nearly one third of the earth's circumference before reaching the very large and magnificent city of Kinsai."

R: The Canaries (Fortunate Islands) are shown 120 degrees east of Quisaya [Kinsai]; therefore Lisbon is 125 degrees from Quisaya, approximately one-third of the earth's circumference (earth's circumference is 360×60 miles, viz 21,600 miles; one-third is 7,200 miles).

8. Q: "It [Kinsai] lies in the Province of Manji."

R: Quisaya is shown in Manji province by Schöner.

9. Q: "near the Province of Cathay."

R: This is what the 1515 globe shows: "Quisaya Manji which is shown in Manji province and shown above Manji is "Chatay" [Cathay].

10. Q: "and from the island of Antilia which you call 'the Island of the Seven Cities,' to the very famous island of Cipangu are ten sections, that is, two thousand five hundred miles."

R: Antilia is shown on the 1520 chart at 335° and Zipangu at 265°, a difference of 120 degrees, which at latitude 15° N is approximately 2,500 miles (one-third of earth's circumference at that latitude).

In sum, Schöner's 1515 and 1520 globes accord completely with Toscanelli's descriptions sent to the king of Portugal and to Christopher Columbus. Toscanelli and Schöner must have been copying from the same globe, a globe that had existed before 1474 (when Toscanelli wrote to Columbus). It appears Toscanelli was telling the truth. In the next two chapters we discover how Schöner got the globe that he copied.

COLUMBUS'S AND MAGELLAN'S WORLD MAPS

Before discussing how Schöner obtained the globe that served as the model for his 1515 and 1520 globes, we should consider some other possible recipients: first, the king of Portugal[1]; second, Columbus[2]; third, the pope[3]; and fourth, Regiomontanus, who appears to have assisted Toscanelli.[4]

Let us consider the king of Portugal.

In my book *1421* I gave a brief description of Magellan quashing a mutiny by claiming to have seen a map in the king of Portugal's library. This story is now fleshed out. (I do not disparage Magellan, who in my eyes stands head and shoulders above all the early European explorers—honest, brave, clever, determined, but above all decent and fair, not least to people who could not protect themselves.)

Magellan's expedition was well provisioned and fitted out (equipped with Portuguese maps)[5] even though he was under the auspices of Spain when he sailed from Sanlúcar de Barrameda on the estuary of the Guadalquivir on September 20, 1519.[6] By the time he and his crew reached the coast of Patagonia, in South America, they had finished their hardtack (biscuits) and were reduced to eating rats[7] (which the sailors caught and sold), the price of which had trebled. Magellan was in desperate trouble. He was halfway through the strait, surrounded by mountains, with no sign of the Pacific.

A mutiny broke out, and Esteban Gómez seized control of one of Magellan's five ships, the *San Antonio*. Pigafetta, the historian aboard Magellan's flagship, tells us what happened next: "We all believed that it [the strait] was a cul-de-sac; but the captain knew that he had to navigate through a very well-concealed strait, having seen it in a chart preserved in the treasury of the King of Portugal, and made by Martin of Bohemia, a man of great parts." As I have been accused of inventing this translation, here is the original: "*Se non fosse stato il sapere del capitano-generale, non si sarebbe passato per quello stretto, perché tutti credevamo che fosse chiuso; ma egli sapea di dover navigare per uno stretto molto nascosto, avendo ciò veduto in una carta serbata nella tesoreria del Re di Portogallo, e fatta da Martino di Boemia, uomo excellentissimo.*"[8]

When writing *1421*, I had tried to find Martin of Bohemia's chart but had been unable to; it seems to have been destroyed or lost. Because the chart has never been found, some have assumed that Magellan was bluffing, pretending he knew where he was so as to quell the mutiny.

However, there are four pieces of convincing corroborative evidence that Magellan *did* have a chart that showed not only the strait but also the way across the Pacific.

The first is described in *1421*. Magellan showed the king of Limasawa in the Philippines a map that, Magellan said, showed how he had reached the Philippines across the Pacific.[9]

The second is the account of the celebrated Portuguese historian Antonio Galvão (also quoted in *1421*), who wrote that the king of Portugal had a map showing the Strait of Magellan:

In the yeere 1428 it is written that Don Peter [Dom Pedro] the King of Portugal's eldest sonne, was a great traveller. He went into England, France, Almaine, and from thence into the Holy Land, and to other places; and came home by Italie, taking Rome and Venice in his way: from whence he brought a map of the world which had all the parts of the world and earth described. The Streight of Magelan was called in it the Dragon's taile.[10]

Third, the strait was mentioned during the examination of Magellan by King Charles V's ministers before Magellan set sail. A globe was produced in which the strait was highlighted: "*de industria dexò el estrecho en blanco.*"

Magellan stressed it was a secret strait: "*estrecho de mar no conocido hasta entonces de ninguna persona*" ("a strait that was known to nobody until now/then" [11]

Finally, the *capitulación,* the contract between the king of Spain and Magellan signed on March 22, 1518, uses the phrase "*para buscar el estrecho de aquéllas mares*"—to go in search of the strait.[12]

So before *1421* was published I sought a map that would have been published before Magellan set sail but still have depicted the strait. There were several candidates. In the Venetian Doges' Palace there is an early-fifteenth-century map showing Asia and the Pacific (described in chapter 7). This map has two roundels, which state how it was composed from information brought home to Venice by Marco Polo and Niccolò da Conti. Marco Polo returned in 1295 and Niccolò da Conti by 1434, possibly as early as 1424.

Despite showing the Pacific and America, the doge's map does not show the southern part of the Americas. There is another map in the map room that does show South America and a route from Atlantic to Pacific, but unfortunately it is undated. Waldseemüller's 1507 world map (see color insert 2) shows South America and the Pacific with remarkable accuracy, but it is centerd on 20° N and stops at 45° S. The strait, which is at 52°40' S, is missing. However, Waldseemüller said in his *Cosmographiae Introductio* that the Americas "have been found to be surrounded on all sides by sea."[13] So Waldseemüller must have known that there was a way from the Atlantic to the Pacific.

The one European map published before Magellan set sail that does show a strait leading from the Atlantic to the Pacific is Johannes Schöner's 1515 globe. This was published before Magellan's examination by Charles V's ministers and before the *capitulación* between Magellan and the king of Spain. It is thus consistent with all the evidence. The authenticity of Schöner's globes has never been challenged. In

1520, before Magellan's expedition returned, Schöner published a second copy of a globe, which shows a similar strait.

If we assume for the moment that Schöner's 1515 globe was the same as that which Toscanelli copied for Columbus, we face two questions: First, what would Columbus's reaction have been? Second, is there a similar map that can be positively identified as having been received and acted upon by Columbus?

Columbus knew the Portuguese were pushing down the coast of Africa to exploit the eastern trade routes to the Indian Ocean and beyond. It seems clear from Toscanelli's letter to Columbus that Columbus was interested in finding a western route to China: "I perceived your magnificent and grand desire to navigate from parts of the east to the west [i.e., to sail westward to China]," Toscanelli wrote, "in the way that was set forth in the letter that I sent you [a copy of the letter to Canon Martinez] and which will be demonstrated better on a round sphere." In short, Toscanelli is clearly helping Columbus achieve his aim of reaching China by sailing west.

Columbus then received the map from Toscanelli (chapter 9, note 1), which indeed shows the way westward to China as Toscanelli described it. However, it also shows an unknown continent (America) between Portugal and China. What would Columbus have made of this new continent? Very likely he would have done his best to get his hands on it. He was a greedy man, as we know from his lawsuit with the king of Spain (*Pleitos de Colón*.)[14]

In the "Privileges and Prerogatives" that Columbus signed with King Ferdinand and Queen Isabella eighteen years later, before his "first voyage" to the Americas, Columbus had abandoned any thought of going to China. He was after the land that had been discovered on the western side of the Atlantic Ocean.

PRIVILEGES AND PREROGRATIVES GRANTED BY THEIR CATHOLIC MAJESTIES TO CHRIS-
TOPHER COLUMBUS: 1492. FERDINAND AND ISABELLA BY THE GRACE OF GOD, KING
AND QUEEN OF CASTILE, OF LEON, OF ARAGON, OF SICILY, OF GRANADA, OF TOLEDO,
OF VALENCIA, OF GALICIA, OF MAJORCA, OF MINORCA, OF SEVILLE, OF SARDINIA, OF

JAEN, OF ALGARVE, OF ALGEZIRA, OF GIBRALTAR, OF THE CANARY ISLANDS, COUNT
AND COUNTESS OF BARCELONA, LORD AND LADY OF BISCAY AND MOLINA, DUKE AND
DUCHESS OF ATHENS AND NEOPATRIA, COUNT AND COUNTESS OF ROUSILLION AND
CERDAIGNE, MARQUESS AND MARCHIONESS OF ORISTAN AND GOCIANO etc.

For as much as you, Christopher Columbus, are going by our command,
with some of our vessels and men, to discover and subdue some islands and
Continent in the ocean, and it is hoped that by God's assistance some of the
said islands and Continent in the ocean will be discovered and conquered by
your means and conduct, therefore it is but just and reasonable that since you
expose yourself to such danger to serve us, you should be rewarded for it. And
we being willing to honour and favour You for the reasons aforesaid; Our will
is, that you, Christopher Columbus, after discovering and conquering the said
islands and Continent in the said ocean, or any of them, shall be our Admiral
of the said islands and Continent you so shall discover and conquer; and that
you be our Admiral, Viceroy, and Governor in them and that for the future
you may call and style yourself D [Don] Christopher Columbus and that your
sons and successors in the said employment may call themselves Dons, Admirals, Viceroys and Governors of them; and that you may exercise the office of
Admiral, with the charge of Viceroy and Governor of the said islands and
Continent. . . .

Given at Granada on the 30th of April in the year of our Lord 1492, I the
Queen, I the King, by their Majesties Command, John Coloma, Secretary to
the King and Queen.[15]

Columbus's diaries show that he sailed with maps of the western Atlantic.[16] The log entry for Wednesday, October, 4, 1492, when he was
approaching the Caribbean,[17] says this: "I should steer west south west
to go there [that is, to reach the islands he is seeking] and in the spheres
which I have seen and in the drawings of Mappae Mundi it is in this
region."[18]

Is there a map we can tie to Columbus before he set sail?

Marcel Destombes described two maps that he had studied in the
Biblioteca Estense Universitaria now in Modena. I quote Arthur Davies' description of Destombes's discovery:

One was a chart of the Atlantic and bordering lands listed as CGA 5A. This map originally extended further north, west and south but had been cut so that it now extends from Normandy to Sierra Leone and eastwards to Naples and Tunis. Destombes concluded from [what Destombes calls] Rhumb lines that the map was designed to extend west as far as the legendary islands of Antilia and Satanaxia (Puerto Rico and Guadeloupe). He [Destombes] assigned his map without hesitation to Bartholomew Columbus on the basis of his excellent lettering and its Genoese style of cartography.[19]

In high excitement, Marcella and I set off for Modena. Dr. Aurelio Aghemo was most courteous and helpful and enabled me to have a photo of two versions[20] of CGA5, a copy of which is reproduced in color insert 2. As may be seen, the two maps have been torn in half and the left halves, which could show the Americas, have been destroyed. We can say for sure this tear is deliberate, for the coast of West Africa down to Cape Blanco (21° N) is shown, as is the Gulf of Guinea farther south. The bit of coast between the two, that is, the coast along the "bulge" of Africa, is missing. Someone does not want people to know what was originally on the left-hand portion of those two maps. So what gives us a lead as to what the missing part once showed?

Clearly it showed the Atlantic—but how much of it and how far west? Did the map originally go as far west as Professor Destombes thought? Did it show the Americas, and if so, how much?

Professor Destombes used what he called rhumb lines to support his supposition. I initially tried a different approach by analyzing what was depicted on CGA5A, which from now we will call the Columbus map because of Bartholomew Columbus's writing on it. The map has several distinctive features, not least a mass of names around the Bight of Benin, south of the "bulge" of Africa. My first step was to see if those names corresponded with the names on other maps drawn around 1480–1485, the most likely date of the Columbus map (Professor Davies indicates that Columbus had his map before 1492).

I quickly found that the Waldseemüller (1507) and the Columbus map shared common names in Guinea, from Rio de Lago to Capo di Monte, though the Columbus map showed more names and much more detail. I then reduced the Columbus map and the Waldseemüller to the same scale and cut out West Africa from the Columbus map, placing it on top of the Waldseemüller, so names common to both were in the same place. Finally I projected the rhumb lines from the Columbus map onto the Waldseemüller. Five sets terminated precisely and neatly on Cuba and South America from the Waldseemüller (using the Canaries as 0° W, as Waldseemüller did)—see color insert 2.

Destombes was quite right—the rhumb lines extended to Antilia and Satanazes and farther—to the Pacific coast of South America. It cannot be a coincidence that all the ends of the rhumb lines fall on a circle. In my submission, this is the evidence that the Columbus brothers had a map that showed the Americas. Columbus himself acknowledged in his logs that he had seen Caribbean islands on a world map. He was also contracted to become viceroy of land across the ocean. This hypothesis is further supported by Schöner's 1515 copy of a globe, which shows the Americas, and accords precisely with Toscanelli's description.

Moreover, as we will see in the next chapter, the Columbus map, Schöner's globe, and the Waldseemüller are all derived from the same source.

Let's turn now to Johannes Schöner, who must have been a recipient of the original globe because his drawing matches Toscanelli's description. Schöner certainly could not have met Toscanelli or the Chinese ambassador. He was not born until January 16, 1477, in Karlsstadt, in what is now the German province of Thuringen. He attended school nearby at Erfurt. The area, as I know well, is a pleasant wooded countryside famous for its plums. It is about as far from the sea as is possible in Europe, with no nautical tradition whatsoever.

Johannes does not appear to have been a renowned scholar; he left school to study at the University of Erfurt but seems to have flunked his exams—he left with no degree. He was ordained a priest in 1515 and became a prebend, an apprentice, at the church of Saint Jacob Bamberg. He was punished for failing to celebrate mass and relegated to the small village of Kirchenbach, where he was detailed to officiate at early-morning mass.[21] How, one may wonder, did this priest produce not only maps of South America and the Antarctic before Magellan set sail, but also elaborate star globes of the Southern Hemisphere?[22]

There are no prizes for guessing the obvious answer: he must have copied them. But from whom?

In January 1472, Toscanelli's friend Regiomontanus had a printing press installed in Nuremberg, as earlier described. When Regiomontanus died in 1475, his press reverted to Bernard Walther, who had provided the finance for it. In a letter to a friend on July 4, 1471, Regiomontanus wrote:

> Quite recently I have made observations in the city of Nuremberg . . . for I have chosen it as my permanent home not only on account of the availability of instruments, particularly the astronomical instruments on which the entire science is based, but also on account of the great ease of all sorts of communication with learned men living everywhere, since the place is regarded as the centre of Europe because of the journeys of the merchants.[23]

In 1495, Johannes Schöner also moved to Nuremberg, where he studied practical astronomy under the same Bernard Walther who had financed Regiomontanus and taken back his printing press. When Walther died, Schöner inherited Regiomontanus's library and printing press as well as Regiomontanus's nautical instruments, globes, and treatises; Schöner published Regiomontanus's *Tabula* and his book on spherical triangles. All of these legacies are now in the Austrian National Library in Vienna.[24]

Regiomontanus had intended to publish his own world map but died before doing so.[25] Schöner inherited this unpublished map and published it under his own name. Hence his 1515 and 1520 copies. After Magellan returned, Schöner published his 1523 globe, which he maintained did not improve upon his 1515 and 1520 (pre-Magellan) maps.[26] The 1523 globe did, however, correct the width of the Pacific across which Magellan had by then (1523) sailed.

Finally, is there any corroborative evidence that Pope Eugenius IV or his successors obtained a world map showing the Americas before Columbus set sail for the Americas?

After Columbus's death, his family instituted legal proceedings against the Spanish monarchy, the *Pleitos de Colón* (Pleadings of Columbus). Evidence was given at these proceedings on behalf of Martín Alonso Pinzón, Columbus's flag captain. Pinzón's son stated that his father had seen a copy of a map of the Americas at the papal court in Rome and had based his own expedition to the Americas upon it.[27] However, his father had decided to join Columbus's expedition instead.

From Schöner, Magellan, Columbus, Regiomontanus, and Pinzón, we now have evidence corroborating the existence, noted by Toscanelli in his letters, of a world map showing the Americas. Toscanelli told the truth. He had met the Chinese ambassador, who had given him a globe or map showing the way to the Americas and around the world. We must now find the original that Toscanelli copied.

THE WORLD MAPS
OF JOHANNES SCHÖNER,
MARTIN WALDSEEMÜLLER,
AND ADMIRAL
ZHENG HE

In 1507 Johannes Schöner bound the different sheets of Waldseemüller's 1507 world map together and placed them inside a cover. This is
the set preserved at the Library of Congress in Washington, D.C.
Waldseemüller's world map shows South America and the Pacific.
The first question is, how did Waldseemüller know of the Americas
and the Pacific before Magellan set sail? The second is, how did
Schöner get a copy of Waldseemüller's sheets in order to bind them?

Martin Waldseemüller was born at Wolfenweiler near Freiberg in
1475, two years before Schöner. His birthplace is about 250 miles from
Schöner's birthplace. Waldseemüller spent his working life as a canon
at Saint-Dié. In 1487 he entered the University of Freiberg to study theology. There is no evidence that Waldseemüller was a particularly
clever student or even that he obtained a degree. In 1514, as a clerk of
the diocese of Constance, he applied for a canonry at Saint-Dié and
obtained the post. He died there in 1522.

Waldseemüller had about a thousand copies of his 1507 map printed.
In addition to the copy owned by the U.S. Library of Congress, a cut-

out set (ready to be made up into a globe) is owned by the James Ford Bell Library in Minneapolis. A third copy was acquired in 2003 by the well-known map dealer Charles Frodsham, from Christie's auction house.

In the summer of 2004 I carefully examined Waldseemüller's 1507 map. Its significance, of course, is that it showed the Pacific, South America, the Andes, and the Rocky Mountains before either Magellan set sail or Balboa "discovered" the Pacific. So it appeared someone had been in the Pacific before Magellan and had mapped 23,000 miles of American coastline.

On the map, the Americas look nothing like the continents; they appear more like an elongated snake. Waldseemüller had used the most extraordinary method to make his map.[1] It was projected from a globe onto a flat piece of paper using a heart-shaped projection. As a consequence, a degree of longitude near the equator was some ten times what it was near the Poles and, conversely, a degree of latitude near the Poles was some ten times what it was near the equator. Even more curious, longitude scales varied from one part of the map to the other at the same latitude, and South Africa poked out of the bottom for no apparent reason at all. (See color insert 2 and the *1421* website for a picture of the map.)

For several months I tried to make sense of this. How could I convert what Waldseemüller had drawn into a map that we would all understand?

Then, at dawn on a lovely summer's day, a heron arrived for his breakfast and perched very near the gazebo in which I was working. I watched him, admiring his patience as his neck craned over the New River, which runs at the back of our garden. After he pounced, his neck swelled. An electric shock went through my body, and it dawned on me that if I reversed Waldseemüller's process—put back onto a globe what he had laid out on a flat piece of paper, and then photographed it—I might have a map in a form that would make sense to us today.

I rushed into the basement that serves as our *1421* offices and photo-copied Waldseemüller's map into black and white, using blue lines to emphasize longitude and red for latitude (see color insert 2). Then I went down the coast of South America and marked points *a, b, c,* and so on every ten degrees of longitude (yellow points). On a separate piece of paper I wrote the latitudes and longitudes of each yellow point. I repeated the process for the Pacific coast of South America and North America, then concluded with the Atlantic coast of North America. Next, I transposed these points *a, b, c,* and so on onto a globe, connecting the points. Then I photographed the globe (see color insert 2).

There on the globe was the world that Waldseemüller had originally copied: an extraordinary likeness of North and South America, which we would recognize today, with the correct landmass, shape, and position relative to Africa. Before Magellan set sail, Waldseemüller had produced a wonderful map of the Americas from a globe.

So how did this clerk in holy orders with no known knowledge of map collecting or cartography, working in what was then the landlocked backwater of Saint-Dié, manage to produce a globe with the first accurate description of the Americas?

Waldseemüller initially said he he got his information from Amerigo Vespucci. Assuming that Vespucci reached 45° S, and that Waldseemüller had received his reports, Waldseemüller could have obtained from him the information necessary to draw the Atlantic coast of South America. Vespucci was an excellent navigator and had Regiomotanus's ephemeris tables, which enabled him to calculate latitude and longitude. Yet Vespucci never claimed to have reached the Pacific. He specifically told the Florentine ambassador that he had failed to find the passage that led from the Atlantic to the Pacific, the passage we now call the Strait of Magellan.

Waldseemüller's map shows the Pacific, the Andes up to Ecuador, and then the Sierra Madre of Mexico and the Sierra Nevada of California. So for him to have credited Vespucci for his depiction of Pacific America (a credit he later withdrew) is nonsense. Waldseemüller must have copied his map—but from whose globe, and when?

There is a host of evidence suggesting that Waldseemüller got his information from the same source as Schöner.

First, Schöner's globe of 1515 and the globe shown on Waldseemüller's map of 1507 are the same.

Both show:

1. "Zipangi" to the west of North America in the same incorrect position.
2. The same shape for North and South America, a continent whose width was unknown to Europeans.
3. The same inaccurate distances from Europe to Kinsai in China.
4. The same understatement of the width of the Pacific—an ocean unknown to Europeans at that time.
5. The same names (described by Toscanelli) for China: India Meridionalis, India Superior, India.
6. The same names for Chinese provinces (also used by Toscanelli): Cyamba Provinca Magna, Chatay, Chairah.
7. The same names for towns (see Toscanelli's letters): Qinsay, Cyamba.
8. Islands in the same position with the same names: Java Major, Java Minor, Peutah, Neevra, Angama, Candin.
9. Both show Quinsay (described by Toscanelli); Waldseemüller has more detail—

WALDSEEMÜLLER	SCHÖNER
QINSAY: "PER CIVITAS HABER IN TITAN AU TUO 100 MILITARI ET IN EA 12M PONTES" Translation: [Qinsay] is treated by the citizens as the son of Uranus (Heaven) and,	"This city is approximately one hundred miles in circumference and possesses 10 marble bridges and its name means the Heavenly City in our language."

astonishingly (AU)
is of 100 military
miles and has
12m. bridges.

10.   Both Waldseemüller and Schöner show the island of Cipangu
      (Japan), but Waldseemüller gives more names and details.

WALDSEEMÜLLER	SCHÖNER
"ERIT AURUM IN COPIA MANA . . . LAPIDES PAOCOS DE OMNI GENE." Zipangu has gold in abundance . . . precious stones and pearls.	[Per Toscanelli:] Cipangu "is very rich in gold, pearls and precious stones."

11.   Both have the same latitude error for the north coast of South
      America.

In Summary, the two globes, Schöner and Waldseemüller, are so
similar that they must have been copied from the same original source,
which must also be Toscanelli's source—Toscanelli's names and descriptions being the same as Schöner's and Waldseemüller's.

The way to put this assertion to the test was to visit Saint-Dié to in-
vestigate Waldseemüller's background and working practices—in particular whether he had used an earlier globe and if so how he obtained
it.[2] My thoughts were that Regiomontanus or Schöner may have bought
the master globe to Saint-Dié from either Nuremberg or Florence. Accordingly we decided to travel to Saint-Dié, which is in a deep valley in
the heart of the Vosges Mountains, by the alpine road from Florence to
where it joined the road from Nuremberg.

Before we set off I spent a month reading up on the history of Lorraine in the 1500s, which revealed the ruler of Saint-Dié, René II of Lorraine, to have been a cultured and influential figure with a symbolic importance to fellow rulers of France, Florence, and Spain, for René was king of Jerusalem—a title he had obtained from his ancestors—the spoils of war from the Second Crusade. I also learned that Saint-Dié had rich silver mines, which had flourished in the early 1500s on account of the Portuguese having found gold mines as their explorers pushed down the west coast of Africa. With abundant supplies, the price of gold in relation to silver had fallen and the mines at Sainte-Marie-aux-Mines near Saint-Dié were working at full capacity to produce sufficient silver. Although at that time France had incorporated Burgundy, Lorraine was still part of the Holy Roman Empire, a relatively independent state between France, Venice, and Florence. Venice at the time was highly unpopular in Europe.

I found that there were a considerable number of well-written histories of Lorraine, the mines, and Saint-Dié's unique role in naming America. The best-known author appeared to be Dr. Albert Ronsin, the honorary conservator of the library and museum of Saint-Dié. I hoped to be able to meet Dr. Ronsin during my visit.

Marcella and I started our journey on August 15, 2007, after a celebration mass for the Assumption of the Virgin Mary. By the time we reached the Alps, heavy rain had reduced visibility to a few yards. As we climbed high into the mountains, the rain became torrential. Our car, loaded with innumerable suitcases of clothing and books, objected to the onerous conditions. The fan belt broke and we shuddered to a halt in a cloud of sparks—now we really felt like medieval travelers! We were able to appreciate the stamina of those who had made the journey across the Alps and through the Vosges to Saint-Dié.

Three days later, with a new fan belt, we were on the move again. By the time we had passed Colmar and joined the Nuremberg–Saint-Dié road at Sélestat, the rain had returned with a vengeance. The tunnel through the Vosges at Sainte-Marie-aux-Mines was flooded, leaving no alternative but to take the mountain pass of Sainte-Marie. The mist that shrouded the mountains reminded me that landlocked Saint-Dié had no seafaring tradition, and Waldseemüller never saw the sea.

We entered Saint-Dié in a gray gloom, the flooded streets reflecting our somber mood. The old town had disappeared, for the Gestapo in a final act of barbaric cowardice at the end of the battle of the Vosges in 1944 had set fire to the place and blown up the cathedral. Nothing is left of the Saint-Dié of Waldseemüller's time. However, our spirits leapt on entering the main north-south street, for there were bold signs that stated: AMERICA 1507–2007—SAINT-DIÉ and underneath: LE BAPTÊME DE L'AMERIQUE À SAINT DIÉ-DES-VOSGES ET LE CONTEXT HISTORIQUE ET CULTURAL EN LORRAINE VERS 2007—MUSÉE PIERRE-NOËL (The baptism of America at Saint-Dié in the cultural and historical context of Lorraine in 2007)[3]

Needless to say, we followed the signs to the Musée Pierre-Noël opposite the cathedral, arriving with an hour to spare before the museum closed.

In high excitement I pulled out my working papers relating to Waldseemüller's 1507 map (see color insert 2) and spread them on the floor before starting a search for Waldseemüller's papers. Standing beside a large-scale version of Waldseemüller's 1507 map was Monsieur Benoit Larger, who came over to see what I was up to. Monsieur Larger offered to show us around the exhibition, and we gratefully accepted. He put aside the next day for us.

Everything that I had hoped to find in several days of research was packed into half a dozen well-organized and well-lit rooms. The excellent exhibition offered a detailed history of Lorraine in the early 1500s, and the role and personality of Duke René II, who used his wealth from mines to finance a group of scholars to promote his passion for geography and cartography.

Monsieur Larger could not have been more helpful. We were permitted to take photographs of the entire exhibition, tape-record our guided tour, obtain photocopies of all material, and purchase a host of books written by those who had made Saint-Dié and the naming and discovery of America in 1507 their life's work. We left with a large suitcase of well-documented research that would have taken me years to collect without such assistance.

The key to the whole operation of producing the 1507 map was the team of people that René and the manager of the mines assembled in 1505. Monsieur Larger explained the composition and characters of this group. The world authority on Waldseemüller's role within this group was Dr. Albert Ronsin, whom I had hoped to see. Sadly, he had died shortly after the exhibition opened, but his legacy lived on in the exhibition brochure. Dr. Ronsin wrote in a beautiful simple style: here I have translated his article from page 98 of the brochure;

Saint-Dié gives a name to the New World.

The birth and baptism of a continent. The representation and naming of the continent of America in the documents printed at Saint-Dié in 1507

The Canon of the Church of Saint-Dié Vautrin Lud, a passionate geographer, heard of a work which was to be published in Strasbourg in 1505 by the young Savant Matthias Ringman. This document "De Ora Antartica" was one of the 14 editions in the Latin language usually published under the title "Mundus Novus," an account of the third voyage of Amerigo Vespucci in 1501–1502 under the auspices of the king of Portugal, Manuel I. On this expedition, Vespucci's fleet sailed along the Atlantic seaboard of Brazil then down to Argentina—from 5 to 52 degrees south. Vespucci reported his proceedings to Lorenzo Pietro Francisco de Medici, head of the trading house which Vespucci served. Vespucci was convinced that the lands past which he had sailed were part of a new continent hitherto unknown to Europeans.

Vautrin, astonished by Vespucci's revelations, decided to set up a school at Saint-Dié and to gather there a group of savants. He obtained the services of Matthias Ringmann, a classical scholar who ran a printing works in Strasbourg, and also the services of Martin Waldseemüller, a German-speaking cartographer well known to educated Alsatian people.

"With his nephew Nicholas Lud, who was secretary to the Duke of Lorraine and his colleague at the Monastery of Saint-Dié, Jean-Basin de Sandaucourt, a well-known classicist, Vautrin Lud, Ringmann and Waldseemüller formed a little group of savants who took the name "Gymnase Vosgien."

Through the intermediary of his sovereign René II Duke of Lorraine, Vautrin Lud obtained two further documents from Lisbon. Vespucci's account written in 1504 to the Head of Florence, Gonfalier Pier Soderini, of his four voyages carried out between 1497 and 1504 under the flag of the king of

Castile with the blessing of the king of Portugal. This document confirmed the discovery of a new continent: [the second document] was a marine chart, published in a cartographic workshop in Lisbon on which was printed the information given in the accounts of Vespucci's voyages. This chart seemed to be very similar to Nicholas Caverio's chart of 1502.

On receipt of these documents, Martin Waldseemüller constructed a little terrestrial globe on which he showed four continents; the new continent in the Western Atlantic he named America, shown twice. This continent was separated by another ocean from Asia. This "Globe Vert" is now owned by the Bibliothèque Nationale de France; it was probably offered to Duke René II of Lorraine by the group at Saint Dié in thanks for sponsoring their work.

Dr. Ronsin, whose book *Le nom de l'Amérique: L'invention des Chanoines et savants de Saint-Dié* I have been quoting, includes a photo of one side of this green globe; please compare it with the diagram I constructed in 2004 when converting what is on Waldseemüller's chart back onto a globe. As may be seen, in his book, Dr. Ronsin has this caption underneath the picture of Waldseemüller's globe, which states: "*Waldseemüller's Green Globe* of diameter of 240mm, the green globe was made at Saint-Dié by Waldseemüller in 1505 or 1506 after receiving a Portuguese chart and the text of the descriptions of Vespucci from his voyages. It was to be offered to the Duke of Lorraine, Rene II, Protector of the group of savants of Saint-Dié."

I now ask the reader to return to Toscanelli's letter of 1474 to Canon Martins of Portugal in which he sends the king of Portugal a chart derived from a globe. All of Toscanelli's descriptions correspond precisely with what is shown on what is known as Waldseemüller's Green Globe. Toscanelli wrote that from Lisbon to Kinsai was nearly one-third of the earth's circumference (on Waldseemüller's globe it is 120 degrees); from Antilia to Cipangu was 2,500 miles. It is as if Toscanelli had Waldseemüller's Green Globe in front of him. Put another way, Waldseemüller's 1506 Green Globe is a direct copy of that which Toscanelli had, and from which Toscanelli and Regiomontanus drew the chart he sent to the king of Portugal in 1474 following his meeting with the Chinese ambassador in 1434. Here again is the letter, which I have annotated:

To Fernan, Canon of Lisbon (1), Paulus the physician [i.e., Toscanelli] sends greetings. It pleased me to hear of your intimacy and friendship with your great and powerful King (2). Often before I have spoken of the sea route from here to India (3), the land of spices: a route which is shorter than that of Guinea (4). You tell me that His Highness wishes me to explain this in greater detail so that it will be easier to understand and take this route. Although I could show this on a globe (5) representing the earth, I have decided to do it more simply and clearly by demonstrating the way on a nautical chart (6). I therefore send His Majesty a chart drawn by my own hand (7), on which I have indicated the western coast line from Ireland in the north (8) to the end of Guinea, and the islands which lie upon this path (9). Opposite them, directed to the west, I have indicated the beginning of India [i.e., China, using the nomenclature of the fifteenth century] (10), together with the islands (11) and places you will come to: how far you should keep from the Arctic pole (12) and the equator; and how many leagues you must cover before you come to these places, which are most rich in all kinds of spices (13), gems (14) and precious stones (15). And be not amazed when I say that spices grow in lands to the West (16), even though we usually say to the East: for he who sails west will always find these lands (17), and he who travels east by land will always find the same lands in the east (18).

The upright lines on this chart show the distance from east to west (19), whereas the cross lines show the distance from north to south (20). The chart also indicates various places in India which may be reached if one meets with a storm or head wind or any other misfortune (21).

That you may know as much about these places as possible, you should know that the only people living on any of these islands are merchants who travel there.

There are said to be as many ships, mariners and goods there as in the rest of the world put together especially in the principal port called Zaiton (22) where they load and unload one hundred great ships of pepper every year, not to mention many other ships with other spices. That country has many inhabitants, provinces (23), kingdoms and innumerable cities (24) all of which are ruled by a prince known as The Grand Khan, which in our language means "The King of Kings" (25), who mainly reside in the Province of Cathay (26) whose forefathers greatly desired to make contact with the Christian world (27), and some two hundred years ago they sent ambassadors to the Pope (28), asking him to send them many learned men who could instruct them in our faith; but these ambassadors [the Polos] met with difficulties on the way (29), and had to turn back without reaching Rome. In the days of Pope Eugenius (30) [1431–1447], there came a Chinese ambassador to him (31), who told him of their great feelings of friendship to all the Christians (32), and I had a long conversation with the ambassador about many things (33): about the vast size of the royal buildings (34), about the amazing length and breadth of their rivers (35), and about the great number of cities on their banks (36)—so great a number that along one river there were two hundred cities with very long, wide bridges of marble that were adorned with many pillars (37). This country is richer than any other yet discovered, not only could it provide great profit and many valuable things, but also possesses gold and silver (38) and precious stones and all kinds of spice in large quantities (39)—things which do not reach our countries at present. And there are also many scholars, philosophers, astronomers (40), and other men skilled in the natural sciences (41) who govern that great kingdom and conduct its wars.

From the city of Lisbon to the west, the chart shows twenty-six sections, of two hundred and fifty miles each—altogether nearly one-third of the earth's circumference (42) before reaching the very large and magnificent city of Kinsai (43). This city is approximately one hundred miles in circumference and possesses ten marble bridges (44) and its name means "the Heavenly City" (44) in our language. Amazing things have been related about its vast buildings (45), its artistic treasures (46), and its revenues. It lies in the Province of Manji (47), near the Province of Cathay (48), where the King chiefly resides. And from the island of Antillia which you call "the Island of the Seven Cities" (49), to the very famous island Cipangu are ten sections, that is, two thousand five hundred miles (50). The island is very rich in gold, pearls and precious stones and its temples and palaces are covered in gold (51). But since the route to this place is not yet known (52), all these things remain hidden and secret; and yet one may go there in great safety.

I could still tell of many other things, but as I have already told you of them in person (53), now to you a man of good judgement I will dilate no further on this subject. I try to answer your questions as well as the lack of time and my work would have permitted me, but I am always prepared to serve His Highness and answer his questions at greater length should he so wish.

Written in Florence on the twenty-fifth of June 1474.

1. *"To Fernan, Canon of Lisbon . . .":* Canon Fernan Martins was at the time confessor to King Alfonso V of Portugal. He and Toscanelli had previously met on the death bed of Nicholas of Cusa (described later).

2. *"your great and powerful King":* King Alfonso, under whose leadership the Portuguese continued down the east coast of Africa and across the Atlantic to Central America and Brazil.

3. *"the sea route from here to India":* India, as may be seen from Waldseemüller's globe and map, in those days denoted China and Southeast Asia—further evidence that Waldseemüller and Toscanelli were copying from the same globe.

4. *"a route which is shorter than that of Guinea":* This is what the Waldseemüller globe shows—it accords with Toscanelli's description.

5. *"I could show this on a globe representing the earth":* The Green Globe was Waldseemüller's blueprint for his 1507 map. Toscanelli and Waldseemüller were copying from the same globe.

6. *"I have decided to do it more simply and clearly by demonstrating the way on a nautical chart":* Toscanelli was working like Waldseemüller. They were copying from the same globe.

7. *"I therefore send his Majesty a chart drawn by my own hand":* According to Uzielli, Toscanelli was helped by Regiomontanus.

8. *"on which I have indicated the western coastline from Ireland in the north":* This is what the Green Globe shows.

9. *"to the end of Guinea, and the islands which lie upon this path":* This is what the Green Globe shows.

10. *"opposite them, directed to the west, I have indicated the beginning of India":* The Green Globe and map show China as India: India "Meridionales" and "India Superior." Both Waldseemüller and Schöner use these names.

11. *"together with the islands":* Many islands are shown on the Pacific as yet undiscovered by Europeans.

12. *"how far you should keep from the Arctic Pole":* Columbus and

King Alfonso are being shown a route leading into the Pacific at about 10° N (Raspadura Canal) as well as one via the "Straights of Magellan."

13. *". . . these places, which are most rich in all kinds of spices"*: Marco Polo: "The pepper consumed daily in the city of Kinsai for its own use amounts to 43 cart loads."

14. *"gems"*: Marco Polo: "All the treasures that come from India— precious stones, pearls and other rarities are brought here [to Khan-Balik]."

15. *"and precious stones"*: Marco Polo

16. *"I say that spices grow in lands to the West"*: By sailing west, the spice lands can be reached as shown on the Green Globe and the Toscanelli description of his chart.

17. *"for he who sails west will always find these lands"*: As shown on the Green Globe and the Toscanelli description of his chart.

18. *"and he who travels east by land will always find the same lands in the east"*: This is what the Green Globe and Toscanelli chart show.

19. *"The upright lines on this chart show the distance from east to west"*: Longitude lines are drawn on the Green Globe and the Toscanelli description of his chart.

20. *"whereas the cross lines show the distance from north to south"*: Latitude lines are drawn on the Green Globe and described by Toscanelli.

21. *"The chart also indicates various places in India which may be reached if one meets with a storm or head wind"*: A number of ports are shown on the Green Globe and described by Toscanelli.

22. *"as many ships, mariners and goods there as in the rest of the world put together especially in the principal port called Zaiton"*: Marco Polo describes Zaiton: "For one spice ship that goes to Alexandria or elsewhere to pick up pepper for export to Christendom, Zaiton is visited by a hundred . . . it is one of the two ports in the world with the biggest flow of merchandise."

23. *"That country has many inhabitants, provinces"*: Marco Polo: "The traveller passes through a fine country full of thriving towns and villages, living by commerce and industry." Many

names of provinces are shown on the chart, as are the
descriptions of inhabitants.

24. *"and innumerable cities"*: Marco Polo: "This city (Soo Chow)
exercises authority over sixteen others, all busy centres of trade
and industry." Numerous cities are shown on the chart.

25. *"all of which are ruled by a prince known as The Grand Khan"*:
Marco Polo: "The people are idolaters using paper money and
subject to the Great Khan and amply provided with all the
means of life."

26. *"who mainly reside in the Province of Cathay"*: Marco Polo: "The
westward road extends for ten days journey through Cathay . . .
all the way it runs through a country of splendid cities and fine
towns with thriving trades and industries, through well filled
fields and vineyards."

27. *"whose forefathers greatly desired to make contact with the
Christian world"*: Marco Polo describes how Kubilai Khan sent
Nicolo and Maffeo Polo on a mission to the pope inviting the
pope to send "a hundred learned men learned in the Christian
religion" to China.

28. *"some two hundred years ago [around 1274] they sent ambassadors
to the Pope"*: The Polos arrived at Acre, an eastern outpost of
Christendom, from China in 1269 but found Pope Clement IV
had died. His successor, Gregory X, could muster only two
learned men. The Polos returned to China in 1273–1274,
reporting to Kublai Khan in Kemenfu.

29. *"but these ambassadors met with difficulties on the way"*: The
difficulties were caused by the invasion of the sultan of Egypt
into Armenia "and wrought great havoc on the country, and
the emissaries [Polos] went into peril of their lives." Marco's
account.

30. *"In the days of Pope Eugenius"*: Eugenius was anointed pope on
March 3, 1431.

31. *"there came a Chinese ambassador to him"*: Zheng He was
appointed ambassador to inform the papacy that the reign of
the Xuan De emperor had commenced. He sailed from China

in 1432. Eugenius moved the Papal Court to Florence in 1434.

32. *"who told him of their great feelings of friendship to all the Christians"*: Zheng He was very tolerant of all religions—he was a Muslim who practiced Buddhism as well. He deliberately sought out Christian navigators for his fleet, searching Quanzhou for them.

33. *"and I had a long conversation with the ambassador about many things"*: Zheng He had set up a languages school in Nanjing, where fourteen languages could be studied, including Latin. Toscanelli, the pope, and Alberti all spoke and wrote Latin fluently.

34. *"about the vast size of the royal buildings"*: Marco Polo: "You must know that for three months in the year . . . the Great Khan lives in the capital city Cathay, whose name is Khan-Balik." Zhu Di had rebuilt Khan-Balik as Beijing; the size of his royal palaces in the Forbidden City is described in *1421*.

35. *"about the amazing length and breadth of their rivers"*: Waldsee-müller drew several of these rivers; some span sixty degrees of longitude—a length one-sixth of the world. Marco Polo: "This river runs for such a distance and through so many regions and there are so many cities on its banks . . . it exceeds all the rivers of the Christians put together and their seas into the bargain."

36. *"about the great number of cities on their banks"*: Waldseemüller depicts many of these cities—Qinsai, Syrngia, Cianfu, Aio, Tangui, Civi, Cyamba, Cyamba Portus. Marco Polo: "There are so many cities on its banks . . . more than 200 cities all having more ships."

37. *"very long, wide bridges of marble that were adorned with many pillars"*: Marco Polo: "On each side of the bridge is a wall of marble slabs and columns . . . at the foot of the column is a marble lion and on top of the column another of great beauty and size and fine workmanship."

38. *"possesses gold and silk and precious stones"*: Marco Polo: "They have gold in great abundance, because it is found there in measureless quantities—there is a place called Ydifu in which

there is a very rich silver mine providing great quantities of silver."

39. *"all kinds of spice in large quantities"*: Marco Polo: "According to figures ascertained by Messer Marco from an official of the Great Khan's customs, the pepper consumed daily in the city of Kinsai for its own use amounts to 43 cart loads, each cart load consisting of 223 lbs."

40. *"And there are also many scholars, philosophers"*: Guo Shoujing in mathematics and astronomy; Confucius in philosophy; Lao-tzu in war; Zhu Siben in cartography; Ch'iao Wei Yo in civil engineering; and Bi Sheng in printing, are but a few such learned men.

41. *"other men skilled in the natural sciences"*: Marco Polo: "Men of the province of Manzi . . . among them are wise philosophers and natural physicians with a great knowledge of nature."

42. *"From the city of Lisbon to the west the chart shows twenty six sections of two hundred and fifty miles each—altogether nearly one third of the Earth's circumference"*: This is what the Green Globe shows and Toscanelli describes.

43. *"the very large and magnificent city of Kinsai"*: Waldseemüller draws Kinsai and describes it (Qinsay) as "treated by the citizens as the son of Uranus (heaven)."

44. *"This city is approximately one hundred miles in circumference"*: Waldseemüller: "Is of one hundred military miles and has twelve bridges."

44. *"and its name means 'the Heavenly City' "*: Waldseemüller description.

45. *"it's vast buildings"*: Marco Polo: "On the river bank are constructed large stone buildings in which all the merchants . . . store their wares . . . in each of these squares, three days a week there is a gathering of forty or fifty thousand people."

46. *"its artistic treasures"*: Marco Polo: "All these ten squares are surrounded by high buildings and below these are shops in which every sort of craft is practiced and every sort of luxury is on sale including spices, gems and pearls."

47. *"It lies in the Province of Manji"*: This is what the globe shows and Toscanelli describes.

48. *"near the Province of Cathay"*: Again, this is what the globe shows and Toscanelli describes.

49. *"And from the island of Antillia which you call 'the Island of the Seven Cities' "*: There are several Portuguese accounts calling Antilia (Puerto Rico) "Island of the Seven Cities."

50. *"two thousand five hundred miles"*: This is what the Green Globe shows and Toscanelli describes.

51. *"The island is very rich in gold, pearls and precious stones and its temples and palaces are covered with gold"*: Waldseemüller describes gold on his map of Cipangu. By 1434, Kyoto had many temples gilded in gold.

52. *"the route to this place is not yet known"*: Toscanelli's letter was sent eighteen years before Columbus "discovered" the Americas and forty-five years before Magellan "discovered" the "Straights of Magellan."

53. *"I have already told you of them in person"*: Toscanelli's first meetings with Canon Martins were when Nicholas of Cusa died.

I include Marco Polo's descriptions because they support Toscanelli's credibility. Obviously if Toscanelli had said he was told something that could not be true, he would not be believed, but everything Toscanelli described can be verified by either Waldseemüller or Marco Polo. His account rings true time and time again.

We can go further. Waldseemüller's map of 1507 finishes in the south at about 50° S—before the strait that bears Magellan's name. Waldseemüller's "Green Globe" of 1506 shows this strait—a strait Magellan claimed to have seen on a marine chart in the king of Portugal's library before he set sail. This strait was also shown on the map of the world that Dom Pedro brought back to Portugal from Venice in 1428. "The Straight of Magellan was called in it the Dragon's tail" (Galvão), which in my view is what Tierra del Fuego looks like on the 1506 Green Globe.

Before reaching Saint-Dié I had never heard of Waldseemüller's

Green Globe of 1506. Although I was sure it must be genuine, because it accorded with my reconstruction of Waldseemüller's map onto a globe (see color insert 2), not least in the latitude errors of the north coast of South America and the longitude errors of South America below 40° S, nonetheless I wanted to be sure that there was independent authentication that the Green Globe was Waldseemüller's and was dated 1505–1506. Monsieur Larger told me that no less an authority than Dr. Monique Pelletier had verified the Green Globe. Dr. Pelletier, now retired, is one of the world's leading cartographers. She was head of the Department of Maps and Charts of France's Bibliothèque Nationale de France and chair of the International Cartographic Association Standing Commission in the History of Cartography from 1988 to 1995. (The Green Globe is owned by the Bibliothèque Nationale.)

On return to London I took the train to Paris and arrived at the Bibliothèque Nationale in less than three hours. There Dr. Helene Richard, conservator of the maps division, kindly arranged for me to have some stunning photos of Waldseemüller's Green Globe and a copy of Dr. Pelletier's opinion as to why she validated it. Essentially she found that more than one hundred names on Waldseemüller's 1506 globe and 1507 map are the same (please see our website for Dr. Pelletier's opinion and color insert 2).

It seems to me that Dr. Ronsin's research and Dr. Pelletier's validation are of enormous importance—it is no longer merely my claim that Waldseemüller must have copied from a globe when publishing his 1507 map, nor is it any longer merely my claim that the globe from which he copied was the same globe from which Toscanelli copied—one has only to read Toscanelli's description while studying the Green Globe to form an opinion.

The whole scenario is now unveiled. As Dr. Ronson says, Waldseemüller received from Portugal a copy of the master globe. This was a copy of the one that Toscanelli sent to Portugal after he received it from the Chinese in 1434. Waldseemüller, as Dr. Ronson says, added in the results of Vespucci's voyages down the Atlantic seaboard of South America. He also incorporates Martellus's 1489 map of the

Indian Ocean, South Africa, and Southeast Asia, and publishes the results in his 1507 map.

The first European depiction of the Americas was not that shown in the 1507 map purchased by the Library of Congress, it was that shown on the 1506 Green Globe. The first map of the Americas was neither of these; it was an even earlier Chinese globe, which will now be described.

Chinese Knowledge of the World in 1434

Waldseemüller's Green Globe of 1506 shows North and South America, the Pacific, and all continents of the world in their correct relative positions. However, Waldseemüller (doubtless in good faith) incorporated the Martellus forgery extending Africa to 55° S at a time when Europeans knew that Dias had rounded the Cape of Good Hope at 34°22' S in 1488. An account of Martellus's forgery uncovered by Professor Arthur Davies is described on pages 429–34 of *1421*.

The depiction of South and Central America is accurate. As earlier stated, Waldseemüller obtained the information to draw the Americas from the king of Portugal, who in turn was sent it by Toscanelli following his 1434 meeting with the Chinese ambassador.

Hence an examination of America shown in the 1506 Green Globe should give a snapshot of Chinese knowledge of the Americas in 1434, the time of Zheng He's final voyage. Moreover, by comparing the Green Globe with Zheng He's 1418 map and with the earlier *Shanhai Yudi Quantu* (*ca.* 1405) we will be able to see the evolution of Chinese knowledge of the Americas resulting from Zheng He's voyages. We can go back even further to the Chinese maps before Christ (the Harris maps), Marco Polo's maps of North America found by Dr. Gunnar Thompson, Zhu Siben's 1320 maps (Liu Gang research), and the Doges' Palace map (before 1428).

Let us begin with a comparison of the later maps of the Americas— Marco Polo, the later *Shanhai Yudi Quantu* (1418), and the Green Globe.

The Marco Polo map (Map with a ship) (research of Dr. Gunnar Thompson) is reputed to be either a Marco Polo map made circa 1297 or a copy made by his daughter Bellela a few years later. It is a "sketch map," produced not for scientific accuracy but as part of an illustration that included a Venetian ship and Marco's personal anagram. It shows China, Siberia, Alaska, and the northwest Pacific coast as far south as Oregon. Corroborative evidence for this map comes from the map of North America in the Doges' Palace, which specifically says the map was created from evidence brought home by Marco Polo and Niccolò da Conti. Visitors can see the map (and read the roundels crediting Marco Polo) in the Doges' Palace map room today, and in color insert 2.

The first *Shanhai Yudi Quantu* (Gunnar Thompson research—circa 1405; reproduced by Wang Qi circa 1601) seems to mark the transition from somewhat crude Yuan dynasty maps (Marco Polo's) to the Chinese maps created as a result of Zheng He's voyages. Both Zheng He's 1418 map and the Green Globe show the influence of the *Shanhai Yudi Quantu* in the longitudes of the Americas. Then we come to the 1418 hemisphere map (Liu Gang research), and finally the Green Globe.

A comparison between the *Shanhai Yudi Quantu* and the 1418 maps should reflect the knowledge gained from Zheng He's voyages in the period 1400–1418; a comparison between the 1418 map and the Green Globe (stripping out the knowledge Waldseemüller obviously gained from Columbus and Vespucci) should reflect the knowledge gained from Zheng He's voyages between 1418 and 1434.

There has been a dramatic improvement in the knowledge of the true size of the Americas between the *Shanhai Yudi Quantu* and 1418 maps.

The Strait of Magellan is shown on the Green Globe but not on the 1418 map. Vespucci told the Florentine ambassador that he had not found the straits; the Green Globe was published before Magellan set sail. So it appears the strait was discovered by Zheng He's fleets between 1418 and 1434, as was the Antarctic, which is much more accurately drawn on the Green Globe than on the 1418 map—Europeans did not chart the Antarctic until three centuries after the Green Globe.

The Green Globe shows a sea passage through Central America at about 10° N linking the Caribbean with the Pacific—which the 1418 map does not. This passage still exists today after heavy rain; it is called the Raspadura Canal. I have spoken to a distinguished explorer, Tony Morrison, who has seen it (details on our website). It links the San Juan and Atrato Rivers. Columbus in his fourth voyage and Vespucci in his first searched for it. Had Vespucci continued for another two hundred miles, he would have found it. My belief is that Zheng He's fleets either discovered this canal or had it dug out between 1418 and 1434.

What is consistently wrong in all the world maps made or derived from the Chinese—Marco Polo, Doges' Palace, *Shanhai Yudi Quantu,* 1418, Schöner's globes, and the Green Globe—is an underestimate of the width of the Pacific. We know Zheng He could accurately calculate longitude, so errors after 1418 are inexplicable.

Despite this serious shortcoming, the importance of the globe Toscanelli received from the Chinese ambassador, which he copied and sent to the king of Portugal, cannot be underestimated. Columbus knew where America was and that by sailing west from Spain for some 70 degrees longitude, he would find the continent and could become her viceroy.

Similarly, Magellan knew that by sailing along the coast of South America to 52°40' S he would find the strait leading to the Pacific, which he could then cross to return home via the Spice Islands.

"The Strait of Magellan" and the Antarctic

Before seeing the Green Globe, I had studied the Piri Reis map, published in 1513 before Magellan set sail. My analysis of that map (pages 148–150 of *1421*) made it clear that the cartographer of the original map from which the Piri Reis was copied had drawn the east coast of Patagonia with considerable accuracy. The prominent features of the coastline headlands, bays, rivers, estuaries, and ports tallied from Cape Blanco in the north to the entrance of the Strait of Magellan in the south. Furthermore, the Piri Reis did show the "Strait of Magellan." I was sure back in 2001 when analyzing the Piri Reis that the Chinese fleet had sailed through the Paso Ancho into the Paso del Hombre, then due south into the Canal Magdalena. They then had altered course to due west into the Canal Cockburn and the Pacific.

An examination of the Green Globe of 1506 leads me to believe that it too shows the same route from the Bahía Grande on the Atlantic through the strait into the Pacific. The Green Globe, like the Piri Reis, shows features of Patagonia, notably the Santa Cruz and Deseado Rivers, the Golfo de Penas, and Tierra del Fuego.

I feel sure that one day the logs and navigational charts of Hong Bao's squadron will be found describing their passage through the Strait of Magellan between 1418 and 1428.

The Green Globe shows the Antarctic mountains of the Vinson Massif, sixteen thousand feet high at 70° W, and the Ellsworth Mountains at 85° W. Schöner's 1515 globe (like the Green Globe) shows the Ross Sea clear of ice to within three hundred nautical miles of the South Pole. In my submission, Zheng He's fleets did explore Antarctica. The Chinese had, at that time, steppe ponies, which could be fitted with special snowshoes that would have enabled them to reach the South Pole. (Captain Scott copied the shoes, but unfortunately they were fitted the wrong way around.)

The European discovery of the Americas and the first circumnavigation of the world came as a direct consequence of the generosity of Zheng He's emissary, who gave the Chinese globe of the world to the pope in 1434.

TOSCANELLI'S NEW
ASTRONOMY

R elations between China and the West began long before 1434.
The Catholic Encyclopedia presents a concise summary:

> Some commentators have found China in this passage of Isaias (xlix, 12):
> "these from the land of Sinim." Ptolomy divides Eastern Asia into the country
> of Sinae and Serice . . . with its chief city Sera. Strabo, Virgil, Horace, Pom-
> ponius Mela, Pliny, and Ammianus speak of the Seres, and they are men-
> tioned by Florence among the nations which sent special embassies to Rome
> at the time of Augustus. The Chinese called the eastern part of the Roman
> Empire *Ta Ts'in* (Syria, Egypt, and Asia Minor), *Fu-lin* during the Middle
> Ages. The monk Cosmos had a correct idea of the position of China (sixth
> century). The Byzantine writer, Theophylactis Simocatta (seventh century)
> gave an account of China under the name *Taugas*. There is a Chinese record
> of a Roman Embassy in A.D. 166.[1]

Tai Peng Wang kindly provided Chinese descriptions of papal envoys.[2] The ambassador who reached Florence in 1434 was by no means
the first. According to Yu Lizi, Yuan China called the Papal States "the
country of Farang" and the Papal States as a whole "Fulin" or "Farang."[3] The official Ming history states that diplomatic exchanges between the Papal States and Ming China began as early as 1371, when
Hong Wu, Zhu Di's father, assigned a foreigner from Fulin or Farang

called Nei Kulan (Nicholas?) as the Chinese ambassador to the Papal States to inform the pope of the dynastic change in China. Later on, Hong Wu appointed a delegation led by Pula (Paul?), who brought gifts and tribute to Farang.

After 1371, diplomacy between China and Europe was a two-way street, with the Papal States and China exchanging ambassadors. Yan Congjian in volume 11 of the *Shuyu Zhouzi Lu* described the visit of the Chinese ambassador to the Papal States in the reign of Zhu Di.

Yan Congjian starts by commenting that Italy's climate was rather cold, then continues:

> Unlike China, the houses here are made of cement but without roof tiles. The people make wine with grapes. Their musical instruments include clarinet, violin, drum and so on. The King [the pope] wears red and yellow shirts. He wraps his head with golden thread woven silk. In March every year the Pope will go to the church to perform his Easter services. As a rule he will be sitting on a red-coloured carrier carried by men to the church. All his prominent ministers [cardinals] dress like the King [the pope] either in green or beige or pink or dark purple and wrap their heads. They ride horses when going out. . . . Minor offences are usually punished up to two hundred times. Capital offences, however, are punishable with death usually drowning the offenders in the sea. These [Papal] states are peace-loving. As is often the case when a minor dispute or rivalry arose, the disputing states only waged a war of words in the exchange of diplomatic despatches. But if there were a serious conflict erupted, they were prepared to go as far as war. They made gold and silver coinage as their monetary currencies. But unlike the Chinese coinage, which can be stringed as a unit to count, there are no holes in their coinage for such purpose. On the back of the money is the face of the king [the pope] bearing his title and name. The law forbids any monetary coinage made privately. The land of Fulin produces gold, silver, pearls, western cloth, horses, camels, olives, dates and grapes.[4]

Yan Congjian's descriptions are reflected in a Pinturicchio fresco of Aeneas Sylvius Piccolomini, the future Pope Pius II.[5] Born in 1405 to a distinguished Sienese family, Aeneas was educated at the universities of Siena and Florence. Between 1431 and 1445, he opposed Eugenius IV. In 1445 he suddenly changed sides. He took orders in 1456, became a bishop in 1450 and a cardinal in 1456, and was named pope upon the death of Calixtus III in 1458.

Pinturicchio paints Pius II being carried on a throne into the Basilica of Saint John Lateran, Rome (where Pisanello was also sketching). The pope wears a red-lined cloak, and his hat is wrapped with golden thread. Before him are his cardinals in green, beige, pink, and blue, their heads covered in white tricorn hats. (See colour insert 3.)

A Ming dynasty book, *Profiles of Foreign Countries,* attests to continued diplomatic exchanges between Ming China and the Catholic Church in Italy.[6] This Chinese primary source includes "Lumi" among the foreign nations that paid China an official visit and rendered tribute during Zhu Di's reign (1403–1424). Lumi is Rome. The name is derived from Lumei, which is what the Song author Zhao Ruqua (1170–1228) called Rome. In his 1225 book *Zhufan Zhi* (Description of various barbarians), Zhao wrote that "all men are wearing turbans as their headwear. In winter they will be wearing coloured fur or leather coats to keep warm. One of their staple foods is the dish of spaghetti with a sauce of meat. They too have silver and gold currencies used as money. There are forty thousand weaver households in the country living on weaving brocades."[7] Clearly, the Chinese were not strangers to the Papal States.

Now for some detective work to see what Pope Eugenius IV, Toscanelli, and his friends Regiomontanus, Alberti, and Nicholas of Cusa learned from Zheng He's delegate besides obtaining world maps.

After the Chinese ambassador had presented his power of attorney (represented by the brass medallion described in chapter 2) to Eugenius IV, he would have formally presented the Xuan De astronomical calendar, which would have established the precise date of the inauguration of the emperor—"when everything would start anew."

Zheng He and the fleet had spent two years preparing to leave China and nearly three years reaching Florence. By the time they arrived in 1434 at the court of Eugenius IV, it had been nine years since the emperor's inauguration. Foreign rulers also had to know the date of the emperor's birth, which was calculated from conception. In the

One of Pisanello's sketches showing a Mongol face.

case of Zhu Zhanji, this would have been 1398. So the calendar had to go back thirty-six years. To certify that the emperor had continued to hold the mandate of heaven during that period, the calendar would also need to show that the prediction of solar and lunar eclipses, comets, positions of planets and stars and untoward lunar conjunctions (the moon with Mercury) had been accurate throughout those thirty-six years—thousands of pieces of astronomical data had to be included.

However, the calendar also had to predict the future. This required that it contain astronomical calculations of the accurate positions of sun and moon, tables of the five planets, the positions of stars and comets, dates of solstices and equinoxes, and a method of adapting those dates and times to the latitude of Florence. We know from the *Yuan Shi-lu,* the official history of Yuan dynasty, that this astronomical data was included in the *Shoushi* calendar, and one can see a copy of the 1408 calendar in the Pepys Museum in Cambridge, England. Two pages are shown on our *1434* website.

When the Chinese visited Florence in 1434, Toscanelli was in his prime, thirty-seven years old. Since graduating from university twenty years earlier, he had worked with Brunelleschi, a mathematical genius, and other leading intellectuals of the day. In particular, Toscanelli and Brunelleschi had, for the previous thirteen years, been collaborating on the complex spherical trigonometry required to build Florence's great dome over Santa Maria del Fiore. Toscanelli thus had ample opportunity to observe and accurately map the heavens in detail before the Chinese visit, but neither he nor any other of his circle did so. Toscanelli was a secretive bachelor who lived with his parents until they died, after which he lived with his brother's family. Although he never cited a particular influence or source for the prodigious mathematical and astronomical skills he displayed after 1434, he did bequeath a considerable collection of books, research papers, astronomical instruments, and world maps to his monastery. All but one of these have disappeared. Aside from that one remaining record—a manuscript housed at the Biblioteca Nazionale Centrale in Florence—we are left primarily with admiring references to him in letters among his friends. But we do know a bit about his actions. Did he behave differently after 1434? If so, how?

Jane Jervis, in "Toscanelli's Cometary Observations: Some New Evidence"[8] examined Toscanelli's surviving manuscript, a collection of folios. She compared the writing on the folios with that on the letters from Toscanelli to Columbus and Canon Martins and concluded that all but three of the folios were written by Toscanelli. Jervis then compared Toscanelli's study of two comets—one in 1433, before the Chinese visit, and another in 1456, after the visit. Folios 246 and 248 describe the 1433 comet; folios 246, 252, and 257 describe the 1456 comet.

The first comet pass was on Sunday, October 4, 1433, in the first hour of the night. Toscanelli's observations consist of a freehand drawing. He did not align the comet's positions with any stars or planets. No times are listed, nor are right ascensions or declinations of the stars or comets.

This is in stark contrast with Toscanelli's treatment, twenty-three years later, of the 1456 comet. Folios 246r and v, 252, and 257 contain a wealth of evidence. For the 1456 comet, he uses a Jacob's staff to give the comet's altitude (declination) and longitude (right ascension) to within ten minutes of arc.[9] Times are now given, as are the declination and right ascensions of the stars (Chinese methods). To achieve this radical improvement in technique, Toscanelli must have had a clock, an accurate measuring device, astronomical tables, and an instrument to show the position of the comet relative to stars and planets.

If true, James Beck's (see page 93) deduction that Alberti was assisted by Toscanelli in drawing the precise positions of stars, moon, and sun at noon on July 6, 1439 on the dome in the Sacristy of San Lorenzo similarly suggests a great leap in Toscanelli's scientific capabilities. For many years prior to 1434, Toscanelli had the opportunity to use the dome of Santa Maria del Fiore for astronomical observations. Yet he never did.

By 1475, Toscanelli had adopted a Chinese type of camera obscura, a slit of light and a bronzina (bronze casting), which he inserted in the lantern of the dome of the Florence cathedral. The pinhole camera has several advantages when measuring objects illuminated by the sun. The edges of the circle receive less exposure than the center. Since the focal length of an object's edges is greater than that of its center, the center is "zoomed in." Shadows cast by the sun, or vision of the sun itself, thus appear sharper, thinner, and clearer.

By the early Ming dynasty, Zheng He's astronomers had refined this camera obscura and used it in conjunction with an improved gnomon to enable measurement of the middle of the shadow of the sun within one-hundredth of an inch. Toscanelli used the Chinese method in a most ingenious way, adapting the dome of Santa Maria de Fiore as a solar observatory.

Between May 20 and July 20 the sun at noon shines through the windows of the lantern on the top of the dome. Toscanelli had the lantern windows covered in fabric with a small slit to allow sunlight through at noon. After passing through the slit, the sunlight became a beam. A bronzina was positioned so that the beam landed on it, and in the center of the bronzina was a hole. As the beam struck the bronzina, the hole would channel it down to the marble floor three hundred feet below. On the floor, Toscanelli drew a north-south meridian line, with incisions to note the position of the sun at the summer solstice. Regiomontanus said that using the meridian line, Toscanelli could measure the sun's altitude (and hence declination) to within two seconds of arc.

In 1754 a Sicilian Jesuit priest, Leonardo Ximénes, experimented with Toscanelli's instrument. Ximenes compared data from the solstices in Toscanelli's era to his own measurements of 1756. He found that Toscanelli was able to determine not only the height of the sun at the summer solstice but also the change in height over the years, which resulted from the change in the shape of the earth's elliptical passage around the sun.

The minute differences in the sun's altitude from one year to another preoccupied Regiomontanus as well, as he said:

> Most astronomers considered the maximum declination of the sun in our days is 24 degrees and 2 minutes but my teacher Peurbach and I have ascertained with instruments that it is 23 degrees and 28 minutes as I have often heard Master Paolo the Florentine [Toscanelli] and Battista Alberti say that by diligent observation they found 23 degrees 30 minutes, the figure I have decided to register in our table.[10]

What is so important to Toscanelli and Regiomontanus about the precise declination of the sun? When I first joined the Royal Navy in 1953, sailors trooped to the Far East by passenger liner rather than by aircraft. Each day at noon, the ship's navigator, captain, and officer of the watch would march resplendent in white uniforms on to the open bridge and stand side by side looking at the sun. Shortly before noon they would start taking the altitude of the sun with their sextants. Just before it was at its highest they would cry, "Now! now! now!" Upon the final *Now!* they would read out the sun's maximum altitude taken from their sextants. They would then declare the distance traveled from the previous noon. The lucky sweepstakes winner would be announced over the ship's address system and would be expected to buy drinks all around.

Distance from one day to the next was calculated by the difference in the ship's latitude. There is a simple formula: Latitude equals 90—sun's max altitude±declination. Declination tables of the sun are issued for each day of the year, so with the sun's altitude, the navigator can determine latitude. It's that simple.

However, this was not what Regiomontanus, Toscanelli, and Alberti were after. A few miles' difference (between 23°28 and 23°30) was in itself completely unimportant to Toscanelli. Instead, he, Alberti, and Regiomontanus were interested in the change in the sun's declination. A copy of that change can be seen in Needham's graph, by kind permission of Cambridge University Press. It shows the change in the sun's declination from 2000 B.C. to the present day, determined by Greek and Chinese astronomers for the earlier measurements and by European astronomers for the later ones, ending with Cassini.

From this graph, we can see that Toscanelli's figure—23°30—was recorded by the great Islamic astronomer Ulugh Begh also used 23°30 in his massive study completed in Samarkand in 1421—some fifty years before Toscanelli's measurement. (Regiomontanus's figure of 23°28 was determined by Cassini two hundred years after Toscanelli, so it would have been inaccurate had Regiomontanus used it.)

This is not some mathematical quibble. If the sun circled the earth, there would be no change in declination. A recognition of the change—the flatter the earth's trajectory, the smaller the declination—is tantamount to recognition that the earth revolves around the sun in an ellipse.

Their obsession with measuring the change in declination is evidence that Toscanelli, Alberti, and Regiomontanus understood that Aristotle and Ptolomy, who believed the sun revolved in a circle around the earth, were wrong. Consequently, Europeans who followed Toscanelli and Regiomontanus were basing their astronomy on a Chinese, rather than a Greek, foundation. This foundation also enabled Regiomontanus to produce tables to determine latitude in different parts of the world, which he published in 1474. Columbus and Vespucci used them, as described in chapter 21.

The exercises at Santa Maria del Fiore could be duplicated to observe the movement of the moon and produce equations of time of the moon. These, in turn, could be used in combination with the positions of stars to determine longitude (see chapter 4). Regiomontanus produced such tables, and Columbus and Vespucci used them to calculate longitude in the New World. Dias used them to determine the latitude of the Cape of Good Hope.

Each of the instruments Toscanelli used in his observations at Santa Maria del Fiore—camera obscura, gnomon, and clock—was used by Zheng He's navigators, as were the instruments Toscanelli used to determine the passage of the 1456 comet—Jacob's staff, clock, and torquetum. All of Toscanelli's discoveries—declination of the sun, obliquity of the ecliptic, passage of comets, ephemeris tables of the stars and planets—were contained in the 1408 *Shoushi* astronomical calendar presented to the pope. They were copied and published in Europe by Regiomontanus in 1474.

In his letter to Columbus, Toscanelli said he had received "the most copious and good and true information from distinguished men of great learning who have come here in the Court of Rome [Florence] from the said parts [China]." In his letter to Canon Martins, Toscanelli described his long conversation with the ambassador from China who had visited the pope, and he cited the "many scholars, philosophers, astronomers and other men skilled in the natural sciences" who then governed China.

In my submission, Toscanelli must have obtained his copious new knowledge of astronomy from the "distinguished men of great learning" who had arrived in Florence from China.

Res ipsa loquitur! "The thing speaks for itself."

THE FLORENTINE MATHEMATICIANS: TOSCANELLI, ALBERTI, NICHOLAS OF CUSA, AND REGIOMONTANUS

Before Toscanelli met the Chinese ambassador, Europe's knowledge of the universe was based on Ptolomy.[1] Ptolomy held that the planets were borne in revolving crystalline spheres that rotated in perfect circles around the earth, which was at the center of the universe. However, many European astronomers realized this did not square with their observations that planets have irregular paths. To resolve this conflict, medieval European astronomers introduced the notions of equants, deferants, and epicycles. Applying these peculiar explanations of planetary motion enabled astronomers to account for the irregular motion of the planets while holding fast to the belief that the heavens rotated around the earth.

To believe, on the other hand, that the earth was merely one planet among many revolving round the sun required a radical change in thought. This intellectual revolution was led by Nicholas of Cusa.[2] Nicholas was born in 1401 on the River Moselle. He died in Umbria in 1464. His father, Johann Cryfts, was a boatman. In 1416 Nicholas matriculated at the University of Heidelberg, and a year later he left for Padua, where he graduated in 1424 with a doctorate in canon law. He also studied Latin, Greek, Hebrew, and, in his later years, Arabic.

While at Padua, Nicholas became a close friend of Toscanelli, who was also a student there. Throughout his life, he remained a devoted follower of Toscanelli, with whom he frequently collaborated on new ideas. At the height of his fame, Nicholas dedicated his treatise *De Geometricis transmutationibus* to Toscanelli and wrote in the flyleaf, *"Ad pavlum magistri dominici physicum Florentinum"* (To the Master Scientist, the Florentine Doctor Paolo).[3]

Nicholas had a huge and independent intellect. He published a dozen mathematical and scientific treatises; his collected works were contained in the *Incunabula,* published before 1476 and sadly, now lost. In his later life he believed that the earth was not the center of the universe and was not at rest. Celestial bodies were not strictly spherical, nor were their orbits circular. To Nicholas, the difference between theory and appearance was explained by relative motion. Nicholas was prime minister in Rome with great influence.

By 1444, Nicholas possessed one of the two known torquetums based upon the Chinese equatorial system.[4] In effect, this was an analog computer. By measuring the angular distance between the moon and a selected star that crossed the local meridian, and by knowing the equation of time of the moon and the declination and right ascension of the selected star, one could calculate longitude (see page 34).

During Nicholas's era, the Alfonsine tables based on Ptolomy were the standard work on the positions of the sun, moon, and planets. Nicholas realized these tables were highly inaccurate, a finding he published in 1436 in his *Reparatio calendarii.*[5] This realization led him to his revolutionary theory that the earth was not at the center of the universe, was not at rest, and had unfixed poles. His work had a huge influence on Regiomontanus—not least in saying, "the earth which cannot be at the centre, cannot lack all motion."

Regiomontanus

Johann Müller was born in 1436 in Königsberg, which means "king's mountain"—Johann adopted the Latin version of the name, Regio-montanus.[6] The son of a miller, he was recognized as a mathematical and astronomical genius when young. He entered the University of Leipzig at age eleven, studying there from 1447 until 1450. In April 1450 he entered the University of Vienna, where he became a pupil of the celebrated astronomer and mathematician Peurbach.[7] He was awarded his master's degree in 1457. Peurbach and Regiomontanus collaborated to make detailed observations of Mars, which showed that the Alfonsine tables (based upon the earth being at the center of the universe) were seriously in error. This was confirmed when the two observed an eclipse of the moon that was later than the tables predicted. From that time, Regiomontanus realized as Nicholas of Cusa had done that the old Ptolemaic systems of predicting the courses of the moon and planets did not stand up to serious investiga-tion. From his early life, again like Nicholas of Cusa, he started col-lecting instruments such as a torquetum for his observations. Although Regiomontanus was some forty years younger than To-scanelli, Nicholas of Cusa, and Alberti, he became part of their group in the late 1450s and early 1460s, when they used to meet at Nicholas's house in Rome. There are numerous references in Regiomontanus's writing to the influence Toscanelli and Nicholas of Cusa had on his work.[8] Some of these will be quoted as we go along.

In 1457, at age twenty-one, Regiomontanus was appointed to the arts facility of the University of Vienna. The following year he gave a talk on perspective. He was now working on math, astronomy, and con-structing instruments. Between 1461 and 1465 he was mostly in Rome; the following two years he seems to have disappeared—nobody knows where he went. In 1467 he published part of his work on sine tables and spherical trigonometry, and in 1471 he had constructed instruments and written scripta. In 1472 he published *A New Theory of Planets* (by

Peurbach), and then in 1474 his own *Calendarum* and *Ephemerides ab Anno* tables.[9] These two were his legacy—of monumental importance in enabling European mariners to determine latitude and longitude and their position at sea. He died in Rome on July 6, 1476, and a number of his works were published after his death.

Regiomontanus's output after his master Peurbach died in 1461 (when Regiomontanus was twenty-five) up until his own death in 1476, at forty, was prodigious and mind-blowing. He was an intellectual giant, the equivalent of Newton or Guo Shoujing. Had he lived another thirty years, I believe he would have rivaled or eclipsed Newton. I have the greatest trepidation in attempting to do him justice, and have spent many sleepless nights trying to write this chapter—not least because I am not a mathematician.

We can reasonably start with his achievements, then go on to consider the possible sources he used and finally attempt to summarize his legacy. Doubtless critics will make the point that it is arrogant of me to even attempt to evaluate the achievements of such a brilliant figure— that such a task should be left to professional mathematicians. This is a fair point. In defense, I offer that I have spent years in practical astro-navigation, using the moon, planets, and stars to find our position at sea, and should be qualified to recognize the huge strides Regiomontanus made in this science.

So here goes. In the course of fifteen years following Peurbach's death, Regiomontanus provided first and foremost ephemeris tables— that is, tables of the positions of moon, sun, planets, and stars that were of sufficient accuracy to enable captains and navigators to predict when eclipses would occur, times of sunrise, sunset, moonrise, and moonset, the positions of planets relative to one another and to the moon. So accurate were these tables—for thirty years from 1475—that navigators could calculate their latitude and longitude at sea without using clocks. They could, therefore, for the first time, find their way to the New World, accurately chart what they had found, and return home in safety. With this and the Chinese world maps, European exploration could now start in earnest. And it did. Dias, for example, calculated the true latitude of the Cape of Good Hope using Regiomontanus's tables.[10] He reported this to the king of Portugal, who knew for the first time how far the captains had to travel south to get to the Indian Ocean. Regiomontanus's ephemeris tables were 800 pages long and contained 300,000 calculations. Regiomontanus could be said to have been a walking computer on that account alone.

He had the energy and skill to devise and make a whole range of nautical and mathematical instruments, the two most fundamentally important being the clock (which was smashed on his death) and the equatorial torquetum.[11] Regiomontanus's torquetum has been described in chapter 4—it enabled him to transfer stars whose coordinates had been fixed by the Arab ecliptic method or by the Byzantine and Greek horizon method into Chinese coordinates of declination and right ascension, the system used down to our present day.

Of Regiomontanus's designs, his observatory[12] and printing press[13] stand out for their practical use. Ephemeris tables could not have been produced to give accurate results had they not been printed. Similarly, Regiomontanus needed his observatory to check on the accuracy of the predictions in his tables. He made telescopes to see the stars; astrolabes to measure angles between stars, planets, and moon; portable sundials for gathering information on the sun's height at different times of day and for different times of the year—even tables to enable bell ringers to forecast times of sunset and hence announce vespers.

The most astonishing discovery was Regiomontanus's revolutionary idea (enlarging on Nicholas of Cusa's) that the earth was not at the center of the universe, the sun was. And further, that the earth and planets circled the sun. This statement will perhaps create an uproar; so I present here my evidence.

First of all, Regiomontanus knew that the planetary system that had been in use in Europe since the time of Ptolomy—in which the earth was in the center and sun and planets rotated around it—did not work. The results of the Ptolemaic system were contained in the Alfonsine tables, which he and Peurbach had studied for years. The predictions contained in these tables were inaccurate. Adding equants, deferents, and other weird corrections failed to correct the errors.

Second, there is no doubt that Regiomontanus knew of Nicholas of

Cusa's work. Nicholas suggested that the sun was at the center of the universe and the earth and planets rotated around it. Regiomontanus describes planetary orbits: "What will you say about the longitudinal motion of Venus? It is chained to the Sun which is not the case for the three superior planets (Mars, Jupiter, Saturn). Therefore it has a longitudinal motion different from those three planets. Furthermore, the superior planets are tied to the Sun via epicyclic motions, which is not true for Venus."[14]

Regiomontanus's opinion that the sun is at the center of the universe is clearly expressed in folio 47v: "Because the Sun is the source of heat and light, it must be at the centre of the planets, like the King in his Kingdom, like the heart in the body."[15]

Regiomontanus also had views on the orbital velocity of planets around the sun: "Moreover the assumption that Venus and Mercury would move more rapidly if they were below the Sun is untenable. On the contrary, at times they move faster in their orbits, at times slower." This foreshadows Kepler.

Regiomontanus realized that the stars were at an almost infinite distance from the solar system: "Nature may well have assigned some unknown motion to the stars; it is now and will henceforth be very difficult to determine the amount of this motion due to its small size."

He later refined this: "It is necessary to alter the motion of the stars a little because of the Earth's motion" (Zinner, p. 182).

The only possible motion of the earth relative to the stars is that around the sun, it cannot by definition refer to the circular motion of the earth around its own axis. This in my view is corroborated by Regiomontanus's written comment alongside Archimedes' account of Aristarchus' assumption that the earth circles around an immobile sun, which is at the center of a fixed stellar sphere. Regiomontanus wrote:

"Aristarchus Samius" (Heroic Aristarchus)[16]

Unfortunately, Regiomontanus's works after the date of this comment are missing.

It seems to me that Regiomontanus's near obsession with measuring the change in the declination of the sun can only be understood if he had appreciated that the earth traveled in an ellipse around the sun and that the shape of this ellipse was changing with time. He wrote: "It will be beautiful to preserve the variations in planetary motions by means of concentric circles. We have already made a way for the sun and the moon; for the rest the cornerstone has been laid, from which one can obtain the equations for these planets by this table."[17]

Before discussing Regiomontanus's masterpiece, his ephemeris tables, we should attempt to address the $100,000 question—from where did he get his knowledge? Undoubtedly Regiomontanus studied Greek and Roman works extensively—Ptolomy for years and years, and he copied out Archimedes' and Eutocius' work on cylinders, measurements of the circle, on spheres and spheroids. Regiomontanus could read and write Greek and Latin fluently. He could also read Arabic. He had mastered a wide range of Arabic work, not least of which was al-Bitruji's planetary theory. However, Regiomontanus adopted the Chinese equatorial system of planet and star coordinates; he rejected the Arabic, Greek, and Byzantine coordinate systems. He borrowed heavily from Toscanelli, including his and Alberti's calculations of the earth's changing ellipse around the sun, and he adopted Toscanelli and the Chinese measurement of the declination of the sun. His work on spherical triangles had been foreshadowed by Guo Shoujing's. If Uzielli is correct, Regiomontanus collaborated with Toscanelli on drawing the map of the world that was sent to the king of Portugal—a map copied from the Chinese, something Regiomontanus must have known.

Regiomontanus repeatedly refers to Toscanelli's work—on spherical trigonometry, declination tables, instruments, and comets. When doing so, he must have known of Toscanelli's meetings with the Chinese—and of the enormous transfer of knowledge from them.

Regiomontanus also had intimate knowledge of Chinese mathematical work, which he acquired directly or through Toscanelli. Among that knowledge was the Chinese remainder theorem.

Regiomontanus's Knowledge of Chinese Mathematics

Regiomontanus corresponded on a regular basis with Italian astronomer Francesco Bianchini.[18] In 1463 he set Bianchini this problem: "I ask for a number that when divided by 17 leaves a remainder of 15; the same number when divided by 13 leaves a remainder of 11; the same number divided by 10 leaves the remainder of 3. I ask you what is that number" (GM translation of Latin).

Bianchini replied: "To this problem many solutions can be given with different numbers—such as 1,103, 3313 and many others. However I do not want to be put to the trouble of finding the other numbers."

Regiomontanus answered: "You have rightly given the smallest number I asked for as 1,103 and the second 3,313. This is enough because such numbers of which the smallest is 1,103 are infinite. If we should add a number made up by multiplying the three divisions, namely, 17, 13, 10, we should arrive at the second number, 3,313, by adding this number again [viz 2210] we should get the third [which would be 5,523]."

Regiomontanus then drew in the margin:

17	170
13	13
	——
10	510
	17
	——
	2210

It is obvious from Bianchini's reply that he did not understand the Chinese remainder theorem (if he had, he would have realized how easy the solution was and not said, "I do not want to be put to the trouble of finding the other numbers."

On the other hand, it is obvious that Regiomontanus had the complete solution to the problem—as the mathematician Curtze summarizes:[19]

"[Regiomontanus] knew thoroughly the remainder problem, the ta yen rule of the Chinese."

The Ta-Yen rule is contained in the *Shu-shu Chiu-chang* of Ch'in

Chiu-shao, published in 1247.[20]

It follows that Regiomontanus must have been aware of this Chinese book of 1247 unless he had quite independently thought up the Ta-Yen rule, which he never claimed to have done.

Regiomontanus's knowledge of the *Shu-shu Chiu-chang* would explain a lot. Needham tells us that the first section of this book is concerned with indeterminate analyses such as the Ta-Yen rule.[21] In the later stages of the book comes an explanation of how to calculate complex areas and volumes such as the diameter and circumference of a circular walled city, problems of allocation of irrigation water, and the flow rate of dykes. The book contains methods of resolving the depth of rain in various types and shapes of rain gauge—all problems relevant to cartographic surveying, in which we know Regiomontanus took a deep interest.

The implications of Regiomontanus knowing of this massive book, which was the fruit of the work of thirty Chinese schools of mathematics, could be of great importance. It is a subject beyond the capacity of a person of my age. I hope young mathematicians will take up the challenge. It may lead to a major revision of Ernst Zinner's majestic work on Regiomontanus.

It seems to me we may obtain a snapshot of a part of what Regiomontanus inherited from the Chinese through Toscanelli (rather than through Greek and Arab astronomers) by comparing Zheng He's ephemeris tables[22] with Regiomontanus's ephemeris tables.[23]

Regiomontanus's tables are double pages for each month with a horizontal line for each day. Zheng He's have one double page for each month with a vertical line for each day. On the left-hand side of each of Regiomontanus's pages are the true positions of the sun, moon, and the planets Saturn, Jupiter, Mars, Venus, and Mercury, and the lunar nodes where the moon crosses the ecliptic. On the right-hand side are positions of the sun relative to the moon, times of full and new moon, positions of the moon relative to the planets, and positions of planets relative to one another. Feast days are given, as are other important days in the medieval European calendar.

Zheng He's 1408 tables have an average of twenty-eight columns of information for each day (as opposed to Regiomontanus's eight columns). Zheng He's tables have the same planetary information as Regiomontanus's—for Saturn, Jupiter, Mars, Venus, and Mercury, and also, like Regiomontanus's, positions of the sun and moon. The difference between the two is that Zheng He's gave auspicious days for planting seed, visiting Grandmother, and so on, rather than religious feast days. Zheng He's have double the amount of information. The astonishing similarity between the two could be a coincidence—but the 1408 tables came first, printed before Gutenberg.

Zinner and others claim that Regiomontanus's tables with 300,000 numbers over a thirty-one-year period were the result of using the Alfonsine (Greek/Arabic) tables amended by observation. If Regiomontanus's tables were based on the Alfonsine tables, they would have been useless for predicting positions of sun, moon, and planets with sufficient accuracy to predict eclipses and hence longitude, as the Alfonsine tables were based on a wholly faulty structure of the universe, with the earth as its center and planets revolving round it.

Furthermore, Regiomontanus well knew that using the old Alfonsine tables would be useless. In his calendar for 1475–1531 he pointed out that in thirty of the fifty-six years between 1475 and 1531, the date of Easter (the most important day in the Catholic Church) was wrong in the Alfonsine tables. (Because of the sensitivity of this information it was omitted from the German edition of Regiomontanus's calendar.) To base his ephemeris on tables he knew to be inaccurate would have been completely illogical. Regiomontanus had to use a new source.

Zheng He's ephemeris tables, on the other hand, were based on Guo Shoujing—which relied on a true understanding of the earth's and planets' rotation around the sun as the center of the solar system. In my submission, Zinner's claim that Regiomontanus's tables were based upon his personal observations also breaks down because he did not have time to make the necessary observations. Regiomontanus died in 1475. His tables continued for another fifty-six years; one can see his amendments in red in the tables, and these cover only five of the fifty-six years.

I hope the accuracy of Zheng He's and Regiomontanus's ephemeris tables will be subjected to a test by the "Starry Night" computer program and compared with the Almagest ephemeris calculator (based on the Alfonsine tables), but this may not occur until the tables are translated and before this book goes to press. In the meantime we need a check into the accuracy of Regiomontanus's tables in calculating eclipses, planetary positions, and longitude. If based upon Zheng He's, they would work; if upon the Alfonsine tables, they would not.

Fortunately, Columbus, Vespucci, and others did use Regiomontanus's ephemeris tables to predict eclipses, latitude, and longitude for years after Regiomontanus died.

Dias used the tables correctly to carefully calculate the latitude of the Cape of Good Hope at 34°22 on his voyage of 1487.[24] Christopher Columbus and his brother Bartholomew were present when Dias returned and presented his calculations to the king of Portugal.[25]

Columbus used Regiomontanus's ephemeris tables, as we know from tables that today are in Seville Cathedral with Columbus's writing on them.[26] Columbus referred to the ephemeris entry for January 17, 1493, when Jupiter would be in opposition to the sun and moon; he knew of Regiomontanus's explanation of how to calculate longitude from a lunar eclipse. His brother Bartholomew wrote: *"Almanach pasadoen ephemeredes. Jo de monte Regio [Regiomontanus] ab anno 1482 usque ad 1506."*[27]

Columbus's first known calculation of longitude using Regiomontanus's method of observing lunar eclipses (whose times Columbus obtained from the ephemeris tables) was on September 14, 1494, twenty years after Regiomontanus had entered the figures in the tables.[28] Columbus was on the island of Saya, to the west of Puerto Rico. ("Saya" on Pizzigano's 1424 chart.) Regiomontanus explains how to calculate longitude by lunar eclipses at the front of the tables.

Using this explanation, through no fault of his own, Columbus used the wrong prime meridian (Cadiz) in his calculations rather than Nuremberg, which was Regiomontanus's prime meridian. In his introduction to the ephemeris tables Regiomontanus does not mention this—one has to go to near the back of eight hundred pages to find this out. Columbus had another go on February 29, 1504, using the tables to predict a solar eclipse in Jamaica and to calculate longitude.[29] He made the same understandable mistake again. Schroeter's tables enable us to know the accuracy of Regiomontanus's tables when predicting these eclipses on September 14, 1494, and February 29, 1504—delays of thirty minutes and eleven minutes respectively, and that twenty and thirty years after Regiomontanus had entered the figures—fantastic accuracy, which in my view demolishes the case that Regiomontanus's ephemerides can have been based upon the Alfonsine tables, which got the date of Easter wrong thirty times between 1475 and 1531. Regiomontanus must have gotten his information from Toscanelli.

Vespucci used Regiomontanus's ephemeris tables to calculate longitude on August 23, 1499, when the tables stated the moon would cross Mars between midnight and 1 A.M. Vespucci observed that at "1 ½ hours after sundown the moon was slightly over one degree east of Mars and by midnight had moved to 5 ½ degrees from Mars rather than in line with Mars at midnight at Nuremberg."[30] He incorrectly calculated the lunar motion compared to Mars and also used the wrong meridian—again Regiomontanus had not made this clear. In doing so he placed the wrong longitude for where he was (the River Amazon). Using the correct figures, in my view, demolishes the argument that Regiomontanus's tables were based upon the Alfonsine tables. Likewise Columbus's longitude errors almost disappear if he had used the correct zero point.

From the publication of Regiomontanus's ephemeris tables in 1474, Europeans could for the first time calculate latitude and longitude, know their position at sea, get to the New World, accurately chart it, and return home in safety—a revolution in exploration.

Regiomontanus's tables were improved upon by Nevil Maskelyne. These were published in 1767 and remained in use by Royal Navy captains and navigators well after Harrison's chronometer was introduced.[31]

The great Captain Cook observed and calculated more than six hundred lunar distances to obtain the longitude of Strip Cove in New Zealand, and in 1777 he made one thousand lunar observations to determine the longitude of Tonga.[32] Maskelyne's tables were absorbed into the *Nautical Almanac* in which lunar-distance tables were incorporated until being phased out in 1907. (They were still in the library at Dartmouth when I learned navigation there in 1954.) With accurate instruments, the tables produced astonishingly good results. William Lambert reports (observations January 21, 1793) that without using clocks the longitude of the Capitol in Washington, D.C., was 76°46 by using the moon and Aldebaran; 76°54 on October 20, 1804, by using the Pleiades and the moon; 77°01 on September 17, 1811, by using an eclipse of the sun; 76°57 on January 12, 1813 by using Taurus and the moon.[33] The true figure is 77°00 W.[34] Hence five different methods, which could have been employed using Regiomontanus's ephemeris tables by different people, gave a maximum error of 14— around eight nautical miles without using clocks or chronometers. Harrison's chronometer was useful but not essential in mapping the world.

Maps

Once Regiomontanus was able to calculate latitude and longitude, he could construct maps. He produced the first European map with accurate latitudes and longitudes in 1450. Its accuracy rivaled the Chinese map of 1137 which showed China mapped accurately with latitude and longitude and is held in the British Museum (Needham).

Regiomontanus was fully aware that he was remaking European astronomy. Zinner cites his drive to banish the errors of Ptolomy and centuries of misunderstanding:

> He had in mind, as his life's goal, the improvement of the planetary theory and planetary tables; he knew of their defects only too well. He wanted to have the best and most error-free editions of ancient manuscripts at the disposal of his contemporaries, so he intended to compose almanacs which represented celestial events in an errorless manner and which would be important aids for predictions and determination of positions. . . . He spoke of the sun as the king among the planets. He connected the three outer planets with the

sun by means of epicyclic motion, whereas Venus was linked to the sun in other ways. Hence the special position of the sun was clear to him, in those days.

In addition, there came the realisation that the planetary tables were unsatisfactory. Later on, in his letters to Bianchini in 1463–64, he was quite clear about the fact that many of Ptolomy's assumptions could not be correct, not only about the obliquity of the ecliptic but also about the paths of the planets themselves. If the planets really did move along epicycles, then their apparent diameters would have to change in a way that is completely contrary to observations.[35]

Just as the Aristotelian/Ptolomeic paradigm of the universe was shelved after 1434, so were Arabic methods of astronomy and astronavigation. The Arab system, with its azimuth star coordinate system and reliance on the ecliptic, had been brought to Beijing by Jamal ad-Din in 1269. It lasted only nine years. After Guo Shoujing was commissioned to produce the *Shoushi* calendar in 1276, he jettisoned the Arab ecliptic coordinates and built the simplified equatorial torquetum later used by Nicholas of Cusa and Regiomontanus.[36]

After the torquetum was introduced to Europe, astrolabes, on which Arabic and European astronomers had lavished all their mathematical art, passed out of favor. Guo Shoujing's torquetum—forerunner of modern European instruments such as the astrocompass—lived on.

From there on, European astronomers followed Chinese methods.

LEON BATTISTA
ALBERTI AND
LEONARDO DA VINCI

L eon Battista Alberti (February 14, 1404–April 25, 1472) has been heralded as the "universal man" of the early Renaissance and described as "the prophet of the new grand style in art" inaugurated by Leonardo da Vinci.[1] His range of abilities was astounding.

Alberti was born in Genoa, the son of a wealthy Florentine banker, Lorenzo Alberti. His mother, Bianca Fieschl, was a widow from Bologna. When he was very young the family moved to Venice, where his father ran the family bank. A ban (a common political occurrence in those days) on the family was lifted in 1428, leaving the young Alberti free to return to Florence.

He benefited from the finest education available. From 1414 to 1418 he studied classics at the famous school of Gasparino Barzizza in Padua and later attained his master's in law at the University of Bologna. In 1430 he moved to Rome, where he prepared legal briefs for Pope Eugenius IV and met Nicholas of Cusa who was prime minister. In June 1434, Eugenius IV was forced to leave Rome for Florence because of a disagreement with the Church Council. Alberti joined him and was appointed canon of Santa Maria del Fiore when the cathedral was near completion. In Florence, he was introduced to both Filippo Brunelleschi (1377–1446) and Paolo Toscanelli, who had assisted Brunelleschi with the mathematics for the cathedral dome. Alberti became lifelong friends with both and part of the group of friends and admirers surrounding Toscanelli.[2]

Before moving to Florence, Alberti had written treatises on the use and disadvantages of the study of letters; two dialogues, *Deiphira* and *Ecatonfilea* (love scenes); a thesis, *Intercenale*; a book about the family, *Della famiglia*; and a life of Saint Potitus, *Vitas Potiti*.

After 1434, however, he began producing a range of works in mathematics, astronomy, architecture, and cryptography.[3] His biographer Joan Gadol describes Alberti's influence:

> [Most astronomers considered] "the maximum declination of the sun in our days is 24 degrees and 2 minutes, but my teachers [Peurbach] and I have ascertained with instruments that it is 23 degrees and 28 minutes and I have often heard Magister Paolo the Florentine and Battista Alberti say that by diligent observation they found that it did not exceed 23 degrees and 30 minutes, the figure I have decided to register in our table."[4]

This description is significant for several reasons. First, Regiomontanus, disciple of Toscanelli and a very accomplished astronomer, credits Alberti as one, as well. Second, he depicts the astronomers arguing about two minutes of declination, which means they must have had very accurate instruments to determine the altitude of the sun at its meridian passage at noon. Third, it suggests they had solved the declination problem with all that implies. Finally, and most important of all, it tells us that they are working on the obliquity of the ecliptic.

Gadol considered that Alberti's entirely new knowledge of the universe, which he had gained from Toscanelli, enabled him to develop many of his ideas by using an astrolabe—in architecture, in perspective, even in cryptography.

At least a decade before Alberti's great works on painting and sculpture, *De pictura* (1435), which he translated into an Italian version, *Della pittura*, the following year, and *De statua* (*ca.* 1446), Florentine artists had been experimenting with perspective. However, the current consensus seems to be that Brunelleschi, Masaccio, and Donatello were intuitive geniuses who developed the *costruzione legittima*, a method of determining perspective with the use of pinhole cameras and mirrors, but did not know the mathematics of the *costruzione abbreviata* developed later by Alberti.

Before considering Alberti's great works, perhaps one should consider how so many brilliant people appeared on the European stage at the same time. Toscanelli, Regiomontanus, Alberti, Francesco di Giorgio, and Leonardo da Vinci revolutionized European thought—in knowledge of the universe and the solar system, in astronomy, mathematics, physics, architecture, cartography, surveying, town planning, sculpture, painting, even cryptography. How did they all appear in the same small area of northern Italy? Did God wave a magic wand over Tuscany?

Undoubtedly, one reason was money. In the 1430s Venice was the wealthiest city in Europe, followed by Paris and Nuremburg. Venetian wealth spilled into Florence. The Medicis were the richest family in Europe. They made their money from banking, a part of which involved lending out money and charging interest for doing so—usury in the eyes of the Church. To atone for their sins, the Medicis sponsored a whole range of religious works—building and embellishing first chapels and later hospitals and libraries. They engaged the best artists to paint frescoes of the stars and planets. They employed people to search out books and maps and scholars to translate books of the ancients.

There were many scholars to employ. Italy boasted some of the oldest European universities—Bologna was nearly as old as Paris—and there were many of them. Tuscany probably had a higher proportion of postgraduates (to use a modern term) than anywhere else on earth. To those who could not afford a university education, the Church offered a free alternative. The religious orders, first Benedictines, then Cistercians, Franciscans, Dominicans, and Jesuits, offered not only a first-class religious training but a practical one for daily life. Benedictines not only prayed but ran highly successful and profitable farms pioneering research into animal husbandry, crop improvements, honey production, fish and poultry breeding, even genetic engineering. Benedictines in time became bankers to small farms, so improving agriculture. As one religious order followed another, the quality of education continuously improved, culminating in the superb education that the Jesuits brought to peoples of the New World. Benedictines, Cistercians, Franciscans, and Dominicans all had their principal bases in Burgundy and northern Italy.

This was the loam in which the seeds of Chinese ideas and inventions were propagated. We should not underestimate the pollination of ideas that resulted from the continuous intellectual interchange among these geniuses. Toscanelli and Regiomontanus collaborated on world maps; determining the declination of the sun; changes in the obliquity of the ecliptic; comets; spherical trigonometry; torquetums; and astronomical instruments. Alberti exchanged ideas on astronomy, mathematics, and trigonometry with Regiomontanus and Toscanelli, on locks and canals with Francesco di Giorgio, and on raising sunken ships with Francesco and Taccola. Nicholas of Cusa discussed astronomy with Toscanelli, Alberti, and Regiomontanus. Members of the group dedicated their books to one another.

They prayed at the same cathedral, Santa Maria del Fiore, ate at the *mensa* in Florence's Palazzo Vecchio, and dined with the Medicis. Nicholas of Cusa's home in Rome was the gathering place for men of influence and science—including Bruni, Alberti, Regiomontanus, and Toscanelli. There were several occasions at which Alberti and Nicholas of Cusa met over the years; during the Council of Florence—Alberti was at Ferrara with Eugenius IV, as was Nicholas of Cusa. The historian Giovanni Santinello draws a number of parallels between Alberti's writings on beauty, art, and perspective and Nicholas of Cusa's.[5]

De Pictura

Alberti's masterpiece, *De pictura,* is generally accepted by art historians of the Renaissance as the most important book on painting ever written. Leonardo da Vinci repeatedly refers to it, sometimes quoting it word for word. It seems appropriate to analyze how Alberti came to write the book, not least because of its impact on the development of Leonardo's genius and the book's influence on the future course of the Renaissance. In my opinion, Alberti would have realized from his and Toscanelli's study of the *Shoushi* astronomical calendar that the earth traveled in an ellipse around the sun while rotating on its axis and that the planets also rotated round the sun in ellipses, and this would have been a seismic shock. That Alberti knew how the solar system worked is evidenced by his painting in the San Lorenzo Baptistry of the heavens of the sun, moon, and stars on July 6, 1439, at noon (see page 92). Not only did this new knowledge overturn the authority of Ptolomy and Aristotle, but it knocked over the entire hierarchical order of the universe and replaced it with a conception of a harmonious and, above all, mathematical world order. Mathematics brought systematic order into the plan of the heavens and revealed a connection between astronomical data and physical research—quite literally a shattering revelation. If the workings and motions of the heavens could be explained in a mathematical rather than a religious context, then surely architecture, engineering, painting, even cryptography could also be explained by mathematics—hence *De pictura,* which gives the first rational and systematic exposition of the rules for perspective. To quote Joan Gadol again:

> [Alberti's] major accomplishment of this Florentine period (1434–1436) was theoretical. By bringing his humanistic and mathematical learning to bear upon the practice of painting and sculpture, Alberti fathered the new, mathematically inspired techniques of these arts and developed the aesthetic implications of this renascent artistic reliance upon geometry.
>
> The sculptural counterpart to the theory of perspective appeared somewhat later in *Della Statua.* Treating the statue as another kind of geometric imitation of nature, he devised an equally ingenious method of mensuration for the sculptor and worked out the first Renaissance canon of proportions.[6]

Alberti, as Joan Gadol so succinctly writes, went beyond the bounds of astronomy to determine its relation with mathematics and then mathematics to develop painting and architecture, cartography and surveying—even engineering design.

Leonardo da Vinci made great use of *Della pittura* [the Italian translation of *De pictura*] in his own treatise on painting, using the same terms, and ideas, even some of Alberti's phrases. For example, Leonardo says the perspective picture is to look as if it were drawn "on a glass through which the objects are seen" (Gadol p. 9), which was a term used by Alberti; and then again when defining painter's perspective as "a sort of visual geometry." Leonardo follows Alberti's theory and principles in every detail: "The sciences have no certainty except when one applies one of the mathematical sciences" . . . and again, to quote Leonardo, "painting must be founded on sound theory and to this perspective is the guide and gateway." Jakob Burckhardt portrayed Alberti in *The Civilization of the Renaissance in Italy* as a truly universal genius and considered Leonardo da Vinci was to Alberti as finisher to the beginner.

Leonardo's use of perspective to create sublime paintings and architecture, and to illustrate his mechanical drawings, is his legacy to mankind.

Alberti's intellectual achievements were truly awesome. As Grayson art historian of medieval Italy, so clearly explains, he introduced the concept of the picture plane as a window on which the observer can see the scene lying beyond it and thus laid the foundations of linear perspective. Alberti then codified the basic geometry so that linear perspective became mathematically coherent.

He wrote a ten-volume architectural treatise covering all aspects of Renaissance architecture—town planning, building designs, water and sewage treatment, public spaces, methods of construction. *De re aedificatoria* (On the art of building) became a standard reference book that spread Renaissance building techniques throughout Italy.

He drew the stars on the ceiling of the San Lorenzo Baptistry as they were seen on July 6, 1439, probably assisted by his friend Toscanelli. He collaborated with Toscanelli and Regiomontanus in helping determine Regiomontanus's declination of the sun, the obliquity of the ecliptic, and the change in its obliquity. He composed the first European treatise on cryptography, "*De componendis cifris.*"

Could one man really cover such a vast array of subject matter ranging from the invention of polyalphabetic substitutes and the cryptic code to new mathematical models for treating perspective?

Alberti was, like Regiomontanus, Toscanelli, Di Giorgio, and Taccola, remarkably reticent in crediting others for the source of his inspiration. Of obvious interest to me was any possible link between Alberti and Zheng He's delegation's visit to Florence in 1434, not least because Alberti as notary to Pope Eugenius IV would have attended meetings between the pope and the Chinese. Moreover, Alberti's writings before 1434 were on domestic themes—his explosion of astronomical, mathematical, and cartographic works all came after 1434.

I started my search by looking into Alberti's work on cryptography, in particular Chinese cryptography of the early fifteenth century. Zheng He would have been likely to have used cryptography for transmitting intelligence reports to the emperor and to his admirals and captains. I could find no translated works.

Then, when researching Regiomontanus's life and works, as recounted in the previous chapter, I came upon the curious fact that Regiomontanus had mastered the Chinese remainder theorem, unique to China at the time. His source for this (as far as I know, the unique source) was the *Shu-shu Chiu-chang* of Ch'in Chiu-shao, published in 1247, which contains a detailed explanation of the Ta-Yen rule.

The *Shu-shu Chiu-chang* is a massive book, the Chinese equivalent to Alberti's *De re aedificatoria,* but published two centuries earlier. With feverish excitement I hurried off to the British Library and read Needham's description of this work—a bombshell; as far as I could see, the genesis of Alberti's work in relation to perspective contained in *Ludi matematici* is in the Chinese book. It is clear to me that both Alberti and his friend Regiomontanus may have had access to this book, which contained not only rules for perspective and the Chinese remainder theorem (for cryptographic analysis) but all aspects of town planning. On our *1434* website are pictures taken from Alberti's *Ludi matematici* and Ch'in Chiu-shao's book side by side, describing ways of measuring height, depth, distance, and weight by mathematical and geometric means.

Let us start with the basic stages of Alberti's work on perspective, the building blocks for his works *De statua* and *De pictura.*

As a first stage: Alberti draws a large rectangle like a window frame, through which he can see the subject he wishes to paint or

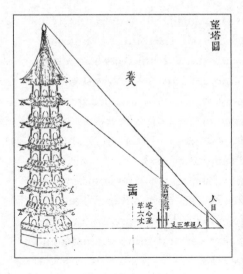

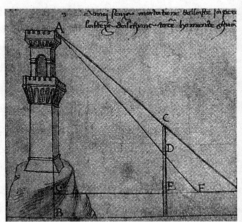

The Chinese, and later the Sienese engineers, used very similar methods for constructing towers and measuring their heights.

create. For the second stage, he selects the largest human he wishes to paint seen through the picture frame. The height of this person is divided into three equal parts, which form the basic unit of measurement, called a braccia.

In the third stage, he makes the center point of the picture frame, which should be no higher than three braccia above the ground.

In the fourth stage, he divides the base line into braccia.

In the fifth stage: He draws straight lines from this center point to each of the braccia on the base line.

For illustrations of the above, please visit our website.

Now to compare where Alberti has gotten with the Chinese method illustrated in the *Shu-shu Chiu-chang*.

The first comparison is illustrated by the method for finding the height of a tower (as explained in Alberti's *Ludi matematici, ca.* 1450):

Stick an arrow or a rod into the ground (c-d) so as to form a straight perpen-
dicular line along which to take sightings to the tower (a-b). Mark the rod
with wax where the line of sight to the top of the tower crosses it (f). The triangle formed by the arrow, ground and eye is the geometric counterpart of
the triangle formed by the tower, ground and eye (abc) hence it can be used to
find the height of the tower (ab). ab divided by bc equals fc divided by ce.

This is how Alberti "discovered" the rules of projection, which since
then have formed the basis of perspective for sculptors and painters.

However, Alberti had not made an original discovery. The same
explanation from Liu Hui in the third century is illustrated in the *Shu-
shu Chiu-chang*. In this book the calculations are called "the method of
double differences," that is, the properties of right-angled triangles.
There are illustrations depicting methods for calculating the heights of
islands seen from the sea; the height of a tree on a hill; the size of a
distant walled city; the depth of a ravine; the height of a tower; the
breadth of a river mouth; the depth of a transparent pool. This trigonometry was invented by Euclid, and Alberti could have obtained his
ideas from him as well as from the Chinese—he never acknowledged
his sources.

However, the links between Chinese sources and Alberti go much
further than trigonometry. Alberti used the same instruments as Toscanelli and adopted similar mathematics. Alberti's method of perspective was brilliant. He realized that perspective was determined not
only by the size of the object viewed and its distance from the beholder
but also by the height of the observer relative to the viewed object and
the angle from which the viewer was looking at the object. In short,
each figure in a crowd when the crowd is viewed in depth would need
a different rule of perspective.

By now I was beginning to feel uncomfortable about the amount of
knowledge that it seemed Florentine mathematicians had copied from
the Chinese—Taccola, Francesco di Giorgio, and Alberti from the
Shu-shu Chiu-chang for mathematics, surveying, perspective cartography, and cryptography; Regiomontanus from Guo Shoujing's work on
spherical trigonometry, Toscanelli and Nicholas of Cusa for Guo

Shoujing's work on astronomy. I could explain one or two Chinese manuals coming into the hands of Venetians and Florentines—but this many, in so many different fields? It seemed too much of a coincidence—too good to be true! On the other hand, there was Toscanelli's evidence about the transfer of knowledge that was unquestionably true—evidenced by maps, which do not lie.

It seemed sensible at this stage to see the original books in China, not only Needham's accounts. Could these have been taken out of context in some way? Perhaps there were also many Chinese inventions that had never been copied by Europeans. Perhaps those that were was just a huge coincidence. Ian Hudson, who has been in charge of our research team and website for five years, volunteered to go to China to inspect the original books that I believed Europeans had copied—by visiting libraries in mainland China and Hong Kong.

He found there were, as far as we can see, no anomalies—first it seemed everything that Taccola, di Giorgio, Regiomontanus, Alberti, and Leonardo da Vinci had "invented" was already there in Chinese books, notably ephemeris tables, maps, mathematical treatises, and the production of civil and military machines. So how was the transfer effected? I had many sleepless nights of worry before the penny dropped—all of these books were reproduced in parts of the *Yongle Dadian,* which Zheng He would have carried. Zheng He's representatives would have undoubtedly told the pope and Toscanelli about the *Yongle Dadian*—as evidenced by Toscanelli's comment, China was indeed ruled by "astronomers and mathematicians of great learning."

Alberti also applied his mathematical ability to surveying, and is cited by many as being the father of modern surveying. Here again, he makes a complete break with the past. His map of Rome bears almost no relation to Ptolemy's system of mapping. He rejects Ptolemy's rectangular coordinates and uses the astrolabe to find the relative positions of points on the ground, just as a navigator would—he takes sightings from more than one vantage point. As Joan Gadol says, "He first set forth these ideas in *Descriptio urbis Romae,* the brief Latin treatise written in the 1440s." Gadol believes Alberti's *Descriptio urbis Romae* and *Ludi matematici* were among the earliest works in surveying land areas by sightings and mapping by scale pictures. He believes Regiomontanus, Schöner, and Waldseemüller followed Alberti's work.

Leonardo's map of Pisa and the mouth of the Arno is thought to be the first modern map to show contours of land by using different shades of color. Leonardo followed Alberti in the principles used in surveying, as he did in rules of perspective.

LEONARDO DA VINCI AND CHINESE INVENTIONS

In my youth, Leonardo da Vinci seemed the greatest genius of all time. An extraordinary inventor of every sort of machine, a magnificent sculptor, one of the world's greatest painters, and the finest illustrator and draftsman who ever lived. When our daughters were young, Marcella and I made a point of taking them to as many exhibitions of Leonardo's work as we could—in London, Paris, Rome, Milan, Le Clos Lucé, and Amboise.

Then, as my knowledge of Chinese inventions slowly expanded, particularly with information provided by friends of our website, I began to wonder. More and more of Leonardo's inventions appear to have been invented previously by the Chinese. I began to question whether there might be a connection—did Leonardo learn from the Chinese? The *1421* team and I examined the subject for years but came to no conclusions.

Leonardo drew all the essential components of machines with extraordinary clarity—showing how toothed wheels, gear wheels, and pinions were used in mills, lifting machines, and machine tools. He described how and why teeth could transfer power, the efficacy of antifriction teeth, the transmission of power from one plane to another, and continuous rotary motion. He drew and described ratchets, pins, axles, cams, and camshafts. Pulleys were an integral part of many of his mechanisms; he produced different systems and applications for them.

Some of the earliest known examples of gear wheels in China have been dated to ca. 50 B.C.

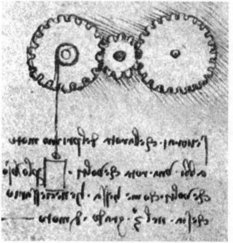

A toothed gear wheel, as drawn by Leonardo in the Madrid Codices.

All these devices had been used in China for a very long time. In the *Tso Chuan* are illustrations of bronze ratchets and gear wheels from as early as 200 B.C. that have been discovered in China.

Axles from the third and fourth centuries B.C. have been excavated from the royal tombs at Hui Hsien. By the second century B.C., in the Han dynasty, complex forms of cam-shaped rocking levers for the triggers of crossbows were in use. The *Hsun I Hsiang Fa Yao*, written in about A.D. 1090, illustrates a chain drive. By the eleventh century A.D. flywheels were used in China for grinding. The earliest archaeological evidence of a pulley is a draw well representing a pulley system of the Han dynasty.

One of Leonardo's best-known inventions was the paddle-wheel boat. The paddle-wheel mechanism was fundamental to China's early naval supremacy. The sight of a boat traveling forward at great speed

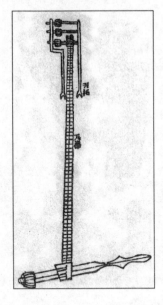

Left: The oldest known illustration of an endless power-transmitting chain drive from Su Sung's Hsun I Hsiang Fa Yaoch drawn in A.D. 1090.

Below: Leonardo da Vinci's illustration of a chain drive (Madrid Codices).

seemingly without oars or sails was terrifying to those in its path. The first record of the existence of paddle-wheel boats occurs in a Chinese account of a naval action under the command of Wang Chen-o, an admiral of the Liu Sung dynasty in A.D. 418.[1] "These vessels later reached enormous proportions: one monster from the Southern Sung dynasty was said to have been 300 feet long. It was crewed by 1000 men and powered by thirty-two paddle wheels."[2]

Leonardo is renowned for his drawings of different forms of manned flight, notably his helicopter and parachutes and his attempts at wings. By Leonardo's day, the kite had been in use for hundreds of years. "China is the homeland of the kite . . . the oldest heavier-than-air craft that gains lift from the wind. It is believed that the kite was invented some 3000 years ago by Lu Ban . . . c.507–444 bc a Chinese master carpenter of the Lu State in the Spring and Autumn period. It was said

Left: Drawing of a Sung paddle-wheel warship.

Right: Along with the other Renaissance engineers Leonardo penned his own version of the paddleboat.

that Lu Ban made a magpie out of bamboo pieces, which could fly. The master carpenter was also the first to use the kite in military reconnaissance."[3]

Parachutes were in use in China fifteen hundred years before Leonardo.

According to the historical records by Sima Qian of the Western Han dynasty, Shun, a legendary monarch in ancient China was deeply hated by his father, a blind old man. When Shun was working on top of a high granary, his father set fire to the granary from below, intending to kill Shun. Holding two cone-shaped bamboo hats in his hands, Shun flew down and landed safely. This book also describes how more recently (in 1214) a thief managed to steal the leg of a statue from the top of a mosque. When caught he admitted to using two umbrellas as a parachute to save himself from injury on his descent.[4]

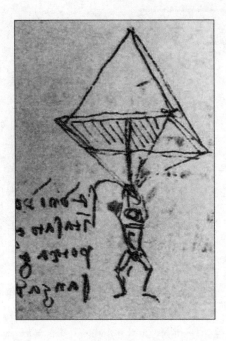

The parachute is a small detail on a folio of the largest collection
of da Vinci's notebooks, the Codex Atlanticus.

Hot-air balloons were known in the second century A.D. in China.
The contents of an egg were removed from the shell, then a little mug-
wort tinder was ignited inside the hole so as to cause a strong air current. The egg rose up in the air and flew away."[5]

The Chinese had made use of the essential principle of the helicopter rotor from the fourth century A.D., a fact noted by the philoso-
pher and alchemist Ko Hung. By then, helicopter toys, like whirligigs,
were popular in China, a common name being "bamboo dragonfly."
The toy was a bamboo with a cord wound around it and with blades
sticking out from the bamboo at an angle. When the cord was
pulled, the bamboo and blades rotated and the toy ascended as the
air was pushed downwards. Needham describes a number of examples of rotating blades being used for flight, often in the form of flying cars.[6]

Leonardo devoted much time to the possibilities of manned flight.

A pictorial version of the aerial car, from the *Shan Hai Ching Kuang Chu.* "The skill of the Chi-Kung people is truly marvellous; by studying the winds they created and built flying wheels, with which they can ride along the paths of the whirlwinds. . . ." "The artist here has drawn the aerial car with two wheels, but both seem to be intended to represent screw-bladed rotors. . . ." (Text of the −2nd century, or earlier, plus 17th-century commentary).

The earliest Chinese description of the concept occurred in the accounts of the short-lived and obscure Northern Chi dynasty (ninth century B.C.), when the emperor Kao Yang "caused many prisoners condemned to death to be brought forward, had them harnessed with great bamboo mats as wings, and ordered them to fly to the ground from the top of the tower. . . . All the prisoners died but the emperor contemplated the spectacle with enjoyment and much laughter."[7]

A later description comes from Marco Polo in the Z manuscript.

And so we will tell you how when any ship must go on a voyage, they prove whether her business will go well or ill. The men of the ship will have a bundle or a grating of willow stem and at each corner and side of this framework

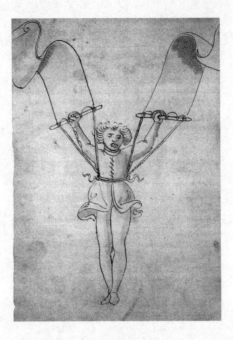

The idea of a man using wings for flight existed in Chinese legend
hundreds of years before this fifteenth century Sienese flying man.

will be tied a cord and they will all be tied at the end of a long rope. Next they
will find some fool or drunkard and will bind him on the hurdle, since no-
one in his right mind or with his wits about him would expose himself to that
peril. And this is done when a strong wind prevails. Then the framework being set up opposite the wind, the wind lifts it and carries it up into the sky,
while the men hold on by the long rope. And, if while this is in the air, the
hurdle leans towards the way of the wind, they pull the rope to them a little so
that it is set again upright, after which they let out some more rope and it rises
higher. And if again it tips, once more they pull on the rope until the frame is
upright and climbing, and then they yield rope again, so that in this manner
it would rise so high that it could not be seen, if only the rope were long
enough. The augury they interpret thus: if the hurdle going straight up makes
for the sky they say the ship for which the test has been made will have a
quick and prosperous voyage. . . . But if the hurdle has not been able to go up,
no merchant will be willing to enter the ship.[8]

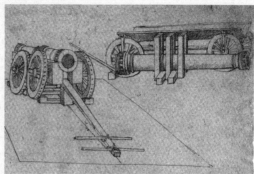

Left: One of the many weapons mastered by China before Europe was
the cannon.

Right: The dismountable cannon appears in da Vinci's notebook and in
those of many other Renaissance engineers.

Leonardo drew an array of gunpowder weapons, including three
variations of the machine gun, which can be seen in the fire lances
used in China since A.D. 950.

The Genius of China states:

Fire lances with several barrels were frequently used and they were built so that
when one fire-tube had exhausted itself, a fuse ignited the next, and so on. One
triple barrelled fire lance was called the "triple resister" and another was called
"the three eyed lance of the beginning of the dynasty . . ." One curious weapon
was the "thunder fire whip" a fire lance in the shape of a sword, three feet two
inches long tapering into a muzzle. It discharged three lead balls the size of
coins. . . . There were also huge batteries of fire lances which could be fired simultaneously from mobile racks . . . a great frame with several wheels would
hold many layers of sixteen fire lances one after the other. . . . When the enemy

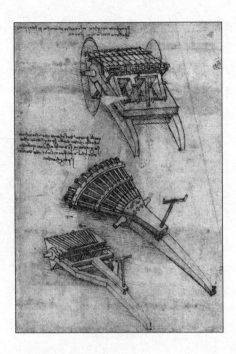

Leonardo's multibarreled machine gun was essentially a reworking
of a concept that had been used by the Chinese for centuries beforehand.

approaches the gate, all the weapons are fired in a single moment, giving the
noise like a great peal of thunder, so that his men and horses are all blown to
pieces. You can then open the city gates and relaxing, talk and laugh as if nothing had happened; this is the very best device for the guarding of cities.[9]

Leonardo also drew different types of cannons, mortars, and bombards.
The Chinese use of bombards is well catalogued throughout the ages.[10]

Leonardo designed many different types of bridges, including suspension bridges. The first mention of a suspension bridge with cables
and planking appears in 25 B.C. "Travellers go step by step here, clasp-
ing each other for safety and rope suspension bridges are stretched
across the chasms from side to side."[11]

By the seventh century China had segmental arch bridges. The
Ponte Vecchio in Florence is a copy of a bridge in Quanzhou.

Leonardo was extremely curious about printing. He was eager to reproduce his drawings faithfully while saving time and labor through increased automation. The printing press by his time was in use all over China. Moveable type, however, was a relatively recent development; we shall return to this in later chapters.

Comparisons of the machines of Leonardo with earlier machines from China reveal close similarities in toothed wheels and gear wheels, ratchets, pins, and axles, cams and cam-shaped rocking levers, flywheels, crankshaft systems, balls and chains, spoke wheels, well pulleys, chain devices, suspension bridges, segmented arch bridges, contour maps, parachutes, hot-air balloons, "helicopters," multibarreled machine guns, dismountable cannons, armored cars, catapults, barrage cannons and bombards, paddle-wheel boats, swing bridges, printing presses, odometers, compasses and dividers, canals and locks.

Even the most devoted supporter of Leonardo (like my family and I!) must surely wonder whether his work's amazing similarity to Chinese engineering could be the product of coincidence.

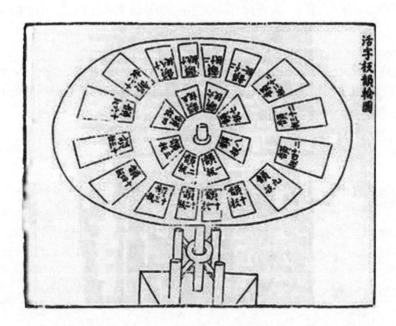

A revolving-type table printing press found in the *Nung Shu*, 1313.
The *Nung Shu* was printed using a similar device.

Was there any connection between the Chinese visit of 1434 and Leonardo's designs sixty years later? For many years I searched for clues in Leonardo's life but could find none. He was extraordinarily observant and inquisitive and certainly was fascinated by Greek and Roman art and architecture, literature, and science, including the works of Aristotle and Ptolomy. He is said to have slept with copies of Vitruvius's works beneath his pillow. But illustrated examples of the Greeks and Romans did not account for a quarter of Leonardo's engineering devices shown on the *1434* website.

Moreover, whether Leonardo appreciated it or not, he was surrounded by evidence of the Chinese impact on the Renaissance, such as Alberti's books on perspective in painting and architecture. The basis of Alberti's work was the mathematics he had acquired from the Chinese explanation of the solar system. Replacing the ecliptic coordinate system used by the Arabs, Greeks, and Romans with the Chinese equatorial system was a fundamental break with the old world, overturning the authority of Aristotle and Ptolomy.

However, that is a far cry from claiming that Leonardo copied existing Chinese inventions. One thing we can be sure of: Leonardo did not meet anyone from Zheng He's fleets when they visited Florence in 1434. So it appeared that the similarities noted above were due to an extraordinary series of coincidences. Years of research by the *1421* team had apparently been fruitless.

MATTHAEUS ET NICOLAUS POLI SAECULO XIII AD CUBLAUM VENIUNT
SCYTHARUM REGEM DIUQUE COMMORATI EIDEM IN SINIS DEVINCEN-
DIS AUXILIO SUNT. PROFECTI DEINDE LEGATI AD PONTIFICEM RE-
DEUNT CUM MARCO ADOLESCENTE. HIC IN AULA VERSATUS CUM
PATRE ET PATRUO PER ANNOS XXVII EXPLORATA SINENSI
PROVINCIA INDIISQUE REGIS JUSSU PERLUSTRATIS SINGULA
RETULIT IN COMMENTARIUM SUMMA FIDE. CAETERIS
DEINCEPS NOVI ORBIS SCRUTATORIBUS DOCUMENTUM
ET INCITAMENTUM. EX QUO TABULA HAEC
DEPROMPTA QUA MARI QUA TERRA ITER
FECERIT RESQUE GESTAS SUIS
LOCIS DESIGNAT.

ISOLE DE
NASCO

VENETA NAVIS URBIS MEXICELIS
PRAETER/UCTA EST MANILLAM
EX PINAS. INCERTUM PER FRETO
TER BONAE SPEI PROMONTORIO

MARE

GIAPAN
ZIPANGRI
de M.POLO

NUOVA SPAGNA

TERRE INCOGNITE
D'ANTROPOFAGI

CALIFORNIA

Quivira

Rio Perutlo

Quivira

Totonteac

Rio Grande

Grandes Corrientes

ORIENTALES INDIAS HAC TABULA
EXPRESSAS PEREGRINATIONIBUS ET
SCRIPTIS ILLUSTRARUNT ENARRATIS
INDORUM MORIBUS ET INSTITUTIS REM
MERCATORIAM ADIUVERE SAECULO XVI
NICOLAUS DE COMITIBUS EDITO ITINE
RARIO LUSITANE POSTMODUM VERSO
NOVAM LUCEM NAUTIS ALLATURO SAE-
CULO XVI CAESAR DE FEDERICIS IN-
SUPER ET JAPONENSIBUS EX ALIENA
FIDE MEMORATIS MERCATORUM OPE
GASPAR BALBUS GEMMARIUS ATQUE ITE-
RATA NAVIGATIONE ALOYSIUS RONCINOT
TUS DENIQUE NICOLAUS MANUTIUS IN
AULA MOGOLI REGIS DIUTISSIME VER-
SATUS OMNIGENAM EARUM REGIO-
NUM HISTORIAM SAECULO XVII.
CONSCRIPSIT QUAE IN BIBLIO-
ECA D. MARCI SERVATUR.

This map in the Doge's Palace clearly depicts the northwest coastline of Canada and North America set "upside down"—with north at the bottom, as was the practice of Chinese cartographers. The roundels describe the sources of the information used to draw it: Marco Polo and Niccolò da Conti.

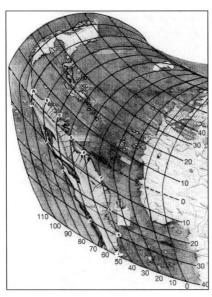 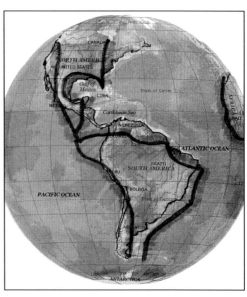

Detailed working shows the conversion of Waldseemüeller's map into a globe with striking results.

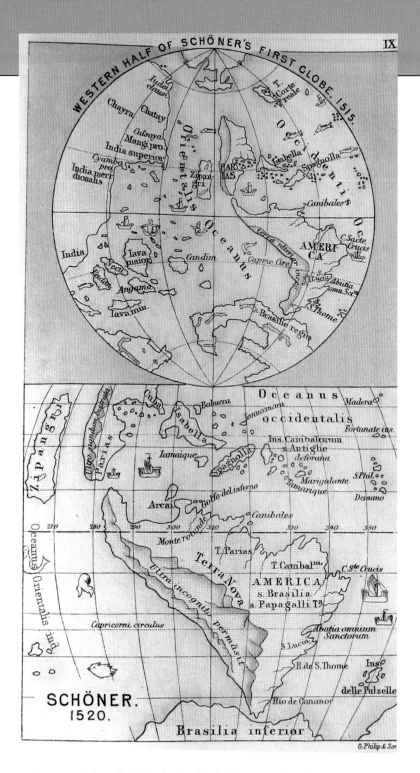

Schöener's globes of 1515 and 1520 clearly depict North and South America, and the desolate Straits of Magellan (OPPOSITE, BELOW), supposedly "first discovered" after the maps had already been drawn.

Universalis Cosmographiae, Waldseemüeller's map of 1507, and his green globe of 1505/06 clearly depict the Americas with remarkable accuracy for the time, and corroborate Toscanelli's story of meeting the Chinese delegation in Florence.

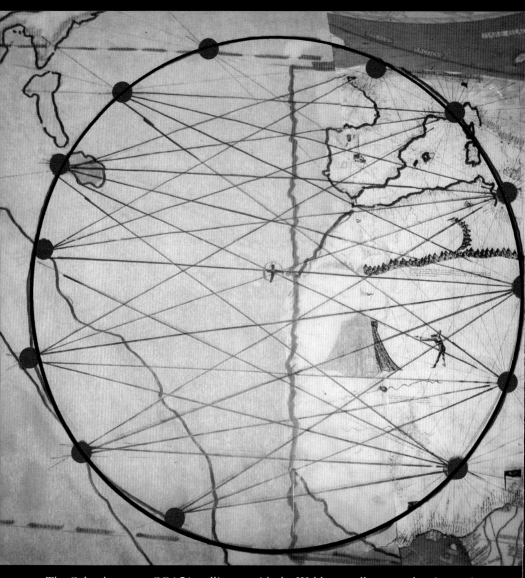

The Columbus map, CGA5A, tallies up with the Waldseemüeller map, showing curious "rhumb" lines that extend out across the Atlantic, all ending on a circle.

LEONARDO, DI GIORGIO, TACCOLA, AND ALBERTI

T hen I had a stroke of luck. While on holiday in Toledo in 2005, Marcella and I happened upon a wonderful exhibition about Leonardo da Vinci. It was here that I was first introduced to the great works of Francesco di Giorgio Martini and the profound influence that these had on Leonardo.

In my ignorance, I had never heard of Francesco di Giorgio. Yet it was obvious that he was important; he had taught Leonardo about waterways. I decided to find out more on our return to London.

In the wonderful British Library I found first that Francesco seemed to have invented the parachute before Leonardo. For what follows I am indebted to Lynn White, Jr., author of "The Invention of the Parachute" in *Technology and Culture*. Dr. White wrote:

> The first known European parachute has been that sketched by Leonardo in the Codex Atlanticus on Folio 381v, that Carlo Pedretti dates circa 1485.... However, British Museum Additional Manuscript 34113, folio 200v. shows a parachute which may be in a somewhat independent tradition since it is conical.
>
> This rich and massive volume [in the British Library] seems to have been unnoticed by historians of technology. Can it be dated and placed?
>
> The Manuscript [34113], a quarto of 261 folios of paper, was purchased by the British Museum in 1891.... Folios 21r. to 250v. [are] a treatise on mechanics, hydraulics, etc. with a multitude of drawings....

Folios 22r. to 53v. are nearly identical in content and sequence with Florence, Biblioteca Nazionale Manuscript Palatinum 766, an autograph of the famous Sienese engineer Mariano detto il Taccola (who died in the 1450's), that was dated by him (on folio 45v) to 19 Jan. 1433. Most of the remaining material in British Museum Additional Manuscript 34113 as far as folio 250v. [the parachute drawings are in folio 200v. and 189v.] is the sort of thing we have come to associate with manuscripts long credited to Francesco di Giorgio of Siena (1439–1501). Indeed folio 129r. [before parachute drawings] is entitled "Della providentia della chuerra sicondo Maestro Francesco da Siena," and on folio 194v. [after parachute drawing], next to the picture of a large file, is written "Lima sorda sichondo il detto Maestro Francesco di Giorgio da Siena."[1]

Dr. White analyzed the watermarks of the paper on which the parachute drawings appear. He concluded:

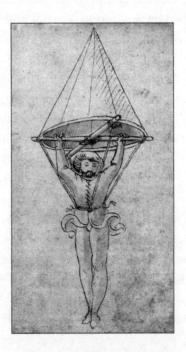

Probably drawn by di Giorgio, this parachute differs in shape
from that of Leonardo's.

Consequently the drawing on folio 200v. [parachute] may be placed reasonably in the 1470's or not much later, if we are to believe the watermarks. . . .

Our new parachute is, therefore, at the latest, contemporary with and probably slightly earlier than that of Leonardo. . . . It is indicative of Leonardo's perceptiveness that he picked up this idea so quickly and that he began to make it more sophisticated.

So it seems Leonardo learned not only about canals and aqueducts from Francesco di Giorgio but also about parachutes. What else? Back to the British Library!

Dr. Ladislao Reti, an expert on Leonardo, has this to say about Francesco di Giorgio Martini's "Treatise on Engineering and Its Plagiarists":

Francesco di Giorgio Martini (1439–1501) the great Sienese painter, sculptor and architect, was also interested as were several of his contemporary fellow craftsmen, in the study and development of mechanical devices. This was in accordance with the still flourishing Vitruvian tradition. His engineering treatise, still little known, is mainly dedicated to civil and military architecture and contains hundred of small but perfectly drawn illustrations showing war machines of every kind, as well as cranes, mills, pumps etc. . . . Although a number of studies have been published about the artistic and architectural work of Francesco di Giorgio, his work in technology has only occasionally been noticed.[2]

Dr. Reti then lists the libraries and museums in which Francesco's *Trattato di architettura civile e militare* is held and continued:[3]

There is also an incomplete manuscript[3] that once belonged to Leonardo da Vinci. This latter is of particular interest because Leonardo added marginal notes and sketches; the manuscript is now in the Laurenziana Library in Florence (Codex Mediceo Laurenziano 361 formerly Ashb.361 [293]). In addition several old copies of the treatise or its drawings are to be found in other Italian libraries, reflecting the early interest aroused by Francesco's work.

These Trattato manuscripts, especially those parts dealing with mechanical engineering and technology, have never been adequately studied or fully published. A fairly accurate picture of Francesco di Giorgio Martini's work was first made available to scholars in 1841 when Carlo Promis, using the Codex owned by Saluzzo, published the Trattato for the first time (Trattato di Architettura Civile e Militare edited by Carlo Promis (2 vol., Turin, 1841). . . .

Further confusion was caused by the fact that the Codex Saluzziano [quoted above] and the Codex Laurenziano [the one owned by Leonardo da Vinci] in spite of being written by the same hand, and containing almost identical drawings, were, for a long time, not attributed to the same author [Francesco di Giorgio]. Early interest was aroused by the Laurenziana Codex because of the marginalia added by Leonardo (p. 288).

Dr. Reti then lists the contents of the *Trattato* (p. 290):

In these folios we can identify no less than 50 different types of flour and roller mills including horizontal windmills . . . sawmills, pile drivers, weight transporting machines, as well as all kinds of winches and cranes; roller-bearings and antifriction devices; mechanical cars . . . a great number of pumps and water lifting devices. . . . and an extremely interesting water or mud-lifting machine that must be characterized as the prototype of the centrifugal pump. . . . [Francesco] described original war machines offensive and defensive, including the hydraulic recoil system for guns. There are also devices for diving and swimming almost identical with those drawn by Leonardo da Vinci in his Manuscript B.

Comparisons of Francesco di Giorgio's and Leonardo's machines are available on our *1434* website.

Leonardo's Helicopter and Parachutes

Apart from copying di Giorgio's parachute, Leonardo's helicopter was not original. His proposed helicopter is shown on the cover of this book. In *"Helicopters and Whirligigs,"* Dr. Reti argues that a model helicopter in the form of a children's whirligig toy appeared in Italy circa

1440 from China and provided the theoretical basis for Leonardo's famous helicopter project.[4]

Dr. Reti contends that it was first drawn in 1438 in the Munich manuscript of Mariano Taccola (see *1434* website).

Clearly, Francesco di Giorgio was an astonishingly innovative designer and engineer. His *Trattato di architettura* still exists in several versions. Marcella and I have examined the copy in Florence once owned and annotated by Leonardo. We were astounded by the range of his drawings; it seemed to us that Leonardo was a consummate three-dimensional draftsman who had taken Francesco's drawings of his machines and made even better drawings of them. Leonardo's role, in our eyes, was changed; he was a superb illustrator rather than the inventor. For as far as we could see, almost all of his machines had been previously invented by Francesco di Giorgio.

This was quite a shock. We decided to unwind in a nearby mountain village, Colle val d'Elsa,[5] the birthplace of Arnolfo di Cambio, the genius who designed Renaissance Florence. His home was once the palace of silk merchants, the Salvestrinis. Today it is a hotel where we had the good fortune to stay in a room with walls three feet thick, which had once been Arnolfo's bedroom. We had a view of a classic Tuscan valley—the hills rolling away like long green ocean swells; the crests of the waves; the stone farmhouses surrounded by vineyards and olive groves. The crowing of cockerels, the bray of a donkey, and the laughter of distant unseen children floated across the sunlit land. We had a panoramic view of the valley far below. Around us huddled the town in which Arnolfo grew up—a mass of fortified towers within the protection of sturdy stone walls, a veritable fortress.

We had dinner al fresco in the square, the walls and flagstone floor still pulsating with heat. After a splendid bottle of Dolcetto, a dark red, dry, sparkling wine, we asked local people what they knew of Francesco di Giorgio. He appeared to be as famous as Leonardo or Mariano Taccola. This was another surprise—who was Mariano Taccola, known as "the Crow" or "the Jackdaw"? Was he called Jackdaw because of his beak or because he "jackdawed" the work of others?

At dawn, we left for Siena and Florence to view Taccola's drawings.

The trip yielded another bombshell: Taccola seemed to have invented everything that Francesco di Giorgio later drew; di Giorgio had obviously copied Taccola.

Mariano di Jacopo ditto Taccola was christened in Siena, near Florence, on February 4, 1382.[6] His father was a wine dealer. His sister Francesca had married into the comfortable family of a silk trader.

Siena[7] had been built on a hill for protection. The land beneath was swamp. Obtaining clean fresh water and draining the swamps were constant necessities. Hence it was natural for a well-educated young man to be acquainted with aqueducts, fountains, water mains, and pumps, as well as the medieval weapons deployed to protect the town—trebuchets and the like.

A prosperous town threatened by Rome from the south and Florence from the north, Siena was a "free city" of the Holy Roman Empire, but Sigismund, the emperor,[8] was too weak to protect her. (In Taccola's time the emperor was preoccupied with the Hussite wars.)

In 1408, Taccola married Madonna Nanna, the daughter of a leather merchant, which enabled him to move up the social scale. In 1410, he was nominated for entry into the Sienese Guild of Judges and Notaries, where his apprenticeship lasted six or seven years. He seemed to have had a penchant for failing his exams. In 1424, Taccola became secretary of a prestigious charitable institution, the Casa di Misericordia, an appointment he held for ten years. As such, he would have become acquainted with influential visitors to Siena—such as Pope Eugenius IV, Giovanni Battisa Alberti (in 1443), and the Florentines Brunellschi and Toscanelli.

In 1427, Taccola began to keep technical notebooks, containing knowledge he had acquired "with long labour." As Prager and Scaglia explain, Taccola's early entries in his notebook are about the defense of Siena and the operation of harbors.[9]

Between 1430 and his death in 1454, Taccola produced a series of amazing drawings that were published in two volumes, De ingeneis[10] (Of four books) and De machinis,[11] and an addendum. The range of his subjects is quite extraordinary. Book 1 of De ingeneis contains harbors, bucket pumps, mounted gunners, bellows for furnaces, underwater divers, fulling mills, and siphons. Book 2 features cisterns, piston pumps, dragons, amphibious machines with soldiers, and ox-powered gin mills. Book 3 includes chain pumps, tide mills, variable-speed hoists, winches, quarrying machines, flotation machines to recover sunken columns, builders' cranes, mechanical ladders, sailing carts, and amphibious vehicles. In Book 4 he tackles trigonometrical surveying, tunneling, machines for extracting posts, treasure-hunting tools, windmills and watermills, pictures of monkeys, camels, and elephants, trebuchets, armored ships, paddle boats, roof-beam joists, and reflective mirrors. *De ingeneis* was followed (*ca.* 1438) by *De machinis,* a volume of drawings of mostly military machines (described in chapter 19).

Prager and Scaglia describe Taccola as a pivotal figure in the development of European technology. In their view, Taccola ensured that the long stagnation of many technical practices of the Middle Ages

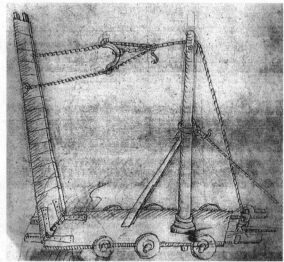

Left: An articulated siege ladder as featured in the general collection of Chinese Classics of Science and Technology.

Right: Taccola's articulated siege ladder is one of many military inventions that bear a striking resemblance to Chinese versions.

came to an end. His *De ingeneis* became the starting point for a long line of copybooks.

So how did a clerk of works of a small mountain town suddenly produce books of drawings of such a huge range of inventions, including a helicopter and military machines that were at that time unknown in Siena?

We could profitably start with the dates of Taccola's books. Prager and Scaglia, in my opinion the leading authorities on Taccola, put publication of books 1 and 2 of his *De ingeneis* at around 1429–1433. Taccola began books 3 and 4 around 1434 or 1438 and continued working on them until his death in 1454; *De machinis* was begun after 1438 and the addenda drawings around *1435*.

According to Prager and Scaglia, the addenda drawings, which were inserted in all four books after about 1435, represent a significant change for Taccola. The new technique is very characteristic of soldiers and engines in small scale, the sketches inserted and annotated with small handwriting in the last two books and in the sequel. Sketches of engines, mainly military in function, may be seen on almost all pages of books 1 and 2; they always surround primary drawings, often in copious array. This paragraph seems to me to mean that another author (Francesco di Giorgio) had begun to annotate Taccola's drawings in books 1 and 2.

Taccola's drawings were certainly added to by Francesco after 1435. In his marvelous book *The Art of Invention: Leonardo and the Renaissance Engineers,* Paolo Galluzzi writes:

> The final pages of Taccola's autograph manuscripts *De Ingeneis* I-II carries
> a series of notes and drawings in the hand of Francesco di Giorgio (fig. 26).
> No document better expresses the continuity of the Sienese tradition of
> engineering studies. They offer us a snapshot, so to speak, of the actual
> moment when the heritage was passed on from Taccola to Francesco di
> Giorgio.[11]

A reproduction of this snapshot of history is shown by kind permission of the Istituto e Museo di Storia della Scienza, Florence, on our

LEONARDO, DI GIORGIO, TACCOLA, AND ALBERTI

1434 website. So we can say at this stage Leonardo had di Giorgio's book of Machines, which were adaptations of Taccola's drawings.

Francesco di Giorgio Pillages Taccola's Work

Di Giorgio was a wholesale plagiarizer. Here are eight examples of his pillaging of Taccola's work, which he never acknowledged.

Francesco's picture of a collapsing tower is almost identical to Taccola's; Francesco similarly copies Taccola's underwater swimmers and floating riders on horseback (see the *1434* website).

Francesco, whose drawings were made after Taccola's, employs the same distinctive trebuchet as Taccola. His hoists and mills, which transform vertical power to horizontal, and paddle-wheel boats copy

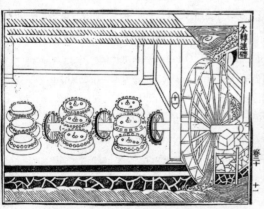

Left: Chinese water-powered vertical and horizontal rice grinding mills.

Right: Di Giorgio's design shows a similar method of
converting vertical energy to horizontal.

Taccola's, as do his devices for measuring distances, his weight-driven wheels, and his ox-drawn pumps. Several examples are shown on our *1434* website.

Francesco di Giorgio Improves on Taccola

Francesco was a very good draftsman. He improved on Taccola—as can be seen in almost every drawing shown. Furthermore, he adds details to improve the quality of the illustration. Galluzzi writes:[12]

> Many of the 1,200 odd drawings and practically all the notes [of di Giorgio's *Codicetto*] are in fact derived from Taccola's manuscripts. But hardly any of the drawings or notes are slavish copies. . . . The drawings are obviously modeled on Taccola but Francesco often adds or omits details and in some cases introduces significant changes. . . . Other people's ideas and procedures were shamelessly plundered even by artists like Francesco. . . . [He] never mentioned the name of his source in the works he later authored. (p 36)
>
> From the . . . small manuscript [*Codicetto*] onward, in the series of drawings and notes based on Taccola's manuscripts, we find an increasingly frequent recurrence of devices not dealt with by Taccola. The drawings are carefully drafted without annotations and clearly focus on four topics: machines for shifting and lifting weights, devices for raising water, mills and wagons with complex transmission systems. . . . There is something illogical and incomprehensible about the abrupt switches between the series of faithful reproductions from Taccola and the presentation of a multitude of innovative projects. For these are not only "new" machines but devices of far more advanced mechanical design than Taccola's. . . . his devices feature complex gear mechanisms whose careful and highly varied arrangements are calculated to transmit to any level and at any desired velocity the motion produced by any source. As we know of no precedents that could have inspired Francesco, we are led to assume that they are his original contribution.[13]

Galluzzi then adds this note: "Scaglia, who describes these projects as a 'machine complex' or 'gear pump and mill complexes' doubts they can be attributed to Francesco. In her view Francesco probably compiled many of these designs, already developed by the late 1460's 'in workshop booklets prepared by carpenters and mill wrights.'"[14]

Galluzzi is clearly puzzled by Francesco's improvements on Taccola, which, knowing of no precedents, he attributes to Francesco's genius. But were there no precedents? Scaglia believes he compiled his designs from workshop booklets. What workshop booklets were available?

My first thought was Roman or Greek booklets. The Renaissance, after all, is said to have been a rebirth of Roman and Greek ideas. Leonardo was said to have slept with all nine volumes of Vitruvius's *De architettura* under his pillow. Taccola described himself as the Archimedes of Siena.

Our research team spent weeks in the British Library investigating whether Taccola and Francesco could have copied their array of machines and inventions from Greeks and Romans. Vitruvius was quickly ruled out—he showed no drawings of machines. Our team next searched Archimedes, Vegetius, Dinocrates, Ctesibus, Hero, Athanaeus, and Apollodorus of Damascus but drew a blank. Scaglia, too, found few classical sources for Taccola's work. "He does not seem to have had direct access to the writings of Archimedes, Hero, Euclid, Vitruvius and *The Mechanical Problems*," she concludes.

A number of Taccola's drawings and di Giorgio's copies were of gunpowder weapons, which, of course, were unknown to Greece and Rome. This suggested a Chinese source. If there was such a source, could we find it in order to compare it with Taccola and di Giorgio? This was our next line of inquiry. It took months.

If such a Chinese book had existed in Florence in Taccola's time, it must have been a printed copy—it would have been inconceivable for Zheng He's fleets to have carted the original book of drawings around the oceans. Like the astronomical calendar and ephemeris tables given to Toscanelli and the pope, it seemed likely that the drawings of machines would also be printed.

We looked for printed books of machines widely available in China at the time of Zheng He's voyages. The British Library's electronic database has a number of articles on Ming printing. *The Harvard Journal of Asiatic Studies* provides a good summary:[15]

Coming down the centuries we have definitive proof of the manufacture and application of wooden type early in the fourteenth century, as recorded by Wang Chen, a magistrate of Ching-te in Anhwei, from 1285 to 1301. At this place, Wang was writing what was to be his great work, the Nung-shu or Writings on Agriculture, an early and very thorough manual on the arts of husbandry. Because of the large number of characters to be employed, Wang conceived the idea of using movable type instead of the ordinary blocks, thereby reducing labor and expense. In his experiments Wang made more than 60,000 separate types, the cutting of which entailed no less than two years. . . .

In order to record for posterity his experiments in the manufacture of wooden movable type, he included a detailed account of them in his block-print edition, the preface of which was dated 1313.

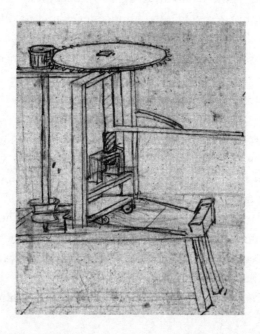

Although perhaps not in da Vinci's hand, this drawing of a printing press appears in his notebooks.

The Source of Taccola and Francesco's Inventions: the *Nung Shu*[16]

So in 1313, the world saw its first mass-produced book: the *Nung Shu*. (Needham implies it became a bestseller.)

Although Mao's Red Guards made bonfires of these *Nung Shu* books, Graham Hutt of the British Library kindly helped us find copies. With mounting anticipation I put a weekend aside to study a copy of the *Nung Shu* and any drawings it might contain.

Opening the book was one of the most thrilling moments in my seventeen years of research. The first drawing was of two horses pulling a mill to grind corn, just as Taccola[17] and di Giorgio[18] had depicted. With feverish excitement I turned the pages—it was obvious that we had found the source for their machines.

Needham organizes the machines illustrated in the *Nung Shu* under various rubrics:

> The *Nung Shu,* on the other hand, shows us no less than 265 diagrams and illustrations of agricultural implements and machines. . . . His *Nung Shu* is the greatest, though not the largest, of all works on agriculture and agricultural engineering in China, holding a unique position on account of its date [1313].
>
> And hence its freedom from occidental influences."[19]

As far as I can see, every variation of shafts, wheels, and cranks "invented" and drawn by Taccola and Francesco is illustrated in the *Nung Shu*. This is epitomized in the horizontal water-powered turbine used in the blast furnace.[20] This complex and sophisticated machine has a horizontal water-drive wheel to which is attached a drive belt. The drive belt powers a subsidiary shaft attached by a pulley to an eccentric crank linked by a crank joint and pushes (through rocking rollers and a piston rod) a fan bellows, which pumps air into the furnace. As Needham says: "We have here a conversion of rotary to longitudinal reciprocating motion in a heavy duty machine by the classical method later characteristic of the steam engine, transmission of power taking place, however in the reverse direction. Thus the great historical significance of this mechanism lies in its morphological paternity of steam power."

As far as I can determine, every type of powered transmission described by Taccola and di Giorgio is shown in the *Nung Shu*. There are several examples shown on the *1434* website.

In di Giorgio's column hoist[21] the enmeshing gear wheels, right-angle gearing, pinwheel, and pin drum are employed.

In his illustration of carts with steering gear[22] *(Codicetto)* he shows a crank arm fitted with connecting rods, and enmeshing gear wheels transform horizontal to vertical power.

Taccola's drawings of reversible hoists[23] *(De ingeneis)* show flat teeth with enmeshing gear wheels transferring horizontal to vertical power,

A Chinese bucket pump.

So many of Taccola's ideas, including the bucket pump and waterwheel, are uncannily similar to the *Nung Shu* illustrations.

together with a differential windlass and counterweight. Taccola shows the same.

The "vertical waterwheel with vanes"[24] illustrates vertical power being transferred to horizontal by enmeshing gear wheels, cranks and connecting rods, cam and cam followers, and right-angle gears.

Di Giorgio's chain pump activated by animal-powered horizontal wheel[25] has scoop wheels on spokes, eccentric lugs, bucket pumps, and continuous drive belts.

That di Giorgio plagiarized both Taccola and the *Nung Shu* is, in my opinion, supported by the following passage from Galluzzi (p. 42):

> The four basic categories of Francesco's machines exhibit some interesting new features. First the inclusion of written commentaries enhances the

A Chinese animal-powered chain pump.

Taccola's illustration of an animal-powered chain pump is strikingly similar to the Chinese version.

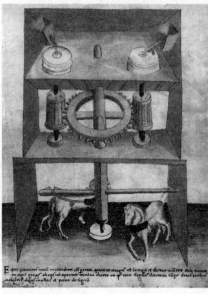

Left: Beasts of burden made much better workers than humans for some jobs!

Right: Santini's design mimics and then develops the process somewhat.

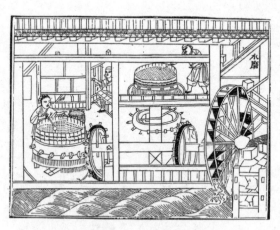

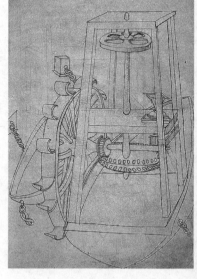

Left: The vertical waterwheel is shown to have many applications in the *Nung Shu*.

Right: A similar vertical waterwheel is found in Taccola's treatise on machines.

graphic representations of the devices with lexical information of major interest, data on materials and dimensions, special construction hints, and specific applications [the *Nung Shu* contains written commentaries]. . . . In some drawings of mills he introduces quantitative analysis on the relationships between teeth, wheel, and pinion diameters.

The author was clearly intent, however, on defining criteria to organise his material—a concern virtually absent not only from Taccola's work and Francesco's early writings but also from all prior books about machines [the *Nung Shu* is organized by criteria]. . . .

The section on mills was most heavily expanded reaching 58 separate items. . . . The chapter on pumps was similarly expanded in the *Trattato* I, which discusses a vast range of this kind of device. Conversely the section on carts and "pulling and lifting devices" was reduced. . . . In particular the number of machines for lifting and moving columns and obelisks was drastically cut. The tendency to narrow the discussion to basic examples of each machine type gathered considerable momentum in the so called second draft of the work (*Trattato* II). . . . Only ten illustrations of mills survived, but now they were strictly arranged by energy source: overshot bucket water wheel, horizontal paddle (a ritrecine) wheel, horizontal axis windmill, crank shaft (a frucatoio) mill with a flywheel bearing metal spheres, human-powered and animal powered mills (three designs with different transmission systems) and lastly the horse-powered tread wheel (two designs; one in which the animal moves the wheel from the inside, the other in which the animal applies pressure on the outer rim). [All these mills illustrated by Francesco appear in the *Nung Shu*.][26]

Galluzzi p. 44 continues:

The successive drafts of the *Trattato* therefore chart the evolution of Francesco's technological method from a potentially infinite series of exampla to the definition of a limited number of "types." Each of these embodied the basic principles of a specific technical system which could then vary ad infinitum to suit the craftsman's needs. [As di Giorgio himself confirms in *Trattato* II:] "and with these we conclude the section on instruments for pulling weights in construction work, since from these one can easily derive the others."[27]

A Chinese chain pump from the *Nung Shu*.

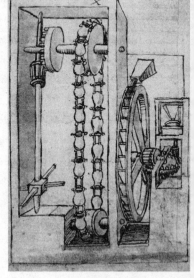

Di Giorgio's chain pump is a copy of Taccola's and almost identical to the Chinese illustration.

In my opinion di Giorgio started with the animal-powered machines shown in the *Nung Shu,* which he copied. He then copied from *Nung Shu* the basic Chinese water-powered machines using horizontal and vertical waterwheels. Next he adapted the horizontal and vertical waterwheels of the *Nung Shu* to power a whole range of mills and pumps—just as Galluzzi describes.

He did this by using the basic principles shown in the *Nung Shu,* that is, converting water power from horizontal to vertical through enmeshing gear wheels. Francesco changed power ratios through different sizes of gear wheels and also changed direction through cam shafts and rocker bearings so as to devise an array of water- and animal-powered sawmills and all manner of pumping systems.[28]

Galluzzi successfully summarizes Francesco's adaptations; Francesco himself says, "From these we can easily derive the others."

Leonardo da Vinci Develops Francesco di Giorgio's Machines

In *The Art of Invention* Galluzzi reevaluates Leonardo's place in light of the earlier work of Taccola and di Giorgio:

"Leonardo ceases to be a visionary prophet in the desert. Rather he appears as the man who most eloquently expressed—both with words and above all images—the utopian vision about the practical potential of technology that were enthusiastically shared by many 'artist engineers' of the fifteenth century."[29]

Leonardo no longer appears as the iconic, singular genius. Instead, as Galluzzi writes, he "emerges as the culmination, as the most mature and original product of a collective development lasting several decades to which many highly talented figures made sizable contributions."[30]

I believe Leonardo's machines were superbly illustrated copies and improvements of di Giorgio's. He brought his brilliant and incisive mind to penetrate the essentials of these machines, which he regarded not as magic creations deposited from heaven but as assemblages of parts. According to Galluzzi, he was able to perceive that an infinite variety of machines could be derived from a finite number of mechanisms, which he defines as "elements of machines." As Galluzzi writes, his vision of the anatomy of machines and man was enshrined in a series of masterly drawings that mark the birth of modern scientific illustration.

By comparing Leonardo's drawings with the *Nung Shu,* we have verified that each element of a machine superbly illustrated by Leonardo had previously been illustrated by the Chinese in a much simpler manual.

In summary, Leonardo's body of work rested on a vast foundation of work previously done by others. His mechanical drawings of flour and roller mills, water mills and sawmills, pile drivers, weight-transporting machines, all kinds of winders and cranes, mechanized cars, pumps, water-lifting devices, and dredgers were developments and improvements upon Francesco di Giorgio's *Trattato di architettura civile e militare.* Leonardo's rules for perspective for painting and sculpture were derived from Alberti's *De pictura* and *De statua*. His parachute was based on di Giorgio's. His helicopter was modeled on a Chinese toy imported to Italy circa 1440 and drawn by Taccola.[31] His work on canals, locks, aqueducts, and fountains originated from his meeting in Pavia with di Giorgio in 1490 (discussed in more detail in chapter 18). His cartography evolved from Alberti's *Descriptio urbis Romae*. His military machines were copies of Taccola's and di Giorgio's—but brilliantly drawn.

Leonardo's three-dimensional illustrations of the components of man and machines are a unique and brilliant contribution to civilization—as are his sublime sculptures and paintings. In my eyes, he remains the greatest genius who ever lived. However, it is time to recognize the Chinese contributions to his work. Without these contributions, the history of the Renaissance would have been very different, and Leonardo almost certainly would not have developed the full range of his talents.

SILK AND RICE

By the time the *Nung Shu* was published in 1313, the Chinese had been spinning yarns for a thousand years, using all sorts of materials. Silk was the finest and most valuable; scrapings of hides were the heaviest and cheapest. Needham produces diagrams of an array of hand-powered and water-powered spinning machines with single and multiple looms.[1]

China had been exporting silk to Italy for a millennium by the time Taccola and Franceso di Giorgio appeared. In 115 B.C., Mithridates II of Persia made a commercial treaty with the Han emperor Wu Ti. In the next century, Julius Caesar possessed silk curtains.[2] By the reign of Augustus, wealthy people were buried in Chinese silk.[3]

In return for fine silk, Chinese merchants sought gold, silver, coral, and glass. Chinese regarded high-quality glassware as a great luxury and were prepared to pay accordingly. During the Tang dynasty, monks smuggled silkworms from China to the West. Pictures of quilling machines, which wind silk thread onto bobbins, can be seen in the stained-glass windows of the Chartres cathedral, dating between 1240 and 1245. A clear illustration of the Chinese model is shown in *The Genius of China*.[4]

By the time Zheng He's fleet visited in 1434, Europeans had silkworms and knew how to wind silk thread and to make silk cloth, but in small quantities. The illustrations and descriptions in the *Nung Shu* showed how the whole Chinese process—production of silk thread, the dyeing and weaving of fine silk cloth, winding the silk threads onto bobbins—could be coupled with water power to expand production enormously.

Figures tell the story: In 1418, Venetian merchants paid tax on a mere three hundred pounds of silk. In 1441, the Florentine government passed a law requiring farmers to plant between 5 and 50 mulberry trees per hectare, depending on the yield from their farms.[5] Tens of thousands of mulberry trees were planted in northern Italy between 1465 and 1474. This period coincided with (or was one of the reasons for) a reversal of Venetian foreign policy. After the death of Doge Mocenigo in 1424, Venice under Francesco Foscari decided to become a land power in northern Italy. Verona, Vicenza, and the Po wetlands came into the Pax Venetica and the northern Po area was planted with

Inventions such as Chinese water-powered threshers and mills facilitated the mass production of silk and rice.

thousands upon thousands of mulberry trees as well as rice (described in chapter 18).

The first Italian hydraulic silk mill, in Verona, is described in 1456. It is a Chinese machine. John Hobson in *The Eastern Origins of Western Civilisation* summarizes the spread of Italian silk-weaving machines to northern Europe: "The invention of the silk filatures (reeling machines) had been made in China in 1090. The Chinese machines comprised a treadle operated silk-reeling frame with a ramping board and a roller system. The Italian model resembled the Chinese right down to the smallest detail such as the lever joined to the crank. And significantly the Italian machines more or less replicated the Chinese right down to the eighteenth century."[6] As Hobson points out, the great British mills set up by John Lombe were copies of "Chinese"-designed silk mills in Italy. Lombe's machines became the blue-

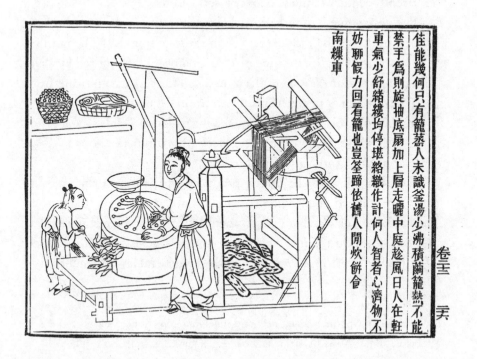

The daily chores of a Chinese housewife.

print for the British cotton industry, whose products later swamped the world.

The combination of abundant mulberry leaves and mechanical reeling and weaving machines led to soaring silk production in Florence and Venice. The Italian mulberry was much more prolific than the Chinese. Florence manufacturing switched from wool to silk. Sericulture spread from Tuscany first to the Po Valley and then to the "terra firma" north of Venice. Alberti wrote there were "so many mulberry trees to feed the worms from which the silk is obtained that it is a marvellous thing." Estimated production of raw silk in the Verona district rose from 20,000 light pounds in 1530 to 150,000 in 1608. Vicenza produced 60,000 light pounds in 1504 and double that amount by 1608. As printing got under way in Venice, publications in clear and simple language explained how best to tend mulberry trees and feed and care for silkworms. Titles such as *Il vermicella dalla seta* (The little silkworm) were remarkably similar to fourteenth-century Chinese books on sericulture.

The development of sericulture led to more and better spinning machines. In the 1450s, Vicenza had eight shops of spinners. The number rose to ten in 1507, thirty-three in 1543, and over one hundred by 1596. Silk production in Verona underwent a similar expansion, rising from eight silk spinners in the 1420s to twelve in 1456, when Verona's first hydraulic mill, on the Adige, was commissioned (Mola, 237). After that, the industry exploded; there were fifty spinners' shops in 1543, seventy in 1549, and eighty-eight in 1559.

The raw silk and silk thread produced in the terra firma encouraged a new breed of entrepreneurs to buy silk. Many were financed by the Medicis. The Venetian government took a close interest in regulating the silk industry in its territory, issuing patents, which increased after the 1440s. In 1474, Venice published a general law of patents:

> The decision has been made that, by the authority of this council, any person
> in this city who makes any new and ingenious contrivance, not made here
> before in our domains, shall, as soon as it is perfected so that it can be used
> and exercised, give notice of the same to the office of our Provveditori di
> Commune, it being forbidden up to ten years for any other person in any ter-

ritory and place or ours to make a contrivance without the content and license of the author. . . . But our government will be free, at its complete discretion, to take and use for its needs any of the said contrivances and instruments, with this condition, however, that no one other than the inventors shall operate them.[7]

By these means, first Venice and Florence, then the whole of Italy came to dominate the raw-silk market of Europe—much as eastern Asia dominates the global market today.

Rice

Florence's silk-based economic boom required more workers, and more workers required more food. As Braudel has pointed out, the yield from rice fields is some several times that of wheat.[8]

Rice had been known in the Mediterranean world since the Roman era, but it was used only for medicinal purposes. The first known reference to rice being grown in northern Italy is a letter of September 27, 1475, from the ruler of Milan, Galeazzo Sforza, to the duke of Ferrara concerning twelve sacks of Asian (*Oryza Sativa*) rice grown in the Po Valley.

Rice is the basic food of southern China. The *Nung Shu* included much advice from Wang Chen about wet rice cultivation, including how to husband and control water supplies from the great rivers that carry melted snow from the Mongolian plateau eastward to the sea.

> Cultivators of rice build surface tanks and reservoirs to store water, and dykes and sluices to stop its flow (when necessary). . . . The land is divided into small patches, and after ploughing and harrowing, water is let into the fields and the seeds sown. When the plants grow five or six inches tall, they are planted out. All farmers south of the river [Yangtze] now use this method. When the plants attain a height of seven or eight inches, the ground is hoed, and after hoeing the water is let go from the fields, so as to dry them. Then when the plants begin to flower and seed, water is again let in.

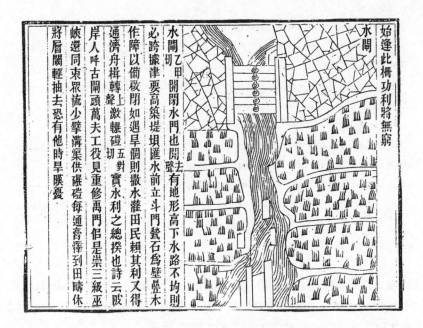

Chinese irrigation design.

The *Nung Shu* illustrates all manner of techniques for the vital task of regulating water supply to the rice fields—many types of bucket and chain pumps, locks and sluices, dams and conduit channels. Buckets, pallets, and chain pumps are a theme,[9] as are bamboo "water palisades," which acted as weirs.

As described in the previous chapter, Taccola and Francesco di Giorgio drew an array of pumps as well as dams and sluice gates.[10] The chain pumps first shown in the drawings of Taccola are still in use today in northeastern Italy, where the local people call them "Tartar" pumps. Since Taccola and Francesco's drawings of chain and bucket pumps were shown in chapter 16, in this chapter only piston pumps will be described.

Sheldon Shapiro in his article "The Origin of the Suction Pump" notes:

Not until the early fifteenth century does the first evidence of the valved piston appear. It turns up in a drawing (Fig. 4) by the Siennese engineer, Mariano

Jacopo Taccola [in Munich Ms. 1435] whose still unpublished notebooks are of the greatest importance for the history of technology. In this drawing dating from about 1433, the valve in the piston is clear. Therefore, although a text and other details are lacking this drawing represents the first suction pump on record; it is unintelligible in any other terms.

The first detailed drawings of suction pumps date from the period 1475–1480; Francesco di Giorgio Martini in the last book of his *Trattato di Architettura* written about 1475 shows several suction pumps. In the most mechanically perfect pump the distance from the sump to the chamber seems only a foot or two, instead of the 32 feet possible, thus showing an imperfect understanding of the nature of this new type of pump.[11]

A Chinese chain pump used for irrigation purposes.

Clearly Franceso did not know how it worked; he must have copied a drawing.

As Needham points out, suction pumps in China are first described in the *Wu Ching Tsung Yao* (Collection of the most important military techniques, published in 1044). Here Needham describes the process:

> For syringes (*chi thung*) one uses long pieces of (hollow) bamboo; opening a hole in the bottom (septum) and wrapping silk floss round a piston-rod (*shui kan*) inside (to form the piston). Then from the hole water may be shot forth. . . . . In the 11th century . . . the military encyclopaedia just mentioned gives us elsewhere a very remarkable account of a flamethrower for naphtha which constituted a liquid piston pump of ingenious design.[12]

Di Giorgio's piston pump is shown in the copy of his *Trattato di architettura* owned by Leonardo da Vinci, which is now in the Laurenzian Library in Florence. Leonardo improved upon di Giorgio's drawings.

In many ways, the Po resembles a smaller version of the Yangtze. Both rivers carry melting snows from the mountains eastward to the sea. Both suffer from flash floods and are controlled by a network of canals, locks, sluices, and dams. The waters of both are used to form extensive rice fields. The exact date when the Po was first utilized for rice is not known. Clearly it predated the 1475 letter, but by how much? I suggest it was after 1435, when Taccola's first drawings of pumps appear, and probably after 1438, when his drawings of lock and sluice gates first appear.

The combination of booming silk production in Florence and Venice and adequate food for the silk workers enabled "an extraordinary increase in silk production" between 1441 and 1461.[13] By the 1480s silk had become "the main source of employment" for Florentine workers. The rise in silk production was mirrored by the rise in the Medici family's wealth, which was largely a product of financing the export of fine silk cloth. Florence had acquired the port of Pisa in 1405 and Leghorn in 1421 and could thereafter export her cloths to northern Europe.

The Florentine Renaissance was fueled by wealth, especially that of the Medicis. The family was in exile when Pope Eugenius IV moved the pontificate from Rome to Florence in 1434, interceded with the opponents of the Medicis, and enabled the family to return to Florence. The Medicis once again became papal bankers and soon controlled Florence. As the future Pope Pius II said, "Political questions are settled at his [Cosimo's] house. The man he chooses holds office. . . . He it is who decides peace and war and controls the laws. . . . he is king in everything but name."[14]

Christopher Hibbert, in *The House of Medici; Its Rise and Fall,* writes of Cosimo de' Medici: "Foreign rulers were advised to communicate with him personally and not to waste their time by approaching anyone else in Florence when any important decision was required. As the Florentine historian, Francesco Guicciardini, observed, 'He had a reputation such as probably no private citizen has ever enjoyed from the fall of Rome to our own day.' "[15]

Cosimo was at the heart of western Christendom. When popes visited Florence, they stayed in Medici palaces, enjoyed Medici hospitality, accepted Medici loans, and, in return, granted highly valuable concessions. For example, in 1460 huge deposits of alum, an essential ingredient in fulling cloth, were found near Civitavecchia in the Papal States. In 1466 the Medicis signed an agreement with the papacy giving them and their partners the sole right to mine alum and sell it abroad.

Hibbert wrote, "the French historian, Philippe de Commines, described the bank . . . as the greatest commercial house that had ever been anywhere. 'The Medici name gave their servants and agents so much credit,' Commines wrote, 'that what I have seen in Flanders and England almost passes belief.' "[16]

By the 1450s, Florence had silk and food. The Medicis had derived unprecedented riches from the silk trade and had used their wealth to fund astronomers, mathematicians, engineers, sculptors, artists, explorers, cartographers, historians, librarians, archaeologists, and geographers. The Renaissance was in full flood—thanks in part to Chinese inventions and plants—use of machines powered by wind and water, Chinese rice, mulberry trees, and silkworms.

GRAND CANALS: CHINA
AND LOMBARDY

On New Year's Day 1991, it was savagely cold in Beijing. Marcella and I had spent the night watching sensuous Tang dynasty dancers in their shimmering peacock-blue dresses—a memorable display. I had a bad headache, for obvious reasons, and found the cold that froze my nostrils a pleasant sensation. In those days there were few cars; Beijing streets were a tangled mass of bicycles, their riders swathed in baggy blue jackets and head scarves angled against the biting wind. The trees—stubby pines for the most part—stooped before the wind and glinted with ice crystals. We drove to the southwest of Beijing to board a huge military aircraft that would take us down to Xian.

By the time we took off, the sun was rising in the east, sparkling on the frozen Grand Canal. We flew south over the silver pencil of the canal on our way down to the Yellow River, then turned to the southwest above the river to Xian.

What a prodigious undertaking this Grand Canal was—dug, according to popular fable, "by a million people with teaspoons." That is probably a serious underestimate: the workforce is likely to have been nearer five million. Like the Great Wall, the Grand Canal is the result of the obsession of many emperors over thousands of years. They dug in sections, gradually extending, deepening, and widening the canal so that it now links the rice lands of the south with Beijing via the Yangtze, Huang He, and Yellow Rivers.

The canal was started nearly 2,500 years ago and greatly extended during the Sui dynasty (A.D. 581–618),[1] when Emperor Yang enslaved his people to link his new capital of Luoyang to Xian (in those days called Changan).[2] Over two decades, he extended the canal down to Hangzhou, enabling Yangtze junks to travel up the canal to ports along the Yellow River. The canal crossed major rivers, traveling from the Tibetan highlands to the sea.

By the Tang dynasty (A.D. 618–907), 100,000 tons of grain were transported northward each year. Kublai Khan extended the canal to Beijing in the north and built a number of locks—there are more than thirty today—rising to 130 feet above sea level.[3] Marco Polo was much impressed by the flat canal barges being towed by horses: "This magnificent work is deserving of admiration and not so much from the manner in which it is conducted through the country, or its vast extent, as from its utility and the benefit it produces to those cities which lie on its course."[4]

Crossing so many rivers, particularly the Yellow, entailed major engineering challenges. The water level varied enormously depending on the time of year and the amount of snow that had melted in the mountains of Tibet and was carried down the rivers to the sea. Other difficulties arose with the need to carry ships uphill as they neared Beijing. In *The Genius of China,* Robert Temple outlines the problem and the response:[5]

The canal pound lock was invented in China in 984 A.D. The inventor was Ch'iao Wei-Yo, who in 983 was appointed Assistant Commissioner of Transport for Huainan. The impetus for his invention was concern over the enormous amounts of grain which were being stolen during canal transport at that time. Grain was the normal tax payment throughout China's history. Movement of the grain to central repositories and warehouses was the lifeblood of the Empire, and any substantial interruption of this process was a very serious social and political problem.

Until 984, boats could only move between lower and higher water levels in canals over double slipways. Chinese boats had no keels and were nearly flat-bottomed. A form of portage had been developed in China, therefore, whereby spillways originally designed to regulate water flow were elongated in gentle ramps both front and back, leading into the water. A boat would come along and be attached to ropes turned by ox-powered capstans. Within two or three minutes, the boat would be hauled up a ramp to the higher level and for a moment would balance precariously in the air. Then it would shoot forward like an arrow out of a bow and scud along the canal to a level several feet higher than it had started. Passengers and crew had to lash themselves tightly to the boat to avoid being hurled into the air and injured. The great disadvantage of this ingenious technique was that boats often split apart or were seriously damaged by the wear and tear of being dragged up the stone ramps. Whenever a boat broke up on a ramp, the contents would promptly be stolen by organised gangs—including corrupt officials—who waited for just such an occurrence. Sometimes apparently the ships were roughly handled on purpose, or were artificially weakened or had even been chosen for their weaknesses so that an "accident" of this kind could be brought about intentionally.

Ch'iao Wei-Yo determined to wipe out this practice. He therefore invented the pound lock so that double slipways would not be needed. Here is how the official history of the time relates the story: "Ch'iao Wei-Yo therefore first ordered the construction of two gates at the third dam along the west river (near Huai-Yin). The distance between the two gates was rather more than fifty paces [250 feet], and the whole space was covered over with a great roof like a shed. The gates were hanging gates: when they were closed the water accumulated like a tide until the required level was reached, and then when the time came it was allowed to flow out. He also built a horizontal bridge between the banks and added dykes of earth with stone revetments to protect their foundations. After this was done to all the double slipways the previous corruption was completely eliminated, and the passage of the boats went on without the slightest impediment."

Pound locks made true summit canals possible. Water levels could differ by four of five feet at each lock without any problems at all. Over a stretch of territory, therefore, a canal could rise more than one hundred feet above sea level, as was the case with the Grand Canal, for instance (rising 138 feet above sea level). This made possible a vast extension of the canal network and freed hydraulic engineers from many awkward topographical restrictions.

The pound locks also conserved water, as Shen Kua relates in *Dream Pool Essays* of 1086:[6]

> It was found that the work of five hundred labourers was saved each year, and miscellaneous expenditure amounting to one million two hundred and fifty thousand cash as well. With the old method of hauling the boats over, burdens of not more than twenty-one tons of rice per vessel could be transported, but after the double gates were completed, boats carrying twenty-eight tons were brought into use, and later on the cargo weights increased more and more. Nowadays [circa 1086] government boats carry up to forty-nine tons and private boats as much as eight hundred bags weighing one hundred and thirteen tons.

Not surprisingly, the *Nung Shu,* the Chinese agricultural treatise published in 1313, illustrated Chinese lock and sluice gates, which were essential to irrigating rice fields and controlling the water levels in canals. Needham states:

> There is no doubt that throughout Chinese history the most typical form of sluice and lock gate was what is called the stop-log gate . . . two vertical grooves fashioned in wood or stone face each other across the waterway, and in them slide a series of logs or baulks let down or withdrawn as desired by ropes attached to each end. Windlasses or pulleys in wood or stone mountings like cranes on each bank helped to fit or remove the gate planks. This system was sometimes improved by fastening all baulks together to form a continuous surface and then raising or lowering it in the grooves by means of bolts. . . .
>
> The oldest illustration of this kind we have found is in the *Nung Shu* Ch. 18, p 4b, the date of which (+1313) deprives Jacopo Mariano Taccola of the honour of having been the first to illustrate a dam with a sluice gate.[7]

So by the time Zheng He's junks visited Venice in 1434 the Chinese had hundreds of years' experience in building canals and locks and operating them in all kinds of conditions—dried-up rivers in summer and torrents in spring.

Lombardy

The geography and climate of Lombardy, the region between the foot-hills of the Alps and the River Po, resembles that of eastern China. The Po carries melted snow from the great lakes, especially Lake Maggiore, first southward, then east across the flat plain to the Po delta south of Venice. For centuries, the river has provided a means of transporting goods, including wood and marble, from the mountains to the cities of the plains, and her waters have produced fertile land.

Canals have played an important role in the development of commerce, agriculture, and industry in Lombardy. The impetus for Lombardy's first major canal appears to have been the capture of Milan by the Holy Roman Emperor Barbarossa in 1161.[8] Milan built substantial defenses, collecting water from local streams to form wide moats around the city. Milan also needed a secure supply of drinking water, and the best available was the River Ticino, which flowed from Lake Maggiore into the Po sixteen miles from Milan. This led to the first canal linking the Ticino with Milan—a huge undertaking for Europeans. The work was completed in about 1180, long before the Chinese arrived in 1434.

The largest canal of this system was called the Naviglio Grande (Grand Canal). It was small, of varying depth, depending on the amount of water coming from the mountains. It had no locks and therefore navigation was hazardous and seasonal. All of this was revolutionized around the year 1450.

This time, the impetus came from Francesco Sforza, a determined and clever leader who seized the throne from Filippo Visconti on his death in 1447. Sforza cut the Naviglio Grande, which promptly deprived Milan of its drinking water. Moreover, the mills alongside the canal lost their power supply so they could no longer grind grain. Milan capitulated and Francesco entered the city as conqueror in 1450. He was proclaimed Duke and created the house of Sforza.

Sforza set about providing Milan with continuous supplies of drinking water, hydropower, and the ability to transfer goods and food throughout the year. Sforza had inherited a canal in the west that connected Milan to Lake Maggiore, but it had no locks and depended on the variable height of water from the mountains. It was useless for navigation. He decided to equip it with locks and transform it into an all-season, all-weather canal.

He planned to build the Bereguardo Canal in the south, in order to link Milan with Pavia, and in the north a link between Milan and the River Adda, which flowed out of Lake Como. This grand scheme would create a waterway from Lake Maggiore in the west all the way to Lake Como in the east, which could provide water for Milan and serve as a navigation system linking the Adriatic with Lombardy. The problem, of course, was that in 1452 when the plan was conceived, Italians had no method of building locks. Without locks, canals could not function—especially not the Bereguardo Canal, which had a fall of eighty-two feet and spring weather that brought melted snow in abundance down from the mountains.

There are no prizes for guessing who provided the design for the locks: it was our old friends, Taccola,[9] Francesco di Giorgio, and Leon Battista Alberti. Francesco, as described in chapter 16, copied and improved upon Taccola's work. We presume he, like Taccola, had access to and copied from the *Nung Shu*. In chapter 16 we described di Giorgio's *Trattato di Architettura*, notably the copy marked Codex Laurenziano, which was owned by Leonardo da Vinci and is now found in the Laurenzian Library in Florence. Also deposited with that document is di Giorgio's *Trattato dei Pondi Leve e Tirari*.[10] One of the last descriptions in the Laurenziana Codex, no. 361, concerns a series of lock gates:

If along a river. . . . we wish to conduct boats, when due to little water and an incline it might be impossible to navigate, it is necessary to determine the fall. . . . Let us suppose that the first part of the river has a drop of thirty piede: construct at that point a high door in the manner of a portcullis. . . . with windlasses to raise it, and in this manner lay off the entire length of the river and all its falls with such doors. After the boat enters, and the door is closed, the boat will soon rise . . . and will be able to enter the second chamber . . . and so step by step you will be able to take the boat to wherever you wish. Should you desire to return down, by opening each door, the boat with the water will be led to the next door, and so from one to the other it will be possible to return to the sea. All boats should be made with flat bottoms, so that they will float on little water.[11]

This description is accompanied by a picture showing a lock system with no fewer than four locks. The date of the picture, from the Hans Lee Laurenziana Codex,[12] is about 1450—a date fixed by the description of the destruction of central Ragusa (Dubrovnik).

Sforza and his architect, Bertola de Novale, now had illustrations of how to build locks. At first they found them puzzling. Here is William Parsons's[13] description: "But the details of the locks were not understood and the contractors refused to move. So Berenzo de Passaro wrote further urgent requests to the Duke to send Bertola with the necessary explanations."[14]

Parsons continues:

By 1461 the canal was completed as is shown by another letter by Lorenzo, in which he complains of defects in the locks and asks again that Bertola be sent to remedy the troubles. In this letter he writes of the locks being two *braccia* deeper than the bottom of the canal [which must refer to the height of fall]. The defects were said to be in the gates: their hinges were weak and the gates themselves could not withstand the water pressure.[15]

After 1461, locks were built on the canal between Milan and the Adda River, which was later called the Martesana. Bertola was engaged in the construction of at least five canals of major navigable importance, all requiring locks. He constructed no fewer than eighteen locks on the Bereguardo Canal and five more near Parma. Chinese canal- and lock-building techniques had been imported into Lombardy through Taccola Francesco di Giorgio and the *Nung Shu*.

An examination of the history of canals in Lombardy also illustrates the close connection between Taccola, Francesco di Giorgio, Leon Battista Alberti, and Leonardo da Vinci. Alberti, who was the notary to Pope Eugenius IV and would have likely attended the meeting between Eugenius and the Chinese ambassador, also designed locks. William Parsons said of Alberti:

The year 1446 saw him re-established in Rome, a friend of Nicholas V, and started on his engineering work—an attempt to recover the sunken galley in Lake Nemi [Alberti used a drawing virtually identical to that of Taccola and Francesco], which only lately has been accomplished. . . . This was followed by the work on which his fame depends, *De re aedificatoria* (written about 1452). From several references to it by other writers, it is certain that the contents were made available to scholars then or soon after. This fact is important because it fixes the date when the canal lock was first described. . . . Leon Batista continued thus: "Also, if you wish you can make two gates cutting the river in two places . . . that a boat can lie for its full length between the two: and if the said boat desires to ascend when it arrives at the place, close the lower barrier and open the upper one, and conversely, when it is descending, close the upper and open the lower one. Thus the said boat shall have enough water to float it easily to the main canal, because the closing of the upper gate restrains the water from pushing it too violently, with fear of grounding." . . . We are sure that Bastista's *Aedificatoria* was written about 1452, and that its contents were known to many engineers.[16]

In other words, both Francesco and Alberti have described the same lock systems that are described in the *Nung Shu*.

It is therefore incorrect to credit Leonardo da Vinci with the invention of locks. As we know, his handwriting appears on the Laurenziano Codex of Francesco (as described in chapter 16). We also know that Leonardo learned much about waterways from his meeting in Pavia with di Giorgio. It is fair to say that Leonardo's drawings of canals are the most elegant by far, but Leonardo did not invent locks, despite centuries of credit for the breakthrough.

Nevertheless, the introduction of locks, which enabled an all-weather, all-season system of navigable canals to be constructed in northern Italy, was of immense importance to the economic development of Lombardy. The introduction of Chinese rice, mulberry trees, and silk was all the more valuable once the rice could be carried downriver on the Po. Marble, too, could be transported from the mountains to the new cities of northern Italy. Italy now possessed an array of Chinese inventions—water-powered machines such as mills and pumps to grind corn and spin silk. After 1434, Italy was on her way to becoming Europe's first industrial nation.

Europe's First Industrial Nation

The wonderful rich legacy based on rice and silk, canals and steel, is visible today. During most summers of the past forty-two years Marcella and I have driven through Burgundy across the Col de Larche to her home in the Piedmont to stay with her family in the foothills of the Alps. We would drive eastward to Venice across the Po Valley through miles upon miles of golden rice fields irrigated by the famous canals fed by alpine snowmelt.

We would start our journey at dawn, the lanes full of puttering trac tors. After four hours, Mantua would appear, a ghostly silhouette suspended from the sky, a light fog sitting on the lakes that surround the town. Medieval town builders exploited the loops of the Po and her tributary the Mincio to create a series of lakes that form Mantua's defenses. Cremona, Pavia, Verona, and Milan were also built on loops of the Po tributaries that wound their way across the fields of Lombardy. Mantua's historic town center is typical of these medieval cities. The Piazza Erbe is an ensemble of enchanting pastel buildings. It leads to the equally beautiful Mantegna and Sordello Squares, each more imposing than the last, each surrounded by superb medieval and Renaissance buildings. At the east side of Sordello Square stands the ducal palace of the Gonzagas,[17] the princely family who ruled this town in the Middle Ages. One great hall leads to another, each covered from floor to ceiling with frescoes, fantastic Renaissance masterpieces—fables by Pisanello and Mantegna, portraits of the Gonzaga family, tapestries depicting the lives of the apostles. The most astonishing impact comes from differing styles being linked to form a harmonious single ensemble. The Gonzagas were clearly a family of enormous wealth and great discernment.

In Verona the Scaglieri[18] ruling family, like the Gonzagas, patronized brilliant artists. This comes as a surprise, for Verona, Mantua, Milan, Urbino, and Ferrara had a different lifestyle than that of republican Florence and Venice. Instead of a wealthy mercantile class engaged in international trade, rulers and aristocracy in these northern cities lived on their wits, often acting as mercenaries to Venice. However, these mini-states lay on trade routes. Milan and Verona controlled the approach to the principal alpine passes and were in a position to gather taxes and tolls from overland traffic between Venice and northern Europe. Each had a little army. The money the rulers lavished on Renaissance artists was undoubtedly part of their foreign policy—to appear wealthier and more important than they really were so as to impress their powerful neighbors, Venice and Florence. Today we are the beneficiaries of this largesse. These sumptuous Italian cities are stuffed with Renaissance masterpieces; one could spend a lifetime in each.[19]

The wealth of modern Italy remains visible in the houses of farmers and middle-class people—huge by the standards of northern Europe, and superbly finished. People wear expensive clothes, and the women exquisitely turned out, presenting the renowned *bella figura*.

To me, the wealth of northern Italy, particularly that of Piedmont, is epitomized in the food. One enters what appears to be a farmhouse; often no name discloses the restaurant within. The place is packed; there are no menus and no price lists—one just chooses a table and sits down. Our favorite is the Nonna, in the foothills of the Alps near Pian Fei. A bottle of slightly sparkling dry deep red wine made from Nebbiolo grapes is brought, together with a plate of Parma ham and salami. Then come crudités with *bagna cauda*, a sauce of garlic, anchovies, tuna, and olive oil, followed by pasta. Several courses—roast kid, guinea fowl, wild boar, suckling pig, and wild rabbit with chestnuts follow. Dessert is frequently the local raspberries and the famous chestnuts boiled with white *vino* and mixed with cream. One is handed the bill, usually about twenty euros a head for twelve courses.

To me there is no place on earth with a higher standard of living than the Piedmont with her huge houses, wonderful food, historic cities, good-natured and charming people—a life based upon natural wealth in a region whose advanced methods of farming and industrialization came six hundred years ago.

FIREARMS AND STEEL

There is substantial evidence that an illustration of a blast furnace in the *Nung Shu* was copied by Taccola and Alberti and built in northern Italy. As a result, for the first time Europeans had the capacity to produce sufficient quantities of high-quality iron and steel to make reliable modern firearms.[1]

One of the first descriptions of an Italian steel-making furnace comes from the Florentine architect Antonio di Piero Averlino, who was called "Filarete."[2] Filarete was born in Florence around 1400. His major work was *Ospedale Maggiore,* a treatise on the reorganization of hospitals and sanitary engineering. Fearing that his readers might find this tome a little too heavy, he provided a series of diversions for relief. One such diversion is his account of a visit to a hammer mill and smelter in Ferriere.[3] Dr. John Spencer[4], chairman of the Allen Memorial Art Museum, asserts that

the technique of smelting iron in the fifteenth century as described by Filarete does not differ markedly from the standard method of extraction that obtains from his own day until the eighteenth century. In barest outline he informs us that the ore was first improved by roasting it with lime, perhaps in an attempt to reduce the high sulphur content, which he notes at various points in the process. The resulting product was ground, sifted and prepared for the charge (p. 206) . . . clear layers of charcoal were alternated in

The harnessing of water power could raise and drop these triangulated tilt hammers with great force.

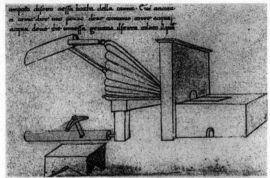

An illustration of a water-powered smithy bellows, forge and hammermill at Grottaferrata near Rome.

the [smelter] stack with layers of ore-lime mixture. The air blast necessary for efficient reduction was provided by an ingenious arrangement of bellows blowing alternatively through a common tuyère. . . . When the molten pig iron had cooled it was melted again and carried to a finery where it was shaped.

Filarete's description of the smelter raises several significant points and poses several problems. His description of the hammer mill at Grotta Ferrata records one of the earliest instances of fining which was already, apparently, well developed. The bellows seem to be quite unique and again a very early example of a sophisticated innovation. . . .[5]

This smelter was not the only Chinese contribution to making iron and steel in northern Italy in the 1450s. Theodore A. Wertime, author

The ingenious water-powered bellows enabled higher temperatures to facilitate iron smelting.

Taccola's similar water-powered bellows are found in his Codex Latinus Monacensis, Munich.

of *The Coming of the Age of Steel,* explored this "oriental influence" in his paper "Asian Influences on European Metallurgy":

> There is no question that Filarete, a trained observer, found here [at Ferriere] an unusual furnace assemblage. But what it was we shall never precisely know, although one suspects oriental influence from the technological context of Filarete's impressions....
>
> Needham is quite right in speaking of the "clustering" of technology, particularly at such moments of technical invention and interchange as the tenth to fifteenth centuries A.D. As noted in *The Coming of the Age of Steel*—with quite conservative interpretations—fifteenth century Italy exhibited an unusual number of metallurgical traits associated with non-European techniques of making cast iron:

1. The employment of the molten bath of cast iron for carburising wrought iron to steel, identified by Needham as an early Chinese process, which in Europe came to be known as the "Brescian" or "Bergamasque" process[6]

2. The early and continued casting of cooking ware and cannons of iron;

3. The Cannechio, a distinctive inverted conical shape in European blast furnaces, with antecedents more probably Chinese than Persian;

4. The granulation of new cast iron for shot or for making iron suitable for fining, not unlike north Persian traditions;

5. Iron filings as an ingredient in fire works, reflecting the heritage of "Chinese fire." . . .

In Italy the evidences of clustering are impressive and force one to ponder most deeply on the course by which societies came to reshape both their mechanisms and their techniques to new purposes. . . .

. . . Filarete may indeed have seen the last vestiges of a large and varied cluster of practices in the Asian manner, associated with the new product "cast iron."[7]

The Medicis financed technical improvements in hardening steel. Suzanne Butters, in "The Triumph of Vulcan: Sculptors' Tools, Porphyry, and the Prince in Ducal Florence," describes a Medici stoneworker, Tadda, experimenting with procedures for tempering steel in order to make chisels hard enough to cut porphyry—the hardest material then used in art.[8] Having devised cast iron and steel of sufficient hardness and strength to enable them to make firearms, the Florentines next needed better gunpowder.

Gunpowder, muskets, and cannons were all Chinese inventions. Gunpowder was first made in the Tang dynasty and improved in the Song.[9] Its main ingredients were sulphur, saltpeter, and charcoal. The Chinese term *huo yao* means "the drug that fires." (Chinese alchemists had originally thought that sulphur and saltpeter were drugs and that gunpowder could treat skin infections.) In their search for an elixir, the alchemists had found that sulphur was flammable. They mixed it with saltpeter to control its volatility by causing partial combustion, a process called "controlling sulphur."[10] They found that by adding charcoal

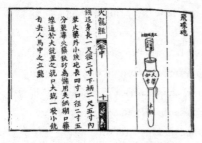

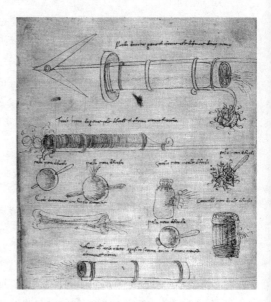

Left: The Wei Yuan Cannon and a similar mountable mobile cannon.

Right: Drawings of cannon balls and petards featured in the Sienese engineers' treatises on warfare.

to the saltpeter-sulphur mix, they could cause an explosion. Armorers then worked on the proportions to obtain the most explosive mixture.

The development of gunpowder in China went hand in hand with the development of firearms. During the Northern Song (A.D. 960–1127), Emperor Zhanzon (also known as Chao Heng) set up China's first arms factory, employing some forty thousand workers. Three different types of gunpowder were perfected: one for cannon, another for fireballs, and another for poisoned smoke bombs.[11] The ratio of saltpeter to sulfur and charcoal varied for each type. Perhaps the most famous weapon developed during the Northern Song was the fire gun, the precursor of modern firearms. The Yuan emperors deployed these weapons in the thirteenth century in central Asia.

China had invented flamethrowers by A.D. 975. Here is a description of a battle on the Yangtze presented by Shih Hsu Pai in his book *Talks at Fisherman's Rock*:

Chu Lung-Pin as Admiral was attacked by the Sung emperor's forces in strength. Chu was in command of a large warship more than ten decks high, with flags flying and drums beating. The imperial ships were smaller but they came down the river attacking fiercely, and the arrows flew so fast that the ships under Admiral Chu were like porcupines. Chu hardly knew what to do. So he quickly projected petrol from flame-throwers to destroy the enemy. The Sung forces could not have withstood this, but all of a sudden a north wind sprang up and swept the smoke and flames over the sky towards his own ships and men. As many as 150,000 soldiers and sailors caught in this are overwhelmed, whereupon Chu, being overcome with grief, flung himself into the flames and died.[12]

Excavations of Kublai Khan's fleet, which was wrecked in 1281 by a *kamikaze* wind off Takashima, Japan, have revealed that the fleet was armed with exploding mortar bombs. The Chinese used this weapon against the Mongols in 1232 in the siege of the northern capital, Kaifeng. Chinese history tells us:

Among the weapons of the defenders there was the heaven-shaking thunder crash bomb. It consisted of gunpowder put into an iron container; then when the fuse was lit and the projectile shot off there was a great explosion the noise whereof was like thunder, audible for more than a hundred li [about forty miles] and the vegetation was scorched and blasted by the heat over an area of more than half a mou [many acres]. When hit, even iron armour was quite pierced through.[13]

Rockets and gunpowder missiles had been known since 1264. In his thirteenth-century book *Customs and Institutions of the Old Capital,* Chou describes gunpowder weapons. "Some of these were like wheels and revolving things, others like comets and others again shooting along the surface of the water."[14]

Gunpowder was used in celebrations, as well, though not always with the intended results. Here is Robert Temple's account of the empress's retirement party at the Imperial Palace in 1264. "A display of fireworks was given in the courtyard. One of these, of the 'ground rat' type went straight to the steps of the throne of the Emperor's Mother, and gave her quite a fright. She stood up in anger, gathered her skirts around her, and stopped the feast."[15]

By Zheng He's era, China had acquired centuries of experience in producing all manner of gunpowder weapons. Zheng He's fleets were armed with rockets that sent sprays of burning paper and gunpowder to set fire to the enemies' sails; grenades soaked in poison; mortars packed with chemicals and human excrement; shells filled with iron bolts to scythe men to pieces; archers with flaming arrows; sea mines to protect his ships; flamethrowers to incinerate the opposition; and rocket batteries to terrify them. Heaven help their enemies![16]

Europeans could hardly have failed to notice this terrifying armory when they met Zheng He's fleets, whether in Calicut, Cairo, Alexandria, Venice, or The Hague.

The first European books on gunpowder weapons were published in about 1440, one by an anonymous Hussite engineer, the second by the Venetian Giovanni Fontana, and the third by our old friend Mariano di Jacopo ditto Taccola.

Fontana described and illustrated many machines, which he called "innovations of impiety no less than genius." He marveled that so much explosive force could be generated by such a weak powder.[17] *Ex quibus est orrida machina quam bombardam appellamus ad dirvendam omnem fortem dvrittiem etiam marmoream turrem non minus impietatis quam ingenii fuisse existimo qui primo adinvenerit tantam vim habeat a pusillo pulvere."[18]*

By the time Fontana's book was published, some gunpowder weapons had already been used in Italy, including rockets at the battle of Chioggia in 1380. It could have been mere coincidence that his book appeared shortly after Zheng He's visit to Venice. However, Fontana's *Liber de omnibus rebus naturalibus* throws out a number of other clues.

First, he exhibited knowledge of America forty years before Columbus "discovered" it. Describing the Atlantic, he wrote, *"Et ab eius occasu finitur pro parte etiam terra incognita"* (In the west the Atlantic is bordered by an unknown land).[19]

Second, he knew of Australia two centuries before Tasman. Fontana wrote that "recent cosmographs and especially those who owe their information to true experience and distant travel and diligent navigation have found beyond the equinoctial circle to the south (south of 23°20 S) a notable habitable region not covered by water and many famous islands."[20]

Third, he exhibited a solid knowledge of the Indian Ocean forty years before Vasco da Gama's exploration of the area. Taking the evidence as a whole—that Zheng He's gunners would have used all the machines described in Fontana's book and would have carried many of them aboard, that Fontana's book was published in Venice shortly after Zheng He's squadron reached Venice, and that Fontana knew of America, the Indian Ocean, and Australia, all at that time unknown to Europeans, it seems to me reasonable to assume that Fontana gained his knowledge of many gunpowder weapons from Zheng He's gunners.

Taccola provides corroborative evidence. He introduced Europe to a Chinese innovation from the early 1400s—a derivation of arsenic to improve the power of gunpowder. As Needham writes:

> *München Codex 197* is a composite work, the notebook of a military engineer writing in German, the Anonymous Hussite, and that of an Italian, probably Marianus Jacobus Taccola, writing in Latin; it contains dates such as + 1427, +1438 and + 1441. It gives gunpowder formulae and describes guns with accompanying illustrations. A curious feature, very Chinese (cf. pp. 114, 361), is the addition of arsenic sulphides to the powder; this dates from fire-lance days but probably had the effect of making it more brisant, hence it could have been useful in bombs and grenades. The +15th century Paris MS, supposedly before +1453, *De Re Militari,* perhaps by Paolo Santini, shows a gun on a carriage with a shield at the front, mortars shooting incendiary "bombs" almost vertically to nearby targets, a bombard with a tail (cebotane or tiller), and with a mounted man holding a small gun with a burning match.[21]

Florentines now had steel and gunpowder to enable them to make bombards and cannons, which Francesco di Giorgio quickly put to good use.

Francesco di Giorgio

In the 1430s and 1440s, the gunpowder weapons drawn by Fontana and Taccola had not yet been "invented." However, that changed over the next forty years, as we know from the records of Francesco di Giorgio regarding the siege of Castellina in August 1478. The Pazzis, backed by Pope Sixtus V, had initiated an armed uprising against the Medicis in Florence. The north of Italy was soon ablaze. Southerners seized their chance and marched on Tuscany. Francesco was appointed to defend the Tuscan cities.[22]

Here is Weller's description of the Neapolitan siege of Colle val d'Elsa, a hill town near Florence:

This terrifying prototype "dragon torpedo" would have smashed and sunk enemy boats without mercy.

This European dragon kite does not seem so frightening!

Duke Federigo had with him for siege purposes five bombards with most terrifying names, such as "Cruel," "Desperate," "Victory," "Ruin" and "No nonsense Here" and which, without doubt, were beautifully decorated, as was the fashion with the Italian cannon at this time: they discharged great balls of stone weighing 370–380 pounds, and their own weight was considerable, the tubes, when nine feet long weighed some 14,000 pounds and the tail 11,000, so that it required more than one hundred pairs of buffaloes to drag them into position

The art of casting these early cannons in two portions, the tube and the tail, was pursued in Siena; and though they might not have had much effect on the result of a modern battle, at this time they were a formidable novelty. Francesco di Giorgio in the siege of Castellina (Aug 14–18, 1478) planted a battery of these Sienese and Papal bombards.[23]

Francesco's cannons are illustrated in the Institute and Museum of the History of Science, Florence.[24] Below them is a print of the "thousand

The Chinese may not have invented trebuchets, but they were certainly in widespread use by the fourteenth century.

Di Giorgio's detailed treatise on machines of war included many trebuchets.

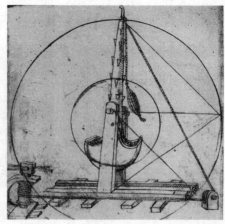

ball thunder cannon," 1300–1350.[25] Taccola's and di Giorgio's drawings are accompanied by the weapons that were fired—exploding missiles and powder kegs.

The Chinese had dozens of illustrations of exploding missiles and powder kegs in the *Huo Lung Chung* published circa 1421; and in the *Wu Ching Tsung Yao*, a Sung dynasty manual originally of 1044 updated in 1412. The "bamboo fire kite" and "iron beaked firebird," incendiary projectors and "thunderclap bomb" from the *Wu Ching Tsung Yao*, and the bone-burning and bruising fire-oil magic bomb from the *Huo Lung Chung* are shown beside di Giorgio's projectiles.

Another interesting similarity between di Giorgio's designs and the Chinese gunpowder cannon may be seen in the curious bulbous shapes of both. Di Giorgio illustrated five different types of bombard in MS Palatino 767 (BNCF p. 163). This curious vase shape is shown in the

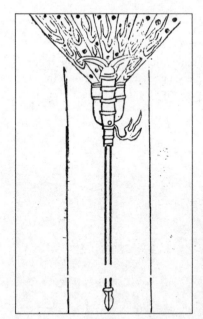

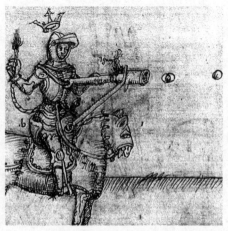

Chinese mastery of gunpowder led to the development of many effective and deadly weapons.

Taccola's fire lances do not seem so fierce!

Huo Lung Chung.[26] At that stage, the Chinese had not yet mastered making steel strong enough to cope with the expansion of gas in the explosion chamber once the gunpowder was ignited. The bulbous shape allowed for thicker metal than in the barrel.

By 1400, the early Ming era, this problem had been solved, enabling the Chinese to produce "thousand ball thunder cannon,"[27] which Francesco copied in his later drawings.[28] Francesco's cannons have beautiful embellishments. However, remove the embellishments, and what remains is the shape of Chinese cannons.

Gunpowder, steel, cannons, and explosive shells were not the only weapons that Taccola, Francesco, and Fontana copied from the Chinese. Within a generation after the Chinese visit of 1434, Florentines were using a variety of Chinese methods to smelt iron and were using Chinese-designed gunpowder to produce exploding shells from cannons identical in design to their Chinese counterparts.

Chinese naval technology had been far superior to that of Europe's for centuries.

An armored boat as featured in a military treatise penned in 15th-century Italy.

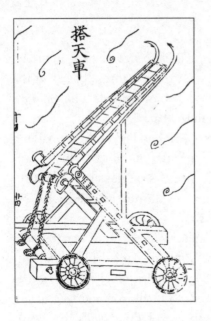

Left: Chinese mobile siege ladders and offensive weaponry.

Right: Di Giorgio's illustration of mobile siege ladders.

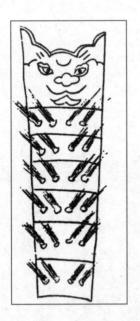
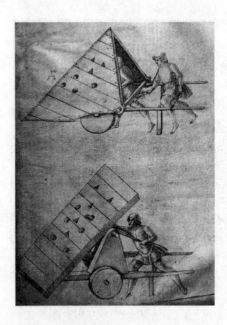

Left: Chinese mobile shields could be effective when both attacking
and defending positions.

Right: Di Giorgio's shields were not as visually arresting.

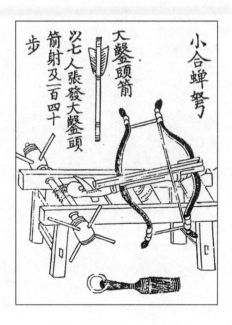
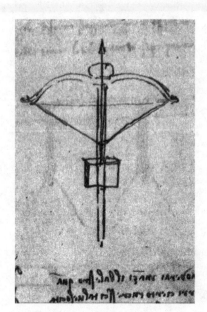

Left: Illustrations of crossbows from the *Nung Shu*.

Right: One of Leonardo's three illustrations of crossbows.

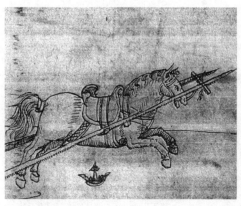

Left: Chinese horses and oxen could become dangerous weapons!

Right: Compare Taccola's drawings—they are strikingly similar.

Both the Chinese and the Europeans used fire-bearing animals to devastating effect.

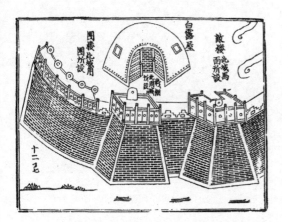

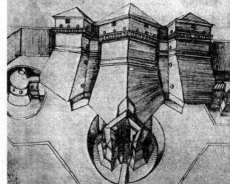

Left: An impregnable border fortress.

Right: A similar fortress by di Giorgio, from his treatise on architecture and machines.

20

PRINTING

T here are many definitions of printing. The one I have adopted is "a process in which ink is set on paper by physical or chemical means." There are four principal methods by which this may be achieved: copper plate, in which the words are engraved on the metal and filled with ink; lithography, a chemical method using the repulsion between grease and water; xylography, or block printing, in which the subject is first carved on a wooden block, which is then coated with ink; and typography, or moveable type printing, in which a separate wooden block is carved for each character or letter.[1]

There is no dispute that block and moveable type printing were invented in China. The Cultural China Series, *Ancient Chinese Inventions,* explains its evolution:

Block printing was probably invented between the Sui and Tang dynasties, based on the technique of transferring texts and pictures cut in relief on seals and stone pillars to other surfaces that was developed in the Spring and Autumn and Warring States periods. The invention of paper and improvement of ink led to the advance of block printing. . . .

Movable type printing was then invented [by] Bi Sheng (*c.* 1051). . . In his *Mengxi Bitan* (Dream Pool Essays), Shen Kuo writes about Bi's moveable type printing . . . made of a mixture of clay and glue hardened by baking. He composed texts by placing the types side by side on an iron plate coated with a mixture of resin, wax, and paper ash. Gently heating this plate and pressing the types with a smooth plate to ensure they are on the same level, and then letting the plate cool, and the type was solidified. Once the impression had been made, the type could be detached by reheating the plate. Bi prepared two iron plates to be used in turn to speed up the whole printing process. He also prepared different numbers of types for characters according to their frequency of use in texts, and arranged them in an orderly way to facilitate composing. Shen noted that this technique was most efficient in printing several hundred or several thousand copies.

After Bi Sheng, other people invented types cut out of wood. In about 1313 Wang Zhen, an agronomist of the Yuan Dynasty, printed his work *Nung Shu* (Treatise on Agriculture) with movable wood types, and wrote about his innovation in an appendix to the treatise. He also invented horizontal compartmented cases that revolved about a vertical axis to permit easier handling of the type. Wang tested his technique, and printed in a month one hundred copies of the 60,000-character *Jing doe Xianzhi* (Jingde County Annals), which was quite a remarkable achievement at that time.[2]

The Development of Printing in the Early Ming Dynasty

According to Joseph Needham:

Ming printing was distinguished by the extended scope of its subject matter and by its technical innovations and artistic refinement. In contrast to that of previous periods, the printing under the Ming included not only the traditional works in classics, history, religion and literary collections but also such new subjects or fields as popular novels, music, industrial arts, accounts of ocean voyages, shipbuilding and scientific treatises from the West, which had never before been seen in print in China. . . .

Ming printers introduced metal typography, improved the multicolour process of block printing, refined the woodcut for book illustrations and used xylography for facsimile reproductions of old editions.[3]

Needham also registered the monumental contributions of Zhu Di. Between 1405 and 1431, Zhu Di assembled a team of three thousand scholars to compile the *Yongle Dadian,* an encyclopedia of a scale and scope unparalleled in history. This gigantic work included a huge amount of information garnered from Zheng He's voyages and included a total of 22,937 passages extracted from more than 7,000 titles from classics, history, philosophy, literature, religion, drama, industrial arts, and agriculture. It was a work of 50 million characters bound in 11,095 volumes, each sixteen inches high and ten inches wide. This massive endeavor was deposited in the Imperial Library in the Forbidden City when it was inaugurated in 1421.

It is generally accepted that moveable block printing reached Europe from China at about the same time that Zheng He's ambassador reached Florence in 1434. There seem to be three principal contenders for the distinction of being the first European to use moveable block printing, the claimants being Laurens Janszoon Coster, Johannes Gutenberg, and an unknown printer in Venice or Florence.

Laurens Jonszoon Coster's Claim

In the center of old Haarlem on the North Sea coast of Holland stands a substantial house just across the square from the Great Church. On its walls the curious may view this inscription:

MEMORIAE SACRUM

TYPOGRAPHIA

ARS ARTIUM OMNIUM

CONSERVATIX

HIC PRIMUM INVENTA

CIRCA ANNUM MCCCCXL

(In sacred memory of typography, the preserver of all other arts, first invented here about the year 1440).[4]

The adherents of Coster, the subject of this inscription, say that he was walking in the woods between 1420 and 1440 when he cut bark from a tree and formed it into mirror images of letters, which he pinned together to print words on paper. His son-in-law helped him to experiment with different inks to improve the quality of the print. Next he carved out pictures and explained them in words. His first printed book was said to be *Spieghel onzer Behoudenisse* (Mirror of our salvation). The papers were printed on one side, and the blank sides were pasted together to form the page. Junius, centuries later, recounts what happened next: "The new invention thrived because of the readiness with which the people bought the novel product. Apprentices were taken on—the beginning of misfortune, for amongst them was a certain Johann. . . . This Johann, after he had learned the art of casting types and combining them—in fact the whole trade—took the first available opportunity of Christmas Eve, when everyone was in Church, to steal the whole type supply with the tools and all the equipment of his master."[5]

The story continues that Johann went first to Amsterdam, then to Cologne, and finally to Mainz, where he opened a printing establishment. Gutenberg financed Johann and eventually acquired his business.

Gutenberg's Claim

Gutenberg was some thirty years younger than Coster. He was born in 1398, of Frielo Gensfleisch (gooseflesh) and Elsa Gutenberg (good hill). In those days, sons could take their mother's maiden name if there was a possibility of the name dying out.[6]

Gutenberg's claim to primacy was carefully examined by Blaise Agüera y Arcas and Paul Needham of Princeton University. They have found by computer analysis that the Gutenberg Bible was not set from moveable type, nor were a dozen of Gutenberg's other early books. If these scholars are correct, Gutenberg's claim is demolished.[7]

The Venetian Claim

Here is a translation of the Venetian Senate decree of October 11, 1441 (prior to Gutenberg):

> Whereas, the art and mystery of making cards and printed figures, which is
> in use at Venice has fallen to decay, and this is in consequence of the great
> quantity of printed playing cards and coloured figures, which are made out-
> side Venice, to which evil it is necessary to apply some remedy in order that
> the said artists who are a great many in family, may find encouragement
> rather than foreigners: let it be ordained and established according to the peti-
> tion that the said Masters have sought, that from this time on, no work of the
> said art that is printed or painted on cloth or paper—that is to say, altar
> pieces, or images, or playing cards or any other thing that may be made by the
> said art, either by painting or by printing—shall be allowed to be brought or
> imported . . . and [if so a fine of] thirty livres and twelve soldi, of which fine
> one third shall go to the State, one third to Giustizieri Vecci, to whom this
> affair is commited and one third to the accuser.[8]

The references above suggest that Venetians had, prior to 1441, been applying the art of printing and colored stenciling for many purposes. After 1441 Venice rapidly became Europe's center of printing. By 1469, the German printer Johann von Speyer had printed an edition of 100 copies of Cicero's *Epistolae ad Familiares*. By 1478, there were twenty-two printing firms operating in Venice, which had printed 72 editions. By 1518, more than 600 editions had been produced. By the turn of the century, this had expanded to 150 presses and 4,000 editions. At this time, books were being published in Latin, Italian, Greek, Hebrew, Arabic, Serbo-Croatian, and Armenian. Venice's low tax rates for foreign firms and the opportunities for profit offered by this great trading city contributed to Venice's rise as printing capital of Europe.[9]

It stands to reason that Zheng He's ambassadors would have made considerable efforts to impart knowledge of printing to Venice. Without printing, the Xuan De astronomical calendar would have had to be copied by hand. The stupid barbarians would inevitably have made mistakes, and those mistakes would have multiplied as copy succeeded copy. Not only would they mess up the calculations of latitude and longitude, but their copies of Chinese maps of the world would grow progressively more inaccurate. To avoid such confusion, it made sense to give the barbarians the knowledge of moveable type printing, along with the astronomical tables and maps. The Chinese could then be confident that Europeans could reach the Middle Kingdom to pay tribute—no further excuses!

The gift of moveable type proved to be of inestimable value apart from its use in cartography and ocean navigation. Printing helped Europeans control the spread of plague by disseminating instructions for combating it. Venice printed edicts in 1456 and 1457, Genoa in 1467, Milan in 1468. Others followed in Siena, Parma, Udine, and Cremona.[10] Plague legislation for the poor came next. Prostitutes were outlawed in Perugia and Siena in 1485, and plague hospitals were set up. Printing was critical to public health.

The Renaissance was not only a revolution in art. It altered European man's idea of his place in the universe, in astronomy, logic, geometry, architecture, engineering, mechanics, anatomy, philosophy, politics, warfare, and music. The printing of books did not produce new ideas. But the introduction of moveable type enabled revolutionary ideas to be spread the length and breadth of Europe.

Printing revolutionized the development of music, too. Musicians could now play together reading from the same score—precisely what the composer had written. The complex music pioneered by the Englishman Dunstable was made possible by the score he wrote for multiple voices. Copying such a score by hand would have been a nightmare. Johann Sebastian Bach completed Dunstable's revolution.

Printing also advanced the voyages of discovery. Knowledge, including Chinese knowledge, could now be made available to numerous explorers. Subsequent explorers' discoveries and exploits could in turn be publicized far and wide. And the romance of exploration fired the imaginations of the people. *The Amadis of Gaul*, relating the imagined adventures of the conquistadores of the New World, gripped public imagination with its tales of flaxen-haired, white-skinned virgins, rubies the size of pigeon's eggs, and men sheathed from head to toe in gold.

Thanks to printing, shipwrights could build to a standard, proven design. Before printing, each ship had been constructed as a copy—a one-off experimental vessel dependent in part on the skill of the copier, a scribe. The firearms and cannons that armed the vessels could now also be made from printed designs that had been tried and tested—a ship master no longer needed to worry whether the barrels of his cannon were sufficiently thick and of suitable iron to avoid an explosion that would kill his own crew. Gun makers could now sell their designs. Ships' captains could sail with printed ephemeris tables enabling them to determine latitude and longitude and their progress to the New World using up-to-date, standardized charts.

The skills of medieval Arab and Chinese doctors could now be disseminated worldwide. For example, by the eleventh century, Chinese doctors understood how to inoculate patients against smallpox. The first Chinese book on forensic medicine, including plague control, was published in 1247.

The extraordinary magnitude and generosity of Chinese gifts to the West made sense from the Chinese emperor's viewpoint. If China was to remain a colossus on the world stage, the barbarians must be bribed and educated to continually render tribute. This voyage, however, proved to be the last. After that, China withdrew into self-imposed isolation. Europe, left to exploit China's lavish gifts, soon became mistress of the world.

CHINA'S CONTRIBUTION
TO THE RENAISSANCE

Maps of the World

After 1434, European world maps changed. There was a shift away from the circular maps centered on Jerusalem, emphasizing religious subjects, to depictions of the world as it really is.

Toscanelli sent Columbus a map of the Americas; Regiomontanus advertised a world map for sale.[1] Magellan possessed a world map. Andrea Bianco showed Florida on his Atlantic chart of 1436 (Newberry Library, Chicago); on his 1448 map, he described Brazil. Then, in 1507, Waldseemüller published his amazing world map accurately rendering North and South America.

All of these maps had something in common: they accurately depicted parts of the New World before Europeans ever reached those parts. The Waldseemüller showed the Pacific before Magellan set sail, Andrea Bianco showed Florida and Antilia fifty-six years before Columbus; the Cantino planisphere of 1502 depicted the Florida coast before Ponce de León "discovered" the place.

There is something else these maps had in common. All are copies in whole or in part of Zheng He's 1418 map. It was a logical and deliberate policy of Zheng He's mission to distribute Chinese maps of the world. For if the barbarians did not have accurate maps, how could they reach the Middle Kingdom to pay tribute?

At the Nanjing conference on Zheng He held in December 2002, Professor Liu Manchum described his research into judicial records of the early Ming dynasty, notably those of Fujian Province.[2] He came across an account of a Brazilian delegation that had reached Fujian in 1507, after a five-year voyage. The delegation bore expensive tribute, notably emeralds, and had their plenipotentiary powers engraved on a golden plate. They had found their way to China by means of a map.

Professor Liu Manchum realized that, at the time the Brazilian delegation left Brazil for China in 1502, Europeans had not reached both Brazil and China by sea.[3] Consequently, the map that guided them from Brazil to China could not have been European. He then searched Zheng He's records and found accounts of his fleets reaching the Americas. He concluded that Zheng He's fleets had reached Brazil before 1434, after which Chinese overseas voyages were prohibited by the emperor. Professor Manchum intended to write a book claiming that Zheng He, not Columbus, discovered the Americas. He then learned of my book *1421* and decided to postpone his own.

Brazil also appears on a Javanese map published before Europeans reached Java. In an April, 1512–letter to King Manuel of Portugal, Alfonso de Albuquerque, the first European to reach Malacca, refers to a world map he has acquired from a Javanese pilot and kept aboard his flagship, the *Fiore de la Mar*. (The *Fiore de la Mar* sank before reaching Portugal.):

I am also sending you an authentic portion of a great map belonging to a Javanese pilot, which shows the Cape of Good Hope, Portugal and the territory of Brasil, the Red Sea and the Persian Gulf and the Spice Islands. It also shows where the Chinese and the Gores sail, with the Rhumbs and the routes taken by their ships and the interiors of the various kingdoms and which kingdoms border on which. It strikes me as the finest piece of work I ever saw and I am sure Your Highness would be delighted to see it. The names were written in Javanese script and I found a Javanese who could read and write the script. I send your Highness this fragment that Francisco Rodrigues copied from the original, in which Your Highness will see where the Chinese and the Gores really come from and the route your ships should follow to reach the spice islands, where the gold mines are located and the islands of Java and Banda, where nutmeg and mace come from and the territory of the King of Siam. You will see the extent of Chinese navigation and where they return to and the point beyond which they will not sail. The main part of the map is lost in the *Fiori de la Mar*. I worked out the meaning of this map with the pilot Pero de Alfoim so that they would be able to explain it to Your Highness. You may take this portion of it as very authentic and accurate because it shows the routes they take in both directions. It does not show the archipelago called Celate which lies between Java and Malacca.

Your Highness's creature and servant, Alfonso de Albuquerque, Caesar of the East.[4]

Albuquerque does not find it necessary to point out that when Europeans first reached the East, the Javanese (and the Chinese) already knew the locations of Portugal and Brazil on a world chart. His letter reveals details of the interiors of kingdoms, implying authentic knowledge. Manuel Stock, to whom I am indebted for this information, has also found a reference to Brazil on a map dated 1447.[5] The Duchess of Medina Sidonia's Library at Sanlucar de Barrameda has maps of Brazil before Dias or Cabral.

In addition to their knowledge of Brazil and a route to the Spice Islands—before European explorers set off for such places—both the Venetians and the Portuguese knew of Australia by 1516 at the latest. Giovanni di Fontana, the Venetian doctor, in 1450 already knew of Australia, the Indian Ocean, and America.[6]

The National Library of Australia holds a letter, dated 1516, written by a Venetian, Andrea Corsali, who had traveled aboard a Portuguese ship. The letter, written from Cochin, is addressed to the doge of Venice. Corsali describes his voyage around the Cape of Good Hope as far as New Guinea and Timor. He illustrates the Southern Cross with sufficient accuracy to prove he must have seen it. The letter asserts that the Portuguese knew of large lands to the south called India Australis (Southern), later referred to as Java la Grande.

Professor Jaime Cortesão, in "The Pre-Columbian Discovery of America," describes the first Portuguese voyage to Brazil and includes a report to King John of Portugal. The King is advised to "please command that they bring you the world map of Pedro Vaz Bisagudo. And Your Highness will be able to see on it the position of this land. Notwithstanding this map does not declare whether this land [Brazil] is inhabited or not. It is an old world-map, but the Mina is registered there."[7]

So here we have a declaration that Brazil was on a world map before the first European expedition there. This squares with Brazil's appearance on Andrea Bianco's map of 1448 and is further proof that the Southern and Western Hemispheres were documented on maps long before European voyages of exploration started.

If, as I claim, Zheng He's 1434 visit provided maps of the world to the barbarians in order to enable them to pay tribute, then the Venetians and the Portuguese would have had knowledge of the New World by 1434.[8] And if the Venetians knew of the New World by 1434, we would expect them to have set sail for it shortly thereafter.

The voyage that is generally accepted as the first to Canada was the ill-fated expedition of Miguel Côrte-Real in 1502. Côrte-Real reached the Gulf of Saint Lawrence. When he arrived there, however, his sailors found a gilded sword hilt and silver trinkets of Venetian manufacture at a native village in Labrador.[9]

Croatian Voyages West

In 1434, the Venetian Empire was at its peak. Venice controlled the Croatian coast. Dalmatian sailors crewed Venetian ships, and Venetian pilots were trained at Perast (see chapters 7 and 13). According to Croatian archives, which Louis Adamic describes in a 1972 publication of *Svetu Magazine*,[10] several Croatian merchant vessels foundered off the Carolina coast in 1449. They were said to be sailing to China via America.

Adamic's search of Croatian archives commenced following conversations with senior citizens who told him of ancestral traditions that Croatians had sailed across the Atlantic in ancient times. The brief account mentioned that three of the five vessels in the expedition were left stranded near Chesapeake Bay; the other two ships sailed back to Dubrovnik. Unfortunately, war with Turkey prevented a relief expedition. Charles Prazak believes the survivors joined the Powhatan tribe and gave their name to Croatan Island.

The crew of a Croatian caravel, *Atlante,* sailed across the Atlantic Ocean and found land in 1484 (Sinovic, 1991). According to historian Charles Prazak, archives reported in *Zajecnicar* (Dec. 2, 1979) tell of several Croatian vessels carrying refugees from Turkish invasions who reached the Carolinas near Roanoke Island in 1470. Prazak (1993) and Sinovic (1991, p. 153) believe these survivors merged with native Algokian tribes and made significant contribution to their culture and language. They have identified the name of one native tribe the Croatoans and an Isle in Cape Hatteras, Croatoan Isle, as derivatives of the Croatian language. . . .

In 1880, historian Hamilton McMillan noted that "Croatoan Indians have traditions which are tied to the individuals, the owners of the destroyed ships from the past."

This story is repeated in the East when Dalmatian ships accompanied the Chinese back to the East and "discovered" a number of Pacific islands to which they gave Dalmatian names—names that were changed to Spanish and Portuguese ones after the First World War.

As noted in my book *1421,* Columbus, Magellan, Albuquerque and Cabral all acknowledged that they had possessed charts of the Caribbean islands, South America, the Pacific, and Brazil, respectively. Toscanelli had sent Columbus a chart following his meeting with the Chinese delegation. Columbus's records, which were acquired by the family of the duchess of Medina-Sidonia, provide ample evidence that Columbus had voyaged to the Americas before 1492.[11] Dr. Marino Ruggiero's book, cites evidence that the pope financed a Columbus voyage to the Americas before 1485.[12]

All of the above confirms that the Venetians and the Portuguese understood world geography after 1434 and before European voyages of exploration started. Surely they received this information from the Chinese.

Zheng He's delegation also provided astronomical knowledge to Alberti, Regiomontanus, and Toscanelli, which Regiomontanus incorporated into his ephemeris tables and Alberti used for multiple purposes. Regiomontanus's tables were issued to Portuguese navigators in 1474 and later to Columbus and Vespucci, who used them to calculate longitude. These tables also enabled sailors to calculate latitude at the meridian passage of the sun by using declination tables. This method was successfully applied by Dias, who accurately determined the latitude of the Cape of Good Hope at 35°20 S.[13]

So not only did Zheng He's delegation show the way to the New World but they provided Europeans with the knowledge to enable them to calculate their latitude and longitude to reach the New World and return home safely.

The transfer of knowledge went further than maps. Nicholas of Cusa was the first European to blow apart Aristotelean and Ptolomaic theories of the universe. He revolutionized knowledge by postulating that the sun, not the earth, was at the center of the solar system, that the earth and planets traveled in an elliptical orbit around it. To reach this conclusion, I submit that both Nicholas of Cusa and Toscanelli used the Chinese astronomical calendar that Zheng He's delegation presented to Pope Eugenius IV.

Regiomontanus's ephemeris tables, with the positions of sun, moon, the five planets, and the stars, contained no information that was not already in the Chinese astronomical calendar, the *Shoushi*. In the forty years after the Chinese visit of 1434, knowledge of the universe was changed as fundamentally as knowledge of the earth.

As Professor Zinner explains, Copernicus could have learned about and been influenced by Regiomontanus. Copernicus studied at the Jagiellonian University in Cracow (1491–1494) and then in Italy, mostly in Bologna (1496–1503).[14] At that time, Cracow was the European university where the teachings of Regiomontanus had gained the surest foothold.[15] Copernicus's interest in sine tables may have been inspired by Regiomontanus's *Tabulae diretorium*, which was printed in 1490 and later found in Cracow.

Zinner describes the connection:

> Copernicus also came under the influence of Regiomontanus in Bologna. Here he obtained Regiomontanus Ephemerides and the Epitome and was presumeably motivated by them to test the Ptolemaic system by observations. And so the same thing happened with Copernicus in 1497 as had happened 40 years earlier with Regiomontanus. By observations, they determined errors and felt compelled to get to the root of these errors.
>
> The similarity goes even further. Both men were busy with extensive sine tables necessary for precise calculations with observational instruments, and—most importantly—both created their own new trigonometry, as the prevailing mathematics was insufficient for their needs.[16]

The use of sine tables and spherical trigonometry to meet the need for precise calculations with observational instruments had all been developed by Guo Shoujing two centuries earlier. Yet Guo Shoujing is not mentioned in European biographies of famous mathematicians.[17]

Zinner continues: (p 184)

> If Copernicus had so many inspirations from Regiomontanus, then it is very likely that he learned through Novara of Regiomontanus' plans for transforming the prevailing planetary theory, and so encouraged him in his own undertaking. . . .
>
> We have to be content with the fact that it is impossible to determine the full scope of Regiomontanus' achievements. His was a gigantic undertaking, intended to be crowned with a planetary theory. In the course of his work he abandoned the prevailing cosmology and was preparing to formulate a new one for the new times. He had the astronomical and mathematical tools to make such a new cosmology; but his efforts were destroyed by an implacable fate [death].[18]

Copernicus's theory "attributed to the earth a daily motion around its own axis and a yearly motion around the stationary sun." He fol-

CHINA'S CONTRIBUTION TO THE RENAISSANCE

lowed Nicholas of Cusa in advancing an idea that had far-reaching implications for modern science. Henceforth, the earth could no longer be considered the center of the cosmos; rather it was one celestial body among many, its orbit subject to mathematical prediction.

Professor Zinner did not know of Guo Shoujing's work. In my submission, we can go further. Did Copernicus directly copy Regiomontanus in proposing his revolutionary theory that the earth and the planets circled the sun and that the sun, not the earth, was at the center of the solar system?

I say he did, and I base my argument on the research of Noel M. Swerdlow, assistant professor of history at the University of Chicago, presented in "The Derivation and First Draft of Copernicus' Planetary Theory"[19]

In his tightly reasoned article, Professor Swerdlow starts with an interesting comment Copernicus made to the pope at the time he published his revolutionary work, *De revolutionibus orbium coelestieum*, in 1543. Copernicus told Pope Paul III of his great reluctance to publish this theory—that the earth was not the center of the cosmos but one celestial body among many—for fear of ridicule by the public. He explained that he had been reluctant "not for just nine years but already in the fourth nine year period—that is," since about 1504, a time after Copernicus had obtained Regiomontanus's *Ephemeris* and *Epitome* in Bologna.

Between 1510 and 1514 Copernicus summarized his new ideas in *De hypothesibus motuum coelestium e se constitutis commentariolus* (A commentary on the theories of the motions of heavenly objects from their arrangements). Its main parts, to quote the *New Encyclopaedia Britannica,* were "the apparent daily motion of the stars, the annual motion of the sun, and the retrogressive behaviour of the planets results from the earth's daily rotation on its axis and yearly revolution around the sun, which is stationary at the centre of the planetary system. The earth therefore is not the centre of the universe but only of the moon's orbit."

To quote Professor Swerdlow, Copernicus, in his *De commentariolus,* says next to nothing about how he arrived at his new theories. He begins with a single principle governing planetary theory, and then raises objections to the theories of his predecessors. Next he explains that he has evolved a planetary theory in conformity with his first principles, and this is followed by a set of seven postulates. These have almost nothing to do with either the principle or the objections, but instead assert the surprising theory that the earth and planets revolve around the sun and give some further consequences of this theory.[20]

Professor Swerdlow continues: (p. 425)

The sources of Copernicus' early planetary theory are relatively few. The derivation for the models for both first and second anomalies and almost the entire contents of the commentariolus seem to depend on three certain and two possible sources. They are the following:

1. Peurbach. . . .

2. Peurbach and Regiomontanus, *The Epitome of the Almagest*. This was begun by Peurbach, who had written the first six books at the time of his death in 1461, and completed by Regiomontanus in 1462 or 1463. . . . I suspect that Regiomontanus not only wrote books VII–XIII of the *Epitome* but also revised Peurbach's version of Books I to VI. . . . This was the book (the *Epitome*) that Copernicus followed even in preference to the *Almagest* in the writing of *De revolutionibus* which is filled with not only information and procedures, but even with close paraphrases from the *Epitome*. In the *Commentariolus* the use of the *Epitome* can be seen most clearly in the section on the length of the tropical and sidereal year and the rate of precession, but, as will often be pointed out in the commentary, the *Epitome* is pertinent to many parts of the *Commentariolus*. Of greater importance for our purpose however are Propositions 1 and 2 of Book XII [by Regiomontanus] which contain **the analysis leading to the heliocentric theory.** . . . The importance of the *Epitome* . . . cannot be overemphasised, nor can its virtues be sufficiently praised . . . the *Epitome* makes one realise what a loss Regiomontanus's early death was to astronomy—a loss not made up for well over a century.[21]

So there we have it—in Professor Swerdlow's opinion Copernicus followed book 11 of Regiomontanus's *Epitome,* which contained the analysis leading to Copernicus's revolutionary theory.

To quote again from the *New Encyclopedia Britannica*:

The Copernican system appealed to a large number of independent-minded astronomers and mathematicians. Its attraction was not only because of its elegance but also in part because of its break with traditional doctrines. In particular, it opposed Aristotle, who had argued cogently for the fixity of the Earth; furthermore it provided an alternative to Ptolemy's geocentric universe. In Western Christendom both these views had been elevated almost to the level of religious dogma; to many thoughtful observers, however, they stifled development and were overdue for rejection.

Scientifically the Copernican theory demanded two important changes in outlook. The first change had to do with the apparent size of the universe. The stars always appeared in precisely the same fixed positions, but if the earth were in orbit around the sun, they should display a small periodic change. Copernicus explained the starry sphere was too far distant for the change to be detected. His theory thus led to the belief in a much larger universe than previously conceived . . .

The second change concerned the reasons why bodies fall to the ground. Aristotle had taught they fall to their "natural place" which was the centre of the universe. But because, according to the heliocentric theory, the Earth no longer coincided with the centre of the universe, a new explanation was needed. This re-examination of the laws governing falling bodies led eventually to the Newtonian concept of universal gravitation.

The dethronement of the Earth from the centre of the universe caused profound shock. No longer could the earth be considered the epitome of creation, for it was only a planet like the other planets. No longer was the earth the centre of all change and decay with the changeless universe accompanying it. And the belief in a correspondence between man, the microcosm, as a mirror of the surrounding universe, the macrocosm, was no longer valid. The successful challenge to the entire system of ancient authority required a complete change in man's philosophical conception of the universe. This is what is rightly called "the Copernican Revolution."

Is it rightly called? Or should it be the Regiomontanus or Guo Shoujing revolution?

Johannes Kepler (1571–1630)

Johannes Kepler is today best known for his three laws of planetary motion. His first law stated that the planets traveled around the sun in elliptical orbits with the sun positioned at one of the ellipse's focal points (Nicholas of Cusa's argument, save for focal point). His second law (which he discussed first) stated that the planets swept out equal areas of their orbits in equal times. He rejected the ancient belief that the planets traveled a circular orbit at constant speed, replacing it with the theory that planets' speeds varied with their distance from the sun—fastest when closest to the sun and slowest when farther away—nothing different from what Guo Shoujing had discovered three centuries earlier about planet Earth.[22]

Kepler had learned Copernican astronomy from Michael Mästlin (1550–1631) when he entered the STIFT, the theological seminary of the University of Tübingen, where he was awarded his master's degree in 1591. He published a textbook of Copernican astronomy written in a question-and-answer form, the *Epitome astronomiae Copernicanae*. In my submission, although Kepler may not have appreciated this, he built on Copernican astronomy, which itself derived from Regiomontanus and Nicholas of Cusa, who obtained their fundamental new ideas from Toscanelli and the Chinese astronomical calendar.

Galileo Galilei

Galileo was born in Pisa in 1564. His father was a musician. He was educated at the University of Vallombrosa near Florence; then in 1581 he enrolled at the University of Pisa to study medicine. He never trained as a mathematician or astronomer.

Galileo's life was dominated by the Copernican revolution. He was the first European to develop a powerful telescope with thirty-two times magnification—a huge advance in astronomical observation. He discovered Jupiter's moons, Saturn, sunspots, and the phases of Venus, publishing his results in *Siderius nuncius* (Starry messenger).[23] This led him to believe Copernican theory was correct; now the trouble started.

The old guard, who had spent their lives teaching Ptolemy's theory that the earth was at the center of the universe, felt their livelihood and reputations threatened. They ganged up on Galileo, gathering support from the Dominicans for his blasphemy in stating that man, God's creation, was not at the center of the universe. The intellectuals and religious fanatics won the day—Copernicus's theory was denounced as "false and erroneous," and by a decree of March 5, 1616, Copernicus's book was suspended. The chief theologian of the Catholic Church, Cardinal Bellarmine, informed Galileo that he must no longer defend Copernicus. Eight years later, Galileo made an attempt to have the 1616 decree lifted. He did get a small waiver—he was entitled to discuss Ptolemy's and Copernicus's theories provided his conclusion was as dictated by the Catholic Church—which was that man cannot presume to know how the world is made because to do so would restrict God's omniscience.

Galileo accepted this restriction and spent the next eight years writing a dialogue comparing the two principal systems—of Ptolomy and Copernicus. The book was hugely popular—a best seller. The Jesuits seemed defeated but they fought back. Galileo's book was so powerfully written it would cause more harm to the establishment view of the cosmos "than Luther and Calvin put together."[24]

The pope ordered a prosecution. This gave the papal lawyers a big legal problem, for Galileo had abided by the decree of 1616. Suddenly a document was "discovered" to the effect that Galileo in the negotiations leading to the degree of 1616 had been prohibited from "teaching or discussing Copernicanism in any way." He had therefore obtained the decree by false pretenses because his book was disguised discussion and teaching. The establishment mounted a show trial, which took place in 1633 when Galileo was in his seventieth year and ill. He was convicted, but his imprisonment was commuted. He was ordered to recant Copernican theory and state that he "abjured cursed and detested" his past errors in supporting Copernicus. While under house arrest he wrote some of his greatest works, summarizing his early experiments. His last big discovery, of the moon's daily and monthly movement, came in 1637, just before he went blind. He died in 1642.

Galileo's monumental achievements were essentially the use of a powerful telescope to discover the heavens and validate Copernicus's work and his pioneering thoughts on gravity. He was the first European who could see that mathematics and physics were part of the same subject and that earthly and heavenly phenomena could be combined into one branch of science, as could experiments with calculation, the concrete and the abstract. Galileo paved the way for Newton.

Galileo is credited with discovering Jupiter's moons, Io, Europa, Callisto, and Ganymede, in 1616. Some scholars contend that the German astronomer Simon Mayer discovered them a few days earlier. In "Ancient Chinese Astronomer Gan De Discovered Jupiter's Satellites 2000 Years Earlier than Galileo," Paul Dong, Rosa Mui, and Zhou Xin Yan cite Professor Xi Zezong of the Chinese Academy of Sciences, stating that a Chinese astronomer, Gan De, had discovered Jupiter's moons in 364 B.C.[25] The basis for this claim can be found in volume 23 of the ancient Chinese astronomical work *Kai Yuan Zhan Jing* (Books of observations from the beginning of history). A passage in it reads, "Gan De said 'In the year of Shau Yo, Xi, Nu, Shu and Wei [Io, Europa, Ganymede, and Callisto] the Annual star was very large and bright. It seemed there was a small red star attached to it side. This is called an alliance.'"

The "annual star" was the ancient Chinese name for Jupiter, the small red star, Jupiter's moon. The authors offer a modern translation of Gan De: "There was a small pink star beside the planet Jupiter. We therefore conclude this is a satellite of Jupiter." (It is still possible today to view Jupiter's satellites with the naked eye in certain places, notably in the Hebei Province of China and from the Sahara and parts of Japan.)

My intention in citing the Chinese observation of Jupiter's moons two thousand years earlier is not to diminish Galileo's enormous achievements but to illustrate how Eurocentric Western historians and astronomers are in not crediting China with astronomy vastly more advanced than Europe's. It seems almost incredible that the Jesuits could have persuaded the Chinese that they knew more about astronomy than the Chinese did, not least in predicting eclipses, something the Chinese had been doing centuries before Jesuits arrived in China.

The Development of Art and Perspective

Leon Battista Alberti, as Pope Eugenius's notary, would have recorded minutes of the meeting between the Chinese ambassador and the pope. As Joan Gadol has so succinctly said, Alberti went beyond the bounds of astronomy to determine its relation with mathematics, and then [used] mathematics to develop painting and architecture, cartography and surveying—even engineering designs and cryptography. Toscanelli, Alberti, Nicholas of Cusa, Regiomontanus, and later Copernicus and Galileo employed the rational conception of space in forming their ideas—a conception to which all were led by the methods of mathematics.[26]

Alberti knew every branch of mathematics—geometry, arithmetic, astronomy, music. In *De pictura,* his system of perspective and human proportions constitute the technical foundations of Renaissance painting and sculpture, introducing to art ideas and values that had far-reaching cultural implications for the age. Alberti's work covered painting, sculpture, architecture, aesthetics, mathematics, cartography, surveying, mechanics, cryptography, literature, and moral philosophy.

Burckhardt regarded the Renaissance pioneered by Alberti as the first age, the genesis of modern European civilization and culture.

Europe Becomes Mistress of the World

It was the combination of a massive transfer of new knowledge from China to Europe and the fact that it came in one short period that sparked the revolution we call the Renaissance.

Not only did kings, captains, and navigators have, for the first time, maps that showed them the true shape of the world, but they also acquired instruments and tables that showed them how to reach those new lands by the quickest route and how to return home in safety.

When they arrived in the New World, an international trading system created by Chinese, Arabs, and Indians awaited them—one that accounted for half the world's gross national product. This system was based upon the transfer of Chinese manufactured goods in exchange for raw materials from the rest of the world. The trading pattern had been built up by thousands of sea voyages over hundreds of years honed by centuries of experience of monsoons and trade winds. When China left the world stage, this trading system was Europe's for the taking.

Europeans found not only rich new lands but the results of sophisticated transplanting and genetic engineering pioneered by the Chinese—maize in Southeast Asia, which originated in America[27] cotton in the Azores, the result of cross-pollination of Indian and American strains; sweet potatoes from South America, which fed indigenous peoples across the Pacific to New Zealand; rice taken from China to Brazil and to "New England"; orchards of citrus trees in the Carolinas, Florida, Peru, West Africa, and Australia.[28]

The same went for animals: vast snail factories in the Paraná River of South America; Asian chickens across South America; American turkeys in India (de l'inde-dinde); Chinese horses in North America; fish farms in New Zealand. Plants that have fed (maize), clothed (cotton), and housed (coconuts) the world for the past six hundred years had been transplanted or transshipped between continents before Europeans arrived in the New World.

Raw materials had been mined and shipped across continents. Europeans found worked gold mines in Australia, iron mines in New Zealand and Nova Scotia, copper in North America, and a sophisticated steel industry in Nigeria.

New methods of cartography enabled Europeans to map the fabulous riches of the New World. Printing enabled news of these exotic discoveries to spread far and wide—not least amongst the newly emergent, brash, competing European nation-states.

At the same moment, Europeans learned of Chinese gunpowder coupled with advanced Chinese weapons—bazookas, mortars, exploding shells, rockets, and cannons. The poor Incas, armed with their feather tunics and clubs, were mown down by the brutal, ruthless, but incredibly brave band of conquistadores under Pizarro. Atahualpa stood no chance; neither did Montezuma. As a result of Pizarro's massacre, Spain gained access to the world's most valuable silver mines, which she grabbed.

Knowledge of printing spread the riches of the New World accurately and rapidly. With gunpowder weapons European rivalry took on a new potency and urgency, resulting in frenetic competition to conquer the New World.

The same dramatic changes can be seen in Europe, not least in food production, mining, and processing of raw materials. The introduction of rice in the Po Valley in the 1440s depended for its success on the aqueducts, canals, and lock systems designed by Leonardo da Vinci and Francesco di Giorgio, coupled with the new Chinese bucket pumps that enabled water to be transferred in a timely and economic way across the rice fields.

Milan's building boom was assisted by harnessing the River Po—through the use of "Chinese" locks and feeder canals. Higher firing temperatures for kilns and smelters were achieved with compressors powered by water turbines. Corn could now be ground by new efficient windmills whose designs had been developed over the centuries by Chinese engineers.

In art and architecture the new rules of perspective explained by the rational mathematics of Alberti and perfected by the genius of Leonardo da Vinci could be applied to create all manner of new buildings—which could be accurately and quickly explained and described by printing. These new ideas spread out from Florence like a forest fire.

Perhaps the most important single transfer of knowledge from China to Europe was that of how the universe worked. Greek and Roman concepts that the earth was at the center and sun and planets rotated around it were replaced by a rational system explained by mathematics. Man now could, and did, look at everything anew and examine his place in the world. This new spirit of inquiry was applied to every aspect of life—in physics, mathematics, science, and technology as well as the arts and religion. Everything could be explained without the blessing of the Church. Thought was freed from centuries of religious dogma.

In the double page diagram in color insert 3, the "inventions" and discoveries of Toscanelli, Alberti, Nicholas of Cusa, Regiomontanus, Taccola, Pisanello, Andrea Bianco, Francesco di Giorgio, and Fontana are shown. As may be seen, they produced little of consequence before 1434 and then came an explosion of new ideas, inventions, and theories.

The transfer of intellectual knowledge in 1434 was between a people who had created their civilization over thousands of years, and a Europe that was just emerging from the thousand-year stagnation following the fall of the Roman Empire. The Chinese seeds fell on very fertile ground.

Until now the Renaissance has been portrayed as a rebirth of the classical European civilizations of Greece and Rome. Chinese influence has been ignored. While Greece and Rome were unquestionably important, in my submission the transfer of Chinese intellectual knowledge was the spark that set the Renaissance ablaze.

It is time for an agonizing reappraisal of the Eurocentric view of history.

III

China's Legacy

TRAGEDY ON THE HIGH SEAS: ZHENG HE'S FLEET DESTROYED BY A TSUNAMI

In 2003, Cedric Bell, a marine engineer, visited his son and family on New Zealand's South Island. Magnetic anomaly surveys he made during his stay threw up an astonishing possibility: a considerable number of junks had been wrecked on the island's southeast coast. Survivors had apparently managed to get ashore and had built stone barracks as living quarters, had sown rice fields and set up fish farms for food and smelters to make iron. Cedric believed an entire Chinese fleet had been wrecked by a colossal storm.

Cedric Bell's report was so far-reaching that at first I was incredulous—my initial reaction was to do nothing. However, a meeting with Mr. Bell convinced me that he was a disciplined practical engineer not given to exaggeration or flights of fancy. So we agreed to embark on a series of independent tests on one barracks block, one wreck, and one smelter; if anyone could disprove his results, we would not publicize his work.

The barracks block was the ruins Cedric had scanned under an Akaroa cricket grounds, where satellite photographs taken in midsummer had shown the grass above the buried walls to be parched; the walls were outlined when looked at from space.

We retained an independent company, GPR Geophysical Services of Auckland, to carry out a ground-penetrating radar survey there. These corroborated Cedric's work, save that one of the walls seemed too straight to be true. We asked the local authorities for underground plans of buried service pipes beneath the cricket pitch. The dead straight wall was one of these, but the barracks' other three outer and interior walls were not. Cedric Bell was vindicated on that one.

We chose the smelter at Le Bons Bay, near Akaroa, because it was on public land, easily visible and accessible, and near iron ore deposits. Moreover, it had a sophisticated design: two streams powered a water turbine, which in turn powered air compressors to raise the firing temperature of the ore. There was a storage house nearby. Accelerometer mass spectrography and carbon-dating tests were conducted by Rafter Radiocarbon Dating Laboratory and by Waikato University (both of international standing and previously unknown to me or Cedric Bell) on different old buildings. The dating certificates can be seen on our website. Cedric Bell's conclusion that this smelter had been worked before Europeans arrived, by an unknown people (the Maoris did not smelt iron), was proved correct; smelting by sophisticated methods with high firing temperatures had been in use before the Maori.

Research by Dr. R. N. Holdaway corroborated this. Asian rat bones he had found in New Zealand were shown by carbon dating to be two thousand years old. As rats cannot swim more than a few yards, humans must have brought them.

The wreck selected for analysis was also in Le Bons Bay, not far from the smelter, covered by sand and underwater other than at low tide. Analysis carried out by GPR showed two foreign objects of the same size and the same position as Cedric Bell's magnetic anomaly survey with the same shapes. (Results are on our website.)

Cedric Bell's survey of a barracks, a smelter, and a wreck had by now been investigated by several methods by different reputable organizations whose results had in broad terms corroborated his work. Their findings disclosed that a sophisticated people who arrived by junks had lived and worked in New Zealand long before the Maoris, the Europeans, or, indeed, before the arrival of Zheng He's fleets.

Our next research was into the Maori people. Who were they? Dr. Geoffrey Chambers and his team, notably Adele Whyte, had conducted

DNA tests to find the answer. They concluded that the Maori mito-chondrial DNA was Chinese from Taiwan, as the foreign minister of New Zealand, Dr. Winston Peters, agreed in his address at the meeting in Malaysia of the Association of Southeast Asian Nations (ASEAN) on July 25, 2006: "My point is very simple, that the indigenous people of New Zealand came from China. . . . DNA is irrefutable evidence."

We now hope the New Zealand government will moderate its approach in representing New Zealand's early history: in particular that sites currently off limits to the New Zealand people will be opened; and that human bones that predate the Maoris' arrival now in possession of the New Zealand government will be DNA-tested. I have offered to pay for these tests, and a distinguished professor of genetics at Oxford University with a worldwide reputation has agreed to conduct them. All we now await is government agreement.

Cedric Bell Returns to New Zealand

After tests on his earlier finds had been concluded, Cedric Bell returned to New Zealand in 2004 and found yet more startling evidence—including wrecked junks impaled upside down high on the cliffs of South Island. The outline of the wooden hull was clearly visible. So was the concrete hull lining, which was proved by analysis to be manmade from a mixture of burnt lime and volcanic ash. Marks were found in the cement where it had been bonded to the hull by rice glue. Some wrecks were charred; some were upside down and tilted as if a giant had hammered them into the cliffs; some rose nearly one hundred feet above the sea. The cliffs sometimes disgorged cannonballs, counterweights, and miscellaneous objects including the remains of a ship's bell, a laminated knife, and a very old Buddhist brooch inscribed with the Chinese word for "mountain."

The only feasible explanation for such widespread destruction was a tsunami. Great waves had smashed the junks into the cliffs, leaving them impaled when the seas subsided. We learned that Professor Ted

Bryant of Wollongong University had published in a carefully documented book, *Tsunami: The Underrated Hazard,* his findings that New Zealand's South Island had been devastated by fires and by a tsunami sometime between 1410 and 1490—dates that he obtained from dendrochronography of the trees. Professor Bryant's book was published well before my own *1421.* As New Zealand lies on a fault line, the tsunami and forest fires could have been caused by a seismic event, as many New Zealand experts, including Dr. J. R. Goff, have argued. However, an earthquake would not explain how the wrecks had been turned to charcoal before being impaled in the cliffs, for it would not cause massively hot fires in the ocean from whence the junks had come.

Professor Bryant's book describes how the Aborigines in Australia and the Maoris in New Zealand both reported a comet being the cause of the "mystic fires." Both Chinese and Mayan astronomers describe a large blue comet seen in Canis Minor for twenty-six consecutive days in June 1430, a date compatible with Professor Bryant's dendrochronography. Then in November 2003 Dallas Abbott and her team at the Lamont-Doherty Earth Observatory, Palisades, New York, announced that they had found that the comet had impacted the sea between Campbell Island and the South Island, blasting a crater twelve kilometers across.

Let us now imagine a fleet of junks sailing north after leaving Campbell Island, homeward bound. Two days out from Auckland Island, the lookout would have reported a group of low-lying islands right ahead (the Snares Islands at 48°10 N, 166°40' E). The fleet would have to alter course to round the islands: one half turns east, the other west, and the two halves are some twenty miles apart centered on position 48°10 N, 166° 55 E.

Then comes the comet, twenty-six times brighter than the sun, its hundred decibels screaming, blowing out the eardrums of the sailors. Its colossal heat sets their skin on fire. Then the comet hits the ocean some sixty miles south of the combined fleet. Gigantic waves, more than six hundred feet high, toss the ships about like matchsticks. The masts and rigging are afire, fanned by four-hundred-mile-an-hour winds. Here is the extract that Dallas Abbott, Andrew Matzen, and Stephen F. Peckar of the Lamont Doherty Earth Observatory and Edward A. Bryant, of the University of Wollongong, Australia, submitted to the meeting of the Geological Society of America in the fall of 2003:

Goff attributes coastal abandonment in New Zealand in 1500 A.D. to an earthquake-induced tsunami event. However, the largest historical earthquake produced maximum tsunami run-ups of forty to sixty metres [150 to 200 feet]. On Stewart Island, New Zealand, beach sand is present ~220 metres [720 feet] above sea level at Hellfire hut and ~150 metres [500 feet] above sea level at Mason Bay. In eastern Australia there are mega tsunami deposits with maximum run ups of 130 metres [425 feet] and a carbon 14 age of about 1503. Mega tsunami deposits occur on the eastern side of Lord Howe Island in the middle of the Tasman Sea, implying a source for the crater further east. We named this source crater Mahuika for the Maori God of Fire. Mahuika crater is approximately 20 kilometres [about 12 miles] wide and at least 153 metres [502 feet] deep. It is on the New Zealand continental shelf 48.3°S and 166°4E. Several pieces of evidence point to Mahuika as the source crater for the 1500 A.D. event. The first is that the crater lies on a great circle path from Australia oriented at about a 45 degree angle to the general trend of the eastern Australia coast. Mega tsunami deposits near Wollongong and at Jervis Bay, Australian suggest a tsunami wave oriented at this angle to the coast. The second is the sub bottom depth of the impact deposits. We have found impact ejecta in all of the dredges near the crater. Because marine sediments are deposited at a rate of about 1 cm [.39 inch] per thousand years, this is expected if the impact deposit is only 500 years old. We are seeking c-14 dates to confirm this. The third is the distribution of tektites, which are found on the opposite side of the crater from the direction of impactor arrival. Although we found impact ejecta in many samples, only some samples contained tektites. All tektite-bearing samples are located SE of the crater, in the opposite direction from SE Australia, where the impact fireball was seen by the Aborigines.

In more recent correspondence, the Lamont-Doherty team has narrowed the dating to 1430–1455. The impact fireball was seen over 1,000 miles away. The tsunami was more than 220 meters (700 feet) high when it reached Stewart Island farther north (beach sand had been carried to that height) and 130 meters (400 feet) when it reached Australia. The wind's maximum velocity would have been 403 miles per hour (Lamont-Doherty calculations). Increased pressure caused by the comet's kinetic energy would have created a Coriolis effect on wind direction. Waves radiating outward from the impact zone running up New Zealand's south coast smashed the ships into the cliffs; many others were hurled ashore on either side of the Tasman Strait in southeast Australia.

Cedric Bell's full report on the junks impaled on New Zealand cliffs is contained on our website www.1421.tv under the heading "Independent Reports" and includes a full schedule of wrecks with the latitude and longitude of each. The eighty wrecks he had discovered by 2004 are from three principal locations: at the Catlins on New Zealand's southeast coast; farther north around Moeraki; and north again around the Banks Peninsula.

The wrecks on Australia's south and east coast can be briefly summarized as follows. The one on the east side of King Island has brass pins similar to those in the Ruapuke wreck. After storms the wreck on the east coast of Tasmania in Storm Bay disgorges Hong Wu (Zhu Di's father) coins. The first settlers to reach Kangaroo Island found feral Chinese pigs. Other feral pigs around Warrnambool have similar flea characteristics (Asian and European pigs have very different fleas). There are a further three unidentified wrecks between Warrnambool and Kangaroo Island. The stretch of coast named the Coorong includes a number of old "Chinaman's" wells. According to the aboriginal people who live along this stretch of coast, foreign people settled among them after a shipwreck that occurred long before Europeans arrived.

The tsunami from the Mahuika impact position would have carried wrecked junks towards Australia. As they approached the coast to the north of the Bass Strait, the coriolis winds would have driven them through the Bass Straits dumping two on Flinders Island, one on the east coast of King Island near the Elephant River, another on the Warrnambool coast, and on Kangaroo Island. Wrecks here are compatible with known facts about the Mahuika comet and resultant tsunami, as are Cedric Bell's discoveries in New Zealand's South Island.

Evidence of the Tsunami: a Wrecked Chinese Fleet in Oregon and British Columbia

On January 31, 2007, Mr. Dave Cotner, an eighty-two-year-old American citizen, e-mailed me from his home in Las Vegas, describing his finding of what he believed were the remains of a very old Chinese junk buried about 130 deep in sand dunes inland some 1,600 yards from the ocean. Like Cedric Bell, Mr. Cotner had made his discovery using the magnetic anomaly system.

I met Mr. Cotner in Las Vegas the following February 20. Together we studied the plans of his findings. The next day, we flew to Coos Bay, Oregon, hired a car and explored the site.

The wreck is in William Tugman State Park, part of the Oregon Dunes National Recreation Area. The location, at approximately 43°30' N, is where the Caribbean explorers Juan Rodriguez Cabrillo and Bartolome Ferrello had reported a wrecked Chinese junk in 1542. Dave Cotner's MAS survey had shown the wreck of a seven-masted wooden ship broken in half lying on its side, listed about twenty degrees to port under twenty to forty feet of sand at about seventy-five feet above sea level. The anchor extends to the northwest of the wreck. When Mr. Cotner originally found the wreck in 1985, he dug an eight-foot hole, put in a pump, and extracted wood. He found the wreck to be a very odd shape, resembling a barge constructed of large (twenty-four inches square) timbers for a keel running its full length. The position of the anchor indicated that it was in use when disaster struck. The position of the anchor relative to the wreck showed that the junk must have been carried sideways to be dumped sixteen hundred yards inshore at an elevation of seventy-five feet by a wave at about that height.

We based our planning on the assumption that the tsunami responsible was a result of the Mahuika comet and therefore would have hit the Oregon coast on its passage from New Zealand on a bearing of about 040. The beach shallows gradually into the ocean over several hundred yards—an ideal condition for a tsunami run-up—there are no outlying islands to blunt the force of the impact.

We decided to start the magnetic anomaly soundings just seaward of the wreck, then move down the sand dunes on a track of 220 degrees toward the ocean. Whenever Mr. Cotner found something we would stop and read out the satellite position and I would take a photograph. (The satellite readings at that stage meant nothing—they were eight- and ten-figure numbers.) On return to shelter we plotted out the magnetic anomalies and realized we had evidence that the junk had broken up on its passage as it was carried by a huge wave from its anchorage onto the sand dunes, littering evidence along its track as it disintegrated.

The shoreline slopes so gently toward the ocean that waves are accentuated—although it was only blowing force five during our visit, the waves were quite ugly. A junk stranded ashore would have been smashed to bits in no time. Ferrello could not possibly have recognized it as a junk 110 years later and must have seen it well inshore; subsequent sandstorms would have covered it in a shroud. We commissioned further testing to obtain a three-dimensional picture of the wreck (as we did at Sacramento) and will approach the authorities with these images requesting permission to excavate them. They corroborate Dave Cotner's MAS survey.

Evidence of the Tsunami in Western Canada: Wrecked Chinese Junks Between 43°N and Vancouver Island

Among numerous reports, here is one made long ago of a wreck on Clatsop Beach north of where the Cotner junk was found. It is a Chinook legend, "First Ship seen by the Clatsop," narrated by Franz Boas which starts with an old woman walking along the beach in search of her lost son. She saw something she thought was a whale. But when she came nearer, she saw two spruce trees standing upright on it. "Behold, it is a monster," she thought.

When she reached the thing she saw that its outer side was all covered in copper. Ropes were tied to these spruce trees, and it was full of iron. Then a bear came out of it. He stood on the thing that lay there. "He looked just like a bear," said the old woman, reporting her find to onlookers, "but his face was that of a human being"[1]

A man climbed up from the beach and went down into the ship. When he looked about in the interior he saw it was full of boxes. He found brass buttons in strings [coins with holes in the middle]—half a fathom long. The Clatsop people gathered the iron, the copper and the brass."

This story is corroborated by the oral history of the Seneca Indians, who say Chinese landed on what is now the Washington-Oregon coast before the Europeans got there. Apparently a small craft landed during summer months and met the local Indian people. A fleet returned during the winter months expecting a similar welcome, but they were wiped out by the Crow people, who had come down from the plains to escape a harsh winter.[2]

Queen Charlotte and Vancouver Islands appear in the Waldseemüeller (1507) and Zatta maps (1776)[3] drawn before western Europeans reached British Columbia, that is, before Vancouver or Cook. Zatta calls Vancouver Island "Colonia dei Chinesi" and gives as authority the Russian explorers who found Chinese there when they arrived in 1728 (Bering) and 1741 (Chirikov). Russian hydrographers in Vladivostok have found Chirikov's drawings of these Chinese people.

Hugo Grotius (1624) reporting Galvão: "The people of China . . . sailed ordinarily the coast, which seems to reach unto 70 degrees towards the north," that is, as far north as the Bering Strait.

When Major Powers of the U.S. Army arrived to take over administration from the Franciscans in the Klamath Valley, Oregon, he found a Chinese colony (40° N). All along the coast from 40° to 50° N there is extensive evidence of wrecked Chinese ships of Zhu Di (1403–1424) and the Xuan De emperor (1426–1435). Both emperors had built massive fleets. Professor Long Fei and Dr. Sally Church of Cambridge University, who examined the *Shi-lu,* Official Shipbuilding Records for 1403–1419, report: 2,726 Junks were built in these sixteen years of which a minimum of 343 and a maximum of 2,020 would have been available to Zheng He.[4]

Evidence of the Tsunami Along the North American West Coast

At Susanville, California, a beautiful Xuan De (1426–1435) brass plate was found buried in woodland.

The University of Oregon Anthropological Paper Number 23 (1981) reports the discovery by Herbert K. Beals and Harvey Steele of Chinese porcelain from the Netarts Sand Spit (45°29' N), 150 miles north of the Cotner Junk: "Between 1956 and 1958 the archaeological site designated 35-TI-I was excavated under the direction of L. S. Crossman of the University of Oregon. In 1958 excavations in House 13 of their site, under the supervision of Thomas M. Newman led to the recovery of 127 fragments of Chinese porcelain."

The report then breaks down the finds into two groups: possible Cheng Hua; Yung Lo (Zhu Di) and Hsuan Te (Xuan De.) The authors conclude: "It is of course possible that early Ming porcelain could have been brought over on Chinese junks or trading journeys in post-Columbian times. This however does appear logically to be doubtful. We can't imagine porcelain for seafaring voyages to be antique especially as antiquity was so highly valued."

The curator of the Tillamook County Pioneer Museum, inland from the Netarts Sand Spit, where the ceramics were found, informed me of a large pulley made of *calophyllum,* an Asian wood found in the sea and given to the Horner Museum at Corvallis.[5] It has been dated 1410.

Ozette, a few days' sailing north of the Cotner Junk, is a Makah village buried by a mudslide in the 1770s. The Department of Anthropology of Washington State University has published three volumes of

Ozette Archaeological Project Research Reports[6] comparing hundreds of reports of people who have contributed since initial excavations were begun in 1966. According to one report, "a section of the hillside above Ozette village gave way . . . and the liquefied clay roared downhill, displacing or crushing everything in its path. This part of the village was densely packed with longhouses."

Excavations of these longhouses and their middens has been carried out methodically and carefully, separating out the different eras. Of relevance to this report is the use of iron tools and the evidence of trade with Japan between 1400 and 1450 (Makah people did not smelt iron).

In an article in *Contributions to Human History*,[7] Royal British Columbia Museum's curator Grant Keddie examines claims that native Indian cultures of the north Pacific coast of North America were influenced by prehistoric contact (i.e., pre-European) with advanced cultures of China. He concludes:

> The native use of large numbers of Chinese coins on the northwest coast as a result of the fur trade is well documented in the journals of early explorers and traders. The manufacturing dates of Chinese coins traded to North American Indians and introduced later by Chinese immigrants were most often a pre-contact (before European) date. . . . It is clear that the temporal and spatial context of late prehistoric trade between Old and New worlds is in need of further study.

Since 1990 when the above report was published a mass of new evidence of pre-Columbus Chinese voyages to the Americas has been found: wrecks at Long Beach, Vancouver Island, said to be carrying rice; a Chinese vase dredged by the trawler *Beaufort Sea* off Ucluelet and another off Tofino (west Vancouver Island); a wreck said to be of a Chinese junk north of Sequim in the Juan de Fuca Strait; a Chinese talisman and lamp (pre-Columbus), bronze figurines of the god Garuda, and ancient Chinese bronzes on Vancouver Island; old Chinese coins at Chinlac; Chinese bronzes hauled up from the Strait of Juan de Fuca; inexplicable stone structures and stone cairns.

Number of Wrecked Junks

Taking all of the above findings into account, it seems that at least thirty junks were wrecked along the coast between 41 and 49° N. If that is so, there should be evidence that a substantial number of survivors got ashore—as was the case following a similar catastrophe in New Zealand (Cedric Bell report).

Chinese Settlements on the Columbia River

Some of the evidence of wrecked junks is near the five-mile-wide entrance to the Columbia River. One hundred fifty miles upriver where the river hooks to the east, just north of Portland, lies Lake Vancouver. There in the narrow valley of Lake River hundreds of ceramic artefacts have been found, fired by "the Washington Potters," a group who appeared from nowhere "around 1400" and disappeared equally suddenly three hundred years later.[8] The U.S. Institute of Archaeological Studies concluded their pottery was Asian in form. A further 120 miles up the Columbia River in an area west of The Dalles is Hog Canyon, where pigs with short legs—said to be Chinese—ran wild until recently.

In lakes beside the Columbia River local people grew a potato-like vegetable called the *wapato,* which is native to China. The Nez Percé Indians, reached from the Columbia River, are well known for their very distinctive spotted horses called Appaloosa, shown in paintings of the Chinese Yuan dynasty.

Evidence along the Columbia River and across British Columbia suggests an old Chinese colony. Squamish Indians have accounts of Chinese traders before Europeans arrived, as do the Haida of Queen Charlotte Island, who describe people sailing from the west toward the sunrise. Nootka folklore has "visitors from afar" who came before the Europeans. The indigenous people of Whidbey Island in Puget Sound believe the Chinese logged off large tracts of forest hundreds of years ago. Totem poles on Vancouver Island and on the Washington coast are identical to those of China's Wuhan Province. Potlach ceremonies in both places are the same. More than thirty words spoken by the Haida people have the same meaning in Chinese—*tsil* (hot); *chin* (wood); *etsu* (grandmother). Olympic State Park has its Ho River and Vancouver Island its China Beach and China Hill. Local people there offer up white dogs as sacrifice "to bring heaven's blessings" as they do in China.

DNA Evidence

Mariana Fernandez-Cobo and colleagues[9] examined the ubiquitous DNA virus polyomavirus JC of Salish people who once lived on the Pacific coast. They describe in layperson's language how they analyzed the urine of these peoples and found that the benign kidney disorder of "Japan" (i.e., Mongolia and Japan) strains MY[ZA] and Tokyo-1 are identical to Salish MT-1 [ZA] and MT-3 [ZA]. In short, the Salish who now live in Montana and the Mongolian/Japanese people tested have the same ancestors.

The Cotner Junk is a vital piece of evidence in many ways. First, it appears to corroborate the extensive evidence of the tsunami that Cedric Bell has found in the wrecked junks in New Zealand. Secondly, it should provide evidence about Zheng He's junks—knowledge that can be passed to builders of a replica for the Beijing Olympic Games. Third, it serves as a focal point in gathering evidence of the voyages of Zheng He to America. Publication of the details of the Cotner Junk will undoubtedly result in a tidal wave of new evidence.

Evidence of Wrecked Chinese Fleets in South America

We have received a great many e-mails relating to pre-Columbian presence of Chinese people and of wrecked junks in South America, especially in Peru. Details may be seen on our website by searching for Peru and Chile. Because I believe that at least one fleet was wrecked by the Mahuika tsunami, we have spent some time narrowing the search. Zheng He's fleets would have traded with the civilizations then existing in South America.

Where those civilizations had their principal ports was determined by the unique geography of South America. The Andes Mountains straddle the equator; as they march south they widen and the coastal plain that starts a hundred miles wide in Ecuador gets narrower and narrower until in Chile it is only twenty miles wide. Where the massif broadens in the south, a grassland plateau some 11,500 feet high emerges between the peaks. Running westward from the high Altiplano down to the sea are innumerable small rivers like legs of a centipede. To the east of the Andes stretches a wide, hot, low plain, which soaks up moist winds from the Atlantic. As the wet winds spread westward they deluge the Brazilian forest with rain before dumping the remainder on the Andes, which, due to their height, falls as snow. In spring between September and April, the winds freshen. For a brief period, snow even reaches the high slopes of the western Andes. When the snow melts in summer, water cascades down the "centipede" rivers into the Pacific. Thus starting at the equator and traveling eastward one encounters an astonishing diversity of climates. First comes the bone-dry strip of coast; then the western slopes of the Andes punctuated every thirty miles or so by rivers full of water some three months of the year; then the high, cold grassy plateau, the Altiplano with plenty of rain for a quarter of the year; and finally the hot, low, wet Amazon jungle.

The bone-dry desert coast exists because of the cold Humboldt Current flowing northward from the Antarctic and a high-pressure system far out in the Pacific, a combination that prevents rainfall. Consequently there is no word for "rain" in either the Quechua or Aymara languages. Instead, in winter the coast is covered by a fine mist, which is burnt off as the sun heats up the land. The Chinese name for this mist is *Peru*.

As the Humboldt Current rises to the surface, it brings millions of tons of plankton from its depths. Small fish feed on the plankton, attracting larger fish, which in turn attract sea lions. The water yields

1,680 kilograms of fish per hectare, almost a thousand times the world average. The most vivid way of seeing this extraordinary richness is by ship (or submarine) from out in the Pacific; the Humboldt Current is delineated by acrobatic displays of huge flocks of seabirds diving into the water to gorge themselves. Millions of these birds nest ashore, producing an endless supply of guano fertilizer.

So the people living along the Pacific coast of southern Ecuador, Peru, and northern Chile had an endless bounty of fish, shellfish, birds, and sea lions for food. Their river valleys were full of water for a quarter of the year, and they had plenty of fertilizer. So it is not surprising that this stretch of coast has produced rich human civilizations since the dawn of time. The land had as much to offer as the Nile, the rivers of Mesopotamia, the Ganges, or the rivers of China. South American civilizations are hence as old as any on the planet: Peru's Caral Supe are about 5,000 years old; Chinese civilization is 3,900 years old; India, 4,600; Egypt, 5,300; and Mesopotamia, 5,700.

The greatest civilizations of the Pacific coast of South America, starting with the sites of Caral and Chavín, were based between the Lambayeque River in northern Peru and the Ica River in southern Peru. South of the Ica the coast narrows considerably, and north of the Lambayeque the Humboldt Current and its fish supplies peter out. Since Peru was home to the richest civilization of them all, this area would have attracted Zheng He.

This part of Peru is awash with evidence of Chinese visitors over the past two thousand years. There are still one hundred villages in the Ancash region of Peru that retain their Chinese names to this day. Inca people have East Asian admixture in their blood to such an extent that their DNA profile could almost be called Chinese. (Professor Gabriel Novick and colleagues—see www.1421.tv, then 'Evidence', then 'Part VII—The Genetic legacy of Zheng He's fleets')[10]

The clearest possible evidence can be seen in Lima's Museo Arqueológico Rafael Larco Herrera, which has 45,000 exhibits from graves of the Cupisnique period (1000 B.C.) through the Moches (A.D. 400–800) and more recent Nasca, Chimu, and Chanca periods. I asked the most helpful curator, Mr. Claudio Huarache, if there were portraits of Chinese merchants found on pottery from the graves. He immediately showed me beautiful paintings of Chinese from Moche, Chanca, and Nasca graves—spanning the past two thousand years and covering the whole coast of Peru north to south. A picture of a Chinese merchant is shown on our website.

Peru appears on Chinese world maps long before the 1418 map (Hendon Harris map collection) and before Zheng He's nautical chart (which also shows Peru—see Liu Gang's 'Map speaks without words' on www.1421.tv). Diego Ribero's master chart of the world of 1529[11] shows the coast of Peru in great detail, with an inscription that describes Peru as "province and cities of Chinese silk." Ribero's map was published before Pizarro (the first European) got to Peru. The Waldseemüller map, also published before Pizarro reached Peru, shows the Andes along the whole length of the South American coast.

So it seems safe to assume that Zheng He knew of Peru before he set sail. He would have visited ports where his fleets could trade. We know from the records of the first Spanish chronicles that in the 1420s the principal trading areas would have been Chan Chan in the north of Peru, then, coming south, Chancay (north of Lima), then Pachacamac in the southern suburbs of modern Lima, then Paracas some 150 miles south of Lima. Chancay suddenly started to mass-produce pottery in the 1420s, some of which they called "china." My first thought was that Chancay was the port Zheng He visited (in medieval Castilian the name means "City of Chinese silk"), but unfortunately the place has been so badly looted it is impossible to be sure. So we need other clues.

The 1418 map has this description alongside Peru: "The local people practise Paracas religion." It also shows a river on the Peruvian coast. When Liu Gang published the map I researched Jesuit and Franciscan records to find when this religion was first mentioned in European annals. To my surprise there were no mentions at all. To find out more we drove south to the Paracas Peninsula, which today is a national reserve protected by the Peruvian government. Here is the Julio Tello site museum, which provided the answer to the riddle. The Paracas people buried their dead in very rich funerary bundles made of a fabric the local cotton and vicuña wool dyed with beautiful natural colors.

A typical scene at the papal court—Pinturicchio depicts the court of Pope Pius II.

lorence and her most famous son, Leonardo da Vinci.

RENAISSANCE MEN AND THEIR OUTPUT BEFORE AND AFTER 1434

1400	**1410**	**1420**

Paolo Toscanelli
1397 - 1481   University 1415 - 1424

Leone Battista Alberti
1404 - 1472

Nicholas of Cusa
1401-1464   University 1417 - 1424

Giovanni di Fontana
c.1400 - c.1455

Pisanello c.1395 - c.1455

Taccola
1382 - 1453

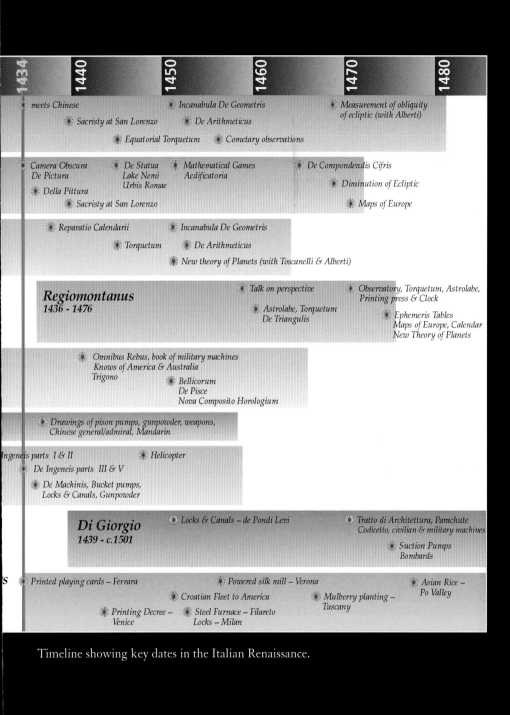

1434 **1440** **1450** **1460** **1470** **1480**

✳ meets Chinese   ✳ Incanabula De Geometris   ✳ Measurement of obliquity
    ✳ Sacristy at San Lorenzo   ✳ De Arithmeticus   of ecliptic (with Alberti)
    ✳ Equatorial Torquetum   ✳ Cometary observations

✳ Camera Obscura   ✳ De Statua   ✳ Mathematical Games   ✳ De Compondendis Cifris
De Pictura   Lake Nemi   Aedificatoria
✳ Della Pittura   Urbis Romae   ✳ Diminution of Ecliptic
    ✳ Sacristy at San Lorenzo   ✳ Maps of Europe

    ✳ Reparatio Calendarii   ✳ Incanabula De Geometris
    ✳ Torquetum   ✳ De Arithmeticus
    ✳ New theory of Planets (with Toscanelli & Alberti)

Regiomontanus
1436 - 1476
    ✳ Talk on perspective   ✳ Observatory, Torquetum, Astrolabe,
    Printing press & Clock
    ✳ Astrolabe, Torquetum
    De Triangulis   ✳ Ephemeris Tables
    Maps of Europe, Calendar
    New Theory of Planets

    ✳ Omnibus Rebus, book of military machines
    Knows of America & Australia
    Trigono   ✳ Bellicorum
    De Pisce
    Nova Composito Horologium

✳ Drawings of pison pumps, gunpowder, weapons,
Chinese general/admiral, Mandarin

Ingeneis parts I & II   ✳ Helicopter
✳ De Ingeneis parts III & V
✳ De Machinis, Bucket pumps,
Locks & Canals, Gunpowder

Di Giorgio
1439 - c.1501
    ✳ Locks & Canals – de Pondi Levi   ✳ Tratto di Architettura, Parachute
    Codicetto, civilian & military machines
    ✳ Suction Pumps
    Bombards

s   ✳ Printed playing cards – Ferrara   ✳ Powered silk mill – Verona   ✳ Asian Rice –
    ✳ Croatian Fleet to America   ✳ Mulberry planting –   Po Valley
    ✳ Printing Decree –   ✳ Steel Furnace – Filareto   Tuscany
    Venice   Locks – Milan

Timeline showing key dates in the Italian Renaissance.

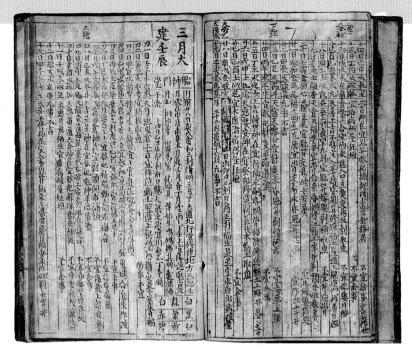

Ephemeris table from the Pepysian Library, Cambridge University.

Gonville & Caius College, Cambridge   23rd May 1953   tel. 3275

Dear Ladborough :

 The printed calendar in the Pepys Collection is the
ephemeris for 1408*, the 25th. year of the Ta T'ung calendar,
which started in 1384 (i.e. the 17th year of the Hung Wu reign-
period of the first Ming Dynasty Emperor, T'ai Tsu). It is
thus an early piece of printing, valuable in itself. *

 The British Museum possesses a copy of a Chinese ephemeris
(I don't know its date) [Birch MSS 4394 fol. 26] on which are
written the words "Lent me by Mr. Robert Boyle, Oct. 29th. 1671". The
writer was probably Robert Hooke, who had a paper on Chinese
language etc. in the Phil. Trans. for 1686. His diary records
his personal acquaintance with one or more Chinese (merchants?)
resident in London at the time.

                    Yours sincerely   Joseph Needham

* N.B. before Gutenberg!   * See note by P. van der Loon.

Needham's postcard is self-explanatory.

Regiomontanus' ephemeris tables.

Chinese astronomy was clearly more advanced than European efforts until after the 1434 Chinese visit to Florence.

Where do future discoveries lead us? To America and beyond...

The fabric was first seen on the Lima market in the late nineteenth century and examined by Max Uhle, a German archeologist, who named it as Early Inca culture.

In 1925, Julio Tello, a Peruvian archeologist, visited the Paracas Peninsula and excavated areas named Cerro Colorado and Wari Kayan. Tello realized what he had found was not Inca in origin but a new culture, which he called Paracas. So Europeans didn't know of this culture until 1925, although the name Paracas appeared on Liu Gang's 1418 map. It seemed to me this could only mean the Paracas Peninsula was known to Zheng He. It was therefore at least arguable that the river shown on the 1418 map was one near Paracas. What other clues were there?

To the north of Paracas is the Cañete River, adjacent to the Peninsular the Pisco, to the south the Ica. The Pisco and Ica Rivers and their tributaries are the same shape as the river in Liu Gang's 1418 map. When Marcella and I visited (May 2006), both were dry, although their valleys were lush and fertile, having received plenty of rain earlier in the year. We traveled up both rivers. The Pisco had once been at least ten miles wide, as one can see from erosion of the cliff banks some twenty miles upriver near Tambo Colorado, where it forks as depicted on the 1418 map. This makes the Pisco River the most likely candidate for being the river on the map. We decided on returning to the United Kingdom to see what the first Spanish to reach the River Pisco found when they arrived a century after Zheng He's voyages.

The most complete account is that of María Rostworowski[12] de Diez Canseco in her *History of the Inca Realm*. After explaining that "Chincha" is the equivalent of "chinchay" (Chinese silk) in medieval Catalan, she describes Inca Tupac Yupanqui's peaceful conquest of the Chinchas and how they were absorbed into the Inca hierarchy and of the courtesies extended first by Tupac Yupuanqui to the Chincha leader and then by Huayna Capac and Atahualpa. She describes the lord of Chincha meeting Pizarro in a litter (carriage without wheels) in the same procession as the emperor Atahualpa—in short, the Chincha lord was of similar status to the Inca chief Atahualpa. Atahualpa explains this by saying that the Chincha lord once had 100,000 ships. Bartholome Ruiz describes capturing a Chincha raft at sea laden with goods of great value. Pizarro's coat of arms includes a Chinese junk (Seville Museum of the Indies).

María Rostworowski found many parallels between Chincha and Chinese peoples. Alone among ancient Peruvian civilizations, the Chinchas were expert at astronavigation using the star Cundri. They were very skilled merchants who traveled as far north as Ecuador and used a type of copper money as international currency. They were expert silver- and goldsmiths. She describes the legends of the Naylamp (in the north), who refer to foreigners arriving before the Spanish by sea in fleets of large rafts. These foreigners settled among them.

Time and time again, Mrs. Rostworowski refers to Chincha as being a rich and prosperous *señorío* (province) of the Incas, to the Chinchas as speaking their own language, Runi Simi, rather than the Quechua of the Incas. Finally she concludes: "Why did the Chincha become seafarers, and how did they learn skills of navigation? Our present knowledge does not permit a satisfactory answer—perhaps they came into contact with navigators from different places who taught them their maritime skills."

The author of *Prehispanic Cultures of Peru*, Justo Cáceres Macedo,[13] emphasizes the importance of Chincha merchants.

> About its [Chincha] origin there is a version according to which outside people [foreigners] conquered the Chincha valley with the aid of an oracle called Chinchacama. Population grew very rapidly and due to that neighbouring valleys formed an alliance with Chincha people, who made expeditions to the sierra to the land of the Collas on the shores of lake Titicaca at the time the Incas were founding Cuzco. At the time of arrival of the Spanish, Chincha was one of the most prosperous and prestigious in the Andes. . . .
>
> Recent studies indicate the existence of an important group of merchants in the Chinchan valley who traded north along the coast as far as Ecuador, south to the Altiplano and along the south coast as far as Valdivia, Chile.
>
> An anonymous manuscript of the 16th Century assures [us] that dealers used a kind of coin and they "bought and sold in copper."

Chincha was conquered by the Incas during Tupac Yupanqui's reign and annexed to the empire in A.D. 1476. When the Incas peacefully conquered the Chincha they took over the site at Tambo Colorado and erected new buildings. Tambo Colorado was an ideal trading site linking the coast with Ayacucho, Abancay, and Cusco on the Altiplano. From the Andes came turquoise, gold, and silver, amethyst and black obsidian, and the magnificent vicuña wool, the world's finest. From the coast came mother-of-pearl, fish, and salt. From the Pisco Valley to both the coast and the Altiplano went a host of plants—fruit and vegetables—grapes, oranges, bananas, dates, cotton, maize, asparagus, and yucca, all of which can be seen growing in valleys today.

Ritual Sacrifice

The 1418 map says that the people of South America practiced ritual sacrifice. Some ten years ago the volcano of Abancay erupted, splattering hot ash on the nearby volcano of Ampato. This melted the snow. Further eruptions threw out of the melted earth a virgin of the sun buried circa 1440 after what is presumed to have been a ritual sacrifice. She has been named Juanita; her perfectly preserved frozen body can be seen in the deep freeze at Arequipa University. In 2000 her body was taken to Tokyo University for DNA tests and carbon dating. She died circa 1440 and hence was conceived about 1425. Her DNA has substantial Chinese (Taiwanese) admixture.

In my opinion the Incas' emperor Atahualpa was correct in saying that the Chincha had once commanded a huge fleet. He was once an admiral in that fleet and when it was wrecked had settled with his people in the Chincha valley, where they prospered as merchants—hence Diego Ribero's description of cities on that coast (prior to Pizarro) as "cities of Chinese silk."

The Inca conquest has always seemed to me extraordinary. They arrived from nowhere around 1400–1450 and within 150 years had conquered an empire in South America about as large as the Roman Empire—and created a system of roads and bridges totaling 18,000 miles—larger than that of the Romans. They were extraordinary administrators, arranging to blend the skills of subjugated people for the common good. It all happened quite suddenly under Pachacuti (1438–1471). Pachacuti overran the Chincha as described, and the Chimu in the north, which gave him the coastal plain as far as Quito in Ecuador. Then he appointed Tupac Yupanqui (1471–1493) to lead armies southward to Chile. Pachacuti overran the Tiwanaku and the Wari. At its greatest extent the Inca Empire stretched 2,600 miles north to south—an empire of some twenty million people—exceeded in extent and numbers only by the Chinese.

Their brilliance as farmers can be seen today by taking a train across the Andes from La Reya down to Machu Picchu. On the high, cool grasslands are herds of alpaca and llama; a thousand metres lower, potatoes are prolific; then maize; fifty miles farther, before the Sacred Valley, is lush grazing; then the Sacred Valley, where coca, bananas, orchids, and peppers grow.

The Incas used the knowledge and skills of their predecessors to enhance the land's fertility. From the Wari they learned how to dig canals, dykes, and aqueducts; from the Chimu they benefited from international trade; from the Tiwanaku of Lake Titicaca, they learned hydroponics and how to grow potatoes in huge quantities. The Moche knew the secrets of cultivating peppers, bananas, and coca. The railroad from Lake Tiwanaku to Machu Picchu is an open museum of Inca farming methods—here aqueducts, terracing, canals, and stone houses are made of cut stone so perfectly fitted today that despite centuries of earthquakes, one could not fit a knife between the cracks.

Why did all the civilizations of South America, save for the Incas, collapse in the 1440s and four decades after that? In my view the Mahuika tsunami was responsible—besides destroying the Chinese fleet, it wrecked the rich cities of the coast, leaving the mountain peoples, the Incas, to take over. I am too old to pursue this line of inquiry, but I hope others will do so.

What is certain is that the Mahuika tsunami destroyed huge Chinese fleets in New Zealand and southern and eastern Australia, in the

Indian Ocean, along the east coast of South Africa, and along the Pacific coasts of North and South America. It was a catastrophe from which China never recovered. There were to be no more great voyages. China withdrew from the world stage to mourn her losses. The great adventure was over.

THE CONQUISTADORES' INHERITANCE: OUR LADY OF VICTORY

Trujillo, Spain, July 25, 1434: The Feast of Saint James

The Pizarro family left their house in the Callera de los Matires at noon. It was but a short walk down a slippery stone path to the Puerta de Santiago. Through it appeared the squat tower of the Church of Santiago where they would attend mass on this, the birthday of Saint James.

One of the most amazing feats of arms in the annals of humankind had its genesis here in this small mountain village in landlocked Extremadura. None of the Pizarro family had seen the sea; their dusty mountain village, Trujillo, had no maritime tradition. Yet the name of Trujillo would soon be stamped upon the length and breadth of the Americas. A son of Trujillo, Francisco Pizarro, would conquer a mighty Inca empire, triumphing over a civilization of 20 million people with a band of 180 comrades.

Extremadura, birthplace of the conquistadores, is a land is of unspeakable beauty and savage cruelty. In spring, it is carpeted with flowers. In summer, wolves trail dying sheep as they plod wearily along Mesta trails in search of pasture. The land's infinite horizons are fringed by mountaintops that are rose pink at dawn, deep velvet by nightfall. At midday, the cracked, red earth vibrates with heat, sending wild pigs scurrying for shelter beneath the olive trees.

In Extremadura, one sees the last vestiges of Roman Spain—remnants of the forest of arbutus, cork, and holm oaks that once covered the whole of the peninsula. The prehistoric *dehesa* is still practiced—thinning forests and scrub by a method of slash and burn. In the everlasting cobalt sky, vultures and imperial eagles wheel, searching for lizards and snakes slithering across the baking sand. Barren rock covers a third of the land. Now and then, chalk-white villages appear splattered on the mountainside, as if thrown by a giant hand.

The name Extremadura was coined as a term of disparagement. *Extremadura* was synonymous with stupidity, backwardness, and barrenness. It suggests a land that has been abandoned—a subject of farce. In the Spanish version of the British comedy series *Fawlty Towers,* Manuel, the idiotic waiter, hails from Extremadura. When Cervantes wanted to create a fool, he, too, chose one from Extremadura.

Today, Extremadura is a thriving, proud, independent region. Like all the regions of Spain, it has its own president and government; it is virtually a nation. In the north, Las Hurdes, the mountains, close in to form one of the most fascinating "lost" regions of Europe, the subject of Luis Buñuel's melancholy film *Las Hurdes: Tierra Sin Pan* (Land without bread). Adjacent to Las Hurdes is La Vera, rich in grapes, cherries, and pears.

Extremadura's history has been determined by its neighbors. To the west lies Portugal, to the north Castile, to the south Andalusia. From each direction, conquering armies have trampled Extremaduran soil, beginning in Carthaginian times right up to the Spanish Civil War in the 1930s. For two thousand years Extremadura peasants have endured armies of strangers occupying their fields, stealing their cattle, raping their women, burning their houses and crops.

Yet this ravaged land was the birthplace of the conquistadores, who conquered the mighty Inca, Maya, and Aztec empires. Extremadurans colonized America from Florida to Tierra del Fuego. Today, the Extremaduran names Trujillo, Guadelupe, and Medellín are found the length and breadth of the Americas, a testament to the courage of those poor, brave, devout men of long ago.

The contrast in 1434 between the wealth of China, or of the great civilizations of the Americas, and the poverty of Extremadura could hardly be greater. As the Inca emperor Viracocha was leading his people into the main square of Cusco on Midsummer's Day 1434, he was adorned in gold and jade jewelry, dressed in clothes of exotic vicuña wool. In Extremadura, Francisco Pizarro's grandfather was attending mass dressed in his poor best. None of the people whose grandchildren would set off to conquer the New World was aware that the Americas existed. Even more extraordinary, almost all of Extremadura's conquistadores came from the most barren part of the region, within a sixty-mile radius of Mérida.

Francisco Pizarro and Francisco de Orellana were born in Trujillo, Hernán Cortés in Medellín, Pedro de Valdivia in Villanueva de la Serena, Vasco Núñez de Balboa and Hernando de Soto in Jerez de los Caballeros. In short, the first colonizers of Florida, Texas, Louisiana, Mexico, Guatemala, Honduras, El Salvador, Panama, Nicaragua, Colombia, Ecuador, Venezuela, Peru, Brazil, and Chile came from the same small arid pocket of land.

Still more astonishing is the number of conquistadores from a single, small mountain village: Trujillo, Hernando de Alarcón, the first European to map California; Nuño de Chávez, founder of Santa Cruz in Bolivia; Diego Garciá de Paredes, founder of Trujillo in Peru; Gonzalo Jiménez de Quesada, Cortés's companion in his conquest of Mexico; Friar Jerónimo de Loaisa, the first archbishop of Lima; Friar Vicente de Valverde, bishop of Cusco; Inez Munoz, the first married woman to settle in Lima; and Francisco de Orellana, discoverer of the Amazon, all lived within a few blocks of the Pizarro family in Trujillo. Did a fairy godmother wave a magic wand on that dusty hillside from whence so many conquistadores came?

I explored Extremadura and Andalusia over many decades seeking an answer to this riddle. Then one cold spring evening, as a dank gray mist settled over the Meseta Central, I came across Nuñez de Balboa's house on a side street of Jerez de los Caballeros. Balboa's bedroom is covered in weeds, devoid of furniture save for a rickety old bed. His family was obviously desperately poor. What gave this illiterate young boy the confidence to sail across thousands of miles of storm-tossed ocean, then to hack his way across almost impenetrable tropical jungle, to discover the Pacific? Then I recalled Pizarro's home, also in a mountain village, also little more than a cowshed, the furniture little more than planks of wood. Did poverty drive the conquistadores' quest?

I decided there and then to explore the birthplaces of Extremadura's most famous sons, starting in the north at Trujillo and working southward through Villanueva de la Serena, Medellín, Mérida, Zafra, and Jerez de los Caballeros. (A visitor who wishes to follow my journey can comfortably do so by car in one day.) I discovered three factors common to all the great conquistadores. Pizarro, Orellana, Balboa, and de Soto were poor; not one of the conquistadore leaders came from the twenty-six great families of Spain. Not only were they poor, but their poverty arose from social injustice.

The Reconquista of Spain from the Muslims had been led by Castile. Extremadura in 1434 was Castile's frontier province. To the south lay Andalusia, the last bastion of the Moors. After the Reconquista, the land the Extremadurans had captured from the Moors was given to Castilian knights. The foot soldiers of Extremadura who had fought so bravely got nothing.

Extremadura had many inhabitants, yet the land belonged to a few Castilian families. In 1434, Castile stretched from the Pyrenees to the Portuguese border in the west, from the coast of Galicia in the north to the Moorish kingdom of Granada in the south. It was said that all this land belonged to eleven families. The duchess of Albuquerque could travel from the Pyrenees to Portugal without leaving her property. As late as 1931, Andalusia belonged to only seventeen families. A few had everything; millions had nothing.

Spain through the centuries has been a class-ridden society. From the fourteenth century, the statute book determined classes and assigned their specific members. The titled class—dukes, marchises, counts, and viscounts—owned the land, controlled tens of thousands of people, and had astonishing power over the government. They lived in castles, aping or surpassing the lifestyle of monarchs. In *The Noble Spaniard,* by Somerset Maugham, a gentleman says, "I can keep my hat on in the presence of the king." It may seem a joke, but members of the twenty-six noble families of Spain were entitled to do so by law.

The injustice of class was encapsulated in a brilliant play, *The Mayor of Zalamea,* by Spain's greatest dramatist, Pedro Calderón de la Barca. Zalamea, in western Extremadura, is a village used by Catholic monarchs as a staging post for their armies en route to Portugal, the Spanish army, consisting of rude private soldiers and officers of minor nobility—hidalgos. The mayor is a man of substance and prestige, *but* he is a peasant. He realizes the army will regard him as a pushover— the key to the girls of the town. The heroine is the most beautiful girl, most at risk, the daughter of an honest, God-fearing farmer named Pedro Crespo. He keeps her hidden in his house. The captain of the army bangs on the door and demands his beautiful daughter. Pedro Crespo refuses, saying "she is my daughter, we are an honourable family, she has her honour and her soul."

But the captain maintains that only hidalgos have honor. He pursues the girl into the woods and rapes her, asserting his *droit de seigneur.*

The Mesta

With that cruel understanding of the Spanish class system, let us revisit the Pizarros. As they walked to mass on that sultry July morning they would have seen in the haze beneath Trujillo a plain stretching to eternity. In the fifteenth century, vast flocks of sheep would have been migrating southward across that plain to their winter pastures. The right of pasturage was another of the spoils that accrued to nobility. After the Castilian nobles seized the huge Moorish estates, they turned them over to sheep ranching. Around 1300, when the Reconquista was practically over, merino sheep were introduced to Spain from North Africa. The kings of Castile then formed the Mesta, an organization to promote sheep farming and wool production, which was dominated by the wealthy families who had seized the land.

The Mesta grew very powerful. For centuries, its iron hand tied the land to sheep grazing, stifling agricultural innovation. Wealth flowed northward and the wretched Extremadurans received little. Over the centuries, impoverishment at the hands of Castile drove peasants to the towns. Even today, an Extremaduran quarter exists in Madrid, where shops, bars, and cafés are full of immigrant families. The harshness of their life is caught in the lilting song *La Vendimia* (The grape harvest):

> *As the carts trundle the roads*
> *They sing the song of autumn*
> *And the vines sing the sad song without their leaves*
> *The boys make off in carts followed by the wind*
> *The leaves sing sad songs.*

The haunting music is repeated in the Hota Extremeña a dance much like the flamenco, heavily influenced by Islamic music.

Class-based injustices were inescapable for poor families like the Pizarros. The Arch of Santiago through which the family walked to mass was owned by the de Chaves family, Castilians who had led the attack that liberated Trujillo from the Moors in 1232. They controlled who passed through it and shut out those who failed to pay their tolls. The family owned an imposing palace that overlooked—and dwarfed—the Pizarro home. In Jerez de los Caballeros, Nuñez de Balboa's hovel was similarly dwarfed by the palaces of the Rianzuela, de Logroño, and Bullon families—all Castilians.

The Virgin Mary's and Saint James's Role in the Reconquista

Despite grinding poverty and inequality, faith seemed to give the conquistadores the courage to overcome any enemy. The conquistadores were marked above all by their faith in the Virgin Mary. She is said to have appeared in the clouds above Trujillo during the battle to capture the town. Today her statue stands high above the Pizarro home, easily visible on the walk to church.

Religious life centred on the Virgin Mary. The coat of arms of the Very Noble and Very Loyal City of Trujillo consists of an image of

Our Lady of Victory on a silver background. The Virgin was intimately engaged in the Reconquista, frequently appearing to assist soldiers in their hour of peril. Likewise, the spiritual heart of the Reconquista was the shrine of the Virgin Mary at the monastery of Guadelupe, on the southeast slope of the mountains of that name. The cult of the Virgin originated there.

After the Reconquista, a period of stagnation began. Castile's expansion had come to a halt. The appearance of the Virgin in Guadalupe gave renewed vitality, a new identity, and focus to people's spiritual endeavors. The conquistadores adopted the Guadalupe Virgin as their protector. In South America her image is everywhere. The Caribbean island where the Portuguese landed in the 1440s was named after the monastery.

The kings of Castile made pilgrimages to Guadalupe, building a *hospederia* to educate the children. Great explorers came to seek the Virgin's assistance before setting off. Columbus received his permission to sail while at Guadalupe. Hernán Cortés, conqueror of Mexico, spent nine days in retreat there, praying before the miraculous image of the Madonna. He later dedicated the greatest pilgrimage shrine in America to Nuestra Señora de Guadalupe.

After the Virgin, the cult of Saint James was another powerful influence on the conquistadores, reaching its apotheosis in the Order of Santiago (Sant Jago=Saint James). In 1434, the order in effect ruled Extremadura as a state within a state.

It had all started with the Reconquista. Islamic armies overran Spain in A.D. 711 after having been invited by squabbling Visigoth princes. It took them seven years to advance to the Pyrenees. It took the Christians seven hundred to expel them. The Reconquista of Spain was tied to Saint James at every step.

The discovery of his body on the Field of Stars in Santiago de Compostela in 889 was the beginning. The news spread rapidly across northern Spain. The whole Christian world wanted to safeguard the apostle's remains and keep the infidels at bay. During this first wave of the Reconquista, the Christian armies were, in effect, followers of local warlords whose principal aim was to enrich themselves at the expense of the Moors. The most powerful warlord, Rodrigo Díaz de Vivar (1040–1099) is the quintessential Castilian hero. His nickname, El Cid (the Lord), was given by the Moors. He would fight anyone—provided he foresaw a profit. A devout Catholic, a devoted husband, and the ideal Castilian knight, El Cid has come to represent the essence of Castilian chivalry and courage.

By 1410, the Moors had been pushed south as far as Antequera, which fell to the Christian army led by the order in that year. By 1434, they were pinned into an enclave bordered by La Línea de la Concepción, Ronda, Antequera, Martos, and Huesca. South of that line, in a pocket shielded by the Sierra Nevada, the Arabs farmed sheep and paid tribute to Castilian overlords.

From Veves, where the order had its headquarters, to the Sierra Nevada, which was the frontier between Christian and Islamic lands, the order held sway. Legacies of that era are evident everywhere—in churches of Santiago from Cáceres in the north to Antequera in the south, fortresses of Santiago from Sanlúcar de Barrameda in the west to Jaén in the east. There are hospitals of Santiago in Zafra and Mérida and seminaries in Caldera de León and Zafra. Virtually every town has its Calle de Santiago.

In 1410, the medieval line of kings of Aragon came to an end when Martin V died without heirs. Civil war loomed. By the Compromise of Caspe in 1412 Ferdinand of Antequera, a member of a junior branch of the Trastamara dynasty, the royal house of Castile, became king of Aragon.

In England, King John married for the second time. His bride, Isabella of Portugal, bore a daughter, also called Isabella. She would eventually defy her advisers and marry Ferdinand of Aragon, putting the seal on a united Spain, one that had been unified for all practical purposes by the Compromise of Caspe.

A unified Spain possessed the prime ingredients for launching voyages of discovery—the Extremadurans. They had the example of their forebear, El Cid, who had achieved his victories over insuperable odds by virtue of superhuman will and courage. And they had the daily reality of no bread.

Save for Cortés, every one of the famous conquistadores we have mentioned came from a poor family; not a single illustrious Castilian family took part in their voyages of exploration. It is no coincidence the conquistadores were intensely legalistic. They negotiated with the monarchy in advance, with the division of spoils spelt out in detail.

For once, Extremadurans could keep the spoils. At home, Extremaduran hidalgos struggled to obtain food for their children. Overseas, conquest, land, and wealth afforded them a purchase on nobility. Embarking on voyages of exploration, the conquistadores could hope for three separate rewards—spiritual salvation for waging war against the infidels, material gain in the form of vast tracts of land and wealth, and, once they returned home, *fama, gloria,* knighthoods, and castles to brighten their twilight years.

The awesome dangers and difficulties the conquistadores faced in exploration must have seemed little different from those they had already encountered in the Reconquista. Provided that they exhibited the same extreme courage as their forebears, they could overcome any obstacle, secure in their faith that the Virgin Mary and Saint James would protect them. In the end, victory would be theirs.

Besides, by 1434, Islam had been squeezed into the southern tip of Spain between the Sierra Nevada and the sea. North of the mountains, there were no lands left to reconquer. For six hundred years, their ancestors had been waging battle; fighting was in their blood.

The hardships of the *tierra sin pan* explain their urge to leave Extremadura but not how the conquistadores overcame their homeland's lack of maritime tradition. That was remedied by the union of Castile with Aragon after the Compromise of Caspe. Having pushed Islam out of Spain, Castile was busy absorbing the immense estates it had recently acquired.

Aragon, on the other hand, had completed her part of the Reconquista two centuries before Castile and used the interim to create a maritime empire. By 1434, she had two centuries of valuable experience. Aragon possessed ships that could sail the world and cartographers who had begun to map the Atlantic and Africa. Her savants knew the earth was round and that the Americas existed across the

Atlantic. Despite this, Aragon was weak; she would be the junior partner doing what Castile required of her.

The conquistadores had the example of the Portuguese before them.
In 1415, Henry the Navigator had taken the colossal gamble of invading Africa, the home of Islam. By 1421, Madeira had been populated,
on the way to becoming a thriving Portuguese colony. Henry's ships
had set sail for the Americas—the Portuguese knew the earth was
round, that the seas did not tumble off the earth, that India and the
East could be reached by rounding Africa.

And what could the conquistadores expect to find when they reached
the fabled Americas, land of Amazons? In an age of romantic literature, their dreams were no doubt fired by the epics such as *The Amadis
of Gaul*. Nubile, sex-mad women awaited them in marble palaces.
Handmaidens would wash their feet and clothe them in golden gowns.
White rubies and green emeralds the size of pigeon eggs would be
theirs for the taking. Small wonder Pizarro had such an easy time se-
lecting two hundred comrades from among the many who answered
his call that blistering summer's morning outside Trujillo's Church of
Santiago.

Fortune favors the brave. The conquistadores found three desperately weakened empires in the Americas. The Aztecs had become
psychopaths—cannibals who ate their fellow tribes in Mexico. Cortés
was welcomed with open arms as millions of Mexicans supported his
invasion. In Central America, the same ghastly cult had poisoned the
Maya. Weakened by civil war, they too offered only token resistance. In
South America, the "mummy cult" of the Incas had reached its inevitable conclusion.

With nowhere to expand, the Incas had taken to fighting one another. They had no iron. An army of padded dolls awaited Pizarro. By
a series of amazing coincidences, each empire succumbed to fatal weak-
ness at the very moment the conquistadores landed. The three fruit
trees had ripened simultaneously, each without thorns. The conquistadores plucked the fruit.

Our quest to rediscover the world of Zheng He's era ends at San
Lúcar de Barrameda, on the estuary of the Guadalquivir. This power-

ful, melancholy river symbolizes the change from Old World to New. Once the grand highway that joined Córdoba, the magnificent capital of Islamic Spain, to the rest of the Islamic world in the East, the river became the link between Seville, capital of New Spain, and her New World colonies in the West.

If the Guadalquivir could speak, she might wearily agree that so extraordinary were the events of Zheng He's era that it seems God had grown tired of his creation and decided to try something new.

The last word goes to Omar Khayyám (circa 1074).

> Those who in ancient ages came
> And those that live in later days
> Depart on their successive ways:
> For all the journey is the same.
>
> This Kingdom of the Earth and Sky
> Remains eternally for none:
> We too must go, as they have gone,
> And others follow by-and-by.

Our long journey of exploration into the medieval world is over. Like our predecessors, we now commend ourselves to God's keeping.

ACKNOWLEDGMENTS

This book is a collective endeavor and could not have been completed without the help of hundreds of people. I am afraid these acknowledgments are likely to be incomplete: if anyone feels aggrieved at being omitted, please let us know. For more extensive acknowledgments, please visit our website.

I am grateful to the following people who conducted major independent research that they funded themselves and that lasted for more than two years:

Lam Yee Din

I had the good fortune to meet Mr. Yam Lee Din in Hong Kong in 2003. Mr. Lam has studied Zheng He maps in exhaustive detail and published his findings in four lengthy papers that are shown on our website. Mr. Lam is, in my opinion, the greatest living expert on Zheng He's voyages. At my suggestion he was invited to deliver his findings to the Library of Congress, which he did on May 16, 2005. His speech was broadcast to China and Asia by Phoenix Television.

Tai Peng Wang

Tai Peng Wang is a historian and journalist based in Vancouver. His family is from Quanzhou, and he can read and speak the version of Mandarin used in his native province. This has been very important in the discussions on the authenticity of the 1418 map, which was created by a Quanzhou cartographer.

Tai Peng Wang has written and published five papers of the greatest importance, particularly his thirty-two-page paper entitled "Zheng He and His Envoys' Visits to Cairo in 1414 and 1433." This is not to imply that Tai Peng Wang agrees with all the statements I have made in this book.

Cedric Bell

Before visiting New Zealand in 2003, Cedric read *1421* and decided to do some research on the beaches of New Zealand's South Island. He sent the results to a company then making a television documentary on *1421*. Cedric had found some forty wrecks buried in sand or in cliffs and also the ruins of barracks that the shipwrecked survivors had built ashore and the remains of smelters built to refine ore. To confirm this, I retained well-known ground-penetrating radar and carbon-dating laboratories to check a wreck, a barracks, and a smelter. The results are on our website *1421,* along with Cedric Bell's research. They show conclusive evidence that Chinese people have been smelting iron in New Zealand for two thousand years. Cedric, in my view, because of his finds and subsequent analysis of wrecks coupled with his experience as a marine engineer, has become the leading authority on the construction of junks in Zheng He's fleets.

Rosanne Hawarden and Dave Bell

Rosanne and Dave have followed through on Cedric Bell's research in New Zealand, investing their own time for four years and without financial support from me. They have done the groundwork that has enabled us to put forward an alternative and less simplistic history of the settlement of New Zealand and the South Pacific—that the original settlers were the Chinese who brought others of South East Asian origin with them. The Polynesians, including the Maori, are their descendents. Rosanne and Dave's work has been of very great importance in furthering *1421* evidence in New Zealand, Australia, and the islands of the South Pacific.

Liu Gang

Mr. Liu Gang, the founding partner of the second-largest law firm in China, has collected maps and works of art for several decades. Five years ago he found in a Shanghai bookstore "Zheng He's 1418 Map of the World," described in detail on our *1421* website. At the time, he knew little of Zheng He and filed the map as a curiosity. In 2005 Liu Gang purchased the Mandarin version of *1421* and realized he owned the first recognizable, accurate world map drawn up after Zheng He's earlier voyages. Please refer to the *1421* website for more about this map and its authenticity.

Dave Cotner

In 1985 Dave Cotner, a retired U.S. Navy pilot, found the wreck of an old ship along the Oregon coast, buried in water beneath thirty feet of sand. The local museum curator classified the wreck as Chinese. When Dave contacted us, we commissioned a well-known firm, GPR Geophysical Services of Portland, Oregon, which conducted the ground-penetrating radar surveys of "Cotner 1" and confirmed in all respects Dave's MAS survey of 1985—position, size, shape, depth, angle, and sitting. Core drilling started in November 2007. The wreck has unfortunately deteriorated into wood slurry. A few small wood chippings have been retrieved, and these will be dated and classified in early 2008. Dave has found a number of other buried wrecks in the area. Very substantial sums will be required to excavate them.

Dr. Gunnar Thompson

Dr. Thompson is an expert in pre-Columbian New World discovery, and his books and research on multicultural findings and early Asian voyages to the Americas have been invaluable to the development of *1434.* In *Secret Voyages,* Thompson provides evidence that between 1277 and 1287 Kublai Khan, emperor of China, dispatched Marco Polo to the Americas, where he reached Hudson Bay. Dr. Thompson presented his findings at the Library of Congress on May 16, 2005. His research can be found at www.marcopolovoyages.com.

Dr. Siu-Leung Lee

Dr. Siu-Leung Lee was born and educated in Hong Kong, where he graduated from the Chinese University. He has a PhD from Purdue University, did postdoctoral research at Yale University, and became a professor of chemistry at Texas A&M University, pioneering in the enzyme biosynthesis of natural products.

Dr. Lee has set up a very popular website called Asiawind (www.asiawind.com). In collaboration with Ms. Fu Yiyao, Dr. Lee published a calligraphy book on Chinese wisdom. He is an internationally known expert on Chinese calligraphy.

Since 2002 Dr. Lee has been a reasoned critic of *1421.* However in 2006 he acquired a medallion that had been found buried near Asheville, North Carolina. Dr. Lee believes this was part of the gifts intended by the Xuan De emperor for American chieftains through his representative. Having found a great deal of corroborative evidence, Dr. Lee now believes that during the Ming dynasty, the Chinese visited North Carolina. In June 2006, he presented his findings at the University of Hong Kong, the Hong Kong History Museum, and the City University of Hong Kong. See Dr. Lee's website for further details.

Paul Chiasson

Paul Chiasson is a fifty-five-year-old Canadian architect born on Cape Breton Island. Paul built up a successful practice with a distinguished list of clients. His specialty became Asian art and architecture.

There is a legend of the local Mi'kmaq people of Cape Breton Island that long ago foreigners came from the other side of the world and settled on a headland now called Cape Dauphin. Five years ago Paul decided to explore the colony where these strangers built their town. On climbing onto the plateau he found the remains of a stone town laid out on Buddhist lines overlooking the Ciboux Islands. Paul's findings are now contained in his best-selling book, *Island of the Seven Cities.*

In 2005 Paul invited Cedric Bell and me to join him on a survey of the site in Cape Dauphin. In my view the site, while Buddhist, is not of Zheng He's era but much older. Eventually I feel it will be shown to be from the voyages of Kublai Khan's fleet.

Charlotte Harris Rees

Charlotte Harris Rees has researched extensively about the early arrival of Chinese to the Americas. As a child she lived in Taiwan then Hong Kong with her Baptist missionary parents Marjorie and Dr. Hendon M. Harris. Dr. Harris's find of an ancient Asian map displaying the western coastline of the Americas led to his 1975 book *The Asiatic Fathers of America: Chinese Discovery and Colonization of Ancient America.* In 2006 Charlotte came out with an edited and abridged version of that book.

The oldest of the Hendon Harris Fusang Maps are Ming Dynasty. They are believed by some to date back to a 2200 B.C. Chinese map. The Harris Map Collection was at the Library of Congress from 2003 through 2006 while it was being studied. It was examined by Dr.

Hwa-Wei Lee, chief of the Asian Division; Dr. John Hebert, chief of Geography and Maps Division; and by Professor Xiaocong Li, from Peking University, Beijing. At my request Charlotte presented her findings at a Library of Congress symposium in May 2005. She continues to write and speak. Her website is www.asiaticfathers.com.

Professor Robert Cribbs

Professor Robert Cribbs is an adjunct professor of engineering at California State University and a visiting professor of scientific archeology and music in Cairo, Egypt. He started, and runs, several corporations involved in medical and industrial ultrasound and high-speed video and radar processing. He also possesses the world's third-largest collection of medieval astrolabes. In consequence he has become, in my opinion, one of the world's leading authorities on the different methods used by ancient and medieval astronomers to determe latitude and longitude, the diminution of the ecliptic, the equations of time of the sun and moon, and the determination of longitude by the slip between sidereal and solar time or by the angular distance between moon, planets, and stars.

Professor Cribbs has explained these methods to me with such clarity that I have been able to explain them to others. Professor Cribbs presented his findings at a seminar on Zheng He held at the Library of Congress on May 16, 2005.

M. Benoît Larger and Dr. Albert Ronsin

M. Larger is a retired French banker living in Saint-Dié-des-Voges. He sponsored an exhibition held at Musée Pierre-Nöel between May and September 2007. The exhibition drew together the work of a group of savants including Martin Waldseemüller who had been recruited by Saint-Dié's ruler, Duke René II, to produce a world map copied from separate maps received from Portugal. This exhibition, which promi-

nently featured the work of Dr. Albert Ronsin, honorary conservator
of the museum, was the collation of the lifetime's research of many
learned scholars into Martin Waldseemüller's maps of 1507 and 1516
and globe of 1506. Their research has been adopted in this book. I am
very grateful for it—it saved me a lifetime of research.

Dr. Tan Ta Sen

Dr. Tan Ta Sen is a leading Singapore businessman who is also president of the International Zheng He Society. This society collates
knowledge relating to Zheng He's voyages between 1403 and 1434. I
have been invited to attend many of the society's meetings and have in
consequence learned a great deal from the experts. Dr. Tan introduced
me to the foreign minister of Singapore, who suggested the *1421* exhibition subsequently held in 2005. Dr. Tan kindly lent several priceless
works of art to this exhibition, financed the production of model junks
of Zheng He's fleet, arranged the loans of very valuable artifacts, and
provided invaluable support in many other ways. The *1421* exhibition
is now in Dr. Tan Ta Sen's museum in Malacca in the former offices
and warehouse of Admiral Zheng He.

Lynda Nutter

Lynda Nutter is a dancer and choreographer who understands Japanese, Chinese, and the Nyungah language of the aboriginal people
who live in the Swan valley east of Perth in Western Australia. Five
years ago Lynda found carved stones that form an astronomical observatory from which longitude may be calculated. These stones have inscriptions in a medieval Chinese script and are at the heart of the
Nyungah territory. Lynda has correlated markings on Zheng He's navigational chart with the coastline around Perth as a result of reading
and translating the Chinese.

Cristopher Pollard

Christopher Pollard has spent a lifetime studying medieval Spain, notably the history of Extremadura. The final chapter of this book is an abridgment of my notes of Christopher's lectures. For those who wish to explore the subject in more depth, Christopher runs Christopher Pollard's Tours based in Taunton, England, and personally leads these tours through the magical cities of medieval Spain.

Libraries

Library of Congress, Washington, D.C.

Owners of Waldseemüller's 1507 and 1516 world maps. The Library of Congress kindly invited me and supporters of *1421* to a symposium on May 16, 2005, on the subject of Zheng He's voyages. They were roundly abused for doing so by critics who claimed that *1421* was a fraudulent book and hence such an august body as the Library of Congress should not give us a platform. The library replied they believed in the basic academic principle of free speech, and the symposium went ahead as planned.

The British Library

The British Library provides a superb service. An array of helpful experts is there to help those of us who cannot speak the language. If by chance the British Library does not hold the book (certain constituent books of the *Yongle Dadian*, for example), one is quickly put in touch with the library that does hold that book. I and five researchers have been using this superb service for years. Without it *1421* and *1434* could not have been written.

The Pepys Library, Magdalene College, Cambridge University

This holds the 1408 astronomical calendar.

Bibliothèque Nationale, Paris

Holder of the Waldseemüller Green Globe of 1506 and Dr. Monique Pelletier's research into the provenance and authenticity of that globe— a vitally important map in the *1434* story.

Hong Kong Central Library

The principal library in Hong Kong is modern and most efficient. The majority of Chinese illustrations found in *1434* came from here and we are indebted for their services.

Library of the Duchess of Medina-Sidonia, Sanlucar de Barrameda, Andalucia, Spain

The duchess's family, hugely wealthy landowners in fifteenth- and sixteenth-century Spain, backed Christopher Columbus and inherited his papers. These describe Columbus's several visits to the Americas before 1492.

The Arquivo Nacional, Torre do Tombo, Lisbon

The repository of records of pre-Columbian Portuguese voyages to the New World. In my submission this will be a gold mine for future research.

My thanks also to the Bodleian Library, Oxford; the School of Oriental and African Studies (SOAS); and the London School of Economics.

Museums, Institutions, and Universities

The British Museum holds a superb collection of Yuan and Ming dynasty ceramics and works of art, not least the Chinese map of the twelfth century that accurately depicts China overlaid with latitude and longitude lines. Some of the ceramics were excavated from remote parts of the world, for example, a fine blue-and-white early-Ming teapot buried in Australia.

Much evidence of the Chinese visits to Venice has been and will continue to be found in the Louvre, Paris—for example, Pisanello's sketches and drawings.

The Musée Pierre-Nöel contains collections of Waldseemüller and his friends and colleagues' memorabilia, the repository of records of Vespucci's voyages, and is the best place to base research on Waldseemüller and his globes and maps.

The Doge's Palace, Venice, holds the world map from India to America, constructed according to notations on the map itself, from information brought to Venice by Niccolò di Conti and Marco Polo. This was copied and given to Dom Pedro in 1428. The map is upside down—as some Chinese maps of that era were.

Chicago University has sponsored the superb electronic database system JSTOR, which has been invaluable to me and the *1421* team.

Surrey University has pioneered a nondestructive system of analysis of materials employing Rutherford backscattering techniques. In broad terms, this enables dating within 5 percent and the capacity to analyze material with sufficient accuracy to determine its origin.

Surrey University has kindly advised us how to utilize this valuable resource, which we believe will prove of great assistance in analyzing artifacts found in or near wrecked junks around the world.

Classic Works Relied Upon for *1434*

Professor Joseph Needham, *Science and Civilisation in China*, Cambridge University Press (various dates past 50 years)

The monumental work of thirty-five volumes is to me one of the most extraordinary pieces of human endeavor ever created. I have read all the volumes over the past fifteen years; without them I would not have started *1421* or *1434*. Needham was a genius; his mind can cover the span of human knowledge from how the Chinese fermented liquor to more obscure aspects of Chinese cryptoanalysis. He has no peer.

John L. Sorenson, emeritus professor of anthropology at Brigham Young University, and Martin H. Raish are authors of the majestic work *Pre-Columbian Contact with the Americas Across the Oceans*. This is an annotated bibliography that briefly describes written works that discuss the transmission of fauna and flora across continents before Columbus. There are some six thousand entries. It seems to me this book demolishes any idea that Europeans can claim to have discovered the New World, and furthermore it seems extraordinary that this book is not in every school in the world. Every time that I give a talk, I do my best to acknowledge Sorenson and Raish. The research team and I are extraordinarily lucky to have had this invaluable resource.

University of Oregon emeritus professor Carl Johannessen, has collaborated with John Sorenson to write and present "Biology Verifies Ancient Voyages." As they say:

> Examination of an extensive literature has revealed conclusive evidence that
> nearly 100 species of plants, a majority of them cultivars, were present in both
> the Eastern and Western hemispheres prior to Columbus's first voyage to the

Americas. The evidence comes from archaeological, historical and linguistic sources, ancient art and conventional natural science studies. . . . the only plausible explanation for these findings is that a considerable number of transoceanic voyages in both directions across both major oceans were completed between the seventh millennium BCE and the European age of discovery.

To me it is no longer arguable to claim any justification whatsoever that Europeans discovered the New World. Sorenson, Raish, and Johannessen have demolished that legend forever.

In *The Art of Invention: Leonardo and Renaissance Engineers,* Professor Paolo Galluzzi describes in 251 pages the contributions that Sienese engineers made to Leonardo da Vinci's work. The book was used by me and the *1434* team as a bible when drawing up chapters 15–20. Galluzzi has an astonishing ability to analyze this fabulous era in Florence. I hope he will not be annoyed by the revelations of the contributions made by the Chinese delegation.

Frank D. Prager and Gustina Scaglia, savants of Italian Renaissance engineering, have written a splendidly readable book, *Mariano Taccola and His Book "De Ingeneis,"* published in 1972. Before Prager and Scaglia's book, only Taccola's books 3 and 4 (*ca.* 1438) had been identified. They have reconstructed for the first time Books 1 and 2. In doing so they have shown how much Francesco di Giorgio adapted from Taccola and the influence that Francesco's work had on Leonardo da Vinci. The book is profusely illustrated, showing the apparently extraordinary explosion of new mechanical and military machines after 1433. We have compared these with those shown in printed Chinese books published before 1420.

Ernst Zinner's great book *Regiomontanus: His Life and Work,* provides a readable, lucid, and comprehensive account of the amazing life of Regiomontanus, whose ideas were later adapted by Copernicus and Galileo—to such an extent that perhaps the Copernican revolution should be renamed. I have quoted and abridged extensively from Zinner.

Joan Gadol has written a fascinating, and illuminating book, *Leon Battista Alberti: Classical Man of the Early Renaissance*. Alberti was notary to Pope Eugenius IV and would have met the Chinese delegation in that capacity. He possessed an enormous intellect and charisma and had a profound influence on Toscanelli, Regiomontanus, Nicholas of Cusa, Taccola, Francesco di Giorgio, and eventually on Leonardo da Vinci. I have quoted extensively from Joan Gadol's wonderful book.

Academic Support

Academic support for the *1421* and *1434* theories are of course of great importance. The following have e-mailed with their interest in *1421* and/ or *1434,* for which I offer my thanks: Professor Yao Jide, Professor Yingsheng Liu, and Professor Fayuan Gao, Professor Liu Xiaohong, Yunnan University; Professor John Coghlan, Melbourne–La Trobe University; Professor Miguel Lizana, University of Salamanca; Professor Arnaiz Villena, Madrid University; Professor Drewry, University of Hull; Professor Ng Chin Keong, director and Professor Yeen Pong Lai, Chinese Heritage Center, Singapore; Professor Ethan Gallogly, Santa Monica College; Professor Hwa-Wei Lee, chief, Asian Division, Library of Congress; Professor Hua Linfu, Remin University, Beijing; Professor Xin Yuan-Ou, Shanghai University; Professor Shi Ping, Naval Command College, China; Professor D. Hendrick, University of Newcastle-upon-Tyne; Professor Zhiguo Gao, China Institute for Marine Affairs; adjunct Professor John S. Lee, Utah Valley State College; Associate Professor Ted Bryant, associate dean of science, University of Wollongong; Professor Bi Quan Zhong; Professor Dobroruka, University of Brasilia; Assistant Professor J. David Van Horn, University of Missouri–Kansas City; professor emeritus of geology Dr. John W. Emerson, Central Missouri State University; Professor Peter N. Peregrine, associate professor and chair, Department of Anthropology, Lawrence University; emeritus professor of anthropology Peter M. Gardner, University of Missouri; Professor Gudrun Thordardottir, University of Reykjavik; J.R. Day, associate professor, division head, Science, Mathematics and Computer Studies, the University of Hong Kong; Professor Goran Malmquist, University of Stockholm; Professor Alex Duffey, chief curator, University of Pretoria; professor of architecture Richard Frewer, University of Hong Kong; Emeritus Professor Peter Gardner, University of Missouri-Columbia; Professor Peter Roepstorff, University of Southern Denmark; Professor Shuxuejun, JiangXi Normal University; Professor Susan Langham, visiting Shenyang University professor of quaternary geology; Professor Jack Ridge, Tufts University; professor of history and political science, Henry Pierson "Pete" French, Jr., State University of New York and Monroe Community College; Adjunct Professor Linda d'Argenio-Cruz, Brooklyn College; Professor Peter L. P. Simpson, Graduate Center, City University of New York; Richard Kanek, retired professor of physics; visiting professor Robin Pingree, Mombassa, University of Plymouth; Professor Jules Janick, James Troop Distinguished Professor in horticulture, Purdue University; Adjunct Professor Anthony Fazio, Graduate Division for Acupuncture and Oriental Medicine, New York Chiropractic College; R. Thomas Berner, professor emeritus of Journalism and American studies, Pennsylvania State University; professor of political science John Lawyer, Bethel University, Saint Paul, Minn.; Paul Winchester, clinical professor of neonatology at Indiana University Medical School; Rosa E. Penna, professor of English literature, Catholic University of Argentina and the University of Buenos Aires; Professor Victor M. Rivera, Baylor College of Medicine; retired professor of anthropology and the founder and director of the Overseas Research Center at Wake Forest University, D. Evans; Patti Grant-Byth, professor of English at Korea University, University of Minnesota; John Splettstoesser, retired professor of geology and president, American Polar Society, Minnesota; Daniel Mroz, assistant professor of theater, University of Ottawa; Professor John Preston, Eastern Michigan University College of Technology; Professor P. A. McKeown, emeritus professor Cranfield University, U. K.; Niels West, research professor, Department of Marine Affairs, University of Rhode Island; David Greenaway, pro–vice chancellor, professor of economics, University of Nottingham; Dr. Chris Gleed-Owen, research and monitoring officer, the Herpetological Conservation Trust,

Bournemouth; Edwin M. Good, professor emeritus of religious studies and (by courtesy) of classics, Stanford University; Adjunct Professor Pedro Augusto Alves de Inda, University of Caxias do Sul; Associate Professor Anthony Nieli, Pennsylvania College of Technology; Rear Admiral Zheng Ming, adjunct professor of the Naval Engineering University, Beijing; Professor Carol Urness, curator of James Ford Bell Library, University of Minnesota; Professor Roderich Ptak, Munich University; Professor Zheng Wei, director of the Underwater Archaeology Center at the National Museum of Chinese History, Beijing; Professor Chen Xiansi, Professor Chao Zhong Cheng, and Professor Fan Jingming, Nanjing University; Professor Zheng Yi Jun, Shandong University; Professor Zhu Yafei, Beijing University; Professor Tao Jing Yi, Sri Lanka; Professor Xu Yuhu, Taiwan University; Professor Li Dao Gang, Thailand; Professor Sir John Elliott, Oxford University; Professor Mike Baillie, University of Belfast; Dr. Philip Woodworth, visiting professor, University of Liverpool; Professor Sue Povey, University College, London; Professor Christie G. Turner II, Arizona State University; Professor George Maul, Florida Institute of Technology; Professor Jane Stanley, Australian National University; Robert S. Kung, Hong Kong Zheng He Research Association; Dr. John P. Oliver, Department of Astronomy, University of Florida; Dr. Eusebio Dizon, director of underwater research, Museum of Manila; Dr. Joseph McDermott, University of Cambridge; Dr. Konrad Hirschler, London, School of Oriental and African Studies, SOAS; Dr. Taylor Terlecki, Oxford University; Dr. Ilenya Schiavon, the State Archives, Venice; Dr. Marjorie Grice-Hutchinson, University of Malaga; Dr. Linda Clark, University of Westminster; Dr. Robert Massey, Royal Observatory, Greenwich; Dr. Bob Headland, Scott Polar Research Institute, Cambridge; Dr. Muhamed Waley, British Library, London; J. M. Nijman, Amsterdam Polytechnic; Dr. Alan Leibowitz, University of Arizona; Dr. Edgardo Caceres; Dr. Tan Koolin, University of Malaya; Dr. Leo Suryadinata, Institute of Southeast Asian Studies, Singapore.

Visitors to Our Website, www.1421.tv

We cannot possibly mention everybody who has contributed to our research, be it by providing new evidence, ideas for new research, corrections for future editions of books, and constructive criticism. However, we have tried to incorporate as many as possible here, in no particular order. We are most grateful to the following:

Geoff Mandy, who kindly dedicated a great deal of his spare time to organizing the "*1421* Friends" database. Thanks to Geoff, we hope, fingers crossed, that we have not left anyone off the list of acknowledgments either here or on our website.

Those who have kindly agreed to manage independent websites within the *1421* website. This concept was developed to enable people who are interested in specific aspects of the *1421* story to have a chance to advance knowledge in these areas, independently of the *1421* team. All time and effort was dedicated at their own expense, and we are particularly grateful to the following people: Joseph Davis, Mark and Laurie Nickless, Juan Carlos Hoyos, Cathie Kelly, Heather Vallance, Paul Lewis, and Anne Usher.

Those who have helped us out in the field with research include:

Dave Cotner, as mentioned previously; Laszlo, who has found a number of wrecks in the Caribbean, over the past twenty years, which were verified as being *not* of any Spanish, English, or Danish ships yet had Chinese characteristics and bore Chinese artifacts; Dr. John Furry and Dr. Michael Broffman, who set up the "China Landing" website, which has furthered exploration into the mystery of the "Sacramento Junk." For more information please visit www.pinestreetfoundation.org/chinalanding.

The research of Dr. Greg Little and colleagues, who have found widespread evidence in the Caribbean that they believe point to a long-gone maritime culture more sophisticated than the Taino or Carib peoples. More recently we have been told that early tests suggest that the cut stones found date to circa five hundred years ago. For

more information please visit the following links: http://www
.mysterious-america.net/newunderwaterbim.html and http://www.mys
sterious-america.net/bimini-caysal200.html.

Brett Green, whose untiring research against considerable adversity, has provided a host of evidence to support the pre-European Chinese exploration of eastern Australia; William C. Kleisch, Richard Perkins, and Paul McNamee, who have led the search for the elusive Great Dismal Swamp junk, which George Washington's friend saw rise out of the swamp in North Carolina; John Slade, whose research shows the potential for pre-European mining throughout eastern Australia, from the Victorian goldfields to north Queensland; Robertson Shinnick, who found Dr. S. L. Lee's medallion in North Carolina in 1994.

Other notable mentions go to Michael Boss and all of the other contributors to the "Gallery" section of the website—a wealth of beautiful paintings, photos, and artifacts; Jerry Warsing, an independent researcher who was one of the first to come forward and let us know that he had come to the same conclusions that I had, before me. We are most grateful for Jerry's continued support and research in North America. Professor Zhiquiang Zhang, whose independent research on Zheng He's travels has been invaluable to ours. D. H. C Tien and Michael Nation of Chinese Computer Communications, whose pioneering research with "Internet Chinese" may one day enable us all to learn to speak Chinese with the ease and fluency of our mother tongues; Anatole Andro, whose book *The 1421 Heresy* complements *1421* and explores the theory further; the Cantravel group, who have accompanied Marcella and me on many an exciting adventure and contributed a great deal to our research: Gill and Frank Hopkins; Carol and Barry Mellor; Gordon and Elizabeth Hay; John and Heleen Lapthorne, and Malcolm and Angela Potter.

The following people have all helped over the years to add to our ever-increasing wealth of knowledge, free of charge, and in good faith, for which we are extremely grateful: Malcolm Brocklebank, Chiara Condi, Tim Fohl, Robert and MeiLi Hefner, Damon de Laszlo, John

Robinson, Bill Hupy, Greg Jeffrey, Hector Williams, Mary Doerflein, David Borden, Rewi Kemp, Ralph McGeehan, Glen Rawlins, Michael Ferraro, Gerald Thompson, Chung Chee Kit, Howard Smith, Kerson Huang, Al Cornett, Tony Brooks, Barbara McEwan, Nicholas Platt, Zhang Wei, Robin Lind, Gerald Andrew Bottomley, Nicholas Wallis, Ester Daniels, William Li, Malcolm Rayner, J. F. Webb, Commodore Bill Swinley, David Borden, Kathrine Zhou, Janna Carpenter, Guofeng Yang, Jamie Bentley, Martin Tai, Ted Bainbridge, Brian Darcey, Rob Stanley, Jan-Erik Nilsson, J. Phillip Arnold, David Lindsay, Mike Osinski, M. J. Gregory, Philip and Wei Lewis; Roger L. Olesen; Adela C. Y. Lee; Guy Dru Drury; Saro Capozzoli; Tim Richardson; Professor Luis Wanke; José Leon Sanchez; Ted Jeggo; Ng Siong Tee; Goo Si Wei; Paolo Costa; Ric Polansky; Professor Mike Bailie; Dr. Wang Tao; Bill Parkhurst, K'ung-Fu Tzu; Duncan Craig, Nico Conti, Barney Chan, Eric Maskrey, Philip Mulholland, Garry Berteig, George J. Fery, Tony Fletcher, Nancy Yaw Davis, J. Phillip Arnold, Chris Righetti, Andy Drake, Paul Wagner, Jim Mullins, John Braine-Hartnell, Michael Penck, Dr. William Goggins, Russell Parker, Bill Hupy, Gillian Bartlett, Shaka Garendi, Rodney Gordon, Bob Butcher, Karin Harvey, John Weyrich, Edward D. Mitchell, Nicholas Platt, David Turner, Phillip Bramble, Jean Elder, Anton McInerney, Patrick Moran, Joy J. Merz, John S. Marr, Scott McClean, Lynn Canada, Richard Zimmerman, William Vigil, Ric Baez, Terry Jackson, Jefferson Wright, Ean McDonald, Beth Flower Miller, Michael Ernest, Omar M. Zen, Bruce Tickell Taylor, Dr. Edward Tumolo, Marie E. Macozek, John Forrest, Julian Wick, Keith Wise, Bobby Sass, Michael Lane, Mari Stair, David Lorrimer, Mark Simonitsch, Dave Blaine, Daryl F. Mallett, Luis Robles, Barry Wright, Mark Smith, Jeff Spira, Chris Nadolny, Li Huangxi, John Pletcher, Paolo Villegas, Kevin Wilson, Janice Avery Clarke, Patricia Duff, Dan Brech, Matthew Wissell, Harry L. Francis, Yangyong Li, Fred J. Gray, Thomas Herbert, Michael Atkinson, Garth Denning, Janet Miller Wiseman, Dean Pickering, Arjan Wilkie, George Barrett, Mark Newell, Roy Dymond; Kate Meyer; Lawrence Smalheiser; Alice Chan; Desmond Brannigan, and Edward Grice Hutchinson.

Exhibitions and Symposia

The Singapore Tourism Board, in association with Pico Art International, mounted the exhibition "1421: The Year China Sailed the World" between June and August 2005. It was held in a large, specially made pavilion, a replica of that used by the early Ming emperors when touring the country. The pavilion was set up in a beautiful site overlooking Singapore Harbor. Pico, the celebrated exhibition designers, arranged for the loan from all around the world of artifacts that evidenced Zheng He's voyages. The exhibition generated huge publicity and corresponding new evidence from Asia and China. I am indebted to the providers and sponsors of the exhibition. The exhibition has now moved to Dr. Tan Ta Sen's wonderful Cheng Ho Cultural Museum in Malacca.

Laboratories and Testing Institutions

I am indebted to the following institutions for their economical, efficient, courteous, and timely testing of evidence: Rafter Radiocarbon Laboratory, Waikato University, GPR Data LLC, Oregon, GPR Geophysical Services, and Forest Research; Pearson plc. For their financial assistance in providing ground penetrating radar survey of the Sacramento wreck site; Surrey University for establishing the origin of elements in artifacts employing Rutherford backscattering techniques.

HarperCollins Team

For much appreciated help and assistance provided by HarperCollins and its imprint William Morrow in the USA—particularly my editor, Henry Ferris, and his assistant, associate editor Peter Hubbard. Thanks also to Lisa Gallagher, Lynn Grady, Tavia Kowalchuk, and Ben Bruton.

For HarperCollins help and support in the United Kingdom, thanks to Carole Tonkinson, Katy Carrington, Jane Beaton, Anna Gibson, Iain Chapple, and Jessica Carey.

The *1434* Team

Finally, my thanks to the team who have been directly responsible for *1434:*

Midas, led by Steven Williams and assisted in Asia by Kaiiten Communications, have achieved almost unbelievable worldwide publicity—I am told more than 22,000 articles or mentions in print media alone. In acting for me I feel sure Midas did not charge normal commercial rates but what I could afford. Their success has resulted in an endless stream of new evidence and has assisted Transworld (who did a wonderful job with *1421*) selling worldwide literary rights.

Christopher Higham, who handles TV rights, has contributed to worldwide sales by achieving important television documentaries broadcast across America, Europe, the Pacific, Australia, and Asia. This in turn has brought new friends to our website with new ideas and new evidence. Chris has borne his own expenses and contributed his time for five years.

Pedalo has devised websites www.1421.tv and www.gavinmenzies .net to cope with this avalanche of new evidence. Its efforts have resulted in very popular sites—we now have 3,500 visits a day from 120 countries around the world. Pedalo's fee for achieving this was one third that of its nearest competitor.

Luigi Bonomi, my literary agent, principal of LBA, sold *1434* to HarperCollins, the first publisher to be approached. Luigi also sold *1421* to Transworld when he was a partner in Sheil Land. Luigi is, to my mind, the most successful British literary agent—authors take note! Without him there would have been no *1421* and no *1434.*

Frank Lee, an experienced Chinese businessman, sold *1421* film rights to Warner Bros. China and was instrumental in negotiating with Phoenix Television to produce a lengthy Mandarin-language documentary on *1421* and in return set up a Mandarin *1421* website—a great source of new evidence from Mandarin and Cantonese speakers. Frank has in his business career set up a very successful sales team in China and elsewhere in Asia and has a huge network of friends and contacts. He is also a discerning historian and has pioneered a new search engine for Chinese historical records. Frank will take over from me as chief executive of the *1421* and *1434* organizations in late 2008 or early 2009. By then we hope the Warner Bros. film on Zheng He will have been released for distribution.

Wendi Watson and her husband, Mike, have produced the illustrations and diagrams for *1434* as they did for *1421*. Wendi has worked from my original unpromising scrawl with good nature and patience for the past seven years. Her results speak for themselves—in my view Wendi has greatly enhanced the book and made the detailed evidence much easier to assimilate.

Laura Tatham has word-processed *1434* in no fewer than fourteen drafts without once complaining or losing her sense of humor. Laura, who at this writing is approaching her ninetieth year, has supported me by word-processing my scribbles for the past twenty-five years. It is a blessing for me that I have been able to dissuade her from retiring!

Our researchers here—Erica Edes, Antonia Bowen-Jones, Vanessa Stockley, Lorna Lopes, Anna Mandy, Anna Rennie, Susie Sanford, and Leanne Welham—are a testament to today's young people and the British education system. Unlike me, they are university graduates with good honors degrees. They have consistently and without exception shown dedication, responsibility, initiative, and hard work in assembling into a coherent whole a disparate mass of assorted evidence that pours into our computers day after day. They are head and shoulders better than I and many of my friends were at a similar age—we were, for the most part, drunken, irresponsible ruffians.

Their dedication and good nature is also attributable to Ian Hudson, who has led our research team these past five years. Ian has the qualities I lack—good nature, politeness, and common sense. Whatever readers consider we may have achieved is due to Ian as much as to me. The future success of the *1434* team will largely depend on Ian's leadership, just as the *1421* team has these past five years.

And finally, I offer gratitude to my beloved wife, Marcella. Readers will appreciate that it is not an easy decision for a wife to be asked to agree to a husband in his seventies in moderate health plowing his royalties into future research rather than into a pension fund—and in addition taking on new financial obligations for yet further research. In our excitements and setbacks over the past five years since *1421* was published, Marcella has once again supported me to the hilt, enabling this great adventure to continue.

I and this book owe her everything.

Gavin Menzies
London
Feast of All Saints, 2007

NOTES

Introduction

1. Antonio Pigafetta, *Magellan's Voyage*: A Narrative Account of the First Circum-navigation trans. R. A. Skelton. (Cambridge, Mass.: Folio Society 1975) p. 49.

Chapter 1: A Last Voyage

1. Twitchett, *Cambridge History*, vol. 3 p. 231.
2. Private correspondence between author and Mr. Frank Lee, 2005.
3. Tsai, *Perpetual Happiness,* reviewed in *Journal of the American Oriental Society* 122, no.4 (Oct.–Dec. 2002): 849–50. Viewable on JSTOR.
4. Dreyer, *Zheng He,* p. 6.
5. Tamburlaine died in 1405. His son Shah Rokh succeeded him in Persia, as did his grandson Ulugh Begh in Samarkand. Accounts of the accident are based on a Persian fifteenth-century account.
6. Dreyer, pp. 174–182.
7. Cambridge History of China p. 272. Dictionary of Ming Biography, p. 533.
8. Cambridge History of China p 278, 302. Renzong Shi Lu, ch. 1.
9. Cambridge History of China VII 286–8.

Chapter 2: The Emperor's Ambassador

1 & 2. A medallion has been found in North Carolina issued by the Xuan De emperor to his representative. For the arguments put forward about the authenticity of the brass medallion and refutations by Dr. S. L. Lee, refer to Dr. Lee's website Asiawind (see below). I am convinced that the medallion issued by Zhu Zhanji found in North Carolina and now owned by Dr. Lee is genuine for the multiplicity of reasons given by Dr. Lee. Research of Dr. S. L. Lee. See *1421* website, (www.1421.tv), and Asiawind, (http://www.asiawind.com/zhenghe/).

3. Dreyer, *Early Ming*, p.144, translating from *Xuanzong Shi-lu*, The *shi-lus* were true records of the period compiled in a highly formalized mandarin process, summarized after the emperor's death with a *shi-lu* of his reign. *shi-lus* served as the primary source for the official history of the dynasty, frequently compiled during the succeeding dynasty, e.g., by the Qing dynasty for the Ming. Zheng He lived in the reigns of five Ming emperors, four of whom had a *Shi-lu* composed for their reigns.

The *shi-lu* system has several lethal deficiencies. First, succeeding dynasties invariably loathe earlier ones and destroy much that they consider creditable from an earlier dynasty. Second, mandarin education was narrow in the extreme. If something did not appear in a *shi-lu*, it could not have happened. This is epitomized in the absurd conclusion reached by certain mandarin "scholars" that if the *shi-lu* does not say Zheng He's fleets reached America, then they did not. Such a system ignores fleets that sailed to America, got wrecked there, or decided to stay and never returned to China. The *shi-lu* system leaves appalling holes in Chinese history. However, perhaps I should be thankful—if history had been properly recorded in China, Chinese scholars would have written books similar to mine centuries ago! See Dreyer, *Zheng He,* p.144.

4.   This is J. L. L. Duyvendak's translation, in "The True Dates," pp. 341–345, 349. Duyvendak's views on the voyages reached almost mythical status—taken as gospel by historian after historian. In my view Duyvendak's restriction of Zheng He to seven voyages is ludicrous. If one takes the shipbuilding records, there were more than 1,000 ships (and possibly many more) available to Zheng He on each of the "seven voyages" recorded by Duyvendak. It is not remotely possible to control fleets of that size. There were in my view between 20 and 50 fleets at sea continuously between circa 1407 and 1434, under the overall strategic command of Zheng He, who may indeed have received only seven imperial orders. There were hundreds of voyages during those years, not seven. Re "3,000 countries," Duyvendak at p. 345, n. 2, argues that "3000" is a copyist error for "30." He then destroys his argument by showing the Chinese symbol for "3,000" beside one for "30." The "3,000" symbol has an extra bar on top. A "copyist error" would produce "30" from "3,000," not the other way around. The "3000" made by the engraver is clearly deliberate.

5.   Ibid.

6.   Correspondence between author and Mr. Liu Gang. Full text on *1421* website, www.1421.tv. Mr. Liu Gang's translation may be viewed on the *1434* website under the heading "The Real Discoverer of the World—Zheng He."
(See note 20 for '3000' countries)

7.   Liu Gang Research 2006 see 1434 website

8.   Professor Xi Longfei and Dr. Sally Church references are invaluable. They should be read in conjunction with note 9. A full list of references in the *Taizong Shi-lu* to shipbuilding are given in Dreyer, *Zheng He,* p. 116–121.

9.   Chaudhuri, *Trade and Civilisation in the Indian Ocean,* p. 241, Notes, Chapter 7, Note 29, citing Abdu'r Razzaq, *Matla'al Sa'dain* in Elliot and Dowson, eds., *The History of India,* IV, 103.

10.   Camões, K. N. Chaudhuri "Trade and Civilisation in the Indian Ocean," Cambridge University Press, 1985. p. 154

11.   Professor Pan Biao's work was brought to my attention by Tai Peng Wang. Mr. Wang has kindly allowed me to place on our website the article "The Most Startling Discovery from Zheng He's Treasure Shipyards." Professor Pan Biao's work was carried out at the Institute of Wood Material Science of Nanjing Forestry University. They analyzed 236 pieces of wood found at the bottom of no. 6 dry dock in Nanjing, which had been flooded for 600 years. Professor Pan Biao shows that hardwood was imported to China and Java on a massive scale to allow Zheng He's junks to be built in China and repaired in Java. These finds

corroborate the work of Professor Anthony Reid (see n. 11). A combination of
Pan Biao's and Reid's work shows how building such massive fleets resulted in
globalization of the timber trade in Asia. See www.gavinmenzies.net.

12. Reid, *South east Asia in the Age of Commerce,* vol. 2, p. 39. Professor Reid suggests
that the most likely explanation for the flowering of fifteenth-century Javanese
shipbuilding was a "creative melding of Chinese and Javanese marine technology
in the wake of Zheng He expeditions." "In each of the seasons 1406, 1414, 1418
and 1432 fleets of a hundred or more Chinese vessels spent long periods refitting
in the ports of East Java."

13. This exercise took place in the Andaman Sea and Strait of Malacca in January
and February 1969. Singapore and Malaysian armed services participated.

14. This took place in the South China Sea, south of the Anambas Islands, in July
1969.

15. Dreyer, p.127, has a good summary. The names of the vice and rear admirals are
taken from inscriptions on the steles described earlier in the chapter. Dreyer gives
the names at pp. 146, 208–15.

Wang Jinghong's name is sometimes spelled Wang Guitong, Wang Qinglian,
and Wang Zinghong. He was after Zheng He the senior admiral until being
drowned. Hou Xian was later envoy to Tibet and Nepal.

16. For the efforts of the *1421* team in assisting to locate the various remaining pieces
of the *Yongle Dadian* that are scattered around European libraries and universities, please refer to our 1434 website, www.gavinmenzies.net. The National
Library of China will digitize what is left of this massive encyclopedia, which
was twelve times larger than Diderot's eighteenth-century encyclopedia, then the
world's largest outside China.

Currently the National Library in Beijing has 221 books, and 60 are stored in
Taiwan.

The Library of Congress has 41 books, the United Kingdom 51, Germany,
5, and Cornell University, 5. Cornell University has an excellent website,
Explore Cornell-Wason Collection. "Starting in 1403 under the aegis of the
Ming Dynasty Yongle Emperor (reign 1402–1424) the entire intellectual
heritage of China was scrutinised for texts worthy to be included in what was
to become the editorialised expression of Chinese civilization. One hundred
and forty six of the most accomplished scholars of the Chinese empire took
part. (See also Needham Vol 32 p.174–5) After 16 months of work, the
Scholars submitted the final product. . . . " The Emperor however refused the
tome on the grounds that it was not on the grand scale he had envisaged.
Consequently he appointed another editorial committee complete with
commissioners, directors, sub-directors and a staff of no less than 2141
assistants "making 2169 persons in all." The newly assembled committee
expanded greatly on the idea of literature and included sacred texts, medicine,
writings on geography and astronomy, the arts and crafts, history, philosophy
and the by then canonized Confucian texts. . . . The Emperor then ordered
the entire work to be transcribed so that it could be printed which would
facilitate the distribution process."

See e-mails between Lam Yee Din, Tai Pang Weng, Liu Gang, Dr. S. L.
Lee, and Ed Liu at www.gavinmenzies.net. In my opinion the most likely

place to find chunks of the *Yongle Dadian* will be the Louvre. Napoleon took Venetian records to Paris. See Needham, *Science and Civilisation,* vol. 19, and vol. 32, p. 174.

17. See Needham, *Science and Civilisation,* vol 19, p. 49–50, 109–10, and vol. 32, p. 174. In May 1913, Herbert Giles wrote to Cornell University confirming that Cambridge only has one volume. See also e-mails between Lam Yee Din, Tai Pang Weng, Liu Giang, Dr. S. L. Lee, and Ed Liu on 1434 website, www.gavinmenzies.net.

18. Tai Peng Wang kindly brought this research to my attention, as has Lam Yee Din. See *1434* website

19. Needham, *Science and Civilisation,* vol. 32, pp. 100–175; and Temple, *Genius of China,* pp.110–15.
For transcribed copies, see Cornell University Explore Cornell-Wason Collection.

20. Needham, *Science and Civilisation,* vol 19.

21. K. N. Chaudhiri "Trade and Civilisation in the Indian Ocean," Cambridge University Press, 1985. p. 154, Note 29.

Chapter 3: The Fleets Are Prepared for the Voyage to the Barbarians

1. I am Indebted to the research of Tai Peng Wang, whose work has been the foundation for this chapter. See titles of papers in bibliography.

2. Needham Vol 27 p.145

3. Needham Vol 30 pt.2 p.83
For calendars, see Needham, vol. 3, pp. 49, 125, 378–381.

Chapter 4: Zheng He's Navigators' Calculations of Latitude and Longitude

Extensive notes on www.gavinmenzies.net.

Chapter 5: Voyage to the Red Sea

1. Tai Peng Weng,"Zheng He Visit to Cairo," p. 2, n. 18, and "Tale of Globalisation."

2. Nelson had twenty-seven ships at Trafalgar.

3. *Yingzong Shi-lu,* chap. 31, 38, 45.

4. Xi Feilong, Yang Xi, and Tang Xien inTai Peng Wang, "Zheng He Delegation to Papal Court," p. 6, detailing Hong Bao; and "Zheng He and His Envoys" p. 1.

5. Hall, *Empires of the Monsoon,* p. 87–89.

6. Ibid., p. 124.

7. Tai Peng Wang, "Zheng He and His Envoys, p. 1.

8. Ibn Tagri Birdi, *Al Nujun AzZahira Fi Mulek Misr Wal Kahira.*

9. Lam Ye Din and Liu Gang research, on www.gavinmenzies.net. See also Tai Peng Wang, "What Was the Route Taken to Florence", p. 1.

10. Ibn Battuta vol 4, p. 813.

11. *The Travels of Ibn Battuta AD 1325–1354*, vol. 4 Hakluyt Society, 1994), p. 773.

12. Tai Peng Wang, "Zheng He and His Envoys," p. 2. See also S. D. Goitein, "New Light on the Beginnings of Karim Merchants," both available at www.gavinmenzies.net.
13. Tai Pang Weng, "Zheng He and His Envoys," p. 2.
14. Tai Peng Wang, see *1434* website
15. Poole History of Egypt. Frank Cass and Co Ltd London 1894
16. Tai Peng Wang, see *1434* website.
17. On *1434* website.
18. Tai Pang Weng and Lam Yee Din research on *1434* website

Chapter 6: Cairo and the Red Sea Canal

1. This paragraph and indeed much else of chapter 6 is a paraphrase of chapters from James Aldridge's marvelous book *Cairo: Biography of a City*. Macmillan 1969 To my mind this book is the finest travel book ever written. Aldridge has an amazing knack for accurately compressing and summarizing a wealth of information in a few sentences. He is also a brilliant writer, witty without being unkind, choosing with great skill how and when to highlight colorful episodes of Egypt's history. This book is a joy to read, and I have done so many times. I strongly recommend it to anyone thinking of visiting Egypt.
2. Ibid., pp. 5, 27, and 127.
3. Redmount, "Wadi Tumilat"; and Payne, *The Canal Builders*. Payne's chapter entitled "Scorpion and Labyrinth" gives a detailed account of the builders from the pharaohs to Greek and Roman times.
4. *Aldridge, Cairo,* pp. 27, 43, 78, 79.
5. Poole, History of Egypt, p. 20. "In A.H. 23 . . . it ran past Bilbeys to the Crocodile Lake and then . . . to the port at the head of the Red Sea."
6. Aldridge, *Cairo,* p.127; al-Makrizi, *Histoire d'Egypte;* and. Revaisse, "Essai Sur L'Histoire."
7. SSECO. A more extensive report of the proceedings may be found on our website, www.1434.tv. See also Ibn Taghri Birdi, Abi I-Mahasin *"A History of Egypt 1383–1469,"* trans. William Popper (Berkley and Los Angeles: University of California Press, 1958) p. 86.
8. R. L. Hobson, *"Chinese Porcelain from Fustat" Burlington Magazine for Connoisseurs* 61, no. 354. A photograph of a piece of blue and white porcelain of Zhu Di's reign found at Fustat is shown on our 1434 website.
9. Aldridge, *Cairo*. The chapter entitled "Saladin's Cairo," from which this quote is taken, is a sumptuously written description showing Aldridge at the height of his powers.
10. Jacques Berges, quoted in Braudel, *History of Civilisations,* p. 66.

Chapter 7: To Venice of Niccolò da Conti

1. *"Geography of the Mediterranean"*
   The first two paragraphs of this chapter are a paraphrase of the celebrated French historian and politician Fernand Braudel's marvelous work *The Mediterranean in the*

Time of Philip II. I have referred to this masterpiece time and again, for in my view Braudel is perhaps the greatest European historian, capable of summarizing a vast array of disparate facts into a coherent and readable whole.

2. Norwich, *Venice: The Greatness*; Hibbert, *Biography of a City*; Lorenzetti, *Venice and Its Lagoon*; Brion, *Masque of Italy*. See also *Venice and the Islands* (London: 1956), p. 22.

3. Ibid.

4. I am indebted to a number of writers who are household names. Norwich, *Venice* is a classic. Norwich, in his own words, is an "unashamed populariser"— a great achievement. Those who denigrate popularizers have no idea how difficult popularizing is. Another popularizer who is also erudite and who writes in a charming style is Jan Morris. My descriptions of life on Venetian galleys and of harbors within the Venetian Empire are taken largely from her *Venetian Empire*.

5. *Descriptions of the Venetian Empire* Morris, *Venetian Empire*, has colorful descriptions not only of the Venetian in the eastern Mediterranean but also of life aboard Venetian galleys. She brings to life the tough and skillful traders and seamen who made Venice. I have extensively paraphrased her book from p.135 onward. Also Norwich, *Venice*, pp. 39–41.

6. Croatans—see Thompson, *Friar's Map* at pages 171–174

7. See European Journal of Human Genetics, II, p.535–542, entitles "*Y chromosomal heritage of Croatian population and its island isolates,* Lavorka Bara, Marijana Perii and colleagues.
    The DNA reports referred to is on our website, www.gavinmenzies.net.

8. Morris, *Venetian Empire,* p. 107; Brion, *Mask of Italy,* pp. 86, 91; and Alazard, *Venise*, p. 73.

9. Morris, *Venetian Empire,* pp. 160–61. See also J. A. Cuddon, *Jugoslavia: The Companion Guide* (London: 1968) pp. 140–41.

10. Brion, a *Mask of Italy,* pp. 80–83; and Braudel, *Wheels of Commerce*, pp. 99–168.

11. Luca Paccioli, "Summa de arithmetica, geometria, proportioni et proportionalita," in Brion, *Mask of Italy,* p. 91; Alazard, *Venise*, pp. 72–73; and Braudel, *Wheels of Commerce,* pp. 141–68 and 390–424.

12. Brion, *Masque of Italy,* p. 83; and Hibbert, *Biography,* pp. 36–48.

13. Hibbert, *Biography,* pp. 36–40.

14. Brion, *Masque of Italy,* p. 83. See also Mas Latric, *Commerce et expeditions militaire Collection des Documents inedits,* vol. 3 (Paris: 1880).

15. Hutton, *Venice and Venetia,* pp. 30–41. Electa (authors Eugenia Bianchi, Nadia Righi, and Maria Cristina Terzaghi) has produced a beautifully illustrated guide, *Piazza San Marco and Museums,* from which I have extensively quoted. 63 shows the world map in the map room of the Doges' Palace. See descriptions in Hibbert, *Biography,* pp. 57–58.

16. Brion, *Masque of Italy,* with a different translation, p. 84; Norwich, *Venice* See also Peter Lauritzen, *Venice* (New York 1978), p. 87.

17. F. M. Rogers, *The Travels of an Infante, Dom Pedro of Portugal* (Cambridge, Mass.: Harvard University Press, 1961), pp. 45–48, 325.

18. Hall, *Empires of the Monsoon,* pp. 88, 124.

19. Hutton, *Venice and Venetia,* pp. 261, 127. (Vittore Pisano). Olschki, p. 101.

20.   Olschki, "Asiatic Exoticism," p. 105, n. 69.
21.   Origo, "Domestic Enemy."

(Subsidiary Notes for Chapter 7)

a) Pisanello's Drawings in Venice and Florence 1419–1438

Antonio di Bartolomeo Pisano, (later known as Pisanello), was born probably in Verona before 1395. He was painting murals in the Doges' Palace before 1419 in association with or in succession to Gentile de Fabriano. In 1432 he was painting in Rome at Saint John Lateran, and between 1432 and 1438 he painted in Florence. He also painted in Mantua for the Gonzagas, in Ferrara for the Este family, and for the Catholic Church in Verona. He made medals for the Holy Roman Emperor Sigismund of Luxembourg and for the Byzantine emperor John VIII Palaeologus (who attended the Council of Florence in 1438). Pisanello is noted for the power of his sketches from real life. He was one of the greatest exponents of drawing of all time—in the view of some experts almost of the caliber of Leonardo da Vinci. Many consider the quality of his drawings exceeds that of his paintings.

b) The Mongolian General

The Louvre keeps a box of comments for each of Pisanello's sketches. I have read the comments of various experts who have attempted an explanation of where and when Pisanello saw the Mongolian general or whether he saw another sketch or portrait from which he copied. The various opinions are collated and refuted one by one by "D" in a five-page opinion entitled "Pisanello: Quatre têtes d'hommes coiffés d'un bonnet, de profile ou de trois quarts," which includes a bibliography of the twelve experts. I assume D was an expert working at the Louvre; his or her opinion is on our website. As may be seen, D does not consider that the Mongol general was part of the entourage of the Byzantine or Holy Roman Emperor and is unable to offer a solution as to where Pisanello saw him. D also advances an opinion on the second Mongol, whom , as he rightly says, has a retroussé nose.

c) Pisanello's Mandarin Hat

On the 1434 website's extended notes (chap. 7) is a portrait of a wealthy Chinese in a hat (*Bulletin of the Metropolitan Museum of Art* 15 (Jan. 1920), as reported in JSTOR). He wears a typical mandarin hat—black with flaps at the side and front (the front flap can only be clearly seen by viewing the original). These hats are very distinctive, shown in many Chinese paintings of the Ming dynasty and reproduced on the PBS documentary *1421*. They were not worn by any other peoples than Chinese, as far as I am aware. So despite the retroussé nose, in my opinion the figure beneath the Mongol general can only be a mandarin.

d) Pisanello's Dragon-Carrying Ship

This dragon has three claws. In China in the Ming dynasty, five-clawed dragons were for the emperor's use; the imperial family and courtiers were granted four claws or fewer. This drawing, therefore, accords with a dragon ornament owned by a Chinese courtier.

e) Pisanello's Drawing of "Macchina idraulica" (Deganhart 147)

As far as I am aware, this is the first European drawing of a piston pump—preceding Taccola and Leonardo. In the 1430s the piston pump was unknown in Europe but had been in use in China for two hundred years. Pisanello's drawing also shows a bucket pump called in Italy *tartari*.

f) Pisanello's Drawings of Guns with Triple Barrels (Deganhart 139)

Triple-barreled guns were unknown in Italy when Pisanello made this sketch but were in use in China (see chap. 19).

Pisanello's Decorated Gun Barrels (140)
These accord with Francesco di Giorgio's, drawn two decades later.
Pisanello's Portrait of a Wounded Soldier (133)
This is a Mongol.
Pisanello's Painting of the Mongol General
Note his rich silk clothes—mere "Archers" would not have worn these.
Other Pisanello Drawings, Not Yet Analyzed by the Author
Water Buffaloes: Louvre, inv 2409
Tartar pallet pump and water wheels: Louvre, 2284, 2285
Cold Desert Camels: Louvre, inv 2476
Ship with Carved Hull: Louvre, inv 2282 to 2288

Chapter 8: Paolo Toscanelli's Florence

1. I strongly suspect that Brunelleschi and Toscanelli also met the Chinese ambassador and Chinese mathematicians and astronomers in Zhu Di's reign between 1408 and 1413. Chinese records show Zhu Di's emissaries did travel to Rome and Florence in that period, but I have been unable to find any Italian records in support or to give corroborative evidence. Papal records at this time were in a complete mess because of the schism. The Vatican library has no record of Eugenius IV records while in exile in Florence and Ferrara. I have been unable to find records of the Avignon papacy and have not searched records of the Spanish pope. My guess is that if the records eventually turn up, they will be among those of the Council of Constance (1415–1418), when the triple papacy came to an end and Martin V became sole pope.

    Brunelleschi could have obtained his knowledge of spherical trigonometry from the Arabs and of reversible hoists and pinhole cameras from the Romans—but all this and articulated barges and "Chinese" methods of improving mortar at the same time?

2. I have read many books on the Renaissance, as may be expected. Some are brilliantly written. My favorites, from which I have quoted extensively, are: Plumb, *The Horizon Book of the Renaissance* (see pp. 14–19 for Italy after the fall of Rome); Hibbert, *Rise and Fall* (see pp. 32–39 for economic growth and emergence of the Medici's); Hollingsworth, *Patronage* (see pp. 48–55 for Cosimo de' Medici's patronage of Renaissance scholars and in particular the San Lorenzo sacristy); Bruckner, *Renaissance Florence* (see pp. 1–6 for Florence's economic development, notably the River Arno, pp. 42–43 for the role of slaves in economic development; and pp. 216–18 for early communication among social groups); Carmichael, *Plague and the Poor* (see pp. 122–26 for control of the plague by means of printed edicts); and Jardine, *Worldly Goods* (for spreading Renaissance ideas). The next two paragraphs are summaries and extensive quotes from these authors. Their descriptions are extraordinarily vivid and so

revealing that in my view it would be a waste of everyone's time for me to try and improve on them.

3. Plumb, *Horizon Book of the Renaissance*, jacket copy.
4. This paragraph is a summary of Plumb's magnificent book, with many direct quotes. Plumb, it seems to me, has brilliantly highlighted the reasons for divisions of Europe after the fall of Rome. *Horizon Book of the Renaissance.*
5. Bernard Berenson, *Essays in the Study of Sienese Painting.*
6. *Leonard* Olschki, "Asiatic Exoticism."
7. Ibid., p. 105
8. Hibbert, *Rise and Fall;* Plumb, *Horizon Book of the Renaissance*; Hollingsworth, *Patronage;* Bruckner, *Renaissance Florence.*
9. Origo, *Merchant of Prato.*
10. *Rise and Fall;* and Hibbert, Hollingsworth, *Patronage.*
11. Timothy J. McGee, "Dinner Music for the Florentine Signoria, 1350–1450, *Speculum,* 74, no. 1 (Jan. 1999): 95, Viewable on JSTOR.
12. *Rise and Fall;* and Hibbert, Hollingsworth, *Patronage,* pp. 48–55.
13. Hollingsworth, *Patronage,* p. 50.
14. Brown, "Laetentur Caeli."
15. Beck, "Leona Battista Alberti." Toscanelli cometary observations also in G. Celoria, *Sulle osservazioni de comete Fatte da Paulo dal Pozzi Toscanelli* (Milan: 1921).

Chapter 9: Toscanelli Meets the Chinese Ambassador

1. Markham, *Journals of Christopher Columbus.*
   The overwhelming majority of historians consider the letters to Canon Martins and Christopher Columbus to be genuine. In 1905 the French historian Henri Vignaud made an attempt to say that they were forged but as far as I know, no other scholar has supported Vignaud. Recent studies described in chapter 12 show that Toscanelli's writing on his cometary observations is the same as the letters. Moreover, every statement in Toscanelli's letters can be substantiated—for the reasons in chapter 11. If Toscanelli's letters were forgeries, then Waldseemüller's "Green Globe," and map of 1507 would be as well. A host of academics down the centuries and across Europe would have to be party to the forgery. The middle part of Toscanelli's letter to Canon Martins has been found by Harrisse in the Biblioteca Colombina in Seville. This is a copy made by Columbus himself of the letter from Toscanelli to Canon Martins.
2. Johnson, *The Papacy,* pp. 18, 100–3, 106, 115–19, 125.
3. G Lorenzetti, *Venice and Its Lagoon*, pp. 623–58, (map at 660): Palaces 15, 32, 35, 40, 42, 43, 66, and 84 (numbers as shown on map).
4. Same as note 1
5. These words were frequently interchangeable in medieval Europe.
6. See detailed notes for chapter 13 that summarise the cooperation between Toscanelli, Alberti, Nicholas of Cusa, and Regiomontanus. For Uzielli, See Zinner, *Regiomontanus,* p. 59.
7. Ibid.

8. Mr A. G. Self and F. H. H. Guillemard
    See notes 6 to 12 for chapter 10
9. I have seen Schöner's 1520 globe in the basement of the German Historical
    Museum, Nuremberg, courtesy of the curator. It is not on public display, unlike
    Behaim's 1492 globe, also in that museum.

Chapter 10: Columbus's and Magellan's World Maps

1. Vignaud, *Toscanelli and Columbus*, pp. 322, 323.
2. Ibid.
3. "In the time of Eugenius."
4. Zinner, *Regiomontanus,* reporting Uzielli, p. 59.
5. Pigafetta, *Magellan's Voyage,* p. 58; and Pigafetta and Miller, *Straits of Magellan*.
6. Pigafetta, and *1421,* pp. 169–77.
    ii—Magellan / King of Spain Contract March 22nd, 158—"Magellan's terrifying
    circumnavigation of the globe—Over the edge of the world" Bergreen, *Harper
    Perennial, New York, 2004,* p. 34.
7. Pigafetta, *Magellan's Voyage,* p. 56.
8. Ibid., p. 49; Guillemard, *Ferdinand Magellan,* p. 189; and Bergreen, *Over the Edge,*
    p. 32: "[Magellan] intended to go by Cape St. Mary which we call Rio de la Plata,
    and from thence to follow the coast until he hit the Strait."
9. Pigafetta and Miller, *Straits of Magellan*; Griffin, *Portsmouth, 1884,* p. 7; and
    Menzles, *1421,* 169–177.
10. Galvão, *Tratado;* and Antonio Cordeyro, *Historia Insula* (Lisbon: 1717), quoted in
    H. Harrisse, *The Discovery of North America*, (1892), p. 51.
11. Pigafetta, *Magellan's Voyage,* pp. 49, 50, 57; Menzies, *1421,* pp. 169–177; and
    Guillemard, *Ferdinand Magellan,* p. 189.
12. Guillemard, *Ferdinand Magellan,* p. 191. I am indebted to Mr. A. G. Self for
    introducing me to Guillemard's book.
13. *"Hunc in midu terre iam quadri partite conuscitet; sunt tres prime partes continentes
    quarta est insula cu omni quaque mare circudata cinspiciat,"* Martin Waldseemül-
    ler, *Cosmographiae introductio*.
14. Orejon et al., *Pleitos Columbinos*, 8 vols. and Schoenrich, *Legacy of Columbus*.
15. I am indebted to Greg Coelho, who brought this to my attention on March 20,
    2003. Original agreements, April 17 and 30, 1492. The decree confirming the
    favors is in the Archivo General de Indias, Seville. Confirmation came in the
    capitulations of Burgos, April 23 and 30, 1497.
16. Menzles, *1421,* pp. 425–427; and Fernández-Armesto, *Columbus,* p. 75.
17. *The Times Atlas* of *World Exploration,* p. 41. Available on www.1434.tv.
18. Fernández-Armesto, *Columbus,* p. 76.
19. Marcel Destombes, *Une carle interessant des Études Colombiennes conservé a
    Modena* (1952), and Davies, "Behaim, Martellus." See also Ao Vietor, "A Pre-
    Columbian Map of the World c. 1489," *Imago Mundi* 18: p. 458.
20. Correspondence between Dr. Aurelio Aghemo and Marcella Menzies. In
    summer 2006 on www.1434.tv.
21. Zinner, *Regiomontanus*.

22. Schöner's 1520 globe is in the German National Museum, Nuremberg, where it may be viewed courtesy of the curator. It is not on public display. The Behaim globe of 1492 (which does not show the Americas) is on public display there.
23. J. J. O'Connor and E. F. Robertson, "Johann Muller Regiomontanus," website, google "Johann Muller Regiomontanus."
24. In 1656 Emperor Ferdinand III of Austria purchased the Library of George Fugger, which included Schöner's library. The emperor gave the collection to the Hofbibliothek in Vienna, where it remains. The collection contains a chart of stars only visible in the Southern Hemisphere, published before Magellan's circumnavigation.
25. Zinner, *Regiomontanus,* pp. 109–39, 211–37, 242–44.
    Lost works in trade list pp. 115–17.
    Zinner (Regiomontanus) Folio 2, Leipzig 1938, pp. 89–103.
26. Guillemard, *Ferdinand Magellan.*
27. Pinzón was really the organizer of Columbus's 1492 expedition. See Bedini, *Columbus Encyclopedia,* vol. 2. S. V. "Arias Perez Pinzón." The History Co-operative. Seville Pinzón's eldest son testified that in 1492 a friend of his father, employed in the Vatican Library, had given him a copy of a document showing that Japan could be reached by sailing westward across the Atlantic. Impressed, Pinzón showed Columbus the Vatican document and persuaded Columbus to visit the Catholic sovreigns once again. This time he was successful in obtaining their backing.

Chapter 11: The World Maps of Johannes Schöner, Martin Waldseemüller, and Admiral Zheng He

1. This shows the Americas as Waldseemueller drew them on a flat piece of paper which he copied from a globe.
2. At this stage I had no evidence Waldseemüller had copied from a globe, although my experiments had shown he must have done.
3. The exhibition was to celebrate the 500th anniversary of the publication of Waldseemüller's 1507 map. Please see the *1434* website, www.1434.tv, for a reproduction of Waldseemüller's world map and for Dr. Ronsin's description in French of how Waldseemüller obtained it.

Chapter 12: Toscanelli's New Astronomy

1. *The Catholic Encyclopedia*, S. V. "China: Foreign Relations," http://www .newadvent.org/cathen/03663b.htm. See also *1434* website, www.1434. tv.
2. Tai Peng Wang, "Zheng He's Delegation."
3. Ibid.
4. Ibid. See also Zheng Xing Lang, *Zhongxi Jiaotong Chiliao Huibian* (Collected historical sources of the history between China and the West), vol. 1, chap. 6, pp. 331 et seq.)

5. Pinturicchio painting can be seen on the *1434* website, www.1434.tv. *Age of the Renaissance.* Borgia Apartments of the Palazzi Pontifici, in the Vatican.
6. Tai Peng Wang, (V) "Zheng He's Delegation."
7. Tai Peng Wang, "Zheng He, Wang Dayvan." Tai produces evidence that Yuan navigators had mastered astronavigation sufficiently to cross oceans. See Gong Zhen, *Xiyang Banguo Zhi* (Notes on barbarian countries in the western seas) (Beijing: Zhounghua bookshop,). See also Xi Fei Long, Yank Xi, Tang Xiren, eds. *Zhongguo Jishu Shi, Jiaotong Cluan* (The history of Chinese science and technology), vol. on Transportation (Beijing: Science Publisher, 2004), pp. 395–96; and W. Scot Morton and Charlton M. Lewis, *China: Its History and Culture* (New York: McGraw-Hill, 2005), p. 128.
8. Jane Jervis, "Toscanelli's Cometary Observations: Some New Evidence" Annali Del Instituto e Museo Di Storia Della Scienza Di Firenze II (1997).
9. *Right Ascension—its significance, a Chinese method not Arabic nor Babylonian method of celestial coordinates.*
10. Gadol, *Leon Battista Alberti:* p.196. See Zinner, *Regiomontanus,* p. 58.

Chapter 13: The Florentine Mathematicians: Toscanelli, Alberti, Nicholas of Cusa, and Regiomontanus

1. Zinner, *Regiomontanus,* pp. 29, 41, 52–59, 64–65.
2. Ibid., pp. 44, 48, 71, 73–78, 83, 104, 214–515; *The* S. V. "Suggest."
3. Compare with Regiomontanus, "De Triangulis," in Zinner, *Regiomontonus.* p. 55–60.
4. Zinner, *Regiomontenus,* pp. 44, 48, 71–73, 78, 83, 104, 214–515.
5. Zinner, *Regiomontanus,* p. 125; and *The Catholic Encyclopedia,* S. V. "Nicholas of Cusa."
6. Ernst Zinner. I have extensively quoted from his majestic work, *Regiomontanus.* Where Zinner's opinion differs from other experts, I have used Zinner's. My only disagreement with Zinner is with his opinion of which precedent Regiomontanus relied upon for his ephemeris tables. Zinner did not know of Guo Shoujing's work; if he had he, in my view, would have come to the inevitable conclusion that Regiomontanus followed Guo Shoujing.
   Regiomontanus's principal works mentioned in chapter 13 are discussed in Zinner as follows: almanacs: pp. 8–12, 21–37, 40, 85, 104–9, 112–25, 141–49, 153; calendars: pp. 42, 50, 112–42 (see also e-mails between Bodleian Library at Oxford University and author, on www.1434.tv); compass: pp. 16–20; De tranigulis: pp. 51–65; ephemeris tables: pp. 108–28, (see also e-mails between Bodleian Library at Oxford University and author, on www.1434.tv); Epitome of Ptolomy: pp. 2, 29, 41–52, 59; instruments: pp. 135–36, 180–84; maps: pp. 113–16, 148; obliquity of ecliptic: pp. 23, 25, 38, 48, 53–69. See also *Johannes Regiomontanus Calendar Printed in Venice of Aug. 1482,* on *1434* website University of Glasgow, 1999.
7. Zinner, *Regiomontanus,* pp. 1–30, 32, 36–56, 76–78.
8. Ibid., pp. 24, 36, 58–60, 72–77.
9. Ibid., pp. 117–25.
10. Ibid., pp. 121–25.

11. Ibid., pp. 98, 115, 133, 137, 158, 212, 244, 246.
12. Ibid., pp. 95 and 301. See also pp. 131–34, 135 (clock); p. 136 (armillary sphere, pp. 137–38, mirrors, compass; and p. 115, torquetum.
13. Ibid., pp. 112, 113, 301. See also Ernst Zinner, "The Maps of Regiomontanus," *Imago Mundi,* 4 (1947): 31–32.
14. Zinner, *Regiomontanus,* p. 40.
15. Ibid., p. 42.
16. Ibid., p. 183.
17. Ibid., p. 64.
18. Ibid., pp. 365, 370; and Ulrich Libbrecht, *Chinese Mathematics,* 1973 p. 247.
19. See Libbrecht for his discussion on Curtze contribution at p. 247. See Needham S19, p. 40 for the *Shu-shu Chiu-chang* and the evolution of Chinese mathematics from the Sung dynasty through to the Yuan.
20. Ch' in Chiu-Shao Libbrecht, *Chinese Mathematics,* pp. 247–48.
21. Needham, *Science and Civilisation,* vol. 19, pp. 10, 40, 42, 120, 141, 472, 577.
22. Ibid., vol. 30. Photo by kind permission of the Pepys Library, Magdalene College, Cambridge University.
23. Zinner, *Regiomontanus,* p. 117. For Copernicus, see p. 119. Other versions of Regiomontonus's tables can be viewed in the copies held by the Royal Astronomical Society, London, and the John Rylands University, Manchester. Photo by kind permission of the British Library.
24. Davies, "Behain, Martellus."
25. Menzies, *1421,* pp. 430–31.
26. Zinner, *Regiomontanus,* pp. 119–23.
27. Bedini, *Columbus Encyclopedia,* p. 436; and ibid., p. 120.
28. Zinner, *Regiomontonus,* p. 123.
29. Ibid., pp. 119–25.
30. Ibid., p. 123.
31. Lambert, "Abstract."
32. G. W. Littlehales, "The Decline of Lunar Distances," *American Geography Society Bulletin,* 4, no. 2 (1909): 84. Viewable on JSTOR.
33. Lambert, "Abstract."
34. Phillips and Encarta.
35. Zinner, *Regiomontonus,* p. 181.
36. Needham, *Science and Civilisation,* vol. 19, pp. 49–50, 109, 110, and 370–378. See also *Yongle Dadian* (Cambridge: Cambridge University Press), chap. 16, pp. 343, 344.

Chapter 14: Leon Battista Alberti and Leonardo da Vinci

1. Gadol, *Leon Battista Alberti,* introduction.
2. Ibid., pp. 67 and 196.
3. See "Selected Works of Leon Battista Alberti" in bibliography.
4. Zinner, *Regiomontanus,* pp. 24, 36, 58–60, 67–68, 72–77, 130–34, 265; and Gadol, *Leon Battista Alberti,* p. 196.
   Letter of Feb 1464 in 'Vita di LB Alberti at p 373

5. Santinello's parallels are explored in more detail on the *1434* website, chapters 13, 18 and 21.
6. Gadol, *Leon Battista Alberti*, p. 155.

Chapter 15: Leonardo da Vinci and Chinese Inventions

1. Temple, *Genius of China*, p. 192.
2. Peers, Warlords, of China, p. 149.
3. Deng, *Ancient Chinese Inventions*, p. 104.
4. Ibid., pp. 113–14.
5. Ibid., p. 112.
6. See ch. 16 for Leonardo copying Taccola, who drew in 1438 a Chinese helicopter.
7. Temple, *Genius*, p.175.
8. Ibid., p. 177.
9. Ibid., p. 243.
10. Taddei, *Leonardo's Machines*, p. 118.
11. Temple, *Genius*, p. 59.

Chapter 16: Leonardo, di Giorgio, Taccola and Alberti

1. White, "Parachute," pp. 462–67.
2. Reti, "Francesco di Giorgio Martini's Treatise," p. 287.
3. Francesco, Trattato. Copies Biblioteca Nazionale Florence and Biblioteca Communale Siena
4. Reti, "Helicopters and Whirligigs"; Leonardo, "Parachute"; Jackson, "Dragonflies"; and Gablehouse, "Helicopters and Autogiros."
5. See Guidebooks on Siena
6. Prager and Scaglia, *Mariano Taccola*.
7. Please also refer to Modern Guide Book "Siena" Romas, Siena p. 154.
8. Sigismund Faced Uprisings In Bohemia following Jan Huss Murder in 1419 (Following Council of Constance)
9. Prager and Scaglia, "Mariano Taccola."
10. Ibid.; and Galluzzi, *Art of Invention*, p. 118.
11. Prager and Scaglia, *Mariano Taccola. Galluzzi, Art of Invention*, p. 35.
12. Galluzzi, *Art of Invention*, pp. 36–37.
13. Prager and Scaglia, *Mariano Taccola*; and ibid., pp. 37–38.
14. Prager and Scaglia, *Mariano Taccola*, p. 93; and Galluzzi, *Art of Invention*, p. 87. Di Giorgio adapts Taccola—Examples

    i) Di Giorgio's fountain (Ms Ash 4IR) and Taccola's surprise fountain (Ms PAL 767 p.21)
    ii) Taccola's hoists for Mills (III, 36R) and di Giorgio's Mills (Trattato I Ms Ash 361 for 37v)
    iii) Taccola's and di Giorgio's underwater swimmers with breathing (Cod Lat Mon 288800 fol 78R and MS PAL 767 BNCF p.9)

iv)   Floating Riders on Horseback (Taccola II 90V) di Giorgio MS II. I. 141 (BNCF) follow 196v

v)   Paddle wheel boats—Taccola Ms Lat 7239 fol 87r: di Giorgio Ms 197 b21 (BML) fol 45 v

vi)   Devices for measuring distances—Taccola Ms Pal 766 fol 52R : di Giorgio Ms Ash 361 fol 29R

vii)   Drawings of Trebuchet Ms 197.b.21 (BML) fol 3V (di Giorgio) and cod lat Mon 197 II fol 59V (Taccola)

viii)   Underground Mining causing towns to collapse—di Giorgio Ms Ash 361 fol 50R; Taccola Codex lat Mon 28800 fol. 48V

ix)   Transportable crane di Giorgio Ms 197 b.21 fol 11V Taccola Ms PAL 766 for ZOR

x)   Weight driven wheels—Taccola Code lat Mon 197 II fol 57 R: di Giorgio Ms 197 b21 Fol 71 V

xi)   Water mills transforming vertical power to horizontal Taccola Ms Pal 766 Fol 39R: di Giorgio Ms Sal 148 for 34V

xii)   Ox drawn pumps Taccola Ms Lat 7239 p. 32 di Giorgio MS II.1.141 fol 97V

15.   K. T. Wu, and Wu Kuang-Ch'ing, "Ming Printing and Printers," Harvard Journal of Asiatie Studies 7, no. 3 (Feb. 1943): 203–60.

16.   See Needham, *Science and Civilisation*, vols. 19 and 27.

17.   *Taccola MS Lat BNP fol 50R*

18.   Francesco *Di Giorgio MS II 1.141 fol 97v*

19.   Needham, *Science and Civilisation,* vol. 27, figs. 602–27, table 56.

20.   *Nung Shu, ch. 19, pp. 5bb–6a* and NS 183.

21.   *MS Lat Urbinas 1757 Fol 118R*

22.   *Carts with steering gear—Codicetto*

23.   *Reversible hoists—de Ingeneis III 36R* Taccola, *De Ingeneis,* book 2, 96v.

24.   *Ms Ash 361 F 37V*

25.   *Ms Getty GEM fol R*

26.   *Galluzzi, Art of Invention, pp. 42–43.*

27.   Ibid., p. 44.

28.   *361 Fol 46v*

29.   Galluzzi, *Art of Invention,* p. 11.

30.   Ibid., p. 11.

31.   Jackson, "Dragonflies," pp. 1–4; Gablehouse, *Helicopters and Autogiros,* pp. 1–3; and White, "Helicopters and Whirligigs."

Chapter 17: Silk and Rice

1.   *Nung Shu;* and Needham, *Science and Civilization,* vol. 27, p. 104.

2.   Martial, quoted in Thorley, pp. 71–80.

3.   Thorley, "Silk Trade Between China and the Roman Empire at Its Height Circa. A.D. 90–130" *Greece and Rome,* 2nd Series, Vol. 18, No. 1 (1971) p.71–80. See Bibliography.

4.   Temple, "Genius," p. 120, ill. 88.

5. Molà, "Silk Industry," pp. 261 and 218, 220.
6. Hobson, *Eastern Origins,* pp. 128, 342; and Kuhn, "Science V."
7. Molà, "Silk Industry," p. 261.
8. "Braudel, Wheels of Commerce," Fontana, 1985, pp. 405–408.
9. Needham, *Science and Civilisation,* vol. 28, pp. 225 and 340.
10. Ms Ash 361 (BMLF) fol 6V
11. Shapiro, "Suction Pump," p. 571.
12. Needham, *Science and Civilisation,* vol. 27, p. 144.
13. Molà, "Silk Industry," pp. 218–46.
14. Hibbert, *House of Medici,* p. 63.
15. Ibid., p. 63.
16. Ibid., Hibbert, p. 89

Chapter 18: Grand Canals, China and Lombardy

1. Emperor Yang—Sui dynasty. Ancient China," p. 66.
2. Lonely Planet p. 378.
3. Now named Xian. "Ancient China" pp. 63–75. Ancient China-Chinese Civilisation from the origin to the Tang dynasty Barnes & Noble N.Y. 2006.
4. Quoted in Lonely Planet pp.378–79.
5. Temple, *Genius,* pp. 196–97.
6. Needham, *Science and Civilisation,* vol. 28; and ibid., p. 197.
7. Needham, *Science and Civilization,* ch. 28, pp. 358–76.
8. *Barbarossa Capture of Milan* Frederick I (1123–1190) conquered Milan in 1161.
9. *Taccola's Lock Gate Taccola, De ingeneis,* vol. 4; and Parsons, *Engineers,* pp. 367–373.
10. Parsons, *Engineers,* p. 373.
11. Ibid.
12. Ibid., p. 376.
13. Parsons, *Engineers.* Descriptions *Trattato dei Pondi* p. 373; Alberti, pp. 374–75; Bartola, pp. 358–376.
14. Ibid., pp. 372–81; Needham, *Science and Civilisation,* vol. 28, pp. 377–80.
15. Needham, *Science and Civilisation,* vol. 28, pp. 358–76.
16. Parsons, *Engineers,* pp. 374–75.
17. See Mantua L.Santoni Mantua 1989, p. 36 et seq
18. Dixon, *Venice, Vicenza,* p. 112. et seq
19. Ibid.

Chapter 19: Firearms and Steel

1. Spencer, "Filarete's Description"; and Wertime, "Asian Influences" and *Age of Steel.*
2. Ibid.
3. Spencer, "Filarete's Description."
4. Ibid.

5. Ibid.
6. Brescia and Bergamo are towns in northern Italy.
7. Wertime, "Asian Influences," p. 397.
8. Butters, *Triumph of Vulcan.*
9. Needham, *Science and Civilisation,* vol. 30. pt. II
10. *Genius of China,* pp. 224–228.
11. Goodrich, L. Carrington, and Fêng Chia-Shêng. *"The Early Development of Firearms in China." Isis* 36, no. 2 (Jan. 1946): 114–23. Viewable on JSTOR.
12. Temple, *Genius,* p. 230.
13. Ibid., p. 234.
14. Cited in Needham, *Science and Civilisation,* vol. 30, pt. II.
15. Temple, *Genius,* p. 237.
16. Goodrich and Feng, "Early Development."
17. Eichstadt, *Bellifortis*; Thorndike, "Unidentified Work," p. 42.
18. Thorndike, "Unidentified Work," p. 42.
19. Ibid., p. 37.
20. Ibid., p. 38.
21. Needham, *Science and Civilisation,* vol. 30, pt. II, p. 51.
22. A Stuart Weller "Francesco di Giorgio Martini 1439–1501" University of Chicago Press, Chicago Ill 1943 at p. 74.
23. Ibid.
24. Refer to *1434* website under "cannon."
25. *Chien Tzu Lei Phao.*
26. *Huo Lung Chung,* pt. 1, ch. 2, pp. 2, 2a, 10a.
27. Ibid., p. 16a
28. MS 5, IV. 5 (BCS) c. 5R.

Chapter 20: Printing

1. Ottley, and Humphreys, *History.*
2. Needham, *Science and Civilisation*, vol. 32, pp. 100–75; and Deng *Ancient Chinese Inventions,* pp. 21–23.
3. Needham, *Science and Civilisation,* vol. 32, pp. 100–175, esp. p. 172. For *Yongle Dadian* see p. 174, n. c. See also Wu, "Development."
4. Hessel, *Haarlem,* and Humphreys, *History,* p. 55.
5. "The Case of Rival Claimants," p. 170.
6. Bibs. 7, 8, and 9.
7. Blaise Agüeras y Arcas and Paul Needham Reported on Google.
APHA/Grolier Club lecture by Paul Needham and Blaise LECTURE: Agueras y Arcas—(organisation of Book Collectors)
January 2001. New York.
PAPER:
Agüera y Arcas, Blaise; Paul Needham (November 2002). "Computational analytical bibliography". *Proceedings Bibliopolis Conference* The future history of the book, The Hague (Netherlands): Koninklijke Bibliotheek.

8.   Ottley, *Inquiry,* p. 47; and Termanza, "Lettere," vol. 5 p. 321.
9.   "Early Venetian Printing," exhibition, Kings College, London, Dec. 2006.
10.   Carmichael, *Plague and the Poor,* pp. 124–26.

Chapter 21: China's Contribution to the Renaissance

1.   Zinner, *Regiomontanus,* pp. 112–13.
2.   Liu Manchums, evidence at Nanjing Conference Dec 2002.
3.   Ibid.
4.   Villiers and Earle, *Albuquerque,* pp. 29–65; and in Antonio de Bilhao Pato, *Cartas de Afonse de Albuquerque Seguides de dowmentos que as elucidam,* vol. 1, letter 9 (April 1512): pp. 29–65. Translation and research by E Manuel Stock.
5.   *O Brasil invar Portulano do* sec xv (Brasil on a Map of Fifteenth Century)
6.   Thorndike, "Unidentified Work," p. 42.
7.   Corte são, "Pre-Columbian Discovery," p. 39.
8.   Thompson, Friar's Map, pp. 171–74.
9.   Fiske, John.
      The Discovery of America—With Some Account of Ancient America and the Spanish Conquest (two volumes). Boston: Houghton Mifflin, 1892. Reprinted 1920.
10.   Thompson, *Friar's Map,* "Venice Goes West," p. 171. Sinovic, 1991, p. 155.
11.   Duchess of Medina-Sidonia's collection of Columbus record, in her Library at Sanlucar de Barrameda.
12.   Ruggero, Marino, *Cristoforo Colombo: L'ultimo dei Templari.* Milan: Sperling, Kupfer Editori, 2005.
13.   Royal Geographical Society Journal Davies, "Behaim, Martellus and Columbus," 143, pt. 3: 451–59.
14.   *Encyclopedia Britannica, New* "The Copernican Revolution." S. V. "Copernicus, Nicolaus," and also Zinner, *Regiomontanus,* p. 183.
15.   Ibid., Zinner, p. 183.
16.   Ibid.
17.   This is being corrected in the latest edition.
18.   Ernst Zinner, *Regiomontanus,* pp. 184–185.
19.   Swerdlow, "Derivation."
20.   "Derivation."
21.   Ibid.
22.   See Gou Shoujing's third-degree method of interpolation in Aslaksen and Ng Say Tiong, "Calendars, Interpolation."
23.   Siderius. See *New Encyclopedia Brittanica*
24.   *New Encyclopedia Brittanica,* 15th ed., S. V. 1994 "Galilei, Galileo."
25.   Mui, Dong, and Zhou, "Ancient Chinese."
26.   Gadol, *Leon Battista Alberti.*
27.   Sorenson and Raish, *Pre-Columbian Contact;* and Johannesen and Sorenson, Biology
28.   Thompson, *Friar's Map*; and letters to author 2003–2007

Chapter 22: Tragedy on the High Seas: Zheng He's Fleets Destroyed by a Tsunami

This chapter relies heavily on the work of Professor Ted Bryant and Dr. Dallas Abbott and
colleagues; please refer to the Acknowledgments section.

1. Legend of the bear climbing out of a wrecked ship on Clatsop Beach. This is
   Chinook folklore, recounted to us by Catherine Herrold Troeh.
2. The legend is corroborated by a similar one of the Crow people, told to us by
   Frank Fitch.
3. Zatta's map appears on our *1434* website as do drawings of Chinese people made
   during Russian expeditions carried out before Vancouver or Cook.
4. These figures are explained in more detail in chapter 2.
5. This correspondence was in 2002.
6. The relevant part of this is reported on the *1434* website
7. Keddie, Grant, "Contributions to Human History," published by Royal British
   Columbia Museum, No. 3, March 19, 1990.
8. Further details of the Washington potters may be found on our *1434* website
9. Professor Marianna Fernandez Cobo and colleagues (see Bibliography)
10. Professor Gabriel Novick and colleagues (see Bibliography)
11. Diego Ribero's chart of 1529 can be seen on our *1434* website. It contains
    accurate mapping details of places from South America to Indonesia, which in
    1529 had not been "discovered" by Europeans and were unknown to them.
12. Rostowerski, Maria—"History of the Inca Realm", Cambridge University Press, 1999
13. Macedo Justo Cáceres "Pre-Hispanic Cultures of Peru," Peruvian National
    Museum, Lima, Peru, 1985.
    Copper coins—these were the shape of small axes. See our *1434* website for the
    section on coinage.

Chapter 23: The Conquistadores' Inheritance: Our Lady of Victory

This chapter relies heavily on a series of lectures on Medieval Spain given by Dr.
Christopher Pollard at Dillington House near Taunton, Somerset, which the
author was privileged to attend in 1999. Please refer to the acknowledgments
section.

BIBLIOGRAPHY

A. Bibligraphy for Chapters 1–5 inclusive

Dreyer, Edward L. *Zheng He: China and the Oceans in the Early Ming Dynasty, 1405–1433.* London: Pearson Longman, 2006.

Mote, Frederick, and Denis C. Twitchett, eds. *The Cambridge History of China.* Vol. 7, *The Ming Dynasty, 1368–1644.* New York: Cambridge University Press, 1988.

Tsai, Shih-Shan Henry. *Perpetual Happiness: The Ming Emperor Yongle.* Seattle: University of Washington Press, 2001.

Twitchett, Denis C., ed. *The Cambridge History of China.* Vol. 3, *Sui and T'ang China, 589–906 AD.* Cambridge: Cambridge University Press, 1979.

Dreyer, Edward L. *Early Ming History: A Political History, 1355–1435.* Stanford, Calif.: Stanford University Press, 1982.

———. *Zheng He: China and the Oceans in the Early Ming Dynasty, 1405–1433.* London: Pearson Longman, 2006.

J. J. L. Duyvendak. "The True Dates of the Chinese Maritime Expeditions in the Early Fifteenth Century." *T'oung Pou* (Leiden), no. 34 (1938).

Needham, Joseph. *Science and Civilisation in China.* 7 vols. 30 sections. Cambridge: Cambridge University Press, 1956–.

Reid, Anthony. *Southeast Asia in the Age of Commerce, 1450–1680.* Vol. 2, *Expansion and Crisis.* New Haven, Conn.: Yale University Press, 1993.

Tai Peng Wang. Research papers available on www.gavinmenzies.net.

———. "Foreigners in Zheng He's Fleets," Apr. 2006.

———. "A Tale of Globalisation in Ancient Asia," Dec. 3, 2006.

———. "The Real Discoverer of the World," ed. Lin Gang—Zheng He," giving explanations relating to Zheng He 1418 map.

———. "The Most Startling Discovery from Zheng He's Treasure Shipyards by Prof. Pan Biao and My Response."

———. "What Was the Route Taken by the Chinese Delegation to Florence in 1433."

———. "Zheng He and His Envoys' Visits to Cairo in 1414 and 1433."

Temple, Robert. *The Genius of China: 3,000 Years of Science, Discovery & Invention.* London: Prion, 1998.

Needham, Joseph. *Science and Civilisation in China.* Vols. 27 and 30. Cambridge: Cambridge University Press, 1956–.

Paul Lunde. *The Navigator Ahmed Ibn Majid.* Riyadh, Saudi Arabia: Saudi Aramco, 2004.

"A history of the Oversees Chinese in Africa." *African Studies Review,* vol. 44, no. 1, April 2001.

Gang Den. "Yuan marine merchants and overseas voyages." In *Minzu Shi Yanju,* Beijing 2005.

Hall, Richard. *Empires of the Monsoon: A History of the Indian Ocean and Its Invaders.* New York: HarperCollins, 1996.

Ibn Battuta. *The Travels of Ibn Battuta, AD 1325–1354,* Vol. 4. London: Hakluyt Society, 1994.

Poole, Stanley Lane. *A History of Egypt in the Middle Ages.* Frank Cass London 1894. *Yingzong Shi-lu.*

Tai Peng Wang research papers, available on www.gavinmenzies.net.

———. "A Tale of Globalisation in Ancient Asia"

In this paper Tai Peng Wang argues that global trade from the Mediterranean to Australia existed in the Tang dynasty, during which massive quantities of export ceramics were fired in Chinese kilns and carried by Arab dhows and Chinese junks. Quanzhou was the principal port from Tang dynasty onward. Quanzhou became the hub of this trading web (Research paper in full on *1434* website)

- Liu Yu Kun, "Quanzhou Zai Nanhai Jiaotongshi Shang de diwei" (The significance of Quanzhou in the history of Nanhai trade). In *Xuesha Quanzhou* (Quanzhou studies), by Cai Yao Ping, Zhang Ming, and Wu Yuan Peng. Central Historical Text Publisher, 2003, pp. 144–45.

- Wang Gungwu, *The Nanhai Trade: Early Chinese Trade in the South China Sea.* Eastern Universities Press, 2003.

- Edward Schaefer. The Golden Peaches of Samarkand: A study of Tang Exotics. Berkeley and Los Angeles: University of California Press, 1991.

Tai Peng Wang research from papers:

"What was the route taken by the Chinese delegation to Florence in 1433 and what might that be?" and "Zheng He and his Envoys visits to Cairo in 1414 and 1433"

Tai Peng Wang's Main Points Relevant to Chapters 2, 3, 5:

1. Hong Bao was instructed by Zheng He on November 18, 1432, to lead his fleets to Calicut.

2. On arrival Hong Bao learned Calicut was about to send its own fleet to Mecca. Hong Bao immediately sent seven interpreter officials to join the Calicut fleet. Zheng He's fleets arrived in Hormuz on January 16, 1433, and set sail for China on April 9, 1433.

3. Zheng He had been ordered to announce the imperial edict of the Xuan De emperor to Maijia (Mecca), Qianlida (Baghdad), Wusili (Egypt), Mulanpi (Morocco), and Lumi (Florence).

4. Egypt and Morocco had already received the imperial edict but had failed to send tribute to Ming China. See Yan Congjian's firsthand account of the visit to "Fulin" kingdom—the Papal Court.

5. The Chinese were trading within the system created in the Yuan dynasty more than a century earlier.

6. Tianfang is the Mamluk empire—Egypt, Syria, Yemen, Arabia, Libya, and Cyprus.

7. The Chinese used Arabic pilots in the Gulf area: Irena Knehtl, "The Fleet of the Dragon in Yemeni Waters." *The Yemen Times* 874, vol. 13 (5 Sept. 7–Sept. 2005).

8. Frankincense was the most valuable product purchased by the Chinese: ibid.

9. *Zheng He visits Aihdab. Yuanshi Luncong.* "The Relation Between Sudan and China Between the Tang and the End of the Yuan. In *Essays on Yuan History,* vol. 7, pp. 200–6.

10. Karimi in Quanzhou: *Zhu Fan Zhi Zhu Pu*. In Zhao Ruqua, *Profiles of Foreign Barbarian Countries* (Hong Kong: Hong Kong University Center of Asian Studies, 2000), p. 175.

11. Karimi merchants behavior: *Qihai Yangtan* (Setting sail in the seven seas), (Hong Kong: Zhounghua, HK, 1990) p.123, and *Bai Shou Yi Minzhu Zhong Jiao Lunji* (Bai Shou Yi's essays in minorities and their religions) (Beijing: Beijing Teacher Training University, 1992), pp.365, 376.

12. Arabic monsoon calendar: First composed in 1271 by Rasulid rulers of Yemen. See Paul Lunde, "The Navigator Ahmad Ibn Majid."

13. Egypt the target of Zheng He visits: Anatole Andro (Chao C. Chien), *The 1421 Heresy: An Investigation into the Ming Chinese Maritime Survey of the World* (Pasadena, Calif.:, 2005), p. 32.
R. Stephen Humphreys, "Egypt in the World System of the Late Middle Ages" *Cambridge History of Egypt*, vol. 1 *Islamic Egypt 640–1517* (Cambridge: Cambridge University Press, 1998).

14. Egypt visited but has not returned tribute to China: Mosili is Fustat. Misr is Cairo. Jientou is Alexandra. Li Anshan, *Feizhou Huqqiaohuaren Shi: A History of Overseas Chinese in Africa* (Beijing: in "African studies review," vol 44, April 2001, 2000).

15. Misr is Cairo: Janet L. Abu-Lughod, *Cairo: 1001 Years of the City Victorius* (Princeton, N.J.: Princeton University Press, 197), pp.1–30.

16. Cairo in the Yuan Dynasty: Shang Yan Bing, *Yuan Marine Merchants and Overseas Voyages in Ninzu Shi Yanju* (Beijing: Minju Shi Yanj 2002), p. 190.

17. Reciprocal visits between China and Egypt: Teobaldi Filesi, *China and Africa in the Middle Age*," trans. D. Morison (London; Fran Cass, 1972), p. 89, and "Merchants As Diplomatic Relations," Eternal Egypt website.

18. Yuan adopt Islamic astronomy: Yan Congjian, *Shuyu Zhouzi Lu.*

19. Interpreting between Egyptian, Persian, and Chinese: Professor Liu Ying Sheng, *A Compendium of Yuan History*, vol. 10 (Beijing: China Radio and TV Publishing House, 2005), p. 30.

———. "What was the Route Taken by the Chinese Delegation to Florence in 1433"

———. "Zheng He and His Envoys' Visit, to Cario in 1414 and 1433"

———. "Zheng He's Delegation to Papal Court of Florence"

B. Bibliography for Chapter 6

Aldridge, James. *Cairo: Biography of a City.* London: Macmillan, 1969.

Braudel, Fernand. *A History of Civilisations.* Translated by Richard Mayne. London: Penguin Books, 1993.

Payne, Robert. *The Canal Builders.* New York: Macmillan, 1959.

Poole, Stanley Lane. *A History of Egypt in the Middle Ages.* London: Frank Cass, 1894.

Origo, Iris. *The Merchant of Pratoo: Daily Life in a Medieval Italian City.* London: Penguin Books, 1992.

Redmount, Carol A. "The Wadi Tumilat and the Canal of the Pharaohs." *Journal of Near Eastern Studies,* no. 54 (1995).

Al Makrizi, Ahmad Ibn Ali, "Histoire d'Egypt." Translated by Edgard Blocher. Paris, 1908.

K. N. Chandhuri. "A Note on Ibn Taghri Birdi-Description of Chinese ships in Aden and Jedda." *Journal of the Royal Asiatic Society* (1989) SJ 447.

C. Bibliography for Chapter 7

I have been travelling to Venice for fifty years and in total have spent months exploring her canals and museums. As may be expected, I have read a lot of books in that time. Four of these, in my view, give brilliant popular descriptions of this wonderful Byzantine city, half European, half Asian. These are Norwich's *Venice: the Greatness and Fall* and *Venice: the Rise to Empire;* Hibbert's *Venice: Biography of a City;* Lorenzetti's *Venice and Its Lagoon,* the bible of Venice; and *Venice: the Masque of Italy* by Brion. These four know Venice like the back of their hand, and it would be impertinent of me to attempt to improve on their rich descriptions. I have quoted extensively from them.

Alazard, Jean. *La Venise de la Renais sance.* Paris: Hachette, 1956.
Braudel, Fernand. *The Mediterranean in the Time of Philip II.* Translated by Sian Reynolds. London: Fontana, 1966.
———. *The Wheels of Commerce.* London: Penguin Books, 1993. Translated by Richard Mayne.
Brion, Marcel. *Venice: The Masque of Italy.* Translated by Neil Mann. London: Elek Books, 1962.
Hall, Richard. *Empires of the Monsoon: A History of the Indian Ocean and Its Invaders.* New York: HarperCollins, 1996.
Hibbert, Christopher. *Venice: Biography of a City.*
Hutton, Edward. *Venice and Venetia.* New York: W.W. Norton & Co., 1989. London: Hollis and Carter 1954.
Lorenzetti, Giulio. *Venice and Its Lagoon.* Rome: Instituto Poligrafico Dello Stato, 1956.
Morris, Jan. *The Venetian Empire.* London: Penguin Books, 1990.
Norwich, John Julius. *Venice: The Greatness and Fall.* London: Allen Lane, 1981.
———. *Venice: The Rise to Empire.* London: Random House, 1989.
Olschki, Leonardo. "Asiatic Exotioism in Italian Art of the Early Renaissance." *Art Bulletin* 26, no. 2 (June 1994).
Origo, Iris. "The Domestic Enemy: The Eastern Slaves in Tuscany in the Fourteenth and Fifteenth Century." *Speculum: A Journal of Medieval Studies* 30, no. 3 (July 1955).
Riviere-Sestier, M. "Venice and the Islands." London: George G. Harrap & Company 1956.
Thompson, Guinnar PhD. "The Friars MAP of Ancient America 1360 AD." WA: Pub Laura Lee Productions, 1996.

D. Bibliography for Chapters 8 and 9

Beck, James. "Leon Battista Alberti and the Night Sky at San Lorenzo." *Artibus et Historiae* 10, no. 19 (1989): 9–35.
Brown, Patricia Fortini. *"Laetentur Caeli:* The Council of Florence and the Astronomical Fresco in the Old Sacristy." *Journal of the Warburg and Courtauld Institute* 44 (1981): 176 ff.
Bruckner, Gene A. *Renais sance Florence.* Berkeley and Los Angeles: University of California Press, 1969.

Carmichael, Ann G. *Plague and Poor in Renaissance Florence.* Cambridge: Cambridge University Press, 1986.

Hibbert, Christopher. *The House of Medici: Its Rise and Fall 1420–1440.* London: Penguin Books, 1974.

Hollingsworth, Mary. *Patronage in Renaissance Italy.* London: John Murray, 1994.

Jardine, Lisa. *Worldly Goods: A New History of the Renaissance.* London: Macmillan, 1996.

Olschki, Leonardo. "Asiatic Exoticism in Italian Art of the Early Renaissance." *Art Bulletin* 26, no. 2 (June 1994).

Origo, Iris. *The Merchant of Prato: Daily Life in a Medieval Italian City.* London: Penguin Books, 1963.

Plumb, J. H. *The Horizon Book of the Renaissance.* London: Collins, 1961.

Tai Peng Wang. "Zheng He's Delegation to the Papal Court of Florence." This research paper was the stimulus for this book. It is available, with an extensive bibliography, on our website. The main points are as follows:

1. Few know of Toscanelli's letters to the king of Portugal and Christopher Columbus, letters that report Toscanelli meeting the Chinese ambassador. C. R. Markham, trans., *The Journals of Christopher Columbus* Vignaud Henri Hakluyt Society O. viii). Also Vignaud "Toscanelli and Columbus"

2. In the 1430s, China described Florence (seat of the papacy 1434–38) as Fulin or Farang. Yu Lizi, *"Fulin Ji Aishi Shengdi Diwang Bianzheng"* (The correct locations of Fulin countries and the birthplace of Ai Shi during Yuan China), *Haijioshi Yanjiu* (Maritime historical studies) Quanzhou: (1990–1992): 51.

3. Diplomatic exchanges between the papacy and Ming China had started with Hong Wu in 1371. See Zhang Xing Lang: *Zhougxi Jiaotong Shiliao Huibian* (Collected historical sources of the history of contacts between China and the West), vol. 1 pp. 315.

4. There are many Chinese descriptions of the papacy in Hong Wu and Zhu Di's reign. See Zhang Xing Lang, p. 331, and Yan Congjian *Shuyu Zhouzi Lu,* at vol. 2. Also Mingshi *Waigua Zhuan* (Profiles of foreign countries in the Ming history).

5. The papacy paid tribute to China during Zhu Di's reign. *Ming Shi Waigua Zhuan,* vol. 5, p. 47.

6. Lumi was Rome in early Ming descriptions. The name originated in the Song dynasty, (in with Zhao Chinese) Ruqua, who used the name Lumei in his book *Zhufan Zhi: Descriptions of Various Barbarians* (Hong Kong: University of Hong Kong Press, 2000), pp. 231–32. Also see (for cloth) John Rigby Hall, *Renaissance* (New York; 1965), p. 78.

7. The pope sent numerous delegations to China during the early Ming. For William of Prato, see Fang Hao, *Zhongxi Jiatong Shi* (A history of contacts between China and Europe), vol. 3 (Taipei: 1953), pp. 211–17. Following William of Prato, ten cardinals were appointed, one as late 1426. Zhang Guogang and Wu Liwei, *Mengyuan Shidai Xifang Zai Hua Zong Jiao Xiuhui* (The church in Yuan China), in *Haijiao Shi Yanjiu* (Maritime history studies) (Quanzhou: 2003): 62.

8. Wang Tai Peng, "Zheng He, Wang Dayvan and Zheng Yijun: Some Insights." *Asian Culture,* (Singapore, June 2004): pp. 54–62. See also W. Scott Morton and Charlton M. Lewis, *China, Its History and Culture* (New York: McGraw-Hill, 2005), p.128.

   In his paper, Tai Peng Wang produces evidence that Yuan navigators had mastered astronavigation sufficiently to cross oceans. See Gong Zhen, *Xiyang Banguo Zhi* (Notes on barbarian countries in the western seas), Beijing: Zhounghua bookshop.

See also Xi Fei Long, Yang Xi, Tang Xiren, eds., *Zhongguo Jishu Shi, Jiaotong Ch'uan* (The history of Chinese science and technology), vol. on transportation (Beijing: Science Publisher, 2004), pp. 395–96.

9. It would have been natural for the Chinese ambassador to issue the *Datong Li* calendar to the papal court. The *Datong Li* cotains astronomical information the same as that in the *Shoushi*.

10. Joseph Needham has pointed out that the *Shoushi* and other Chinese astronomical calendars were astronomical treatises. Joseph Needham, *Zhougguo Gudai Kexue* (Science in traditional China) (Shanghai: Shanghai Bookshop, 2000), pp. 146–47.

11. Nicholas of Cusa had predated Copernicus in some respects. Jasper Hopkins, "Nicholas of Cusa" in *Dictionary of the Middle Ages*, ed. Joseph R. Strayer (New York: Charles Scribner and Sons, 1987), pp. 122–25. See also Paul Robert Walker, *The Italian Renaissance* (New York: Facts on File, 1995), p. 96.

12. See also Tai Peng Wang, *The Origin of Chinese Kongsi* (Kuala Lumpur: Perland UK Publications, 1994).

Vignaud, Henri. *Toscanelli and Columbus*. London: Sands, 1902.

Slaves in Florence

White, Lynn, J. "Tibet, India and Malaya as Sources of Medieval Technology." *American Historical Review* 65, no. 3 (April 1960): 515–26. Viewable at JSTOR.

Origo, Iris. "The Domestic Enemy: The Eastern Slaves in Tuscany in the Fourteenth and Fifteenth Century." *Speculum* 30 (1955): 321–66.

Vincenzo Lazzari. "Del Traffico e della Condizioni degli Schiavi." In *Venezia Nei Tempi de Mezzo Miscellanea di Storia Italiana* 2 (1862).

Romano, Denis."The Regulation of Domestic Service in Renaissance Florence." *Sixteenth Century Journal* 22, no. 4 (1991).

Man, R. Livi. "La Sciavitu Domestica" (20 Sept. 1920): 139–43. Viewable at JSTOR.

Leonard Olschki: "Asiatic Exoticism in Italian Art of the Renaissance." *The Art Bulletin*, vol. 26, no. 24 (June, 1944), pp. 95–106.

Tai Peng Wang, "1433 Zheng He's Delegation to the Papal Court of Florence"

(2) Toscanelli's observations of comets—Patricia Fortini Brown

(3) "Laetentur Caeli" Patricia Fortini Brown

Johnson, Paul. *The Papacy*. London: Weidenfeld and Nicolson, 1997.

Lorenzetti, Giulio. *Venice and Its Lagoon*. Rome: instituto Poligra Fico Dellostato, 1961. (Trs. J. Guthrie)

Markham, C. R., trans. *The Journal of Christopher Columbus*. London: Hakluyt Society, 1892.

Vignaud, Henri. *Toscanelli and Columbus*. London: Sands, 1902.

Zinner, Ernst. *Regiomontanus: His Life and Work*. Translated by Ezra Brown. Leiden: Elsevier, 1990.

E. Bibliography for Chapters 9–12

Bedini, Silvio A. *The Christopher Columbus Encyclopedia*. 2 vols. New York: Simon & Schuster, 1992.

Bergreen, Lawrence. *Over the Edge of the World: Megellan's Terrifying Circumnavigation of the*

Globe. New York: HarperPerennial, 2004.

Davies, Arthur. "Behaim. Martellus and Columbus." *Geographical Journal* 143.

Fernández-Armesto, Felipé. *Columbus.* London: G. Duckworth, 1996.

Galvão, Antonio. *Tratado dos diversos e desayados caminhos.* Lisbon: 1563.

Guillemard, F. H. H. *The Life of Ferdinand Magellan.* London: G. Philip & Son, 1890.

Menzies, Gavin. *1421: The Year China Discovered America.* New York: William Morrow, 2002.

Orejon, Antonio Muro, et al., eds. *Pleitos Columbinos.* 8 vols. Seville: The History Co-operative, 1964–1984.

Pigafetta, Antonio. *Magellan's Voyage.* Translated by R. A. Skelton. New Haven, Conn.: Yale University Press, 1969.

———. *Magellan's Voyage. A Narrative Account of the First Voyage.* Translated and edited by R. A. Skelton. London: Folio Society, 1975.

Pigafetta, Antonio, Cdr. A. W. Millar. *The Straits of Magellan.* Portsmouth: UK Griffin, 1884.

Schoenrich, Otto. *The Legacy of Columbus: The Historic Litigation Involving His Discoveries, His Will, His Family and His Descendants.* (Jun) 2 vols. Glendale, Calif.: Pub Arthur H Clark, 1949.

Vignaud, Henry. *Toscanelli and Columbus.* London: Sands, 1902.

Zinner, Ernst. *Regiomontanus: His Life and Work.* Translated by Ezra Brown. Leiden: Elsevier, 1990.

Martin Waldseemüller

Far and away the most knowledgeable writer on Waldseemüller and his maps is Dr. Albert Ronsin, conservator of the Biliothèque et Musée de Saint-Dié-des-Vosges. His best-known works relating to Waldseemüller's 1507 map are:

———. "Le baptême du quatrième continene, Amérique." *Historia* 544 (April 1992).

———. "La cartographe à Saint-Dié au debut du XVI siècle." In *Patrimonie et culture en Lorraine.* Metz Serpenoise, 1980.

———. "La contribution alsacienne au baptême de l'Amérique." *Bulletin de la Société Industrielle de Mulhouse* 2 (1985).

———. "Découverte et baptême de l'Amérique." Edited by Georges le Pape. Jarville, editions de l'est 1992.

———. "La Fortune d'un nom": America. In Le baptême de nouveau monde à Saint-Dié-des-Vosges. Grenoble: G. Millon, 1991.

———. "L'imprimerie humaniste à Saint-Dié au XVIe siècle." In *"Mélanges Kolb."* Wiesbaden: G. Pressler, 1969.

Fischer, Joseph, and R. von Weiser. *The Oldest Map with the Name America of the Year 1507 and the Carta Marina of the Year 1516 by M. Waldseemüller.* London: H. Stevens 1903. Fischer found the map.

Harris, Elizabeth. "The Waldseemüller World Map: A Typographic Appraisal." *Imago Mundi* 37 (1985).

Hébert, John R. *The Map That Named America: Martin Waldseemüller 1507 World Map.* Washington, D.C.: Library of Congress.

John Hessler: "Warping Waldseemueller: A Phenomenological and Computational study of the 1507 World map." *Cartographia* 41 (2006): pp.101–113.

Karrow, Robert W. *Mapmakers of the Sixteenth Century and Their Maps.* Chicago: Orbis Press, 1992.

Lestringant, Frank. *Mapping the Renaissance World*. Berkeley: University of California Press, 1994.

Morison, Samuel Eliot. *Admiral of the Ocean Sea: A Life of Christopher Columbus*. Boston: 1942. (Describes Columbus believing he had met Chinese.)

Rae, John. "On the Naming of America." *American Speech* 39, no. 1 (Feb. 1964). Viewable on JSTOR. (This article argues that "America" was not the name given by Waldseemüller but was given by Native Americans who lived in Nicaragua. They used "Amerrique Mountains," which Columbus misheard.

Randles, W. G. L. "South-East Africa as Shown on Selected Printed Maps of the Sixteenth Century." *Imago Mundi* 13 (1956). Viewable on JSTOR.

Ravenstein E. G., "Waldseemüller's Globe of 1507." *Geograph ical Journal* 20, no. 4. Viewable on JSTOR.

Shirley, Rodney W. *The Mapping of the World: Early Printed World Maps 1472–1700*. London: Holland Press, 1983.

Soulsby, Basil H. "The First Map Containing the Name America." *Geographical Journal* 19 (1902). Viewable on JSTOR.

Stevenson, E. L. "Martin Waldseemüller and the Early Lusitano-Germanic Cartography of the New World." *Bulletin of the American Geographical Society* 36.

Waldseemüller, Martin. *Cosmographiae introductio*.

Amerigo Vespucci

Levillier, Roberto. "New Light on Vespucci's Third Voyage." *Imago Mundi* 11 (1954). Viewable on JSTOR.

Markham, C., ed., *Vespucci: The Letters and Other Documents Illustrative of His Career*.

Sarnow, E. and Frubenbach, K. "Mundus Novus," Strasbourg, 1903, subtitle "Ein Bericht Amerigo Vespucci an Lorenzo de Medici Über Seine Reise Nach Brasilien in den Jahren 1501 / 1502."

Thacher, J. Boyd. *The Continent of America: Its Discovery; It's Baptism*. New York: William Evarts Benjamin, 1896.

Part 2–Schoener Johannes Schöner

Cooke, Charles H., ed. *Johan Schoner*. London: Henry Stevens, 1888.

Correr, Ambassador Francesco. Letter to Signoria of Venice. July 16, 1508. In *Raccolta Columbiana*, p. 115. The letter followed Correr's interview with Vespucci; Vespucci had not found the strait leading from the Atlantic to the Pacific.

Nordenskiöld, A. E. "Remarkable Global Map of the Sixteenth Century." *Journal of the American Geography Society* 16 (1884).

Nunn, George E. "The Lost Globe Gores of Johann Schöner, 1523–1524: A Review." *Geographical Review* 17, no. 3 (July 1927). Viewable on JSTOR.

Ronsin, Albert. "Découverte et baptême de l'Amérique." Edited by Georges le Pope. Montreal: Editions Georges Le Pape, 1979.

————. Schöner, Johannes. *Luculentissima Quoeda⁻ Terra Totius Descriptio*. Nuremberg, 1515. Describes the Strait of Magellan.

Settlement of Santa Fe. [Agreement between Catholic Monarchs and Christopher Columbus.] April 17, 1492. Held at Dirección General de Archivos y Bibliotecas. *Capitulaciones del*

Almirante Don Cristóbal Colon y Salvo Conductos Para El Descubrimento de Nuevo Mundo. Madrid, 1970.

Gadol, Joan. *Leon Battista Alberti: Universal Man of the Renaissance.* Chicago: University of Chicago Press, 1969.

Wang, Tai Peng.

———. "Zheng He's Delegation to the Papal Court of Florence, 1433." Research paper. Available on *1434* website.

———. "Zheng He, Wang Dayuan and Zheng Yijun: Some Insights." *Asian Culture.* Singapore, June 2004: 54–62.

Zinner, Ernst. *Regiomontanus: His Life and Work.* Translated by Ezra Brown. Leiden: Elsevier, 1990.

Bedini, Silvio A., ed. *The Christopher Columbus Encyclopedia.* 2 vols. New York: Simon & Schuster, 1992.

Davies, Arthur. "Behain, Martellus and Columbus." RGS. *Geographical Journal,* vol. 143.

Lambert, William. "Abstract of the Calculations to Ascertain the Longitude of the Capitol in the City of Washington from Greenwich Observatory, in England." *Transactions of the American Historical Society.* New series. Vol. 1. Viewable on JSTOR.

Libbrecht, Ulrich. *Chinese Mathematics in the Thirteenth Century.* Cambridge, Mass: MIT Press, 1973.

Menzies, Gavin. *1421: The Year China Discovered America.* New York: William Morrow, 2002.

Needham, Joseph. *Science and Civilisation in China.* Vols. 30 Section. Cambridge: Cambridge University Press, 1950.

Zinner, Ernst. *Regiomontanus: His Life and Work.* Translated by Ezra Brown. Leiden: Elsevier, 1990.

F. Bibliography for Chapters 13–14

Selected Works of Leon Battista Alberti:

De pictura, 1435
Della pittura, 1436
De re aedificatoria, 1452
De statua, ca. 1446
Descriptio urbis Romae, 1447
Ludi matematici, ca. 1450
De componendris cifris, 1467

Gadol, Joan. *Leon Battista Alberti: Universal Man of the Early Renaissance.* Chicago: University of Chicago Press, 1969. There are many excellent books on Alberti. Joan Gadol's is written for people who are neither mathematicians nor knowledgeable about the use of perspective or cryptanalysis. She writes in a beautiful, clear style, and I have used her book extensively.

Grayson, Cecil. "ed Bari Laterza" 1973 "Opere Volgari, Vol Terzo: Trattati D'arte, Ludi Rerum Mathematicarum, Grammatica della Lingua Toscana, Opuscol, Amatori, Lettere."

Needham, Joseph. *Science and Civilisation in China.* 30 vols. Cambridge: Cambridge University Press, 1956.

Zinner, Ernst: *Regiomontanus: His Life and Work.* Translated by Ezra Brown. Leiden: Elsevier,

1990.

G. Bibliography for Chapters 15–16

Paolo Galluzzi. *The Art of Invention: Leonardo and the Renaissance Engineers* (London: Giunti, 1996). This has become the bible for the *1421* team. Galluzzi's book is lavishly illustrated, making it very simple to compare Taccola and Francesco's machines and see the evolution from Taccola to Francesco to Leonardo. We have studied Galluzzi's books with great care, then compared the drawings with Chinese books existing before 1430.

Clark, Kenneth. *Leonardo da Vinci*. Rev. ed. Introduction by Martin Kemp. London: Penguin Books, 1993.

Cianchi, Marco. *Leonardo's Machines*. Florence: Becocci Editore, 1984. This is a very clear and concise summary produced using the Leonardian Library of Vinci.

"Sur les pas de Léonard de Vinci." Gonzague Saint Bris—Presses de la Renaissance. Gonzague's family the Saint Bris owned the château of Clos-Lucé for three centuries.

Cooper, Margaret Rice. *The Inventions of Leonardo da Vinci*. New York: Macmillan, 1965.

Deng Yinke. *Ancient Chinese Inventions*. Hong Kong: China Intercontinental Press, 2005.

Galdi G. P., *Leonardo's Helicopter and Archimedes' Screw: The Principle of Action and Reaction*. Florence: Accademia Leonardo da Vinci, 1991.

Galluzzi, Paolo. *Leonardo, Engineer and Architect*. Montreal, 1987.

Hart, Ivor B. *The World of Leonardo da Vinci, Man of Science, Engineer and Dreamer of Flight*. London: Macdonald, 1961.

Heydenreich, Ludwig, Bern Dibner, and Ladislao Reti. *Leonardo the Inventor*. London: Hutchinson, 1980.

"Parc Leonardo da Vinci—Château du Clos-Lucé—Amboise"—Beaux Arts (Leonardo's home 1516 to 1519, the last 3 years of his life)

Kemp, Martin. *Leonardo da Vinci: Experience, Experiment and Design*. London: V&A Publishing, 2006. This is lavishly illustrated and very readable.

Needham, Joseph. *Science and Civilisation in China*. 7 vols. Cambridge: Cambridge University Press, 1956–.

Pedretti Carlo, and Augusto Marinoni. *Codex Atlanticus*. Milan: Giunti, 2000.

Pedretti, Carlo. "L'elicottero." In *Studi Vinciani*. Geneva, Studi Vinciani: 1957.

Peers, Chris. *Warlords of China 700 BC to AD 1662*.

Reti, Ladislao. "Helicopters and Whirligigs." *Raccolta Vinciana* 20 (1964): 331–38.

Rosheim, Mark Elling. *Leonardo's Lost Robots*. Heidelberg: Springer, 2006.

Saint Bris-Clos-Lucé, Jean. "Leonardo da Vinci's Fabulous Machines at Clos-Lucé in Amboise," *Beaux Arts,* 1995.

Taddei, Mario, and Edoardo Zanon, eds. *Leonardo's Machines: Da Vinci's Inventions Revealed*. Text by Domenico Laurenza. Cincinnati: David and Charles, 2006. This provides a very clear array of illustrations from pp. 18–25.

Temple, Robert. *The Genius of China: 3,000 Years of Science, Discovery & Invention*. London: Prion, 1998.

Wray, William. *Leonardo da Vinci in His Own Words*. New York: Gramercy Books, 2005.

Zollner, Frank, and Johannes Nathan. *Leonardo da Vinci*. Comprehensive, fully illustrated catalogue. Cologne, 2003.

Francesco di Giorgio Martini. *Trattato di architetura*. Presented in Biblioteca Comunale, Siena (first draft); Biblioteca Nazionale Siena; and Laurenziana Library, Florence (Leonardo's copy).

H. Bibliography for Chapters 17–19

Gablehouse, Charles. *Helicopters and Autogiros.* Philadelphia: J.B. Lippincott, 1967.

Galluzzi, Paolo. *The Art of Invention: Leonardo and the Re naissance Engineers.* Florence: Gunti, 1996.

Jackson, Robert. *The Dragonflies—The Story of Helicopters and Autogiros.* Arthur Barker: London, 1971.

Leonardo da Vinci. Codex B (2173). Nell Istito di Franck I. Manoscritti e I disegni di Leonardo da Vinci. Vol. 5. Rome; and Reale Commissione Vinciana, 1941.

Needham, Joseph. *Science and Civilisation in China.* 7 vols. 30 section. Cambridge University Press, 1956–. Vol IV, Pt 2. pp 580–585.

Parsons, William Barclay. *Engineers and Engineering in the Renaissance.* The Williams and Wilkins Company: Baltimore, 1939.

Prager, Frank D., and Giustina Scaglia. *Mariano Taccola and His book De Ingeneis.* Cambridge, Mass.: MIT Press, 1972.

Promis, Carlo, ed. *Vita di Francesco di Giorgio Martini.* Turin, 1841.

Reti, Ladislao. "Francesco di Giorgio Martini's Treatise on Engineering and Its Plagiarists." *Technology and Culture* 4, no. 3 (1963): 287–93. John Hopkins University Press.

———. "Helicopters and Whirligigs." *Raccolta Vinciana* 20 (1964): 331–38.

Singer, Charles. *A History of Technology.* Oxford: Oxford University Press, 1954–58. vol. 2.

Taccola, Mariano di Jacopo ditto.

De Ingereis I and II (c. 1430–1433) III and IV after 1434

De Machinis after 1435 in Biblioteca Nazionale Centrale, Florence.

Wellers, Stuart. *Francesco di Giorgio Martini 1439–1501.* Chicago: University of Chicago Press, 1943. p 340.

White, Lynn, Jr. "Invention of the Parachute." *Technology and Culture* v. 9, no. 3 (July 1968): 462–67. University of Chicago Press

———. *Medieval Technology and Social Change.* Oxford: Oxford University Press, 1962. p 86–87

Braudel, Fernand. "The Mediterranean in the time of Philip II." Translated by Sian Reynolds Fontana. London, 1966.

Hibbert, Christopher. *The House of Medici: Its Rise and Fall, 1420–1440.* London: Penguin Books, 1974.

Hobson, John. *The Eastern Origins of Western Civilization.* Cambridge: Cambridge University Press, 2006.

Molà, Luca. "The Silk Industry of Renaissance Venice." *American Historical Review* 106, no. 3 (June 2001). Viewable on JSTOR. This gives a good chronological description, which I have extensively used.

Needham, Joseph. *Science and Civilisation in China.* 7 vols. Oxford: Oxford University Press, 1956–.

Nung Shu.—

Reti, Ladislao. "Francesco Di Giorgio Martini's Treatise on Engineering and Its Plagiarists." *Technology and Culture* 4, no. 3 (1963): 287–93. John Hopkins University Press.

Shapiro, Sheldon. "The Origin of the Suction Pump." *Technology and Culture* 5, no. 4

(Autumn 1964): 566–74. Viewable on JSTOR. John Hopkins University Press

Temple, Robert. *The Genius of China: 3,000 Years of Science, Discovery & Invention*. London: Prion, 1998.

Thorley, John. "The Silk Trade Between China and the Roman Empire at Its Height Circa A.D 90–130." *Greece and Rome*. 2nd series, vol. 18, no. 1, (April 1971): 71–80. JSTOR.

Dixon, George Campbell. *Venice, Vicenza and Verona*. London: Nicholas Kaye, 1959.

Lonely Planet. *'China' A Travel Survival Guide*. Sydney: Lonely Planet 1988.

Needham, Joseph. *Science and Civilisation in China*. Vol 28. Oxford: Oxford University Press, 1956–.

Parsons, William Barclay. *Engineers and Engineering in the Renaissance*. Rev. ed. Introduction by Robert S. Woodbury. Cambridge, Mass: MIT Press, 1968.

This is the accepted bible. It is very useful for Renaissance engineers but ignores any Chinese input. Parsons sees the Renais sance as a quasi-religious event and Leonardo as a demigod. He ignores the question of how so many new machines managed to appear at the same time in Italy; and of how different artists drew the same entirely new machines in different parts at the same time—viz. the pumps of Taccola, Alberti, Fontana, and Pisanello. The subject of copying from earlier books is not addressed. His explanation of the development of Lombard's canals is excellent.

Payne, Robert. *The Canal Builders*. New York: Macmillan, 1959.

Temple, Robert. *The Genius of China: 3,000 Years of Science Discovery & Invention*. London: Prion, 1998.

Biringuccio, Vannoccio. *Pirotechnia*. Translated by Cyril S. Smith and Martha T. Gnudi. New York, 1942. Viewable on article JSTOR.

Butters, Suzanne. *Triumph of Vulcan—Sculptors' Tools, Porphyry, and the Prince in Ducal Florence*. Florence: Leo S. Olschki, 1996.

"Porphyry, and the Prince in Ducal Florence." *Sixteenth Century Journal* 28, no. 1 (Spring 1997): 286–87. Viewable on JSTOR.

Clagett, Marshall. *The Life and Works of Giovanni Fontana*. Princeton: Princeton University Press, 1976. Fontana's principal works are:

> *Nova compositio horologii* (clocks)
> *Horologium aqueum* (water clock)
> *Tractatus de pisce, cane e volvere* (a treatise on measurement of depths, lengths, surface areas)
> *Bellicorum instrumentorum liber cum figuris et fictitiis literis conscriptus* (written in cipher; see Alberti, *Compondendis cifris*)
> *Secretum de thesauro experimentorum y imaginationis hominum*
> *Notes on Alhazen*
> *Tractatus de trigono balistario* (An extraordinarily detailed handbook of calculating lengths and distances by trigonometry; see Alberti, *De arte pictoria* (*ca.* 1440) and *De sphera solida* (*ca.* 1440).
> *Liber de omnibus rebus naturalibus* (the book analyzed by Lynn Thorndike in "Unidentified Work."

Eichstadt, Konrad Kyser von. *Bellifortis* (War fortifications). 1405. This describes rockets.

Foley, Vernard, and Werner Soedel. "Leonardo's Contributions to Theoretical Mechanics." *Scientific American* (1983): 255. Viewable on JSTOR

Fontana, Giovanni di. *Liber bellicorum instrumentorum*. Munich: Bayerische Staatsbibliothek, c. 1420.

Goodrich, L. Carrington, and Fêng Chia-Shêng. "The Early Development of Firearms in China." *Isis* 36, no. 2 (Jan. 1946): 114–23. Viewable on JSTOR. This has been of major value to our research and makes the following specific points:

- The *Wu Chung Tsung Yao,* compiled in 1044 by Tsêng Kung-Liang, discusses gunpowder manufacture, bombs, trebuchets, and grenades fired by gunpowder.
- Exploding arrows were used in 1126.
- Mortars were used in 1268.
- Exploding cannonballs were in use by 1281.
- A lengthy section on Zhu Di's weapons mentions land mines ("a nest of wasps"). Every unit of 100 men had 20 shields, 30 bows, and 40 firearms.
- Every three years after 1380 the bureau of military weapons turned out 3,000 bronze Ch'ung muskets and 90,000 bullets.
- The exploding weapons after 1403 were manufactured from dried copper with a mixture of refined and unrefined. Fuses were in use from the thirteenth century. The earliest cannons were dated 1356, 1357, and 1377.
- Flame-throwing devices were used from 1000, and bullets since 1259.

Liu Chi. *Huo Lung Ching,* (Fire drake artillery manual). Part 1.

Needham, Joseph. Vol. V, Pt. 7. *Military Technology: The Gunpowder* Epic. Joseph Needham, with the collaboration of Ho Ping-Yu [Ho Peng-Yoke], Lu Gwei-djen and Wang Ling, 1987.

For Leonardo, crossbow, and gunpowder, see arsenic sulphides added to gunpowder, p. 51; trebuchets (Leonardo and Taccola), p. 204; missiles, p. 205; "eruption," mortar, p. 266; trebuchet, p. 281; Seven-barreled Ribaudequin (see Pisanello sketches), p. 322; rocket launcher, p. 487; machine gun, p. 164; mortars, p. 165; handguns, p. 580; aerial cars, p. 571; poisonous projectiles, p. 353; rockets and missiles, p. 516; riffling; p. 411; breechblock, p. 429.

Schubert, H. R. *History of the British Iron and Steel Industry from 450 B.C. to A.D. 1775.* London: Routledge & Kegan Paul, 1957.

Spencer, John R. "Filarete's Description of a Fifteenth Century Italian Iron Smelter at Ferriere." *Technology and Culture* 4, no. 2 (Spring 1963): 201–6. Viewable on JSTOR.

Temple, Robert. *The Genius of China: 3,000 Years of Science, Discovery & Invention.* London: Prion, 1998.

Thorndike, Lynn. "An Unidentified Work by Giovanni di Fontana: *Liber de Omnibus Rebus."* *Lynn Thorndike, Isis* 15, no. 1 (Feb. 1931): 31–46. Viewable on JSTOR. Description of America on p. 37; Australia, p. 38; Indian Ocean, p. 39; Niccolò da Conti, p. 40; gunpowder, p. 42.

A. Stuart Weller, "Francesco di Giorgio Martini 1439–1501". Chicago: University of Chicago Press, 1943.

Wertime, Theodore A. "Asian Influences on European Metallurgy." *Technology and Culture* 5, no. 3 (Summer 1964): pp. 391–97. Viewable on JSTOR.

———. The Coming of the Age of Steel. Chicago: University of Chicago Press, 1962.

White, Lynn Jr. "Tibet, India and Malaya as Sources of Western Medieval Technology." *American Historical Review* 15, no. 3 (April 1960): 520. Viewable on JSTOR.

Wu Chung Tsung Yao. Song dynasty, *ca.* 1044.

Allmand, Christopher. *The New Cambridge Medieval History, Volume 7,* edited by Christopher Allmand. Cambridge University Press, 1998.

Bouchet, Henri. *The Printed Book: Its History, Illustration and Adornment From the Days of Gutenberg to the Present Time.* Translation by Edward Bigmore. New York: Scribner and

Welford, 1887.

Carter, Thomas Francis. *The Invention of Printing in China and Its Spread Westward.* New York: Columbia University Press, 1925.

Carmichael, Ann G. *Plague and the Poor in Renaissance Florence.* Cambridge: Cambridge University Press, 1986.

Deng Yinke. *Ancient Chinese Inventions.* Hong Kong: China Intercontinental Press, 2005.

I. Bibliography for Chapter 20

Hessel, J. H. *Haarlem, The Birthplace of Printing.* London: Elliot Stock and Co., 1887.

Humphreys, H. N. *A History of the Art of Printing.* London: Bernard Quaritch, 1868.

McMurtrie, Douglas. *The Book: The Story of Printing and Bookmaking.* Oxford: Oxford University Press, 1948.

Moran James. *Printing Presses: History and Development from the Fifteenth Century to Modern Times.* London: Faber and Faber, 1973.

Ottley, William Young. *An Inquiry into the Invention of Printing.* London: Joseph Lilly, 1863.

———. *An Inquiry into the Origin and Early History of Engraving upon Copper and in Wood.* London: John and Arthur Arch, 1816.

Needham, Joseph. *Science and Civilisation in China.* Cambridge: Cambridge University Press, 1955. Vol. 32.

Ruppel, A., *Gutenberg: Sein Leben and Sein werk (His Life and His Work),* second edition. Berlin: Mann, 1947.

Singer, Samuel Weller. *Research into the History of Playing Cards.* Oxford University: 1816. You can read the whole book on Google following this link: http://books.google.com☒/books ?id= _WAOAAAAQAAJ&printsec=titlepage.

The Haarlem Legend of the Invention of Printing by Coster. Translated by A Van der Linde. London: Blades, East and Blades, 1871.

Wu, K. T. "The Development of Printing in China." *T'ien Hsia Monthly* 3 (1936).

Wu, K. T., and Wu Kuang-Ch'ing. "Ming Printing and Printers." *Harvard Journal of Asiatic Studies* 7, no. 3. (Feb. 1943): 203–60. Viewable on JSTOR.

J. Bibliography for Chapter 21

Antonio de Bilhao Pato, Raymondo, ed. *Cartas de Alfonso de Albuquerque Seguides de documentos que as elucidam.* 7 vols. Lisbon: 1884–1955. Vol. 1, letter 10 (April 1512), pp. 29–65. Translated by E. Manuel Stock.

Aslaksen, Helmer, and Ng Say Tiong. "Calendars, Interpolation, Gnomons and Armillary Spheres in the Work of Guo Shoujing (1231–1314)." Article. Dept of Mathematics, University of Singpore 2000–2001.

Cortesão, Jaime. "The Pre-Columbian Discovery of America." *Geographical Journal* 89, no. 1:39.

Davies, Arthur. "Behaim, Martellus and Columbus." *Royal Geographical Society Journal* 143, pt. 3: 451–59.

Gadol, Joan. *Leon Battista Alberti: Universal Man of the Early Renaissance.* Chicago: University of Chicago Press, 1969.

Johannessen, Carl, and Sorenson John. Biology Verifies Ancient Voyages. (unpublished)

Sorenson John L. and Martin H. Raish *Pre-Columbian contact with the Americans across the oceans, an annotated bibliography,* second edition, 2 vols. Provo, Utah: Research Press, 1996.

Professor Liu Manchum.

Mui, Rosa, Paul Dong, and Zhou Xin Yan. "Ancient Chinese Astronomer Gan De Discovered Jupiter's Satellites 2000 Years Earlier Than Galileo." Unpublished article sent to author by Rosa Mui on May 22, 2003.

Sorenson, John L., and Martin H. Raish. *Pre-Columbian Contact with the Americans Across the Oceans.* Provo, Utah: Research Press, 1990.

Swerdlow, Noel M. "The Derivation and First Draft of Copernicus's Planetary Theory." *Proceedings of the American Philosophical Society* 117, no. 6 (31 Dec. 1973). Viewable on JSTOR.

Thompson, Gunnar, Ph.D. *The Friar's Map of Ancient America, 1360 AD.* Bellevue, WA: Laura Lee Productions, 1996.

Zinner, Ernst. *Regiomontanus: His Life and Work.* Translated by Ezra Brown. Leiden: Elsevier, 1990.

Antonio de Bilhao Pato, Raymondo, ed. *Cartas de Alfonso de Albuquerque Seguides de documentos que as elucidam.* 7 vols. Lisbon: 1884–1955. Vol. 1, letter 10 (April 1512), pp. 29–65. Translated by E. Manuel Stock.

Aslaksen, Helmer, and Ng Say Tiong. "Calendars, Interpolation, Gnomons and Armillary Spheres in the Work of Guo Shoujing (1231–1314)." Article. Dept of Mathematics, University of Singpore, 2000–2001.

Cortesão, Jaime. "The Pre-Columbian Discovery of America." *Geographical Journal* 89, no. 1:39.

Davies, Arthur. "Behaim, Martellus and Columbus" *Royal Geographical Society Journal* 143, pt. 3: 451–59.

Gadol, Joan. *Leon Battista Alberti: Universal Man of the Early Renaissance.* Chicago: University of Chicago Press, 1969.

Beals, K and Steele, H, University of Oregon Anthropological Paper No. 23, Oregon 1981.

K. Bibliography for Chapter 22

Fernandez-Cobo, Marianna, and colleagues. "Strains of JC Virus in Amerind-speakers of North America (Salish) and South America (Guarani), Na-Dene speakers of New Mexico (Navajo) and modern Japanese suggest links through an Ancestral Asian Population." *American Journal of Physical Anthropology,* 118, 154–168 (2002)

Keddie, Grant. "Contributions to Human History," No. 3, Royal British Columbia Museum, Vancouver, B.C. 1990

Macedo, Justo Caceres. "Pre-Hispanic Cultures of Peru", Peruvian Natural History Museum, Lima, Peru, 1985

Novick, Gabriel and colleagues. "Polymorphic-Alu Insertions and the Asian origin of Native American Populations" in "Human Biology", Vol. 70, No.1, 1988

Rostoworski, Maria. *History of the Inca Realm.* Cambridge: Cambridge University Press, 1999.

PERMISSIONS

I am grateful to the following for permitting me to quote their work:

Chapter 1: Henry Tsai, "Perpetual Happiness: The Ming Emperor Yongle," Seattle: University of Washington Press, 2001; Edward L. Dreyer, "Zheng He: China and the oceans in the early Ming Dynasty, 1405–1433," on page 6 and page 144, Pearson Longman, 2006 (www.ablongman.com).

Chapter 2: Henry Tsai, as above; Edward L. Dreyer, as above; Tai Peng Wang; Joseph Needham, "Science and Civilisation in China," Vol. 19, pp. 49–50 and 109–110 (Vol. 19) and Vol. 32 pp. 100–175, Cambridge University Press, 1954–; Professor Anthony Reid, "South East Asia in the Age of Commerce 1450–1680," Vol. 2, "Expansion and Crisis" on page 39, Yale University Press, 1993; Richard Hall "Empires of the Monsoon—A History of the Indian Ocean and its Invaders," Harper Collins, 1996.

Chapter 3: Thatcher E. Deane, "Instruments and Observations at the Imperial Astronomical Bureau during the Ming Dynasty," on pp. 126–140, Osiris 2nd series, Vol. 9, 1994. JSTOR (University of Chicago Press); Joseph Needham, as above (Spherical Trigonometry), Vol. 19 pp. 49–50 and 109–110, Cambridge University Press, 1954–; "Ancient Chinese Inventions" ed. Deng Yinke, China Intercontinental Press; Rosa Mui, Paul Dong, and Zhou Xin Yam, "Ancient Chinese Astronomer Gan De Discovered Jupiter's Satellites 2000 Years Earlier than Galileo"; Professor Helmer Aslaksen and Ng Say Tiong, "Calendars, Interpolation, Gnomons and Armillary Spheres in the Work of Guo Shou Jing (1231–1314)," Department of Mathematics, National University of Singapore.

Chapter 4: Professor Robert Cribbs.

Chapter 5: Paul Lunde, "The Navigator Ahmad Ibn Majid"; Richard Hall "Empires of the Monsoon" at pp. 88, 128, as above; Ibn Battuta, "The Travels of Ibn Battuta," ad 1325–1354 pp. 773, 813, Trs. H.A.R. Gibb and C.F. Beckingham, 1994, Hakluyt Society, London, 1994. The Hakluyt Society was established in 1846 for the purpose of printing rare or unpublished voyages and travels. For further information please see their website at: www.hakluyt.com; Stanley Lane Pool, "A History of Egypt in the Middle Ages," 1894.

Chapter 6: C. A. Redmount, "The Wadi Tumilat and the Canal of the Pharaohs," Journal of Near Eastern Studies 54, 1995. JSTOR, University of Chicago Press; Stanley Lane Pool, "A History of Egypt in the Middle Ages," as above; James Aldridge, "Cairo: Biography of a City," Macmillan, 1969, reproduced with permission of Palgrave Macmillan; R. L. Hudson, "Chinese Porcelain from Fustat," *The Burlington Magazine for Connoisseurs* Vol. 61, No. 354 (Sept. 1932), JSTOR—The University of Chicago; Fernand Brandel, "A History of Civilisations," Trs. Richard Mayne, 1995, reproduced by permission of Penguin Books Ltd.

Chapter 7: Fernand Brandel, "The Mediterranean in the Time of Philip II," reproduced by permission of Penguin Books Ltd.; John Julius Norwich "A History of Venice," 1983, reproduced by permission of Penguin Books Ltd.; Francis M. Rogers, "The travels of the Infante Dom Pedro of Portugal," pp. 46–49, 256–266, 325, Cambridge, Mass.: Harvard

University Press, Copyright © 1961 by the President and Fellows of Harvard College; European Journal of Human Genetics (2006) 14 (478–487); "Tibet, India and Malaya as Sources of Western Medieval Technology," Lyn White Jr., American Historical Review Vol. 65, No. 3 (1960) JSTOR; Iris Origo, "The Merchant of Prato: Daily Life in a medieval Italian city," 1992, reproduced by permission of Penguin Books Ltd.

Chapter 8: Leonard Olschilli, "Asiatic Exoticism in Italian Art of the Early Renaissance," *The Art Bulletin* Vol. 26, No. 2 (June 1944) JSTOR; Timothy J. McGee "Dinner Music for the Florentine Signoria, 1350–1450," *Speculum* vol. 14, no. 1, Jan 1999, JSTOR; Mary Hollingsworth, "Patronage in Renais sance Italy," John Murray, 1994; James Beck, "Leon Battista Alberti and the 'Night Sky' at San Lorenzo," *Artibus et Historiae,* Vol. 10, No. 19 (1989) JSTOR; Patricia Fortini Brown, "Laetentur Caeli: the Journal of Florence and the Astronomical Fresco in the old society," *Journal of the Warburg and Courtauld Institutes,* Vol. 44, 1981, JSTOR.

Chapter 9: Ernst Zinner, "Regiomontanus: his life and work," Trs. E. Brown, *Isis*, Vol. 83, No. 4 (Dec., 1992), pp. 650–652, Amsterdam.

Chapter 10: Marcel Destombes quoted by Professor Arthur Davies, Royal Geographic Society Records, vol. 143 p. 3; Ernst Zinner "Regiomontanus: his life and work," Trs. E. Brown, as above; "The Catholic Encyclopedia"; Yang Long Shan, "Zhuyn Zhou chui Lu"; Joan Gadol, "Leon Battista Alberti, Universal Man of the Early Renaissance," JSTOR, University of Chicago Press, 1969.

Chapter 13: E. Zinner "Regiomontanus: his life and work," as above.

Chapter 14: Joan Gadol, pp. 155, 159, as above.

Chapter 15: Robert Temple, "The Genius of China: 3,000 Years of Science, Discovery and Invention," pp. 243, 259, an imprint of Carlton Publishing Group, 20 Mortimer St., London W1T 3SW; Chris Peers, "Warlords of China 700 bc to ad 1662," 1998, Arms and Armour Press, Imprint of Cassell Group, Wellington House, 125 Strand, London; "Ancient Chinese Inventions" p. 112, China Intercontinental Press; Lynn White, Jr., "The Invention of the Parachute," Technology and Culture 9:3 (1963), 462–467. © Society for the History of Technology. Reprinted with permission of The John Hopkins University Press; Reti, Ladisloa, "Francesco di Giorgio Martini's Treatise on Engineering and Its Plagiarists," Technology and Culture, 4:3 (1963), 287. © Society for the History of Technology. Reprinted with permission of The John Hopkins University Press; Frank D. Prager and Gustina Scaglia, "Mariano Taccola and his book de Ingeneis," MIT Press, 1972; Paolo Galluzzi, "The Art of Invention: Leonardo and the Renaissance Engineers."

Chapter 17: John Hobson, "The Eastern Origins of Western Civilisation," Cambridge University Press, 2004; Joseph Needham, "Science and Civilisation in China," Vol. 28, p. 225, as above; Sheldon Shapiro, "The Origin of the Suction Pump," Technology and Culture 5, (1964), 571. © Society for the History of Technology. Reprinted with permission of The John Hopkins University Press; Christopher Hibbert, "The Rise and Fall of the House of Medici," 1974, reproduced by permission of Penguin Books Ltd.

Chapter 18: "The Genius of China: 3,000 Years of Science, Discovery and Invention," Robert Temple, as above; Joseph Needham, "Science and Civilisation in China," as above; William Barclay Parsons, "Engineers and Engineering in the Renaissance," Baltimore, 1939.

Chapter 19: John R. Spencer, "Filarete's Description of a Fifteenth Century Italian Iron Smelter at Ferriere," Technology and Culture 4:2 (1963), 201–206. © Society for the History of Technology, reprinted with permission of The John Hopkins University Press; Lyn Thorndyke, "An Unidentified Work by Giovanni da' Fontana: Liber de omnibus rebus naturalibus," *Isis,* Vol. 15, No. 1, Tab. 1031 pp. 31–46, JSTOR; Wertime, Theodore A., "The Coming of Age of Steel," Technology and Culture, 5:3 (1962), pp. 391–397. © Society for the History of Technology, reprinted with permission of The John Hopkins University Press; Robert Temple, "The Genius of China: 3,000 Years of Science, Discovery and Invention," as above; Joseph Needham, as above; Allen Stuart Wellers, "Francesco di Giorgio Martini, 1439–1501," Chicago, 1943.

Chapter 20: "Ancient Chinese Inventions," as above; Joseph Needham, as above.

Chapter 21: Dr. Gunnar Thompson; Ernst Zinner, as above; Noel M. Swerdlow, "The Derivation and First Draft of Copernicus's Planetary Theory: A Translation of the Commentariolus with Commentary," *Proceedings of the American Philosophical Society,* Vol. 117, No. 6, Symposium on Copernicus (Dec. 31, 1973), pp. 423–512, JSTOR, University of Chicago Press; *New Encyclopaedia Britannica,* 15th edition, 1994, Encyclopaedia Britannica, Inc.

PHOTOGRAPH CREDITS

I am very grateful to the following for permitting me to reproduce the beautiful illustrations in this book:

Internal Black-and-White Images

Wendi Watson: Ellipse around the sun diagram; Latitude diagram; Longitude diagram; Position of ships diagram; Ship AB and point C diagram; Lunar mansion; Torquetum diagram; Star map diagram.

The General Collection of Chinese Classics of Science and Technology; The Nung Shu; the Chinese Science and Technological History Review; The Fire Dragon Book: Chinese measuring height; Chinese cannon; Chinese revolving type table printing; Chinese articulated siege ladder; Chinese water powered horizontal wheel; Chinese waterwheel bucket pump; Chinese Ox chain pump; Chinese horse mill; Chinese vertical waterwheel; Chinese chain pump; Chinese water powered machine; Chinese loom and spinning machine; Chinese irrigation; Irrigation wheel; Chinese tilt hammer; Chinese water powered bellow; Chinese cannon balls and petards; Dragon Kite; Chinese trebuchet; Chinese fire lance; Chinese armored ship; Chinese mobile siege ladder; Chinese mobile shield; Chinese crossbow; Chinese animals with spears; Chinese animals with fire; Chinese fortress.

Biblioteca Nacional de España, Madrid: from Leonardo's Madrid Codices: Leonardo tooth geared wheels, fol. 15v; Leonardo cranks, chain drives, fol. 35v; Leonardo crossbow, fol. 51r;

Biblioteca Ambrosiana, Milano: from Leonardo's Codex Atlanticus: Leonardo paddleboat, fol. 954r; Leonardo parachute, fol. 1058v; Leonardo cannon, fol. 154v; Leonardo printing press, fol 358 r-b; Leonardo machine gun, fol. 56v.

Bayerische Staatsbibliothek, Munchen: Taccola's water powered bellows. Codex Latinus Monacensis 197 pt. II, fol. 43v; Taccola fire lance. Codex Latinus Monacensis 197 pt. II, fol. 75v; Taccola horse with spears. Codex Latinus Monacensis 28800, fol. 67v; Taccola dogs with fire. Codex Latinus Monacensis 197 pt. II, fol. 67r.

Biblioteca Comunale, Siena: Italian cannon balls and petards. Ms. D. IV, fol. 48v; Italian armored boat. Ms. S. IV, fol. 49r.

Biblioteque Nationale de France, Paris: Santini horse mill. Manuscript Lat. 7239, fol. 50r; Pisanello Mongol sketches; Alberti sky Canis Major; Pisanello Mongol face.

Biblioteca Apostolica Vaticano: Anonymous Sienese parachute. Ms. Additional, fol. 200v; Di Giorgio water powered horizontal wheel. Ms. Latimus Urbinate 1757, fol. 138r

Biblioteca Medicea Leurenziana, Firenze: Di Giorgio measuring height. Ms. Ashburnham361, fol. 29r; Di Giorgio chain pump. Ms. Ashburnham 361, fol. 35r.

Biblioteca Nazionale Centrale Firenze: Taccola water wheel bucket pump. Manuscritto Palatino 767, p. 11; Taccola ox chain pump. Manuscritto Palatino 766, p. 19; Taccola vertical waterwheel. Ms. Palantino 767, p. 65; Di Giorgio mobile siege ladder. Ms. II.I.141, fol. 201r; Di Giorgio mobile shields. Ms. Palatino 767, p. 143.

British Museum, London: Anonymous Sienese Engineer, flying man. Ms. Additional 34113, fol. 189v; Di Giorgio trebuchet. Ms. 197, b. 21, fol. 3v.

Cambridge University Press: Chinese toothed gear wheels. Needham vol. 4, pt. 2, sect. 27, p. 85; Cranks, chain drive China. Needham vol. 4, pt. 2, sect. 27, p. 102; Chinese paddleboat. Needham p. 431; Chinese flying car. Needham p. 572.

Color Insert Images

I am most grateful to the following for allowing the reproduction of their photographs:

Color insert 1, page 1: Zheng He in Malacca, 2007, © *Ian Hudson*

Color insert 1, page 2–3: 1418 / 1763 Liu Gang map, 2007, © *Liu Gang*

Color insert 1, page 4: Summer Palace, Beijing, bronze figure on marble. © *Library of Congress, Washington, D.C.*; Summer Palace, Beijing, 1902. © *Library of Congress, Washington, D.C.*

Color insert 1, page 5: The Forbidden City, Beijing, 2007. © *Ian Hudson*

Color insert 1, page 6: The Great Wall of China at Simatai, 2007. © *Ian Hudson*; Blue and white porcelain. © *Percival David Foundation.*

Color insert 1, page 7: Chinese junk, 1906. © *Library of Congress, Washington, D.C.*; Camels at sunset, 2007. © *Ian Hudson*

Color insert 1, page 8: Red Sea, 2007. © *Ian Hudson*; Cairo / Nile lithograph. © *Library of Congress, Washington, D.C.*

Color insert 2, page 1:Venice panorama, 1900. © *Library of Congress, Washington, D.C.*

Color insert 2, page 2–3: Venice map, © *Doge's Palace Museum, Venice.*

Color insert 2, page 4: Schöner globes, 1515 and 1520; The Straights of Magellan. Color insert 2, page 5: © *Gavin Menzies*, Waldseemüller map, Americas with new latitudes and longitudes; Map showing Waldseemüller projected onto a globe, as corrected by *Gavin Menzies.*

Color insert 2, page 6–7: The Waldsemüller map of 1507 side by side with the Waldsemüller 1506 "Green Globe," © *Bibliotheque Nacionale de France, Paris.*

Color insert 2, page 8: Map showing CGA5a projected over Waldsemüller. © *Biblioteca Estense, Modena.*

Color insert 3, page 1: Pope Pius II, *Pinturicchio.*

Color insert 3, page 2–3: Florence; Leonardo da Vinci (self) portrait.

Color insert 3, page 4–5: Renaissance timeline. *Wendi Watson and* © *Gavin Menzies*

Color insert 3, page 6: Needham's postcard. © *Pepysian Library, Magdalen College;* 1408 Ephemeris.table, © *Pepysian Library, Magdalen College*

Color insert 3, page 7: Regiomontanus' Ephemeris table, © *British Library*; Armillary sphere at Beijing Observatory. © *Gunnar Thompson.*

Color insert 3, page 8: Submarine surfacing, © *Gavin Menzies*; Dr. S.L. Lee Medallion. © *Dr. S.L. Lee.*

INDEX

Page references in *italics* refer to illustrations.

Harvard Journal of Asiatic Studies, 188
Harvatye Mariakyr, 67, 70–71
Hayashida, Kenzo, 12
Heilbron, John, 91
helicopter rotor, 170, 175, 180–81
"Helicopters and Whirligigs" (Reti),
    180–81
Heliopolis, 50, 51
Henry III, king of France, 71
Henry the Navigator, 287
Henry Tsai, 4
Henry V, king of England, 89
Herodotus, 50–51
Hibbert, Christopher, 205
Himalayan Mountains, 39
Historia Mongalorum (Pian del Carpine), 73
Histories (Herodotus), 50
History of Egypt in the Middle Ages, A
    (Poole), 51
History of the Inca Realm (Rostworowski),
    273
Hobson, John, 199
Holdaway, R. N., 258
Hollingsworth, Mary, 89, 90
Hong Bao, 13, 42, 43, 44, 45, 131
Hong Wu, 4, 17, 18, 19, 132–33, 262
Hooke, Robert, 24, 27
Hormuz, 47, 48
Hormuz, Strait of, 41
House of Medici, The: Its Rise and Fall
    (Hibbert), 205
Hou Xian, 13
Hsuan Te, 266
    see also Xuan De, emperor of China
Huarache, Claudio, 271–72
Hubson, R. L., 53–54
Hudson, Ian, 164
Hui Hsien, 167
Humboldt Current, 270–71
Huo Lung Chung, 226, 227
Hvar, 65, 66, 67, 69, 70, 71, 72

ibn Al-As Amir, 52
Ibn Battutah, 45
Ibn Khusrau, Nasir, 51
Ibn Tagri Birdi, 44
ibn Tulun, Ahmad, 52

Incas, 253, 271, 273–76, 278, 279, 280, 287
incense, 58
India
    ambassadors from, 41
    China known as, 99, 113, 121
    Chinese trade with, 40, 46
    civilization of, 271
    Karim warehouses in, 54
    on map in Venice, 77
    monsoons in, 39
    Nile Canal trade with, 52
    ships from, 39–40
Indian Ocean, 28, 36, 37, 39, 40, 42, 67, 104,
    128, 145, 223, 240, 277
Indians, North American, 264–65, 267,
    268, 269–70
    see also Native Americans
Institute and Museum of the History of
    Science (Istituto e Museo di Storia
    della Scienza), 184, 225
Institute of Archaeological Studies, U.S.,
    268
"Invention of the Parachute, The" (White),
    177
iron, 22, 216–19, 221, 222, 226, 227, 231, 232,
    237, 252, 257, 258, 265, 267
Isabella, queen of Spain, 104–5, 285
Islam, 18–19, 23, 40, 55–56, 57, 139, 283,
    284, 285, 286, 287, 288
    see also Muslims
Itinerarium (William of Rubruck), 73

Jacob of Ancona, 73
Jacob's staff, 16, 137, 140
Jamal ad-Din, 18, 154
James, Saint, 284, 286
Jang Min, 15, 17
Japan, 4, 12, 68, 77, 97, 114, 221, 250, 267,
    269
Jebel Khamish, 43
Jerusalem, 64, 115, 238
Jervis, Jane, 136
Jesuits, 157–58, 249, 251, 272
Jews, 14, 46, 57, 73
Jiegantou Kingdom, 48
Jiménez de Quesada, Gonzalo, 280
Jingdezhen Kilns, 19